THERE IS NO GREATER POLITICAL ENIGMA to the West and no more embarrassing dilemma to Soviet Russia than the Government of Marshal Tito of Jugoslavia.

- Though he claims to be a Communist, he openly defied Stalin and forced the Russians to come to his terms.

- He began the liberalizing movement in his own country, but did not hesitate to suppress ruthlessly writers and party members who criticized his policies.

In the Balkans there is a saying that behind every hero stands a traitor. From one point of view, Tito can be represented as a traitor to his king and his country, the agent of a foreign power which he also betrayed. On the same facts, he appears as a national hero twice over—the partisan leader who drove the Nazis out of Jugoslavia and later defended his country's independence against the military might of Russia.

The story of his life is a spectacular melodrama of victory against staggering odds, the story of a man who forged a nation out of chaos and now holds the fate of his country in precarious balance between East and West.

FOR VERONICA

who knows the people and the places

My warm thanks are due to my secretary, Miss Jeanne Thomlinson, for her kindness and care in preparing the text and to my wife for her invaluable work on the index.

F. M.

TITO

THE MAN WHO DEFIED HITLER AND STALIN

(ORIGINAL TITLE: THE HERETIC)

BY FITZROY MACLEAN

BALLANTINE BOOKS
NEW YORK

ꙅꙅꙅꙅ CONTENTS ꙅꙅꙅꙅ

MAPS

part one

✦ ⧈⧈⧈⧈⧈⧈⧈⧈⧈⧈⧈⧈⧈⧈⧈⧈⧈⧈⧈⧈⧈⧈⧈⧈⧈⧈ ★

OUTSIDE THE LAW

Patriotism to the Soviet State is a revolutionary duty, whereas patriotism to a bourgeois state is treachery.

TROTSKY

Note on the Spelling and Pronunciation of Serbo-Croat Words and Names.

---

s = *s* as in *seven*

š = *sh* as in *ship*

c = *ts* as in *bats*

ć = the same, only softer

j = *y* as in *you*

z = *z* as in *zodiac*

ž = *j* as in French *jour*

nj = *n* as in *new*

g = *g* as in *got*

dj = *g* as in *George*

I 〜〜〜 APOCALYPSE

> And I saw a new heaven and a new earth.
> Revelation xxi, 1

EARLY on Easter morning of the year 1915, during the heavy fighting then in progress on the Carpathian sector of the Eastern front, an Austrian infantry battalion, entrenched on some flat ground near a tributary of the Dniester, was overrun by a regiment of Russian cavalry. A neighboring Austrian battalion had fallen back, leaving a gap in the line, and a party of the enemy, creeping stealthily down from the high ground which they held on the far bank, had crossed the river during the night and advanced under a cover of darkness and of a heavy artillery bombardment to a point on the flank of the Austrian positions. At first light the Russians attacked, frontally and from the rear. The Austrians, in their muddy trenches, were taken completely by surprise. While they were fighting off the frontal attack as best they could, more Russians, wearing the high black sheepskin hats and carrying the long two-pronged lances of the famous Circassian *Dikhaia Divisia* or "Savage Division," suddenly swooped down on them from behind, a yelling, slaughtering horde, their lance points glinting cruelly in the early morning sunlight. In the Austrian trenches there was utter confusion. Most of the officers were farther up the line, where they had gone the night before to celebrate Easter and where they had been caught unawares by the enemy's attack. Regimental Headquarters had long since been overrun. Left to themselves, some of the Austrian noncommissioned officers and men went on fighting; others tried to surrender. The Circassians, for their part, gave no quarter, but killed and killed and killed. It was only when a battalion of Russian infantry finally came on the scene that the carnage was stopped and the surviving Austrians rounded up and taken prisoner.

Among the prisoners was a badly wounded young Croat

3

Feldwebel, or warrant officer, with blue eyes and fair curly hair, named Josip Broz. Two Circassians had engaged him simultaneously. While with rifle and bayonet he was fighting off one, the other had run him through the back with his lance, leaving him bleeding and unconscious in his trench. With the other prisoners, he was taken back to base and thence, by slow and painful stages, to Russia. Thus it was that, on the outbreak of the Russian Revolution two years later, Josip Broz, later to become famous as Marshal Tito of Jugoslavia, found himself in Russia. In this manner the first link was forged in a chain of events which were not to be without their influence on the history of the world.

Of Josip Broz's early life little until recently was generally known. It was as though no great importance attached to his beginnings, as though he had sprung, a fully grown and fully armed revolutionary, from the collective matrix of the Revolution—a purely political phenomenon in relation to whom no human or personal considerations could be of any possible account. Today, the veil has to some extent been lifted on the events of those early years. What stands revealed is neither particularly surprising nor particularly significant, but it may serve to cast some light on the human and personal development of a man whose human and personal characteristics were to prove in the long run of infinitely greater importance than either he or anyone else could possibly have suspected.

Feldwebel Broz had been born twenty-three years earlier, in May, 1892, in the little village of Kumrovec in Croatia, then part of the Austro-Hungarian Empire. He came of a proud, rebellious race, speaking their own Slav language and clinging to their own ancient traditions. At intervals through the centuries the Croats had rebelled against their Austrian or Hungarian rulers, in much the same way as their neighbors the Serbs, also South Slavs, had rebelled against the Turks. Of late they had succeeded in winning certain minor concessions. But this had only encouraged them to press on more vigorously toward what for many had become the ultimate aim: independence from Austria-Hungary and union with their South Slav brothers across the border in Serbia.

Kumrovec was situated on the borders of Croatia and Slovenia, in the Zagorje, or "Land beyond the Mountains," a green, hilly country, plentifully watered by rivers and mountain streams. The village itself lay on a little river, the Sutla, in a pleasant, fertile valley, beneath wooded hills. Its cottages, red-roofed or thatched, their walls painted a variety of bright colors, clustered untidily around the single, muddy village street. Cattle, sheep and horses grazed in the meadows round about. Rows of poplars and willows marked the course of streams and rivulets. Vineyards alternated with orchards and maize fields. Perched on a steep hill above the village stood the little whitewashed church of Saint Roko, while farther away, on another hill, rose Cesargrad, the ruined castle of the Erdödys, once feudal lords of Kumrovec and the country round. Scattered along the length of the valley were other castles and villages, each with its church spire rising above the rooftops.

Josip's father, Franjo Broz, whose forebears had been established in Kumrovec for several hundred years, lived with his wife and children on the outskirts of the village in a low, solidly built, whitewashed house which they shared with some cousins. Each family had two rooms and half the kitchen. Franjo's rooms were on the right as you entered the door. The parents slept in a massive bed in one of the rooms. The newest baby (Josip was the seventh of fifteen children) slept in an equally massive cradle by their side. The rest of the children bedded down where they could: on the floor, on top of the great tiled stove, upstairs in the garret. The furniture was simple and scanty: a table or two and some rough benches. The walls were whitewashed. On the wall in the larger of the two rooms hung a colored waxwork group of the Holy Family with behind it a musical box which played a hymn tune and, beneath, the inscription: *"Jesus, Maria und Josef, erleuchtet, rettet und helfet uns."* There were holy pictures, too, on the tiles of the stove. In the kitchen there were two fireplaces and two ovens, one for each family, and a handmill for grinding the grain. Behind the house lay a patch of garden with a few fruit trees and a well, and beyond that gently sloping maize fields. From the front, you looked across to a high range of wooded hills rising steeply on the other side of the valley.

Franjo, a dark, lanky man with aquiline features and black curly hair, possessed an amiable but unstable disposition and a taste for drink. He farmed a dozen or so acres which he had inherited from his father and, as this did not suffice to feed him and his family, earned what he could by doing odd jobs as a carter. A great talker, he also engaged in occasional deals in cattle and horses and hay and grain. Roaming the countryside in search of clients, he came to spend more and more of his time hanging round fairs and drinking in inns. As time went on, he was very often the worse for drink and almost always in debt. His wife, Marija, a tall, fair-haired, blue-eyed woman from across the border in Slovenia, had a far stronger character. It was she who cuffed the children into obedience and kept things going as best she could, struggling from morning to night to make both ends meet, while her husband's taste for drink grew stronger and the family fortunes rapidly declined.

Eight of Josip's fourteen brothers and sisters died when they were quite small. The seven survivors had a hard life. There was hardly ever enough to eat and they often went hungry. From the age of six or seven they worked for their living, taking the cows to pasture, digging or helping to grind the corn. At night they would scuffle avidly for the last crust or the last morsel of meat, when there was any.

When he was not needed for anything else, little Josip, or Joža as he was called, attended the village school, a low one-storied building a few hundred yards down the street with two rather bleak classrooms and the usual rows of wooden desks. At first school bewildered him, but he was naturally intelligent and soon his marks compared well enough with those of the other children. He stayed at school for four years, leaving when he was twelve. The school records show that by then he was "very good" at gardening, gymnastics and scripture, while his conduct is described as "excellent."

But most of his childhood was spent out-of-doors in the fields. What he liked best of all was looking after his father's horses and he could ride almost as soon as he could walk. He was fond, too, of dogs and was heartbroken one winter when his father, in debt as usual, had to sell their sheep dog, Polak, to pay for some firewood. But, much to Joža's joy, Polak soon ran away from his new master and returned home, where he was welcomed back by the children, who hid him in a cave until the search for him had been abandoned.

On Sundays, their mother, a devout Catholic, would send Joža and his brothers and sisters off to the little white church above the village, where he and another boy, resplendent in surplices and red cassocks, served as acolytes, swinging their censers and rattling off the Latin responses. Joza liked going to church. He liked the singing and the ritual and the smell of incense and he liked being an acolyte. But one day after mass, when he was helping the priest off with his vestments, he happened to fumble with the tapes and the priest, a big surly man, newly arived in the village, boxed his ears. After that Joža refused to serve at the altar and only went to church when he was made to.

Though his conduct at school was stated to be "excellent," his behavior, when he was not under the eyes of his teachers, was, by all accounts, less exemplary. He had an enterprising and independent nature and when there were fights with the boys from the next village or poaching expeditions or raids on a neighbor's orchard he was usually the ringleader. Contemporaries recall the ingenuity which he showed in planning these forays and the agility and resourcefulness with which he carried them out. Though slightly built, he was tough and wiry and perpetually on the move and, when retribution overtook the raiders, it was rarely Joža who suffered. Once, when the owner of an orchard caught him up a pear tree, he dropped out of the branches straight onto the unfortunate man's head, knocking him flat, and then ran away, stopping only to pick up a few more pears as he went.

His elders, in general, found him a nuisance. He was never quiet, always firing a stream of questions at them, or pestering them for more food, or playing tricks of one kind or another. But he was his mother's favorite child, who helped her to forget for a while the worries and troubles which now weighed her down more and more. He had the same fair hair and blue eyes as she had herself and, when he was little, he would ask her to sing him songs or tell him stories or wind up the musical box on the wall for him to listen to. And although his constant escapades were irritating, he was also, when you could get hold of him, a useful little boy who did the jobs he was given willingly and well, often showing an efficiency and an ingenuity beyond his years.

Joža's childhood was a hard one, but there was much about it that was agreeable: roaming through the woods and over the hills; watching the flocks in the valley on hot summer days; swimming or fishing in the river; climbing up to the ruined castle; sitting by the fire in the winter, listening to stories of other countries and other centuries, stories of war and rebellion and adventure. Much of his early childhood was spent with his mother's father, a merry old man who owned sixty acres of pasture and woodland across the border in Slovenia. Joža was devoted to his grandfather and would set off gaily along the white, dusty road lined with fruit trees which wound along the valley of the Sutla through meadows and past farmsteads and then turned sharply into a narrow gorge where the river ran for a space between steep wooded cliffs.

His grandfather shared with him a taste for practical jokes and the two got on splendidly together. In the daytime Joza would look after his horses for him and in the evening after supper the old man and the little boy would laugh and joke together for hours on end. Long afterward, when his grandfather had been dead for many years, Josip found himself looking back on the days they spent together as the happiest of his early life.

Life was hard in Croatia at the turn of the century and it was the intention of Josip's father to send him to seek his fortune in America as soon as he grew up. But, when it came to the point, Franjo Broz could not raise the necessary sum of money and so in 1907, when he was fifteen, young Josip was, on the advice of a cousin, sent off to the nearby town of Sisak to work as a waiter in a café.

The café at Sisak was the best in the town, agreeably situated in a park beside the river. To the little peasant boy, the bright lights of the small provincial town, the gay gypsy band playing under the trees, the smart uniforms of the officers who frequented the café and the even smarter dresses of the ladies who accompanied them were a revelation. But a waiter's life did not suit Josip Broz. It struck him as being a futile occupation that led to nothing. He decided that he must at all costs learn a proper trade. He remembered the short train journey to Sisak. The locomotive, which was the first he had ever seen, had fascinated him. Like other boys, he longed to be an engine driver. Like other boys, he was, as things turned out, unable to satisfy this longing. But he was nonetheless to find scope for his mechanical turn of mind. While working at the café, he made friends with two youths who were apprenticed to a locksmith called Nicholas Karas, who, they told him, might have room for another apprentice. Karas, a big, burly, exuberant man, had his workshop in a little house in a side street with a yard behind it. He was duly approached and, having listened to what Josip had to say, laughingly agreed to accept the fifteen-year-old boy as an apprentice. As usual, Franjo, who came over from Kumrovec to sign the contract of apprenticeship, was short of money and Josip was obliged to buy his first pair of mechanic's overalls out of his own pocket with the money he had earned in tips as a waiter.

Josip enjoyed his three years as an apprentice. The work was hard, but he liked it. He liked the smell of oil, the whir of the lathes and drills and the sparks which flew from the molten metal. He liked, above all, the feeling that he was making something. There were plenty of different things to make. Karas was a kind of general mechanic, who not only constructed locks, but mended bicycles and threshing machines, repaired shotguns and did fancy ironwork. In winter the apprentices slept in the workshop. In summer they slept on some hay in the loft. The food was good and plentiful. Josip made many friends and there was plenty to do in his spare time. On two evenings a week he went to a special school for apprentices where he was able to continue his general education. While he was at Sisak, he took to reading. He read everything he could lay hands on: history, fiction, tales of travel and stories of adventure. He had not enough spare time to read all he wanted. And so he started reading in working hours. One day, as he was sitting beside his lathe immersed in the latest installment of *The Adventures of Sherlock Holmes,* then appearing locally in serial form, the drill he was supposed to be watching broke to bits. At that moment his employer loomed up beside him and with one well-aimed blow knocked him flying. Josip knew he was in the wrong, but he did not like being knocked about. He ran away and took a job at a brickworks. At once he was brought back by the police and sent to jail for breaking his contract. But old Karas bore his truant apprentice no ill will. He sent him his dinner round to the prison, arranged for his release and then took him back to the workshop for the remainder of his apprenticeship. Some weeks later Josip completed his first job as a trained metalworker: a handsome wrought-iron handrail which to this day adorns the staircase of the District Court at Sisak.

His training finished, Josip Broz left Sisak. He wanted to get on in his profession and he wanted to see the world. At eighteen, in 1910, he set out for Agram, now Zagreb, the capital of Croatia, and there found work as a mechanic. Agram, with its wide avenues of chestnut and plane trees, its opera house and its majestic rows of stucco-fronted government buildings, was a fine city. On the hill, dominating the new town, stood the cathedral, newly restored in the Gothic manner, with next to it the palace of the Archbishop. Above that again, against a background of trees and gardens, rose the churches and fortifications and palaces of the old town. In the Ilica, the principal street of the city, elegant townsfolk mingled with peasants in national dress who had come in from the country. Among the carriages which drove up and down it, a few motorcars were beginning to make their appearance. In the cafés scores of prosperous-looking citizens sat, like their even more prosperous counterparts in Vienna, leisurely reading their newspapers and sipping their cream-topped coffee. In the shop windows goods were displayed of which young Broz had never seen the like, luxuries which he did not know existed. In the working-class district where he found a room the poverty and squalor were more familiar, but even there everything was on a larger scale than anything he had ever seen before.

He stayed in Agram for two months. At Sisak some of his fellow mechanics had told him about Socialism and the trade union movement. In Agram he became a member of the Metalworkers' Union and of the Social-Democratic party of Croatia and Slavonia and was given a badge to wear with a hammer and two clasped hands on it. But uppermost in his mind was the desire to save enough money to buy himself a new suit to take home to Kumrovec. He had always longed to have good clothes. He had even thought of becoming a tailor so as to be able to make them for himself. Now, with his accumulated savings of twenty florins, he bought the best suit he could get and hung it up in triumph in his lodgings. But when he came back to his room that night, he found the door open and the suit gone. He had no money left. When he went home for Christmas he was no better dressed than anyone else. But the chicken soup his mother had made for him tasted delicious and his friends and relations were agog to hear his tales of life in the great city.

For two months Josip stayed at home, working as a laborer. But it was not long before he overheard people saying that there was not much point in a boy serving a three-year apprenticeship if he was only going to become an ordinary laborer. And so defiantly he set out once more on his travels, this time wandering farther afield in search of work, to Laibach and Trieste, to Mannheim, Pilsen, Munich and Vienna.

Work was not always easy to find and there were times during these early years when he was without food or shelter for the night. But he was young and determined to make his way in the world and he did not let such minor setbacks deter him. When cash was short he slept in barns and went hungry. Besides, life had its compensations and relaxations. A photograph, taken at this time, shows him wearing the uniform of the "Sokol" Gymnastic Society, a sturdy little figure with a feather in his cap and an expression of defiance on his face. Politically the Sokol was anti-Hapsburg, but what Josip liked best about it was the companionship and the brightly colored uniform and the smart cap with a feather in it and marching briskly along behind the band.

His travels broadened his mind and widened his experience. They also taught him to look after himself. He learned German and Czech and improved his knowledge of engineering. In the evenings he took dancing lessons and soon spun round as skillfully as any Viennese to the waltzes of Johann Strauss and Franz Lehar which in later years were still to remain his favorite tunes. He was no longer a simple country boy. By 1913, when, at the age of twenty-one, he was called up for his two years' military service in the Austrian Army, he was working as a skilled mechanic and test driver at the Daimler works outside Vienna.

As a member of an underprivileged minority, Josip Broz, like the majority of his comrades in the Croat regiment in which he served, had no strong feelings of loyalty toward Austria-Hungary or the Emperor Francis Joseph. Even so he made a good soldier. He was alert both physically and mentally and interested in military matters. Within a year he was sent on a course for noncommissioned officers and, having distinguished himself in a fencing competition at Budapest, was promoted *Stabsfeldwebel* (sergeant major) in the Croat infantry regiment in which he was serving.

As fate would have it, Josip Broz was soon to be given an opportunity of proving his worth as a fighting man. On June 28, 1914, the crisis which had long been brewing in southeastern Europe came to a head. On that day, St. Vitus's Day, the Archduke Franz Ferdinand of Austria, while visiting the town of Sarajevo in the newly annexed province of Bosnia, was shot dead by a young Bosnian Serb named Gavrilo Princip. The assassination, planned by a group of Serb terrorists in Belgrade, gave expression to the national aspirations of the Emperor's South Slav subjects and symbolized their exasperation at the continuance of Hapsburg rule. It also seemed to the Austrian Government to provide a long-sought opportunity of dealing once and for all with their neighbor Serbia, whom they regarded, not without reason, as the chief source of pan-Serb and pan-Slav agitation within their dominions. A stiff Austrian ultimatum was presented in Belgrade. Russia came to the help of Serbia. Germany backed Austria. France and Great Britain mobilized. By the beginning of August Europe was at war.

Not many weeks later, Josip Broz's regiment was sent to the front. In the autumn of 1914 the Russians had advanced over the Carpathians to within 125 miles of Budapest, and Austrian reinforcements were now thrown in to fill the gap and halt their progress. Josip had already seen some fighting against the Serbs not far from Belgrade, but it was on the Carpathian front that he had his first real taste of war.

It was not a very agreeable front nor a very agreeable war. By the time his regiment reached the line the weather was bitterly cold. Both the Austrians and the Russians were badly equipped. On both sides there were severe casualties through frostbite and exposure. There was also much heavy fighting, the Russians throwing vast masses of ill-armed infantry into the attack, often without any preliminary artillery barrage, in an attempt to bear down the enemy by sheer weight of numbers. At night, alone in his observation post, looking out over the snowy, corpse-strewn expanse of no man's land, Feldwebel Broz's thoughts were frequently far from cheerful.

But there is always a certain satisfaction to be derived from doing something that you are good at. Young Broz was good at making raids behind the enemy lines. Country bred and town trained, he was both hardy and alert. He possessed an enterprising nature and an adventurous disposition. He was brave, determined and resourceful. Above all, he was a natural leader and his men followed him gladly. In command of a platoon, he set out night after night on extended raids and reconnaissances bringing back prisoners and information. By the time he was captured in the spring of 1915, he was beginning to get the hang of things.

The war, in short, had done for Josip Broz what it was to do for millions of his contemporaries. It had brought him to maturity before his time. A snapshot taken in the trenches by a friend in the same regiment shows a face that is already full of character. The youthful features beneath the Austrian kepi are stern and concentrated. The eyes that look along the rifle barrel are vigilant, the mouth unusually resolute. It is already a formidable face.

The lance thrust that laid Josip Broz low was a nasty one. It had entered his body just below the left arm, narowly missing his heart and leaving a deep and troublesome wound. On reaching Russia, he was taken to Sviazhesk, a little town on the Volga in the province of Kazan, some five hundred miles east of Moscow. There he spent just over a year in hospital in an old Orthodox monastery, recovering from his wound, from the pneumonia which followed it and finally from typhus caught from his lice-ridden fellow patients. On one of the walls there was a holy picture and at this he would rage in his delirium, accusing the saint which it depicted of trying to steal his belongings. As gradually he got better, he started to teach himself Russian. Two schoolgirls who lived near by, the daughters of a doctor and an engineer, attracted no doubt by the young prisoner's bold bearing and good looks and by his interesting pallor, would bring him Russian books to read, Turgenyev and Tolstoy, and then linger on talking to him.

Despite its hardships, his life as a prisoner possessed certain attractions. He was by race a Slav. And now he was in a Slav country, among fellow Slavs, in Holy Russia. The language, he found, was not so very different from his native Croat. From the first he could understand much of what was said around him and before long he spoke Russian fluently. Now that he was living among them, many hundreds of miles away from the firing line, he found his late enemies pleasant enough companions. There was much about them that was attractive: their kindheartedness; their conviviality; their habit of sitting up all night talking and singing and drinking; the breadth, as they called it, of their nature; their refusal to be put off by what they considered as trifles; their disregard for details; the devastating violence of their emotions; their courage and their immense capacity for endurance.

Their country, too, attracted him. No one with any imagination—and Broz had plenty—can be left completely unmoved by his first contact with the East, and here, in the Government of Kazan, on the fringes of Tartary, he found himself in one of those regions where Europe merges into Asia. There were the dark-skinned Tartars, with their narrow eyes and high cheekbones, riding in from the steppe. There was the great rolling plain, stretching away for thousands of miles, to the Urals, to the Black Sea, to the confines of China and Persia. Everything gave an impression of vastness, of spaciousness, of power. Of power with an undercurrent of anarchy and violence.

Nor did the Russians, for their part, seem to bear him any more ill will than he bore them. They were not by nature a resentful people and the war did not seem to mean more to many of them than it did to him. And, in any case, he was not a *Schwab,* a Hun, but a brother Slav.

And then there was something else. To an intelligent observer—and Broz was not lacking in intelligence—there were signs, daily more evident that in Russia something was stirring, something that the war, with its attendant misfortunes, was rapidly bringing to a head. A variety of factors contributed to the unrest which was beginning everywhere to seep through: widespread dislike of the war and of the sufferings and hardships which it brought in its train; anger at social injustice and at the treachery, the corruption and the inefficiency which existed in high places; a half-baked, sentimental, intellectual radicalism; a deep-seated natural trend toward chaos and revolution; and, finally, the determination of a small, ruthless body of men—some in Russia, some still in exile abroad—to use all these various factors of discontent for purposes of their own.

When at last, in May, 1916, Josip Broz was well enough to leave hospital, he was sent south to Ardatov near Samara in what is now the province of Kuibyshev, and there set to work as a mechanic in a mill. Some months later, toward the end of 1916, he was put in charge of a gang of other prisoners working on the Trans-Siberian Railway between Perm and Ekaterinburg (now Sverdlovsk) and based on the little town of Kungur in the Urals. It was at Kungur that, in March, 1917, while under close arrest for some disciplinary offense, the news reached him that revolution had broken out in Petrograd and Moscow. From the cell in which he was confined he could hear the crowd shouting "Down with the Czar." The Czar, it seemed, had abdicated. A weak Provisional Government had been established under liberal and radical direction, and a Council of Soldiers and Workers Deputies had been formed, repressenting the more extreme revolutionary elements and, in particular, the Bolshevik section of the Social-Democratic party.

From his own experience as an industrial worker before the war, Broz had derived no fondness for capitalists or capitalism, for aristocrats or aristocracy, for emperors or empires. What happened in Russia was, it might be said, no concern of his, but during the two years which he had spent there as a prisoner his sympathies had become engaged on the side of those who were working for the overthrow of the existing order. Rebellion was in the air, rebellion of the poor and downtrodden against the rich and privileged, of the working class against their masters. He was young and the events that were taking place around him were calculated to fire a youthful imagination. It is scarcely surprising that, having once got out of jail, he should have felt impelled to join in.

From the first he sided with the revolutionaries and when, almost immediately, differences arose between the moderates and extremists, it was with the extremists, with the small but well-organized minority of Bolsheviks, that his sympathies lay. Very soon his sympathies got him into trouble. In the excitement of their own domestic affairs, the Provisional Government had little time to bother about prisoners of war. But a prisoner of war who sided actively with their rivals for power was a rather special case, and it was not long before Broz was arrested as a Bolshevik.

He did not remain in prison for long. In the railway workshops he had made friends with an old engineer, who shared his liking for the Bolsheviks. His new-found friend helped him to get out of jail, gave him some civilian clothes and provided him with a letter to his son who was working as an engineer in the great Putilov armament works in Petrograd. Thus equipped, he set out toward the end of June on the long journey westward. At first he walked. Then, two stations down the line, he found a goods train bound for Petrograd. Hidden in a truck among some sacks of grain, he arrived several days later in the capital, where he was made welcome by his friend's son.

The moment of his arrival was a critical one in the history of Russia and indeed of the world. The situation in Petrograd was rapidly getting out of hand. The Provisional Government under Kerenski were fast losing control and power was passing more and more into the hands of the Councils of Workmen and Soldiers and through them into the hands of the Bolsheviks, who used it to create chaos and to render the task of government impossible. Up to now the Bolsheviks had labored under one serious disadvantage: their principal leaders were still abroad. Some, like Lenin, were in Switzerland. Others were in North America. Then in April, with the help of the German General Staff, who arranged for his passage in a sealed train from Switzerland through Germany to Russia, Lenin returned. He was followed within a few weeks by Trotsky and Zinoviev. It was not long before they made their presence felt. Soon the name of Lenin was on everyone's lips.

The Bolsheviks now organized mass demonstrations against the Provisional Government. These were the famous July Demonstrations. Widespread rioting ensued. Josip Broz joined in enthusiastically. When the crowd reached the railway station, they came under heavy machine-gun fire from government troops on the roof of the station buildings. Many of the demonstrators were killed and large-scale arrests of Bolshevik sympathizers ensued. Among those arrested was his friend, the engineer's son, with whom he was staying. In the confusion of the great city, amid all the turmoil of the Revolution, Josip Broz was now on his own.

After some time spent sleeping out under the bridges and hiding where best he could, he eventually decided to try to reach Finland. But at the border he was arrested and sent back to Petrograd, where he was consigned to the damp, rat-infested dungeons of the Fortress of St. Peter and Paul on its island amid the swirling waters of the Neva. There he spent three weeks. By now he spoke Russian fluently and at first his captors refused to believe that he was a foreigner. In the end he succeeded in convincing them that he was a prisoner of war, but the only result of this was that they decided to send him back under guard to his prison camp in Siberia.

Broz was quite ready to go to Siberia, but he preferred to travel independently of the authorities. When the slow-moving, crowded train reached Ekaterinburg, he asked his escort for permission to get some water to make tea, and then, mingling in the throng on the platform, jumped onto a passenger train bound for Omsk that was just pulling out of the station. When a gendarme who joined the train farther down the line asked him whether he had seen an escaped Austrian prisoner, he replied in fluent Russian that he had not.

A day or two later, shortly before reaching Omsk, the train in which Broz was traveling was stopped and boarded by an armed mob. The passengers asked what was happening. The mob replied that the Bolshevik Revolution had broken out and Soviet rule had been established. They, it seemed, had been sent out from Omsk to intercept fugitive members of the bourgeoisie. The date was November 7, 1917.

Having established that he was not a fugitive bourgeois, but an Austrian prisoner of war whose political ideas were in line with their own, the Bolsheviks of Omsk welcomed Broz with open arms. *"Vsio v poriadke,"* they said reassuringly, "Everything is in order." If he liked, they added, he could even join the Red Guard; many of his fellow prisoners of war had already done so. A few days later he was duly enrolled.

Broz was to spend another three years in Russia. They were years of bloodshed and turmoil. He had his share of both.

In 1918 Omsk was recaptured by the Whites and he was forced to go into hiding. He was hidden by a seventeen-year-old Russian girl called Pelagea Byelusnova or Polka for short, a Bolshevik like himself. She had blue eyes and long fair hair and was touchingly beautiful. They fell in love.

Soon the Whites had learned of his presence in Omsk and were searching for him. It was no longer safe for him to stay there. He fled to the nearby steppes. There he fell in with a tribe of Kirghiz nomads, dark-skinned, moon-faced Mongol horsemen, with slit eyes and high cheekbones, who lived, surrounded by their flocks and herds, in little round tents called *kibitkas*. Their chief, Hadji Isaj Djaksembayev, was a man of some standing who possessed a herd of two or three thousand horses, a score of wives and a hundred or so children. Fortunately for Josip Broz, Isaj had recently acquired a motor mill and needed a mechanic. Broz showed what he could do with the mill and was at once taken on. His skill in operating and maintaining it and in repairing such other odd bits of machinery as they possessed struck the simple nomads as miraculous. His horsemanship, too, won their respect. Soon he had achieved a position second only to that of the chief who pressed him to marry some of his handsome though dusky daughters and settle down.

Although he did not accept Isaj's invitation to become a permanent member of the tribe, Broz spent many months with the Kirghiz. He got on well with them and they with him. He learned their language and wore their dress. Their life suited him. In the summer, with their vast herds of horses, they would ride for hundreds of miles across the endless expanse of the steppe. Sometimes they would go out spearing wolves and he would go with them, enjoying the breakneck pursuit over the echoing plain. In the winter, when the temperature dropped far below freezing point, they would dig themselves in and stay where they were, clustered round the fire in their *kibitkas,* talking and telling stories.

In the end the Bolsheviks recaptured Omsk and Broz was free to go back there. The first thing he did was try to get news of Polka. She, too, had fled from Omsk, but at last he found her in a neighboring village. Not long after she became his wife.

Early in 1920 Josip Broz, taking his bride with him, made his way to Petrograd. Thence, some months later, he set out for his own country. He had heard that there too things were moving in a revolutionary direction and he was anxious to get back.*

The events he had lived through had left their mark on Josip Broz. When he had first come to Russia as a prisoner in 1915 he had lacked any very deep convictions, any strong purpose in life, any guiding principle, any cause to which to devote himself. When he left Russia five years later to return home, this was no longer so. He had with his own eyes witnessed the triumph of the Bolshevik Revolution and the establishment of the Soviet State. He had seen the working class, to which he himself belonged, rise and seize power. He had seen, or thought he had seen, the Future—the Future for Russia and for the whole world. He had found a cause by comparison with which family, religion, fatherland counted as nothing, a cause which demanded complete and absolute devotion. He had become a Communist. Henceforward, he had but one aim: to spread the gospel of Communism, to bring about as soon as possible a Communist revolution in his own country. That there might never be such a revolution there, or that, if there were a revolution, it might not succeed, were thoughts which never for one moment entered his mind.

* In his *La Yougoslavie sous la Menace Intérieure et Extérieure* Anton Ciliga states that Broz did not return from Russia until 1925. I have, however, not been able to find independent support for this assertion.

II 52525252 SOLDIER OF THE REVOLUTION

IN company with his wife and with a number of other returning prisoners, Josip Broz, still wearing the sheepskin hat which he had been given when he first joined the Red Guard, traveled back to his own country by way of the Baltic. It was a long and weary journey across a war-battered continent. Finally, in September, 1920, he and Polka, who was now expecting a child, arrived at Kumrovec. The village looked much the same. He went to his father's house, only to be told that his family had moved to another village near by. He made his way there and found his father and one of his brothers sitting down to their evening meal. His mother, they said, had died in 1918. A few hours after their arrival Polka gave birth to a boy, their first child, but the baby died two days later. It had not been a happy homecoming. Even the stories of revolution seemed to have been exaggerated. There had been some rioting among the peasants, but that was all. Sadly the two of them once more collected their belongings and set out for Zagreb to look for work. Broz now discarded his fine fur hat in favor of a less noticeable felt. *"Ne ču da budem karnaval,"* he said to a friend who asked him what he had done with it, "I do not wish to make an exhibition of myself."[1]

There had been many changes in central and eastern Europe during the six years which Josip Broz had spent abroad. The war had now been over for two years. Germany was abased. The old Hapsburg Empire had distintegrated. He himself had become a citizen of the new kingdom of the Serbs, Croats and Slovenes, later to be renamed Jugoslavia.

The creation of a Jugoslav or South Slav State was the culmination of a historical process which had begun some fourteen or fifteen centuries earlier when the forebears of the Slav peoples and races who now inhabit Jugoslavia first migrated there from the steppes and forests of the north. Their history had from the start been turbulent and confused, a tale of bloodshed and violence, of heroism and treachery. Individual

[1] Numbered footnotes will be found in the Appendix, beginning on p. 405.

19

Serb, Croat, Bosnian and Slovene princes and chieftains alter-
nately fought among themselves for supremacy or joined together to fight against one or other of their neighbors. To
attain their own immediate ends, they would enlist the help of
outside powers, of Byzantium or the Turks, Hungary or Venice,
the Emperor or the Pope. And afterward they would again join
forces to throw off the foreign allegiance or alliance which a
short time before they had so readily accepted. They excelled
in the art of playing off one great power against another: Pope
against Emperor, Rome against Byzantium, Teuton against
Turk. Their ultimate purpose, meanwhile, remained constant:
the furtherance of their own interests and the preservation of
their own independence. This purpose they pursued with peculiar vigor and resilience.

But for these small kingdoms and principalities, caught between the conflicting forces of East and West, the struggle
for survival was a hard one. The advance westward of the
Osmanli Turks grew ever harder to check. In 1389 at Kosovo,
on the fatal Field of the Blackbirds, the Serbian Czar Lazar
was defeated and slain and his people passed under Turkish
sway. The neighboring principalities succumbed one after
another. In 1528 Jajce, the last remaining Bosnian stronghold,
fell to the Turks. The whole Balkan Peninsula was now under
alien rule, the Turks spreading out over the south and east,
while the Austrians and Hungarians advance to meet them
from the north and west, and the Venetians established themselves along the Adriatic coast. In this manner the South Slavs
came to be separated from each other, Serbia and Bosnia
falling under Turkish rule, while in the course of time Croatia
and Slovenia became provinces of the Hapsburg Empire. For a
while Dalmatia remained Venetian territory; then it too was
absorbed by Austria-Hungary.

Henceforward, though linked by a common language and
common racial origins, the two main groups of South Slavs
were divided from each other by the frontiers of the great
powers under whose dominion they had fallen and so gradually
grew apart. Under the loose, though sometimes savage rule
of the sultans, the Serbs came to look eastward. Their church
was the Eastern, the Orthodox Church, with the Patriarch of
Constantinople at its head. In Bosnia, many embraced the
faith of their conquerors and became Mohammedans. The
Croats and Slovenes, on the other hand, looked westward to
Vienna. By religion, like their Hapsburg masters, they belonged to the Western Church, the Church of Rome. Already

in the tenth century Pope John X had called the Croats *"specialissimi filii Sanctae Romanae Ecclesiae,"* while their subsequent resistance to the Turks had won them, from Pope Julius II, the proud title of *"Antemurale Christianitatis."* With the passage of time they became, in their standard of civilization and in outlook generally, a Western rather than an Eastern people. While Belgrade remained a Turkish fortress, Zagreb became a European city.

But if in some respects the Serbs lagged behind their Croat and Slovene brothers across the border, they never lost their love of freedom. All through the centuries of Turkish rule, the spirit of independence was kept alive in the hill country of Serbia by little bands of guerrilla fighters, half brigands and half patriots. In their mountain fastnesses, under the rule of their own princes and prince-bishops, the Montenegrins, in particular, held out unsubdued for century after century.

It was thus that, when in the early nineteenth century the Ottoman Empire began to crumble and the new forces of liberalism and nationalism started to spread across Europe from the West, there still remained in Serbia a nucleus of resistance ready to flare up into a full-scale national revolt. In 1804 the Serbs, led by a peasant named Kara Djordje, or Black George, rose and within three years had driven the Turks from Serbia. In 1809 the Turks returned, but Black George drove them out once more, this time with Russian help. In 1813 they returned again in overwhelming force. Black George was defeated and fled abroad and the Turks appointed Miloš Obrenović, a herdsman, to govern the country for them. But in 1815 the Serbs rose yet again, now led by Miloš Obrenović, whom the Turks had themselves made viceroy. In a single campaign Obrenovič expelled the Turks and proclaimed himself Prince of Serbia. The Turks agreed to recognize him and in return he accepted the suzerainty of the Sultan. When in 1817 Black George came back to his native land, he was at once assassinated and his head sent to the Sultan by Miloš Obrenović, who preferred to see his rival liberator safely out of the way and welcomed this opportunity of ingratiating himself with his former enemies.

For the next hundred years Serbia presents an extraordinary picture of violence, intrigue and unrest. Rival dynasties, founded by the two rival peasant-liberators, Kara Djordje and Obrenović, served as rallying points for opposing factions. Power passed from one to the other and back again. Princes and kings, patriarchs, prime ministers and commanders-in-chief followed each other in a bewildering succession, regulated by conspiracy, assassination and the intrigues of the great powers. Public violence and private scandal were the order of the day. In her external relations, Serbia sided first with one great power and then with another, while the great powers, for their part, lent their support first to one Serb faction and then to their opponents. But, however confusing and unedifying these proceedings may seem when examined in detail, regarded as part of a whole, they appear as mere incidents in the struggle of a proud and turbulent people for unity and nationhood.

After fighting side by side with Russia in the Russo-Turkish War of 1877, the Serbs were rewarded in 1878 by the grant of their complete independence from Turkey. As an independent kingdom, Serbia now became an ever greater center of attraction for those South Slavs who still remained under foreign domination. She also became a cause of ever greater concern to Austria-Hungary, who saw in the rise of Serbian nationalism, deliberately fostered by Russia, a direct threat to the security and integrity of her own dominions. Up to the year 1903 Austria's fears were to some extent allayed by the personal hold which she managed to establish on the Obrenović dynasty. In that year, however, King Alexander Obrenović was murdered with extreme brutality by a group of military conspirators and his body, together with that of his wife Draga, thrown down from the palace window into the gardens below. His place was taken by King Peter Karadjordjević, Black George's grandson, whose pro-Russian and anti-Austrian proclivities were well known. Henceforward Austria's attitude toward Serbia became increasingly hostile and the situation in the Balkans increasingly tense.

In 1908 the Austrian Government formally annexed the Slav-populated provinces of Bosnia and Herzegovina which, while remaining nominally part of Turkey, had in 1878 been placed under their administration by the Treaty of Berlin. Outraged at the annexation by Austria of what they regarded as Serbian territory, the Serbs lost no time in compensating themselves elsewhere. In 1912, in alliance with the Montenegrins, the Greeks and the Bulgars, they declared war on Turkey and in the course of a short and spectacularly successful campaign succeeded in wresting from her almost all that remained of Turkey in Europe. In 1913 they fought the Bulgars, their allies of the year before, for the fruits of their common victory and heavily defeated them. They emerged from these struggles with their prestige enhanced, their territory enlarged by the addition of Old Serbia and most of Macedonia and their national consciousness more inflamed than ever. By the summer of 1914 the Austrian Government had decided that the time had come to eliminate the Serbian menace once and for all. The assassination of the Archduke Franz Ferdinand at Sarajevo in June, 1914 gave them the pretext they needed.

From 1914 to 1918 the Serbs fought magnificently against fearful odds. At first they more than held their own against the Austrians. Then an irresistibly strong combined Austro-German force under German command was thrown against them. Their country was overrun and devastated. But still they fought on. After retreating in midwinter on foot through the mountains of Albania to the Adriatic, the main Serbian force was evacuated by the Allies to Salonika whence it fought its way back into Serbia from the south. At no time during the appalling hazards and hardships of the war did the Serbs abandon hope or lose sight of their ultimate aim. They were fighting for their existence as a people and also for unity with the South Slav minorities in Austria-Hungary.

Their aims and hopes were shared by many of their South Slav brothers across the border. In the course of the war large numbers of the Croat and Slovene troops in the Austrian forces deserted to the Allies and a Jugoslav Committee was formed on Allied territory to discuss the establishment of a Jugoslav state. During 1918 a Jugoslav National Council was set up in Zagreb by the Serbs, Croats and Slovenes of the Empire and, after the final collapse of Austria-Hungary, a unified South Slav state was proclaimed jointly by this body and by the Serbian Government. Simultaneously the Montenegrins, who up to now had been independent, formally deposed their king and proclaimed the union of Montenegro with Serbia. On December 16, 1918, a joint session of the Serbian Skupština and the Zagreb Council formally ratified the union and King Peter Karadjordjević became the first king of the new Triune Kingdom of the Serbs, Croats and Slovenes. On his death three years later he was succeeded as king by his son Alexander, a stubborn, courageous, austere man with an autocratic nature and a strong, if narow, sense of duty, who had won universal admiration by his bravery during the war.

The new Jugoslav State was more than twice as large as the old kingdom of Serbia and possessed more than twice the number of inhabitants. With a population of close on twelve million, made up of some five million Serbs, three

million Croats and one million Slovenes, its territories extended
from the frontiers of Italy, Austria and Hungary on the north
to those of Greece and Albania on the south. To the west, its
coastline stretched for four hundred miles along the Adriatic.
To the east, its frontiers marched with those of Rumania and
Bulgaria. Geographically it was a land of infinite diversity. To
the Serbian hills and woodlands and green, rolling countryside, had been added the Alpine valleys and mountains of
Slovenia with their dense pine forests, the rich agricultural
lands of Croatia and Slavonia, the wild hill country of Bosnia,
the tawny uplands of Macedonia, the smiling seacoast and
craggy peaks of Dalmatia and Montenegro. Its inhabitants
differed almost as widely as the regions which they inhabited.
But by origin they were all South Slavs, speaking different
varities of the same South Slav language. And now, after
centures of separation and four years of world-wide bloodshed
and suffering, occasioned, if not caused, by their longing for
national unity, they were at last united in a South Slav state
which in its extent and composition went far to meet their
common hopes and aspirations.

And yet, no sooner were the southern Slavs united than at
once they were violently at variance among themselves. The
Serbs, it is true, were not dissatisfied. They were on top, and
that, they felt, was where they should be. They, after all, had
borne the burden and heat of the day. Their national leaders
had raised the standard of revolt against the Turks a century
before and had carried through to fruition the idea of an independent South Slav state. Their troops had fought for the
greater glory of that state in the Balkan Wars of 1912-13.
They had fought again, side by side with the Allies, in the
European war which followed, at a time when many Croats
and Slovenes had been fighting, not for the Allies, but for
the Austrians. In six years of almost continuous war they had
lost a million dead—a quarter of their country's total population. Now that victory had been won and that, thanks to their
efforts, the South Slavs had at last been reunited, it was, they
felt, right and proper that, in the new state which they had
founded, they should take the lead: right and proper that the
capital should be in Belgrade, a Serbian city, that a Serbian
king should sit upon its throne, that its affairs should be guided
by Serbian statesmen, that its army should be under Serbian
command, that its national church should be the Serbian Orthodox Church. On these terms, they were proud and glad to

welcome their Croat and Slovene brethren to what was a predominantly Serbian fold.

But the Croats and Slovenes—particularly the Croats—
thought otherwise. While the Serbs looked eastward, they had
learned to look westward. They set store by their superior
civilization. It entitled them, they felt, to more of a say in
matters than they were getting. The phrase "A thousand years
of Croat culture" was constantly on their lips. They clung to
their church—the Western Church, the Church of Rome. They
clung to their national leaders, who had played no small part
in the foundation of the new state, and who were now virtually
excluded from the conduct of its affairs.

Already during the negotiations which had preceded the
proclamation of a combined Jugoslav state, the Serbian
Government had let it be seen that they were more interested
in the aggrandizement of Serbia than in bringing about the
union on equal terms of Serbs, Croats and Slovenes. This
first impression was abundantly confirmed by subsequent
events. The old Serbian political parties occupied a dominant
position in the Constituent Assembly which met in Belgrade
in 1921, and the constitution which it promulgated in June of
the same year was strongly centralist in character and deliberately calculated to maintain Serb hegemony. Of the wishes of
the Croat representatives, who favored a federal solution, no
account was taken.

In Croatia, meanwhile, a sweeping victory had been won at
the elections by the Croat Republican Peasant party of Stjepan
Radić. This party, as its name betokened, stood for the Croat
cause and for a Peasant Republic. Stjepan Radić, its leader, a
plump, waggish, moon-faced little man with a pointed beard,
was a true tribune of the people. A fiery, somewhat confused
orator, he enjoyed immense popularity among his fellow peasants in Croatia. While accepting in principle the idea of South
Slav brotherhood, Radic had never shown great enthusiasm
for the new state and by 1921 had already come into serious
conflict with its rulers, by whom he was more than once imprisoned for his political activities.

But repression did nothing to solve the Croat problem.
Soon there were those in Croatia who murmured that things
had been better under the Hapsburgs; who spoke with regret
of the good old days; who spoke without warmth of their
new-found Slav brothers; who spoke, even, of an independent
Croatia.

After the devastation and destruction of the war years, the

new Triune Kingdom stood badly in need of a period of tranquillity. But this was not to be. From the start, the thorny problem of Croatia and of the other nationalities in the new state dominated its political life, keeping it in a perpetual ferment. Nor was this all. The national economy was completely dislocated. There was widespread unemployment among the industrial workers. Demobilized soldiers and returned prisoners of war swelled the ranks of the unemployed. Large areas of the countryside had been laid waste in the fighting, crops destroyed and livestock carried off or slaughtered. Food and raw materials were short, prices high and wages low. There was unrestrained corruption and profiteering. Again and again troops were called out to repress strikes and disturbances.

This uneasy state of affairs lent grist to one mill at any rate. At the elections of 1920 no less than fifty-nine Communist candidates were elected to the Constituent Assembly, while the number of Communist party members throughout the country had soon risen to sixty thousand. Here, too, revolution was in the air.

The Jugoslav communist party, or Socialist Workers' party, as it was at first called, had been formed in Belgrade in April, 1919 from a variety of elements, notably the Serbian Social-Democratic party and various other Socialist parties from the areas formerly under Austro-Hungarian rule. At its First Congress the new party had roundly denounced the old Socialist International for its betrayal of the working class and formally adhered to the new Communist International, or Comintern, which had been founded in Russia only six weeks before. At its Second Congress, held at Vukovar in June, 1920, the party was given a definitely Communist mold and formally assumed the name of Communist party of Jugoslavia. Its statute and organization were remodeled on the Russian pattern and its aim was declared to be the establishment, by revolutionary means, of a Jugoslav Soviet Republic, to be included ultimately in a World Communist Union. A group of delegates who refused to accept the Comintern's Twenty-one Conditions, which included the complete subordination of every Communist party to the Comintern, were formally expelled. Henceforward the first loyalty of Jugoslav Communists, as of all other orthodox Communists everywhere, was to be, not to their own country, but to the Country of the Revolution, to Russia, to the Soviet Union.

To Josip Broz, fresh from Russia, there was nothing shocking about this. On the contrary. The new kingdom of the Serbs, Croats and Slovenes meant no more to him than the old Austro-Hungarian Empire had done. His hopes, his aims, his loyalties lay elsewhere. The new party corresponded exactly to his aspirations. His first act on returning home was to join it. In September, 1920 he was enrolled as a member of the Zagreb branch.

He had by now found work as a machinist in an engineering workshop in Zagreb and had resumed his membership of the Metalworkers' Union. This gave him numerous opportunities for doing what now mattered to him most of all: spreading the new faith. At trade union meetings he would distribute pamphlets and agitate for higher wages and better working conditions. He possessed an agreeable and compelling personality and was popular with his fellow workers, who listened readily to what he had to say. He had a ready sense of humor and was always laughing and joking; he was always glad to do a friend a good turn. He himself saw issues clearly and had the gift of putting them to others in simple terms. His experiences and the burning conviction which he had derived from them lent him assurance. Though still only in his twenties, he spoke with authority. He would speak of the class struggle, and of what he himself had seen in Russia, and of the need for the workers to seize power by armed force. In this period of profound political, social and economic unrest, his words fell on fertile ground. That winter he helped to organize a metalworkers' strike in Zagreb.

But in the new kingdom an agitator's task was becoming increasingly hazardous. From the first the Belgrade Government, warned by what was happening in Russia and elsewhere, had viewed the Communists with fear and detestation. A fresh wave of strikes alarmed them still further. In December, 1920 a proclamation was issued by the Minister of the Interior, severely restricting the activities of the Communist party. Then, in the summer of 1921, a Communist attempt on the life of the Prince Regent, followed a month later by the assassination of the Minister of the Interior by a group of young Communists, gave the authorities the opportunity they wanted. In August, 1921 a Law for the Defense of the State, authorizing drastic measures against terrorists, was passed through Parliament. On the strength of this the fifty-nine Communist Deputies were expelled and the Communist party declared illegal. Its members became liable to immediate arrest and imprisonment. From now onward Josip Broz and his comrades were political outlaws.

Repression often has a stimulating effect. In the case of the Jugoslav Communists this was not so. The party lacked effective leadership. Driven underground or into exile by vigorous police action, its leaders squandered their time and their energies in internal strife, quarreling among themselves, wallowing in every kind of heresy and deviation, neglecting the most promising opportunities for making trouble and leaving the rank and file to fend for themselves as best they could. More and more of their time was spent outside Jugoslavia, in Russia or Austria or Germany, where at successive conferences and congresses they argued endlessly over the merits and demerits of their respective theories and countertheories.

During these early years Josip Broz was not of sufficient standing in the party to take any part in framing policy or to join in the highlevel ideological disputes which fluttered the Comintern dovecotes in Moscow and Vienna. But, though undistinguished as a theoretician, he was already becoming known as a reliable and devoted worker for the cause. At the beginning of 1921 he had left Zagreb and gone, in response to a newspaper advertisement, to work in the pleasant little Croatian village of Veliko Trojstvo at a flour mill belonging to a Jew called Samuel Polak. His job was to look after the fifty-horsepower charcoal-burning engine which worked the mill. The mill was the center of life in the village and in his spare time Broz would sit in the yard and talk to the peasants who had brought their grain to be ground. He would talk to them about present conditions in Jugoslavia, about the high cost of everything and the high level of taxation. He would tell them of his experiences in Russia and about the Revolution and how splendid it all had been, and how Communism was the solution to all their troubles. The peasants listened open-mouthed and sometimes asked questions, to which he always had an answer ready.

In the provinces the Communist party machine had been badly disorganized by the government's repressive measures and individual members had lost touch with each other and with the party. In 1923, however, Josip Broz managed to establish contact with underground party cells in the nearby towns and in 1924 he was elected a member of the underground Regional Party Committee. Henceforward he would from time to time secretly visit Zagreb on behalf of the Regional Committee and make reports to the Provincial Committee for Croatia. A friend who worked with Josip Broz during these early years has described his neat appearance and the clearness and efficiency of his political work. Nothing about him was slipshod or confused; everything was clear, logical and decisive. Doubt or indecision were unknown to him. What he had seen in Russia, the friend records, was still uppermost in his mind and he was profoundly convinced that nothing could prevent the ultimate triumph of the Revolution in his own country.[2]

Meanwhile the police were becoming more and more vigilant. Brož's continual comings and goings soon drew their attention to him. In 1924 he was denounced by the officiating priest for a speech made at a friend's funeral and arrested on a charge of subversive activities. But, luckily for him, the judge who was Orthodox, disliked the priest, who was a Catholic, and he was accordingly released after only a week of prison. He was lucky, too, in his employer. Old Samuel Polak, the mill-owner, was a good-natured man with a large family who turned a blind eye to his mechanics' political activities. "You are a good mechanic," he would say, "and it does not matter to me what you do outside the mill." But in 1925 old Polak died and his son-in-law took over. The new owner was less good-natured and less well disposed to Brož. He did not like his attitude over wage rates. Nor did he like the increasing attention which he was beginning to attract from the police. Things were beginning to get difficult. In the autumn of 1925, at the suggestion of the Provincial Committee of the party, Broz left Veliko Trojstvo.

During the four and a half years they spent there Josip and Polka Broz had had three children, a girl called Zlatica, a boy called Hinko and another boy called Žarko. Little Hinko died of dysentery when he was a few days old. Zlatica, a pretty child with fair hair and blue eyes, who was the delight of her father, lived to be nearly two and then died of diphtheria. Sadly, Broz carried her little body to the graveyard in a small, rough coffin which a friend had made for him. A year later, when he had been able to save enough money, he put up a marble gravestone for Hinko and Zlatica in the little graveyard at Veliko Trojstvo. Engraved on it is a cross with beneath it the following inscription:

Here, in the Peace of God, lie
Zlatica Broz, aged 2 years,
and her brother Hinko, aged 8 days.

> Let there be peace and quiet over your grave.
> We, your sorrowing parents,
> will carry away with us
> all pain and grief.

After the death of their first three children, the birth of Žarko in 1924 was a great joy to his parents. Soon he was a well-built little boy, fair-haired and blue-eyed, with the same striking good looks as his father and mother.

From Veliko Trojstvo Josip Broz went to Kraljevica, a small seaport on the northern Adriatic, where no one knew him. Kraljevica was a pleasant little place, its brightly painted houses clustering round the blue waters of a bay against a background of rocky gray cliffs and green pine woods. Just outside the town, fringed with pine trees, there was a shipyard and here, after making some preliminary inquiries, Broz took work as a mechanic, building and repairing marine engines. Having found a room in a shack on the hill above the little town, he sent for his wife and for Žarko, now nearly two years old. Sometimes, when he had come off work, he would go swimming or fishing with a friend who was a fisherman and had a boat. Or else he would sit at home or outside under the pine trees reading the little collection of books he had brought with him from Veliko Trojstvo. Most of them dealt with social problems and had a left-wing flavor. There was *The Iron Heel* by Jack London, *Women and Socialism* by Bebel, *Mother* by Gorki, and others. When he had read them himself, he would pass them on to the friends he soon made among fellow workers at the shipyard.

But his real task, the task for which he had been sent there, was to organize a trade union branch and a party cell. Wages at the shipyard were bad and the foreign-controlled company which owned it was permanently in arrears with their payment. Men who complained were dismissed. Broz told his fellow workers that, if they were to achieve anything, they must organize. He had a way with him and the men listened to what he said. Soon a branch of the Metalworkers' Union was formed and he himself became a shop steward. He also organized a workers' sports association and a cultural group which gave little concerts. And in this fertile soil he duly planted a secret party cell.

Before long Broz judged that the time was ripe for a showdown. At his behest the party cell organized a two hours' stoppage of work. Alarmed, the management granted some of the workers' demands, but not all. Encouraged by this success, the union called a strike. It lasted nine days, at the end of which the management gave in and agreed to a wage raise and the immediate payment of all arrears. At the same time they put up a list giving the names of a number of workers whose services were no longer required. Near the top was the name of Josip Broz. He was out of a job, but his time at Kraljevica had not been wasted. When in October, 1926 he returned to Zagreb he left behind him an active nucleus of industrial and political unrest.

From Zagreb Broz went to Belgrade and thence to Smederevska Palanka, a little semi-industrial town in the green, rolling country south of the capital, where he found work in the partly French-owned railway repair workshops. Here, once more, he became a shop steward. Before he had been there six months a clash with the management over working conditions led to his dismissal. But once again he left behind him a flourishing party organization among the factory's nine hundred workers.

Returning to Zagreb in April, 1927 Broz reported to the party for fresh instructions. It was only natural that he should do so. He was part of the machine; it was the only authority that he recognized. At party headquarters he was well received. The manner in which he had fulfilled his latest assignments had given proof of his energy, devotion and organizing ability. He was told that he had been chosen by the party, whose influence in the trade union movement was considerable, to take over the post of secretary of the Zagreb branch of the Metalworkers' Union. Thus at thirty-five he became a full-time trade union official or perhaps it would be more correct to say, a full-time party executive. Henceforward the whole of his life was given up to the party.

By now the police, not unnaturally, had come to the conclusion that Josip Broz was something more than a mere trade union organizer. But in order to send him to prison for any length of time, they required, under the Law for the Defense of the State, concrete evidence that he was an active member of the Communist party. In June, 1927, soon after taking over as secretary of his union, he was arrested and removed to jail for interrogation. From Zagreb he was taken to Baker, near Kraljevica, where he was confronted with six of his fellow workers from the shipyard. Someone, it seemed, had admitted to borrowing left-wing literature from him and this had started an investigation. But no one could be found to say that he was a Communist. All seven were taken in chains to the nearby town of Ogulin and put into the ancient Frankopan Tower, overlooking the main square, to await trial.

Soon it became clear that the authorities were in no hurry to bring Broz to trial. It suited them better to keep him in jail. Weeks went by. Finally he decided to force their hand by declaring a hunger strike. After eating nothing for five days, by which time he was barely conscious, he received a visit in prison from the presiding judge, a kindly old liberal, who was worried at the repercussions which might be caused by the death in prison of a popular trade union leader. The judge did his best to persuade him to abandon his strike and start eating again, pointing out that he would do nobody any good by starving himself to death. But Broz did not let himself be put off. "People who fight sometimes die," he replied, and went on repeating that he would only give up his strike if he were brought to trial or released.[3] In the end he won his point. The judge gave him his word that the investigation of his case would soon be concluded, after which he would be brought to trial.

At his trial, which took place in October, 1927, Broz was sentenced to seven months' imprisonment on the charge of distributing subversive literature. On his appealing against this sentence the case was transferred to a higher court and he was for the time being allowed to go free. Pending the hearing of the appeal, he made his way back to Zagreb and resumed his trade union work. In addition to leading the Metalworkers' Union, he was now made secretary of the Leatherworkers' Union. He also began to play an increasingly active part politically and some months later was elected a member of the Central Committee of the Zagreb branch of the party.

Early in 1928 there was a sharp deterioration in the economic situation in Jugoslavia. Wages fell, the cost of living went up, unemployment increased. The result was widespread discontent and unrest, followed by further repressive action on the part of the police. But the Jugoslav Communist party were in no state to exploit this, from their point of view, promising state of affairs. In seven years their membership had dropped from sixty thousand to barely three thousand. At a time when economic depression offered an unusually favorable opportunity of stirring up industrial strife, these internecine feuds and dissensions and the absence of any real leadership effectively paralyzed the activities, not only of the party, but of the Communist-controlled trade unions.

To Josip Broz and other keen party workers like him, who were concerned not so much with abstruse ideological issues as with achieving practical revolutionary results, this state of affairs was deeply distressing. The party was missing its opportunities. Something, they decided, must be done. Their chance came at the Eighth Party Conference for the Zagreb Area which took place at the end of February, 1928.

The Conference was held clandestinely in a small house in the suburbs of Zagreb during the night of February 25-26. The house, which belonged to a woman of secret Communist sympathies, was in an isolated position and was not known to the police as a party meeting place. The thirty-two delegates arrived at it singly and by devious routes, having taken elaborate precautions to ensure that they were not being followed. They were admitted only after giving the appointed password. The Conference was also attended by a Ukrainian known as Milkovich, representing the Comintern. This meant that a detailed report on the Conference and on the attitude of the various delegates would in due course reach Moscow.

After an introductory speech from a dissident dentist, the main proceedings opened with a report by the Branch Secretary who sought to excuse the party's inactivity by blaming it on the extreme vigilance of the police. His remarks were received in unenthusiastic silence, broken only by the footsteps of the lookout man tramping up and down outside. As soon as the Branch Secretary sat down, pandemonium broke loose, the left attacking the right and the right attacking the left. This was the moment for which Josip Broz and his friends had been waiting. Profiting by their opponents' divisions, they rose one after another to attack the Central Committee, charging it with ineffectiveness and with failure to put a stop to the quarrels of right and left. A leading part was taken by Josip Broz himself, who, though now himself a member of the Central Committee, joined vigorously in the attacks on it and concluded by demanding that the Conference should take a firm stand against "fractionalism" and should dispatch a letter direct to the Comintern, condemning not one but both factions.

Although Broz and his friends were in a minority, they had the advantage of knowing exactly what they wanted while their opponents were divided among themselves. They enjoyed yet another advantage. Knowingly or unknowingly, they had the support of the Kremlin and of the man who was rapidly becoming its supreme master, Joseph Stalin, who, for his part, wholeheartedly shared their dislike of factions, greatly preferring a "monolithic" party exclusively under his own personal control.

In the end Broz and his friends got their way. The Branch Secretary's report was rejected, a new Central Committee for the Zagreb Area was elected and Broz appointed Secretary. It was five in the morning when the delegates finally dispersed. Outside it was dark and snow was falling. One by one they trudged off to their homes. It had been a useful night's work.

The new Central Committee soon made their presence felt. Broz's first act as Branch Secretary was to send direct to the Comintern, over the heads of the party leaders, a letter on the lines that he himself had suggested, urging that vigorous steps should be taken to liquidate "fractional strife in the Communist party of Jugoslavia."

Neither the letter nor its author passed unnoticed. In May, 1928 the Executive Committee of the Comintern responded with an "open letter" addressed to the members of the Jugoslav Communist party calling upon them once more to put an end to fractional strife.[4]

Simultaneously the old leadership of the party under Sima Marković was swept away and a new Central Committee appointed. In Moscow, meanwhile, the name of Josip Broz had been noted down for future reference as that of a zealous and dependable servant of the party.

During the year 1928 the internal position in Jugoslavia had grown ever more tense. After a temporary truce, the Croat Peasant party was once more in open opposition. The Croat question was more acute than ever. The economic situation had still further deteriorated. There was widespread unrest and discontent. The police became increasingly active. As Party Secretary of Zagreb, Broz was busier than ever before, moving clandestinely, organizing strikes and demonstrations, distributing arms, and generally doing everything he could to take advantage of what was beginning to look more and more like a revolutionary situation. In Zagreb the May Day demonstration organized by the party led to a clash with the police, in the course of which he himself was arrested and sent to prison for a fortnight. In Belgrade unrest over the Croat question culminated in an outburst of violence. The crisis finally reached its spectacular climax when on June 20, 1928, in the course of a stormy debate in the Skupština, a government supporter drew his pistol and opened fire at the opposition benches, mortally wounding Stjepan Radić and killing outright two other members of the Croat Peasant party. To many, the kingdom of the Serbs, Croats and Slovenes seemed about to disintegrate.

In Zabreb the shooting was the signal for more demonstrations against the regime and for riots lasting three days, in which the Communists, diligently fishing in the troubled waters, took a leading part, handing out such arms as they had and distributing pamphlets calling upon the people to rise against the government. This, in turn, provoked an even sharper reaction on the part of the authorities.

The police were by now searching high and low for Josip Broz, about whom they no longer had any illusions whatever. Hence-forward he lived "illegally," as it was called. He took to wearing glasses and assumed a variety of disguises and false names. An actor from the Zagreb theater showed his friend how best to alter his appearance. He was constantly on the move, never sleeping more than three nights running in the same house. While he snatched a hurried meal or a few hours' sleep, trusted comrades kept watch outside.

He had some narrow escapes. One day the police arrived while he was paying a flying visit to the offices of the Metal-workers' Union. "Is Josip Broz here?" they asked. "Can't you see he isn't?" Broz replied promptly, whereupon, much to his relief, the police saluted and withdrew. On another occasion, when he arrived at his office he found the police already in occupation. This time they recognized him, but he was too quick for them and, jumping out of the window onto the roof of another building, managed to make good his escape. The new Branch Secretary was not an easy man to pin down.

But the police caught up with him in the end. At eleven o'clock on the night of August 4 he was accosted in the street by a man he knew vaguely by sight who gave him a message asking him to come round urgently to 46 Vinogradska Ilica, to a room where he and other party members used occasionally to spend the night. There were some comrades there, the messenger said, who were in trouble and needed his help. Broz had been up all the night before and was feeling tired. Without stopping to check the messenger's credentials, he went round to No. 46. As he entered the room, he was seized by two plain-clothes policemen who handcuffed him and carried him off to Police Headquarters on the Ilica for inter-rogation. He had fallen into a carefully laid trap.

This time the charges brought against him were serious

ones: active membership in the illegal Communist party; the dissemination of Communist propagaanda; the illegal possession of bombs and firearms. After three months in prison, he and five of his associates came up for trial at Zagreb on November 6, 1928.[5]

The trial, which was prominently reported in the local press, was remarkable for one thing in particular: for the first time a prisoner openly glorified the Communist cause. Broz's cross-examination took place on the second day of the trial. The correspondent of *Novosti,* a right-wing newspaper, was struck by the way in which, from the dock, he dominated the proceedings. "Josip Broz," he wrote,

was brought in next. His is undoubtedly the most interesting personality in this trial. His face makes you think of steel. His light gray eyes, behind his spectacles, are cold, but alert and calm. In his case, his attitude in court is perhaps more than a mere pose, for he has been prosecuted before and has already served several sentences for his political beliefs. Many of those present were doubtless aware of the stubbornness with which he maintains his views, and his cross-examination was listened to attentively and in complete silence.

From the very start Broz took the offensive. Asked by the president of the court if he understood the charges preferred against him, he replied that he did, but that he did not consider himself guilty of any crime. "I admit," he went on, "that I am a member of the illegal Communist Party of Jugoslavia. I admit that I have spread Communist propaganda and that I have proclaimed the injustice suffered by the proletariat at the hands of a bourgeois government. I admit that I have expressed that idea in public and in private ever since the Communist party ceased to be legal and became illegal. But I do not recognize your bourgeois court of justice. I consider myself responsible only to my own party."

"Have you ever heard of the Law for the Defense of the State?"

"I have heard of it, but I have not read it. It did not interest me."

"Do you know that it forbids all Communist propaganda?"

"I do. But it is only a temporary law, a law brought in by one class against another, a law that will be swept away."

"But at the present moment it is in force, like the other

laws of this country, and anyone who breaks it ends up in Lepoglava Prison. It is a law that has a long arm."

"I know. But it is not a law that was passed by the people, and I am not in the least afraid of it. It would be a sad thing if the Communist party were to let itself be frightened by a temporary piece of legislation."

"You are obstinately throwing away your young lives to no purpose at all."

"I am quite ready to accept the consequences of my action, whatever they may be."

Asked about Božićković, the landlord of the room in which he had been arrested, Broz denied that Božićković was a Communist. "I don't like," he said, "to think of innocent people suffering."

"But what about the hand grenades under his bed?"

"Do you think," retorted Broz, evading the issue, "that it would only take four hand grenades to overthrow the present regime?"

"Four here, four there, four in every street—and you'd soon see what it would lead to."

"I'll admit anything else you like, but I know nothing about the hand grenades. Although, if they had been mine, I should have been quite ready to admit it. Because, after all, anybody who is oppressed has the right to defend himself, by force of arms if necessary."

"What did you use the room for?"

"To hide our friends when the police were after them."

"Who stayed there?"

"You won't get that out of me."

"And so you know nothing about the hand grenades?"

"Nothing. It would in any case have been very foolish of anyone to keep hand grenades and Communist literature in the same room."*

"They are both useful for the fulfillment of your program. Did you know there was Communist literature in the cupboard?"

"I did."

"Packets addressed to the Communist Youth Organization, to Montenegro, to the Vojvodina, to Macedonia, etc.? And notes of how many leaflets and pamphlets you had sent out?"

"I admitted just now that I had distributed Communist propaganda," said Broz, raising his voice. "Isn't that enough for you? What more do you want me to say? I am not, Mr.

* "They were mine all right," he said years later, on being asked whose the hand grenades really were.

Prosecutor, prepared to go into these matters in detail. You must work out the meaning of the notes you have found for yourself as best you can."

"Are you in communication with Moscow?" asked the president.

"Certainly we are in communication with Moscow. We are Moscow's organization."

"Did you sleep in the room yourself?"

"Yes, for four nights between June 20 and the beginning of August."

"Was it just by chance that the hand grenades were found there?"

"After what had happened on June 20, the blame had to be put on somebody and my guess is that the police planted the arms and the hand grenades on us. I have had some experience of the methods used by the police. They had killed three workers. Therefore they had to pin the blame for something on the workers. Therefore they planted the arms and hand grenades on us."

"I suppose," inquired the public prosecutor, "that you didn't happen to kill the three workers yourselves, so that you could fish in troubled water? By the way, do you know about the leaflets calling a strike for June 20?"

"I do."

"Did you write them?"

"I did not."

"They were found in your room. So was the duplicating machine."

"I don't know who wrote them or who duplicated them. What I do know is that the police treated me in the most savage and inhuman way." And Broz launched into a detailed account of the rough treatment he had received at the hands of the police after his arrest, of his hunger strike and of the despairing screams he had heard coming from the neighboring cells where his fellow prisoners were being interrogated.

"You are simply telling these stories so that people should think you a martyr," interrupted the public prosecutor. "I suppose you hope it will make them send you money from Moscow. All the other prisoners say that they were well treated."

"I have admitted most of the charges against me and I have nothing to fear. I know that I am in for a long stretch in jail anyhow. The others are all afraid of what will happen to them if they say anything. That is why they say they were well treated."

The proceedings concluded on November 9, when the public prosecutor further developed his case against Broz and asked for a heavy sentence under Article I of the Law for the Defense of the State.

It had been Broz's intention to make a speech in reply, a speech telling how he had become a Communist in the first place, of his childhood and youth, of all the oppression and injustice and inequality there was in the world, of the struggle of the poor and unprivileged against the rich and privileged; telling, too, of the part which the Communist party had played, was playing and would play in all this.[6] But he had hardly begun when the president of the court ruled him out of order, refused permission for either counsel to say any more and brought the proceedings to an abrupt conclusion. Whereupon Broz, jumping up, shouted across to the president, "What better proof could there be that this is a police state? Long live the Communist party! Long live the World Revolution!" At this there was some disturbance in court; the president suspended the sitting, and the defendants were forcibly removed by the police.

The sentences were announced in a packed courtroom on Wednesday morning, November 14. They were read out amid complete silence. Under Article I of the Law for the Defense of the State, Josip Broz was sentenced to five years' imprisonment on the grounds that, being an active member of the Communist party, he had rented a room from which, with the help of unknown associates, he had disseminated Communist propaganda; that, with the object of furthering Communist aims he had purchased and hidden four German hand grenades and one revolver and ammunition. To the sentence of five years were added a further five months in respect of the charges brought against him at Ogulin the year before. Two of his fellow defendants were given shorter terms of imprisonment, while the other two were acquitted.

After the sentences had been read out, Broz jumped to his feet and, turning to the crowd, again shouted three times "Long live the Communist party! Long live the Third International!" Then he and his companions were led out.

All this was reported at length in the press, and the published accounts were widely read and passed from hand to hand by discontented people all over the country. As a result, the Communist cause was exalted and to many people Josip Broz became a hero.

Had he taken a different line at his trial, he might have received a shorter sentence. "But," he said afterward to a friend, "our party needed showing that it was a proud thing to be a Communist, that the party deserved unquestioning loyalty and devotion from its members and was worth going to prison for too, without cringing to the bourgeoisie or trying to get your sentence shortened by feigning respect for their courts and their police."[7]

Even in this, whether consciously or unconsciously, Josip Broz was demonstrating his unswerving obedience to the precepts of the Comintern. "In its trials and tribulations," ran a resolution passed by the Executive Committee of the Comintern in April, 1926, "the Jugoslav party must use every platform that offers itself to spread Communist ideas and policy. The party must pay special attention to the behavior of its members in courts of law and at police investigations. Hitherto they have not always taken full advantage of these opportunities of defending the party's ideas before the masses."

Broz served the bulk of his sentence at Lepoglava, a pleasant little town lying at the foot of the mountains on the borders of his native Zagorje. The prison was situated in a former Pauline monastery which had been converted to its present use at the time of the Hapsburgs. Once again his mechanical knowledge stood him in good stead. After a time he was, on the strength of it, put in charge of a small power plant which supplied electricity for the town and prison, and, in return for working it, was allowed books to read and other amenities. His new post allowed him comparative freedom of movement. With a screwdriver in one hand and a test bulb in the other, he was at liberty to wander in and out of the other cells and all over the building. Sometimes he was even sent under escort to the village to carry out repairs. Broz made the best of his opportunities. Before long he had established a Communist cell in the prison and soon its gray walls housed a flourishing party organization. In due course he was even able to re-establish contact with his comrades outside, thanks to a friendly café proprietor in the town who plied his escort with drinks and so kept them occupied downstairs, while he disappeared upstairs, ostensibly to mend the electric light, but in fact to confer with secret Communist emissaries from Zagreb.

In all this he was ably supported by one of his fellow prisoners, a Belgrade Jew by the name of Moša Pijade, who was transferred to Lepoglava from another prison in January, 1930, and thereafter acted as assistant electrician. Pijade, who had been given a fourteen-year sentence in 1925 for illegally editing and printing a Communist newspaper, came of a well-known Sephardic Jewish family, long established in Jugoslavia. He was an odd-looking little man of about forty with a toothbrush mustache, a quizzical expression and rapid birdlike movements. In addition to being a talented writer, he was an impressionist painter of some distinction and amused himself while in prison by painting portraits of his fellow prisoners and of the prison staff. But his real vocation was for Marxist dialectics. He was even now engaged on a translation of the collected works of Marx and Engels and was always ready for an argument on some abstruse point of Marxist doctrine. Broz and he soon became firm friends. Though they had never met before, Broz had heard of him as one of the leading theoreticians of the party, while he in prison had heard of Broz's courageous conduct at his trial. Broz found Pijade's conversation fascinating. Pijade, for his part, was struck by the pertinence and directness of the questions which this untutored mechanic would put in the course of their discussions on Communist theory. A snapshot taken at the time shows this oddly assorted pair standing in front of their power plant, Broz alert and lively-looking, Pijade gazing owl-like through his spectacles, his thoughts seemingly far away in the realm of dialectical materialism.

Broz spent nearly five years at Lepoglava. At the end of this time he was charged with trying to escape and moved to Maribor in Slovenia, then generally regarded as the worst prison in Jugoslavia. Here he had none of the privileges which he had enjoyed up to now. Even so he succeeded in smuggling in and reading the works of left-wing literature which were so dear to him, usually disguised as harmless works of fiction. The treatment of prisoners and the living conditions at Maribor were considerably worse than they had been at Lepoglava. Cigarettes were hard to come by. When they got one, the prisoners would take turns in smoking it, the butt end, with its accumulation of nicotine, being eagerly sought after. In the intervals of making innumerable paper bags, they would wage war against the bedbugs with which the prison swarmed. The most effective method, they found, was to burn them out of their hiding places with a red-hot wire. Sometimes when Broz was alone in his cell, he would listen to the trains shunting on the railway line outside. Now and then the engine driver would be new to his job. The locomotive would start with a roar and stop with a sudden screeching of brakes, jarring to the nerves of a trained mechanic.

But the years which Broz spent in prison were not entirely wasted. They gave him time for thought. For the first time in his active, agitated life he had leisure to read extensively. He used it to continue and complete his modest early education. He read his way through a whole series of massive works on economics and psychology and sociology and political science. He read Shakespeare, and John Stuart Mill *On Liberty,* and a book on Greek Philosophy. He also read and reread the works of Marx and Engels. And he talked it all over with Moša Pijade and other intellectuals. "It was," he said long afterward, "just like being at a university." Asked whether his imprisonment had embittered him or made him hate the then regime more than before, he replied that it had not. "I regarded the whole question," he said, "from a purely realistic and practical point of view. I was trying to overthrow their government. It was only natural that when they caught me they should shut me up. I should have done the same in their place. Indeed I had every intention of doing the same when I *was* in their place."[8]

Broz served the last few months of his sentence in the old Frankopan Tower at Ogulin. When he was finally released in March, 1934, he was told that henceforward he must remain permanently at Kumrovec and report every day to the authorities. While still in prison he had ordered himself a smart new suit and a good pair of brown shoes to wear when he came out. Putting these on, he set out for Kumrovec.

DURING the six years which Josip Broz spent in jail events in the outside world were following the uneasy course which in a score of years was to lead from one world war to another. In 1929 the slump hit the United States. In 1931 the "China incident" led to war in the Far East. In 1933 Hitler came to power in Germany, pledged to overthrow the Versailles settlement and much else besides.

In Jugoslavia matters had finally come to a head at the beginning of 1929. The assassination of Stjepan Radić, which was followed by the withdrawal of the Croat Peasant party deputies from the Skupština, had shown clearly enough that things could not go on as they were. On January 6, 1929, King Alexander, having rejected the demand of the Croat Peasant party for a federal constitution as a condition of their further co-operation, suspended the Constitution, dissolved Parliament, appointed the Commander of the Royal Guard as his Prime Minister and established what was in effect a personal dictatorship. "The machine," he said, in an interview with the correspondent of *Le Matin*, "no longer works."

These were lean years for the Jugoslav Communist party. The Royal Police were more active than ever. Djuro Djaković, the Organizing Secretary, was caught and killed within a few months of taking over. The Political Secretary, Jovan Martinović, after a vain attempt at armed insurrection, fled abroad to Vienna whence he sent confused and hysterical instructions to the rank and file in Jugoslavia. In Vienna, Martinovic and the other leaders soon became absorbed once more in abstruse "fractionalist" disputes and completely lost touch with the party in the country, who were left to fend for themselves as best they could in the face of increasingly rigorous action on the part of the police. The latter now managed to introduce a number of their own informers and *agents provocateurs* into the party, with the result that in two years they succeeded in killing over a hundred of its members and arresting a thousand more—out of a total, it must be remembered, of barely three thousand. To quote the Central Committee's report to the Fifth Party Congress: "Party life in the country died down in 1930 and 1931. Only scattered individual groups existed. Almost the entire leading party cadre, both high and low, were in prison, had been killed, or had emigrated."

Nor was it only the Communists who were adversely affected by what came to be called the Regime of the Sixth of January. The Croat Peasant party also suffered its full share of persecution. Meanwhile many of the more extreme Croat nationalists followed the example of the Communists and went "underground" or into exile, determined to bring about by violence what they had failed to achieve by constitutional means, namely, the independence of Croatia. On January 7, 1929, the day after the suspension of the Constitution, a number of them founded in Zagreb a secret society known as the *Ustaše* or Rebels. Their leader, or *Poglavnik,* was a certain Dr. Ante Pavelić, a plain, gloomy-looking lawyer with flat heavy features and large ears, who had been a Croat member of the Skupština.

Dr. Pavelić did not himself remain in Croatia, but moved two days after the inaugural ceremony to Austria and thence to Italy, where, under the protection of the Italian Government and with Italian financial support, he established at Borgotaro a training center for Ustaše agents who were subsequently sent back to Jugoslavia for the purpose of committing acts of terrorism. A similar Ustaša center was established at Yanka Pusta in Hungary with the approval of the Hungarian Government, who, like the Italians, welcomed any opportunity of making trouble for their Jugoslav neighbors and looked forward hopefully to Jugoslavia's early disappearance from the map. At these and at other camps in Italy and Hungary little bands of desperate men were trained up to form the nucleus of a force which, their leaders hoped, would one day enter Zagreb in triumph as an army of liberation. Meanwhile in twos and threes, they slipped across the frontier to deal death and destruction in their native land and so, in their eyes, to strike a blow for Croatian independence. Soon periodic explosions on Jugoslav trains and in barracks and police stations bore witness to their activity, and in October, 1934 their efforts were crowned by the assassination of King Alexander at Marseilles while he was on a state visit to France.

By a strange turn of fate, Alexander proved more popular

in death than in life. Their king's murder in a foreign land came as a shock to the Jugoslav people. Even in Croatia weeping crowds knelt at the side of the railway line as the train bore his body back to Belgrade. The disorders which his enemies had hoped would break out on his death failed to materialize and he was duly succeeded as king by his son Peter, a schoolboy of eleven. During the young King's minority the regency was assumed by his father's cousin, Paul. Prince Paul, an agreeable, cultivated man with many foreign friends and connections, had spent much of his life abroad. He had fought neither in the Balkan wars nor in the Great War; took more interest in art and literature than in the affairs of state; and felt altogether more at home in a Paris salon or an Oxford common room than in the rough and tumble of Balkan politics, into which, willy-nilly, he was now plunged.

On his release from prison in March, 1934, Josip Broz had gone underground. His parents were both dead. His wife and son were in Russia, whither they had been sent clandestinely by the party while he was in jail. After a brief visit to Kumrovec to see his friends and a short stay with a married sister near by, he had made his way to Zagreb and there established contact with the party organization. Learning that he had disappeared from Kumrovec, the police issued a warrant for his arrest. The news did not disturb him unduly. He grew a mustache, dyed his hair red and put on a pair of spectacles. He also assumed a false name, in fact a whole series of false names, with false papers and false personalities to match. Henceforward he was to live, in the jargon of the party, "illegally."

Josip Broz was now forty-two. His devotion to the Communist cause was, if possible, stronger than ever; indeed he cared for nothing else. All that he had seen, all that he had read, convinced him that in Communism lay the solution to every problem. The constant dangers and difficulties which he had to face meant nothing to him; the cause he served meant everything. To a relative who at this time sought to persuade him to abandon his revolutionary calling and settle down, he explained that if he did not follow what he believed in he would not be able to live with himself—it was stronger than he was.[1] While in prison, he had lost none of his old energy and decisiveness. He was also better educated, more thoughtful, more stable and more mature than when he had

started to serve his sentence six years earlier. These new qualities all helped to fit him for the increasingly important role
which he was henceforth to assume.

The years 1933 and 1934 had witnessed a certain revival
of Communist activity in Jugoslavia. A number of active party
members who had been rounded up by the police in 1928 and
1929 had served their sentences and been released. Fresh
cells were formd and local and provincial party committees
once more set up. But the party leaders and the Central Committee still remained in Austria, out of touch and out of sympathy with the rank and file. Nothing could be undertaken
by the party organizations in Jugoslavia until authority had
first been received from the Central Committee in Vienna,
while the Central Committee, for their part, did nothing without authority from Moscow. Owing to poor communications,
this led to endless delay and confusion.

On resuming contact with the secret party organization in
Zagreb, where his conduct at his trial six years before was
still remembered with enthusiasm, Broz was received with
open arms and was at once elected a member of the new
Provincial Committee for Croatia. For the Provincial Committee, the immediate problem was to establish a firm connection with the Central Committee of the party in Vienna.
So far, almost all the emissaries sent by the Central Committee had been caught by the police. Broz was known as a
resourceful, experienced and above all a practical man. It
was decided that he should go to Vienna for the purpose of
discussing with the Central Committee how regular communications could best be established.

Dressed as a tourist with climbing boots and a rucksack
and armed with a card showing him to be a member of the
Mountaineering Club of Slovenia, Broz set out toward the
end of July, 1934 for the Austrian frontier, accompanied by
a guide who, in return for a large sum of money, had undertaken to show him a short cut across the mountains which
would avoid the frontier posts. But before they had even
reached the dangerous part of their route, the guide, who had
come provided with three bottles of wine, was incapably
drunk and clamoring loudly for more money. In the end
Broz was forced to leave him and go on alone. Somehow he
managed to find his way through the mountains and at length
arrived, hungry and exhausted, on the other side. But, on
reaching the outskirts of the first Austrian village, he was
surprised to be stopped a few seconds later by three young

men carrying rifles. Then he noticed that the young men, who were in civilian clothes, were wearing scarlet armbands with a black swastika on a white ground. Earlier that day— it was July 25—members of the Austrian National Socialist party had assassinated the Chancellor, Dr. Dollfuss, in Vienna and were now trying to seize power all over the country. In this particular village fighting was going on between government troops and the local Nazis, each side holding one end. The Nazis asked Broz what he wanted. He replied that he was a Jugoslav tourist. To this the Nazis retorted that in that case he had better go back to Jugoslavia; for the moment they could spare no time for foreigners. There was nothing for it but to set out again uphill in the direction of the frontier. But, once he was safely out of sight, Broz turned back in the direction of the nearby town of Klagenfurt. Before he had gone much farther he was again stopped, this time by government supporters, who, when he told them that he had been obliged to make a detour in order to avoid the Nazis, let him go again. And so in the end he succeeded in reaching Klagenfurt. There, too, he found fighting in progress, but in the confusion managed to make his way to the railway station, where he caught the train to Vienna.

The first thing to be done on reaching Vienna was to make contact with the Central Committee. For conspiratorial reasons, all he had been told by the party in Zagreb was that, if he visited a certain young Jugoslav girl who was studying the ballet in Vienna, she would give him the information he needed. He duly called on her and was told that she would let him have an answer next day. Meanwhile she gave him an address in the Döblingerstrasse where he could find a "safe" room. Next day came a message to say that the Central Committee would see him.

The Secretary of the Jugoslav Communist party at this time was a large redheaded man with freckles called Milan Gorkić, who had succeeded Martinović at the end of 1932 after one of the Comintern's periodical purges. Though born in Bosnia, Gorkić was by race a Czech, his real name being Cizinski. Before his appointment he had spent twelve years or so working at Comintern Headquarters in Moscow, where, it seemed, he was well thought of. He and the other members of the Central Committee received Broz with apparent enthusiasm, asking innumerable questions about what was happening in Jugoslavia. In Broz's own words, they fell on him "like bees on honey."[2] Broz gave then a frank account of conditions in the country and of the frame of mind of the party. The rank and file, he said, disliked having absentee leaders.

After some weeks spent in discussions in Vienna, Broz was told that he had been co-opted to the Central Committee and might henceforward regard himself as one of the leaders of the party. He was to go back to Jugoslavia and arrange for the holding of clandestine party conferences, first for Croatia and Slovenia and then for the whole country. He was to send reports on these to the Central Committee. With this assignment he returned late in August to Zagreb, again taking the same route by which he had come.

Back in Jugoslavia, Broz lost no time in getting to work. The Party Conference for Croatia was held immediately after his return to Zagreb and a full report dispatched to the Central Committee by a reliable messenger on September 3. He then went to Slovenia, where he reorganized the Provincial Committee and made arrangements for the forthcoming conference. This was held in the second half of September in a country house belonging to the Bishop of Slovenia, whose half-brother was a Communist sympathizer who, unknown to the Bishop, had placed it at the disposal of the party. Thus it was that about thirty delegates from all over Slovenia lived in the Bishop's house in luxury for two days, sleeping in comfortable beds and eating abundant meals off the Bishop's best plate and china, magnificently emblazoned with the episcopal arms.

Broz's chief aim was to collect a nucleus of active and devoted party members capable of overhauling and revitalizing the derelict party organization throughout the country. At the various conferences and meetings which he organized he met some of the new generation of Jugoslav Communists and was able to form some idea of their value. Most of them had, like himself, served prison sentences and undergone the rigors of police interrogation. This was a powerful bond between them. Many had known each other in prison and had belonged to the same illicit party cells and Marxist study groups. All were united by the feeling of comradeship which comes from dangers endured in common. "It was a full, intensive life," one of them said later. "You felt yourself growing up. We came to know the meaning of discipline and comradeship, the sharing of responsibility, the meaning in fact of a collective life. I, for my part, discovered freedom . . . in jail. When we came out, we had learned something, and not only with our heads; we had had actual experience. We were free, just as we had been in prison, because we had learned how to live together and work together for aims we all believed in, even though some of us would have to die before they were achieved."[3] Broz, a keen and exacting judge, took all this in and saw that here were men he could work with, men of an altogether different brand from the group of decaying refugees he had found in Vienna.

At Ljubljana and at the Slovene Party Conference he met a young man whose name was Edvard Kardelj, and who was also known variously as Bevs and Levs and Kristof and Bircs. Kardelj, now in his early twenties, was a short, dark, reserved youth with spectacles and a slight limp. Born in Ljubljana of working-class parents, he had, with several of his friends, joined the illegal Young Communist League at sixteen, when studying to be a schoolteacher. At nineteen, he had been caught by the police, badly tortured and sentenced to two years' hard labor. He had throughout resolutely refused to give any information and had on his release immediately resumed his revolutionary activities. His experiences at the hands of the police had left him with a limp but had not dismayed him. "While I was under torture," he said afterward, "it never for one moment entered my head that I might give in."[4]

What struck Broz most about Kardelj was his steadfastness and his calm, equable temperament. He was also favorably impressed by the quiet efficiency with which he did his work. Efficiency was a quality by which Broz set great store. "Kardelj was so quiet," he said many years later, "that you hardly noticed him at first; but decisions were made, aims were achieved, and then you realized that it was he who had made the proposal, persuaded others to accept it, and put it into effect. No setback dismayed him. He was free of pretense and bluff. He eschewed fractionalism. His mind dwelt on essentials. After my first meeting with him I had no doubt that he was an honest man and a true revolutionary."[5]

Another young Slovene Communist who attracted Broz's attention was Boris Kidrić, the son of a professor at the University of Ljubljana and a friend and contemporary of Kardelj's. "In summing up a man," he said afterward, "I notice how he goes about his work. . . I like people who don't fret and fuss about details, but keep their minds on the task in hand and overcome obstacles as they appear. Kidrić was like that. No difficulties could put him off."[6]

There were others too: in Zagreb, in Ljubljana, in Belgrade and scattered here and there all over the country—young men and women from all walks of life. Peasants, artisans and poor students plotted, schemed and defied authority in company with the sons and daughters of cabinet ministers, generals, rich merchants and high government officials. Most of them had become Communists for two main reasons: because of the poverty, corruption and social injustice which they saw all around them and because of the dislike which many of them, as Croats, Slovenes or even Serbs, felt for the pan-Serb hegemony in Belgrade. Communism, with its flavor of illegality and its promise of revolution, appealed to their innate turbulence, to their natural resentment of authority. Communism, they felt, would get rid of the Belgrade regime and of the *carsija,* the gang of financiers and politicians who in their minds were associated with it. Communism, they firmly believed, would give the people control of their own country and bring them a better standard of living. In a bewildering world, Communism seemed to them the only system that made sense.

Nor did the increasing severity of the Royal Police do anything to undermine their convictions. They were too deeply rooted for that. For them Communism possessed an apocalyptic quality, which seemed to lift them out of the squalor and drabness of their everyday life. It was a cult which brought them spiritual satisfaction, a secular religion which made them feel that they were part of a higher world, a select company especially chosen to redeem humanity. It gave them a sense of their own strength and superiority. It made their less fortunate fellows seem by comparison ignorant, stupid and lost. It furnished them with a revealed theology, with a body of dogma which solved all their problems. It endowed them with a new loyalty, a new morality, a new set of values. It prepared them for any sacrifice on their own part or on the part of others, for any act of deceit or violence. It gave them, finally, something to yearn for, something to look forward to: first, Armageddon, the Revolution, and, after that, the Paradise of a Soviet Jugoslavia.

Up to now there had not been much they could do. Working in teams of three or four, usually out of touch with such central organization as existed, they had distributed leaflets and scribbled Communist slogans on walls. But even these unimportant and unco-ordinated activities and the risks which they involved called for certain qualities and served, in a sense, as a test and a preparation for what was to come.

Early in 1934 effective contact had been established between the underground party organizations in Ljubljana, Zagreb, Belgrade and elsewhere. "We found," to quote Kardelj, "some of our former fellow prisoners among the new leaders. This gave us a feeling of confidence, for we knew them, we knew that we could trust them utterly. It also gave us a feeling of being part of a national movement. All the other parties and religions in the old Jugoslavia were regional. Ours embraced the whole country."[7]

It was at this stage that Josip Broz appeared on the scene, neatly, even smartly, dressed, equipped with credentials from the Central Committee, and with the reputation he had won by his open defiance of the regime at his trial six years earlier. Kardelj has given his own and his comrades' first impressions of him: "We found him very direct of speech and manner. He was in his early forties, about twenty years older than we were, and looked it. But he was not at all like the old-time party leaders, who were nothing but bureaucrats. He did not talk about himself, but you felt that he had experience. He was well versed in Marxist theory, but, when you put a question to him, he did not always answer with a quotation from Marx or Engels, or Lenin—he spoke in practical, common-sense terms. 'That,' he would say, 'is the problem which confronts us. This is what I think ought to be done. Do any of you think differently?' If none of us had any conflicting opinions to put forward, he would urge us to think again. That was (and still is) his method of conducting conferences."[8]

At the Party Conference for Slovenia Broz put forward an idea which was likely to commend itself to an audience of Slovenes, and which also accorded with the current party line. He was, he said, in favor of each natonality or region in Jugoslavia having a Communist party of its own, all of which together would constitute the Communist party of Jugoslavia.* They would thus be laying the foundations of a federal state. He spoke with the authority lent him by his membership of the Central Committee of the party and, more important still, by his own revolutionary past. Though nominally only an observer, he became, in the words of one of those who attended it, "the center of the meeting."[9]

* This proposal was in fact implemented in 1937.

Toward the end of September, Broz returned to Vienna to report in person to the Central Committee, traveling by train on a forged Czech passport. This time, more than ever, he could speak to his fellow members of the Central Committee as the representative of the party in the country, of the party with which they, its nominal leaders, had so completely lost touch.

At the beginning of October, after a few busy days in Vienna, during which he gave an account of his own activities, worked out plans for the subversion of the armed forces, for the formation of "Workers' Defense Companies," for the penetration of the trade unions and for the preparation of strikes, and also discussed arrangements for the forthcoming Fourth Party Conference, Broz again went back to Jugoslavia. But hardly had he arrived there than the news was received of King Alexander's assassination at Marseilles. This was naturally at once followed by an intensive security drive. Broz was well known to the authorities and was by now more heavily compromised than ever. If the police caught him again, he was bound to be sentenced to a long spell in prison—or worse. Of late, he had proved himself of great value to the party. The Central Committee accordingly decided that for the time being he had better leave Jugoslavia. A message was sent to him, instructing him to return at once to Vienna en route for the Soviet Union.

The passport he used for the journey had been hurriedly and not very skillfully forged and on reaching the Austrian border he was disturbed to find that a particularly rigorous investigation of all documents had been instituted. It looked as though he was going to be caught. But, just as the frontier police were coming round, an Austrian woman who was traveling in the same railway carriage gave him her six months' old baby to hold. Broz took the baby on his knee with one hand and handed the frontier guard his passport with the other. The baby chose this moment to relieve itself, ruining Broz's best pair of trousers. This so amused the frontier guard that he scarcely bothered to glance at the passport. A few minutes later they were safely across the frontier.

Owing to the intensified activity of the Austrian police since Dr. Dollfuss's murder in July, it was no longer possible for the Central Committee to meet in Vienna, and the meeting which Broz now attended was held at Brno in Czechoslovakia, whither he traveled under yet another pseudonym and with yet another forged passport—an Austrian passport this time, made out in the name of a barber called Jirechek. At this meeting it was decided that he should spend some time in Moscow in the Jugoslav section of the Comintern. Not long afterward he was on his way to the Soviet Union.

Leaving the last Polish station behind it, the train plunged once more into dark pine forests. The snow was piled high on either side of the track and stretched away dimly under the trees. Suddenly, as they looked out of the windows, the passengers could see that they were approaching a high barbed-wire fence, floodlit and broken at intervals by watchtowers from which machine guns protruded, pointing, like menacing black fingers, across the snow. The train slowed down and then passed through a rather flimsy wooden arch bearing a large red star and the inscription "Greetings to the Workers of Europe." They were in Russia.

It was the first time Broz had been back to the Soviet Union since 1920. For the whole of those fifteen years, during which he had grown from youth to maturity, his thoughts, his hopes and his ambitions had been constantly focused on the Country of the Revolution, on that promised land, where, as a youth, he had found the answer to all his longings, where, in a blinding flash, the Truth, the ultimate Truth had been revealed to him. "In the most trying hours," he wrote long afterward, "through dismal nights and endless interrogation and maltreatment, through days of deadly solitude and close confinement, we were always sustained by the hope that these agonies were not in vain, that far away there was a mighty country, where all the dreams for which we were fighting had been fulfilled. For us, it was the Workers' Fatherland, where labor was honored, where love, comradeship and sincerity prevailed. How I exulted in its might when I came out of prison in 1934 and could listen each night to Radio Moscow and hear the Kremlin clock striking the hours and the stirring strains of the Internationale."[10] And now he was back there, back in the Land of Socialism, back at the center of things.

Frontier guards, their bright green caps adorned with red star, hammer and sickle, and their long gray greatcoats reaching almost to the heels of their soft top boots, boarded the train. One of them saluted and asked Broz for his passport. He handed it over, secure in the knowledge that, even though it was, as usual, forged, here for once was a frontier guard from whom he personally had nothing to fear. A few moments later they steamed into the frontier station of Negoreloye.

Here they changed trains. Outside, on the platform, the cold was intense. In the steam-heated customs building brightly colored murals depicted scenes from Soviet life: a succession of preternaturally happy and healthy soldiers, peasants, workers, old men, women and children, getting in the harvest, driving tractors, building houses and manipulating large and complicated machines. Round the room, in half a dozen languages, golden letters a foot high invited the workers of the world to unite. In the four corners, aspidistras grew in pots. It was all very new and very bright. For Josip Broz, returning after an absence of fifteen years to the Country of the Revolution, all these outward and visible signs of Communist achievement had a special significance. They represented what he himself, all those long years ago, had helped to build. It was what, in time, he hoped to build in his own country, in Jugoslavia. With a feeling of elation he made his way to his sleeping car. It had been built before the Revolution. But before the Revolution it would have been reserved for the idle rich, whereas now all that had been changed. An obsequious conductor, noticing his foreign clothes and securing a tip, showed him to his bunk. Soon they were rattling at a steady twenty-five miles an hour across the snow-covered plain to Moscow.

There had been many changes in the Country of the Revolution since Broz had left it to return home in 1920. In 1924 Lenin had died. Already during his last illness, as he lay paralyzed, the struggle for the succession had begun between Trotsky and Stalin. It had culminated five years later in the triumph of Stalin and the defeat and exile of Trotsky.

All other considerations of Communist doctrine or policy were now subordinated to the attainment of three main aims: first the concentration and maintenance of power in the hands of Stalin himself; secondly, the building up of the military and economic strength of the Soviet Union; and thirdly, the extension of Soviet influence, and, where possible, of Soviet authority, outside the frontiers of the Soviet Union—aims to be pursued by all possible means, subject only to the condition that nothing be undertaken in pursuit of either of the two latter aims which might in any way prejudice the first. For the total opportunism which followed, justification was always ready to hand: only thus could the Revolution be safeguarded and its ultimate triumph assured. It was as simple as that. By such rough and ready means, practice was reconciled with theory, or, perhaps it would be more accurate to say, theory was brought into line with practice.

And indeed the ensuing years were marked by the most complete disregard, not only for ordinary considerations of morality, but for what had once seemed essential tenets of Communist doctrine. These were the years of the first and second Five Year Plans, designed to make the Soviet Union self-sufficient and ready for any contingency—in particular for war. To achieve this end, all means were employed, and the vision of a peaceful, prosperous, classless Utopia rapidly receded into the dim distance. Instead of withering away altogether, as Marx and the prophets had said it would, the state, the Soviet State, grew in stature and in strength until, monstrous, it dominated everything, crushing all other human manifestations out of existence. A powerful army, navy and air force were built up; a vast police force was brought into being. Forced labor was used on an unprecedented scale and treated as expendable. A new, highly privileged managerial class was deliberately created. The Stakhanovite system, used for increasing production, was indistinguishable from capitalist "speeding-up" methods. Agriculture was collectivized, and, in the process, millions of peasants starved to death. The party, the government, the administration, the armed forces, industry, agriculture and every other branch of the national life were swept by periodical purges of "traitors," "wreckers" and "deviationists." By such means Stalin increased the military, industrial and economic potential of the Soviet Union and at the same time maintained and methodically consolidated his own position.

Such was the wider background against which in January, 1935 Josip Broz settled down to work at Comintern Headquarters. After many years spent as a fighter in the front line, he had been promoted a staff officer of the Revolution. It was in some ways not quite the same revolution that had swept him off his feet nearly twenty years before. But it still commanded his entire loyalty.

On the recommendation of the Central Committee of the Jugoslav party he had been appointed to the Balkan Secretariat of the Commintern as *rapporteur* for Jugoslavia. This meant that all reports from Jugoslavia came to him and that he prepared the memoranda which served as a basis for any discussion concerning Jugoslav affairs. Like the gods and demigods of the ancients, the denizens of the Communist Olympus possessed many names: some for use by the initiated and some by the profane, some official and some conspiratorial, some permanent and others temporary. On taking up his new appointment, Josip Broz was given a new name. Henceforth he was known to Moscow as "Comrade Walter."

Of some interest, as showing how he was regarded in his own party at this time, is the confidential report, dated January 16, 1935, which accompanied the Central Committee's recommendation that he should be appointed *rapporteur*. "We," they wrote,

> are agreed that he can take on this job. We leave final decision to you. If he is appointed *rapporteur*, see that people are nice to him. Tell Valija and the rest of them that he is a worker who has spent six years in prison and that perhaps at first he will not be as skillful as some of the more experienced intellectuals. But he knows the party; he represents the best elements among our active workers; and at the end of six or eight months we intend to recall him for important work on the Central Committee. He should therefore not be treated as a minor official, but as a party member who in the near future will be a party leader, and, we hope, a good one.[11]

At this time the Comintern had its seat in a rather dingy building in the Makhovaya across the road from the Kremlin. There Broz was given a room to himself and a secretary and was initiated into the smooth-running office routine of the Communist International, which, with its files and its filing systems, its minutes and its memoranda, its heads of department and deputy heads of department, its ash trays full of cigarette ends and its little glasses of sweet tea brewed at all hours of the day and night, was very much like any other government department anywhere. When he was not at his office, he lived in a small room on the fourth floor of the Hotel Lux in the Ulitsa Gorkovo, a musty old rabbit warren of an hotel, overflowing into several annexes, which served as a dwelling place for most of the more important foreign Communists in Moscow. In its passages he would encounter such giants of the Communist world as Togliatti, Kuusinen, Georgi Dimitrov, José Diaz and Earl Browder. Every morning, like any other conscientious functionary, he would walk down Gorki Street and along the Makhovaya to his office and every night he would return to the Lux. Sometimes, when rubles were short, he would warm something up in his room on a spirit lamp.

Broz had not been to Moscow when he was in Russia before, and at first he spent his spare time seeing the sights of the Soviet capital. First the red basalt mausoleum under the Kremlin walls where Lenin, embalmed, lay eternally in state in his glass case, his carefully trimmed little beard pointing permanently upward, his Slav features set forever in an expression of detached inscrutability. Then the Lenin Museum, the Anti-God Museum, the newest and best-equipped factories and schools and crèches and collective farms, all so different from anything that had existed in Russia when he was last there. So different, that is, in some ways; in others, so surprisingly, so disturbingly like. "I was excited at being back," he said long afterward, "but soon my excitement began to cool off. I saw weaknesses and defects which I had never expected to see. I saw things that were quite different from what I myself had so enthusiastically described in Jugoslavia."[12]

After his initial bout of sight-seeing, Broz settled down to an existence of monastic seclusion spent between Comintern Headquarters and his room at the Lux Hotel. Almost his only relaxation was an occasional visit to the ballet or opera. His marriage had broken up. Six years on her own in Moscow had, he found to his lasting grief, been too much for Polka. The ardent girl-revolutionary of 1917, with her flowing golden hair and her flaming Bolshevik faith, had, like the Revolution itself, suffered a change. On her return to her own country she had found the new Soviet ruling class ready to welcome her literally with open arms. She had availed herself enthusiastically of their welcome—a little too enthusiastically. Amid the material advantages of her new existence she had soon forgotten her husband in jail in Jugoslavia. She had left their son Žarko, now a boy of twelve or fourteen, to run wild and fend for himself. In 1935 she obtained a divorce and soon after married one of her protectors. In the words of a friend, "Bureaucratic society had swallowed her up."

In prison Broz had grown accustomed to solitude and now he spent most of his spare time alone in his room reading.

Ever since he came out of jail, his chief concern had been to learn more, to deepen and broaden the scope of his knowledge. His friends suggested to him that, now he was in Moscow, he should take a regular course of Marxist-Leninist theory, but he preferred to work alone. In addition to politics, philosophy and economics, he made a special study of military science, reading Clausewitz and the Germans, as well as the modern Soviet military theorists. For, after all, was he not a soldier of the Revolution, a soldier who might one day be called upon to fight sword in hand for his beliefs?

In Moscow, Broz resumed his acquaintance with Edvard Kardelj, the young Slovene schoolmaster who had made such a favorable impression on him at the Slovene Party Conference in the autumn and who was now taking a course at the International Leninist School, which existed for the benefit of the higher party cadres from foreign countries. From time to time both gave lectures at one or other of the Comintern's institutes or schools, for which they were paid at a rather low rate in rubles. Like Broz, Kardelj spent every moment of his spare time studying the theory and practice of Marxism-Leninism, and, the more he studied it, the more he wanted to see it applied to his own country. Neither the Russians nor the senior Comintern officials paid much attention to the Jugoslavs, who were left very largely to their own devices. In the evenings Kardelj would sometimes come and visit Broz in his room and the two would talk far into the night about Marxism-Leninism and the prospects of a Communist revolution in Jugoslavia. Kardelj found Broz an agreeable and stimulating companion. He had a sense of humor and a gift of going straight to the point, which contrasted more refreshingly with the turgid and cliché-ridden verbosity of some of their fellow seekers after truth. Soon a firm friendship grew up between them.

Sometimes Broz would talk of Jugoslavia's industrial future and then his eyes would light up. *"Industrializacija!"* he would cry, *"Elektrifikacija,* there is the answer!"[13] And he would speak of Magnitogorsk and Dnieprostroi and of the millions of tons of steel which they produced and of how Jugoslavia, with her rich industrial potentialities, must follow in the same path as the Soviet Union. Then there would be no more exploitation by foreign capitalists, no more poverty or squalor, no more wretched villages full of miserable, struggling peasants.

In August, 1935 the Seventh Congress of the Comintern was held in Moscow, in the Kolonnyi Zal, the great blue and white pillared ballroom of the former Nobles' Club, now the Palace of the Trade Unions. Its basic theme was the formation of a "Popular Front against Fascism." Josip Broz attended the Congress as one of a Jugoslav delegation of seven members. It was at the opening ceremony that he first saw Stalin: a squat Asiatic figure in a plain semimilitary tunic; narrow eyes close set under heavy brows: the downward sweep of his mustache ponderous beneath a hawklike nose; his expression alternating between apparent benignity and bored inscrutability. Next to him sat Nikolai Ivanovich Yezhov, the wistful, wide-eyed little consumptive, who, before himself being sent to his death, was from his desk in the Commissariat of Internal Affairs to institute and preside over a reign of terror unparalleled in the whole bloodstained history of Russia.

For Josip Broz it was a big moment. He was setting eyes for the first time on the Leader of the International Proletariat, the Light of the World, the infallible Master, to whom he and every other orthodox Communist owed absolute, unswerving, unquestioning allegiance. For Stalin the occasion was less important. The proceedings of the Congress, slavishly following a line which he himself had dictated in advance, were of no particular interest to him. In any case the Comintern, the *Lavochka* or "Grocer's Shop," as he contemptuously called it, was an institution for which he had never had much fondness. He had always disliked and distrusted foreigners, especially foreign Communists. As soon as the formal opening of the Congress was over, he left, and did not reappear. As for Josip Broz, sitting spellbound in the body of the hall, Stalin was not remotely aware of his existence. Nor, at that time, did there seem any particular reason why he ever should become aware of it.

To Josip Broz the Seventh Comintern Congress was of more than sentimental interest. It marked a new step forward in his career. At a meeting held on July 27 at which the redheaded Milan Gorkić was elected head of the Jugoslav delegation, he was appointed its secretary. On August 14 the delegation, most of whose members had come, not from Vienna, but "illegally" from Jugoslavia, held another meeting to discuss the appointment of a Jugoslav member of the Executive Committee of the Comintern. This time it was decided, "at the instance of the delegates from Jugoslavia" that the

name of Josip Broz should be proposed as a full member of the
Executive Committee and that of Milan Gorkić as a "candi-
date member." The latent conflict between the rank and file
of the party in Jugoslavia and its absentee leaders was beginning to take concrete shape. It was crystallizing into a
personal conflict between Milan Gorkić and Josip Broz, and
the decision taken at the meeting of August 14 represented
a definite challenge by Broz to Gorkić's leadership of the
party.

But the decision, in the ultimate analysis, did not rest with
the Jugoslav delegation. It rested with the Comintern. And
the officials of the Comintern, who knew Gorkić and had
appointed him Secretary General of the Jugoslav party, saw no
reason as yet to let his supremacy be challenged. Nor, for
that matter, did they see any reason why such a small and
unsatisfactory party should claim two seats on the Executive
Committee. On August 19, on a hint from above, a further
meeting of the Jugoslav delegation was held at which a fresh
resolution was unanimously adopted, admitting that a mistake
had been made and withdrawing Broz's name. And a few days
after that Gorkić was appointed, not a member, but a candi-
date member of the Committee.[14] The Jugoslav delegation had
been put in their place. Comrade Walter, for his part, had
achieved a prominence which he had not possessed before.
Whether a desirable prominence or not, remained to be seen.

Josip Broz spent the whole of 1935 in the Soviet Union,
mastering the latest line and absorbing wisdom at the fountain-
head of Socialist Truth. In Vienna, meanwhile, and in Jugoslavia, the interpretation of the new line was, as might be
expected, giving rise to serious difficulties. Little progress
was made as it was not long before fresh disputes and dissensions had once again broken out in the Central Committee, giving rise to Comintern circles to a feeling of weary
disillusionment and to the saying: "Two Jugoslavs—three
factions."

In April, 1936 Gorkić, anxious to find a way out of the
fresh difficulties that now beset him, resorted to the highly
unorthodox measure of calling a "plenary meeting" of the
Central Committee without notifying most of its members
and, worse still, without informing the Comintern. In due
course, needless to say, news of this meeting, which began
in Vienna and was continued in Prague and which, incidentally, only served to aggravate the existing dissensions in

the party, reached Moscow. There it provoked an explosion of rage. The long and somewhat confused resolution passed at the end of the meeting[15] was found to be chock-full of ideological errors, while the organizers' failure to notify the Comintern of what was afoot was held to constitute "a gross breach of international discipline." Clearly action was called for. It followed promptly. The members of the Jugoslav Politburo were, we are told, at once summoned to Moscow and the leadership of the party "completely renovated."[16]

Under the new dispensation, Gorkić, despite his irregular behavior, remained, strangely enough, Secretary General. But this time Josip Broz, who by now also had friends in high places and had completely mastered the current party line, was appointed to the key post of Organizing Secretary or Orgsec. He had reached (or almost reached) the top of the party hierarchy. The reasons for his promotion are not hard to discern. From the Comintern's point of view, he had an ideal record. He was, in the first place, of working-class origin. He was also a man of action, a practical, efficient man, known for his energy and organizing ability and also for his complete devotion to the Communist cause. Better still, he was no "intellectual." No one was less likely than he to become involved in complicated ideological entanglements or heresies. To him, "fractionalism," whether of the left or the right, was anathema. He had shown that he was a good Stalinist. By good luck or good management, he had contrived to hitch his wagon to that particular star when it was in the ascendant. And it had stayed hitched. He had also managed, thanks partly to the good fortune which for six critical years had kept him in prison, to avoid the most dangerous thing of all: *"somnitelnie sviazi,"* those "dubious connections" which of recent years had been the downfall of so many keen but misguided revolutionaries. And then, during the time he had spent in Moscow, he had, by his enthusiasm, by his loyalty, by his devotion to duty, by the orthodoxy of his views, and by the readiness with which he adjusted them to meet the chops and changes of the party line, earned himself golden opinions and won himself powerful friends. Thus it was that he now stood so high on the ladder, with only one short step between him and the topmost rung of all.

From the first, there was a sharp divergence of opinion between the Secretary General of the Jugoslav party and its new Oragnizing Secretary, the latter maintaining that the right place for the leaders of the party was in Jugoslavia, while the former took the opposite view. Before leaving Moscow in April, 1936 to take up his new appointment Broz put his point of view as forcefully as he could to Georgi Dimitrov. Gorkić was also present and a fierce argument ensued. In the end it was decided that the Central Committee should split. Part of it, led by Broz, would return to Jugoslavia, where they would work underground. The remainder would stay abroad with Gorkić, who would, however, retain the right to veto any decisions taken by the party in Jugoslavia.

For some time past conditions in Vienna had made life there increasingly difficult for the Central Committee. In the summer of 1936, following the advent of power in France of the Front Populaire, it was decided to transfer it to Paris, and Gorkić now moved his headquarters there. Broz, for his part, after visiting Prague, Vienna and Paris, returned clandestinely to Jugoslavia, arriving there toward the end of 1936. Things were still going badly for the party. The police were as active as ever—and more successful. Shortly before Broz's return, 150 party members had been arrested, including the whole of one provincial committee. In Belgrade practically the whole party organization had been wiped out.

As in the past, Broz went first to Zagreb. Thence he sent a message to Belgrade asking that "a responsible comrade" from the capital should report to him there. The comrade who arrived early in 1937 was a Montenegrin intellectual of peasant stock called Milovan Djilas, a tall, good-looking young man of about twenty-five with a sensitive face, the air of a visionary and a shock of wiry jet-black hair like a golliwog. Like most of his contemporaries, he had only recently come out of prison. He and Broz got on well. Neither knew the other's real name; for security reasons it was considered wiser that they should not. But Djilas was impressed by the businesslike and at the same time human approach of this unnamed member of the Central Committee, while Broz was struck by the young man's enthusiasm for the cause and by his lucid account of the party's trials and tribulations in Belgrade. For Djilas's benefit he outlined some of the new measures which he proposed to take. He told him how he intended to give the party a broader and firmer basis and to bring the Central Committee into direct contact with the people. He also spoke of the need for an effective youth organization and before Djilas caught the train back to the capital it was agreed that he should return as soon as possible with a carefully picked student from Belgrade University to take over its leadership. Belgrade University had always possessed a strong radical and revolutionary tradition and had of recent years become an important center of Communist activity, its students, mostly the sons of peasants, helping to spread Communist ideas far and wide throughout Jugoslavia. The University branch of the party had moreover escaped the recent wave of arrests which had crippled the main party organization in Belgrade and was still very largely intact. It provided a promising base on which to build.

On his return to Belgrade, Djilas talked things over with one of the most active surviving members of the local party organization, Aleksandar Ranković, generally known in the Party as "Marko" or "Leko." Ranković was a peasant's son from the nearby Sumadija, shrewd, cunning and hard-headed. Apprenticed to a tailor, he had at nineteen become Secretary of the Young Communist League for Serbia. But he had soon been betrayed to the police, savagely beaten up and sentenced to six years' hard labor. Having completed his sentence, he had now actively resumed his revolutionary activities. At first sight he might well have struck a casual observer as dull: a solidly built, stolid-looking young man with a pallid complexion, heavy features and a long, rather crooked nose. And yet his mouth, when you looked at it, was resolute, the mouth of a man who could bear, and perhaps administer, torture unflinchingly, and his small eyes, when the conversation turned to party matters, glinted with a lively intelligence. A good conspirator, one would say, and a hard man to get the better of. Together he and Djilas chose as head of the Youth Organization a young law student called Ivo Ribar, dark, vital and eloquent, known for his exceptional ability and for his complete devotion to the Communist cause. His father, as it happened, was a prominent liberal politician, Dr. Ivan Ribar, who had been President of the Constituent Assembly of 1920.

In addition to his other duties as Organizing Secretary of the party, Broz had, on leaving Moscow, been given a special task by the Comintern, that of arranging for the recruitment and dispatch of Jugoslav volunteers for the Republican Forces in Spain.

Broz did his job well. The volunteers were collected, provided with funds and smuggled, by a variety of underground routes, to Spain, where they were duly incorporated, with other volunteers from southeastern Europe in the International Brigade. Although some fifteen hundred Jugoslav volunteers reached Spain, in the course of the war, nearly half of these were killed, three hundred wounded and three hundred and fifty interned in French concentration camps.

Broz himself did not fight in Spain. Planning and administration kept him fully occupied. In the course of 1937 he traveled illegally all over Jugoslavia and went several times to Paris to arrange for the passage of Jugoslav volunteers through France and to consult with his colleagues of the Central Committee who were now installed there. In Paris he lived at a little hotel on the Left Bank, plowing through the turgid columns of *l'Humanité* to improve his French, keeping in touch with the Spanish Embassy, and paying occasional pious visits to the cemetery of Père-Lachaise, where the Communards of 1871 had met their end.

His life during this period was one long game of hide and seek with the authorities: up and down the length and breadth of Jugoslavia; back and forth across the frontier; hairbreadth escapes from the police of half a dozen countries; false papers; false passports. The existence, in short, of a professional international revolutionary.

Sometimes even he found these constant changes of name and identity a little confusing. Once he had a very narrow escape. He was traveling back to Jugoslavia from France by the way of Germany. In Paris he had been given a fresh set of forged documents. But the last few days had been tiring and soon after taking his seat in the train he fell heavily asleep. He woke to find a green-uniformed German frontier guard with a swastika badge on his peaked cap shaking him and asking his name. It was then that he realized that in the hurry and confusion of his departure he had forgotten to look at his new passport and did not know what name it bore. It was only by feigning ignorance of the German language that he gained time in which to glance surreptitiously at his passport and thus discover the answer to the all-important question which the Nazi official was repeating with embarrassing insistence.

On another illicit journey some months later he traveled by way of Denmark, using, this time, a Canadian passport. In Copenhagen, a policeman, noticing this, spoke to him in English. He managed to get out a few halting words of broken English in reply. But the Dane was not taken in.

Fortunately for Broz he happened to be an easygoing fellow of left-wing sympathies. "Next time you travel on a false passport, Comrade," he said with a wink, "choose a country whose language you speak."

While he was in Jugoslavia during the summer of 1937 there came to Josip Broz, amid all the cares and worries of his "conspiratorial" existence, a sudden longing to see his own village, to see Kumrovec. Without telling anyone, he set out from Zagreb and, having taken the bus for part of the way, finished the journey on foot, arriving just before sunset. No one recognized him—he had no wish that they should—and, making his solitary way to an orchard on the hillside above his father's old house, he sat down on the ground and silently watched the people of Kumrovec going about their business as the day neared its end. Nothing had changed. There lay the village with its muddy streets and its brightly painted houses. There flowed the Sutla through the meadows where he had once watched his father's horses and cattle. And there went the villagers in their heavy boots and tattered clothes, their backs bent from hard work. There, he reflected, his forebears had lived from one generation to another in this same mud and squalor. His own contemporaries, whom he had grown up with, had for the most part long since left Kumrovec. There was nothing to keep them there and not enough bread to feed them. As he looked at his village in the evening light, he knew full well that in those little houses with their roofs of shingle or thatch there were still children who were hungry, just as he and his brothers and sisters had been hungry, and who one day no doubt would also be forced to leave their village and seek a better life elsewhere.

"I stayed in the orchard," he told a friend afterward, "until it had become quite dark. The dogs were barking ceaselessly from one end of the village to the other, and I thought of everything that I had seen and the poverty and backwardness that had weighed on us for centuries. And I thought, too, of the day when Kumrovec and thousands of other towns and villages like it all over Jugoslavia would rouse themselves from that backwardness, when the young people in them would at last have a chance in life, a chance to live in peace and happiness and to bring up their families. I did not know when that would happen. But I knew very well that it was worth making every effort and every sacrifice to ensure that it did happen."

Next night, back in Zagreb, Broz talked things over with

a friend, a playwright. He told him of the feelings which had assailed him so sharply as he looked out over his own village. "Something," he kept repeating, "must be done. There must be a way." And he spoke of what he had seen in Russia, at Dnieprostroi and Magnitogorsk. "There," he said, "is the answer: *Industrializacija! Elektrifikacija!*"

A few weeks later, while he was still in Jugoslavia, Josip Broz received a message which was of the greatest interest both to the party and to him personally. It came from Paris and it told him that Gorkić, the Secretary General, had been urgently summoned to Moscow. Gorkić, it seemed, did not know why he had been sent for, but expected trouble: as he himself put it, a *golovomoika* or "head-washing." In other words, there might soon be a vacancy at the top of the party.

Gorkić's forebodings were, as it turned out, all too well founded. Not long afterward a telegram arrived in Paris from Moscow, ordering the suppression of a pamphlet that Gorkić had written. Then the news trickled through that his wife, who was Director of the Moscow Park of Rest and Culture, had been arrested as an agent of the British Intelligence Service. Finally a letter was received from Wilhelm Pieck, the head of the Balkan Secretariat of the Comintern, announcing that Gorkić had been dismissed and instructing Broz to take temporary charge of the Central Committee. After a visit to Paris to settle that body's somewhat dislocated affairs, Broz returned to Jugoslavia. There he found a message from the Comintern, summoning him in his turn to Moscow.

Anyone with a less fanatical devotion to the Communist cause, or less self-confident, might have hesitated to go, for Moscow, in the summer of 1937, was not a very healthy place to be summoned to. The great purge, which had begun the year before, was now at its height. It swept through the Soviet hierarchy like a consuming fire. Nobody was safe, from the highest to the lowest. Marshals, generals, admirals, people's commissars, Heroes of Soviet Labor, Heroes of Soviet Art, party functionaries, the Secret Police themselves, all lived in terror of a knock on their door at two in the morning. Denunciation and delation were rife. Everybody was afraid of everybody else, of their colleagues, of their friends, of their own families. Nobody trusted anybody. Fear and suspicion hung over the whole country like a poisonous mist, seeping in everywhere. At the great State Trials, the giants of the past, the flower of the Old Bolsheviks, the friends of Lenin, the men who had made the Revolution, dragged from the cells of the Lubianka, made brief, squalid last appearances, confessing their guilt, bemoaning their sins, begging for punishment. Presidents of the Council of People's Commissars, marshals of the Soviet Union, secretaries of the Communist International, Zinoviev, Kamenev and Radek, Yegorov and Tukhachevski, Bukharin and Rykov, all went the same way: to "liquidation." Others simply disappeared. Sometimes they would be heard of again, and sometimes not. Sometimes, later on, there would be a paragraph in the paper to say that they had committed suicide or died after a short illness. Sometimes the news would seep through that they had been liquidated "administratively." Sometimes they would be given state funerals. Sometimes nothing more would be heard of them at all. Foreign Communists were in the greatest danger of all. One of the underlying reasons for the purge was acute xenophobia. A lifetime of loyal service to the party made no difference. Béla Kun the Hungarian had gone. And Khristo Rakovski from Bulgaria. And a lot of Germans. And now Gorkić and, it seemed probable, most of the other Jugoslavs with him. It was difficult to know whom to trust, whom to confide in, whom to go and see. Dimitrov himself was rumored to be in danger. Anyone might turn out to be a "dubious connection." Anyone might compromise you. Anyone might twist anything you had said to mean anything. Anyone might denounce you.

But Josip Broz, having received the summons, at once obeyed it. It was clear to him that a crisis had been reached in the affairs of the Jugoslav Communist party and it seemed to him that it was his duty to try to save something from the wreck. It was this that decided him to go.

On reaching Moscow he found that his forebodings were more than justified. From what Dimitrov told him, it was clear that the Comintern had reached the point when they were seriously thinking of abolishing the Jugoslav party altogether, as being more trouble than it was worth. Gorkić and most of the other Jugoslavs in Moscow had, it appeared, been arrested. It was desired, said Dimitrov, that he should provisionally take over the post of Secretary General.

"Provisionally . . ." The word was a challenge—a challenge and a threat. Everything he valued, everything he had worked for, for so long, was at stake. Everything depended on him, and on him alone. He was a man who was at his best in a crisis, and this was a crisis with a vengeance—the worst, he said afterward, that he had ever had to face.[18] He told Dimitrov that he accepted the appointment and would make it his business to clear up the mess. "Go ahead," said Dimitrov wearily.[19]

IV ꙡꙡꙡ SECRETARY GENERAL

Josip Broz had become Secretary General of the Jugoslav Communist party at a critical moment in the history of the world. War seemed likely, and war would offer opportunities for revolutionary action which could never occur in peacetime. It was essential that the party should be prepared for any eventuality.

The new Secretary General's first move was characteristic and, in the long run, of great importance. Early in 1938, after a brief visit to Paris, he returned illegally to Jugoslavia, taking the party headquarters with him. He was deeply convinced that the Central Committee must live and work in Jugoslavia. "It is impossible," he wrote later,

> to expect a workers' democratic movement to succeed if its leaders are far from the scene of the struggle. Their presence on the spot is an essential condition for the success of such a movement. To have to wait for instructions from outside, to depend on someone else's brain instead of one's own, can only be disastrous. Moreover, life outside the country, in exile, causes men to decay, whatever their political talents. Political exile spells ruin for a political worker. Even if it means risking his life, it is better that he should be in his own country, among his own people, where he can fight shoulder to shoulder with them and share their good luck and their bad, than that he should be an exile and a wanderer, far from the movement and far from the people.[1]

It is easy to picture the amazement and delight of the rank and file of the party on finding, for the first time for nearly ten years, that the Secretary General and all the other leaders of the party were actually with them in the country, sharing their dangers and directing their activities. This was something new.

Broz's next concern was to put an end to all further "fractional" disputes by giving the party a strong united leadership under his own control. The team he picked were new men with practical experience of active revolutionary work: Edo Kardelj, Milovan Djilas, "Marko" Ranković, Boris Kidrić, Ivo Ribar and others like them. All these were young men still in their twenties. But they had been Communists ever since they left school and nearly all of them had at one time or another gone to prison for their beliefs. Together with their leader they formed a solid group, united by their common experience and in close sympathy with each other. Most of them had worked with Broz during the years since 1934 and were well known to him for their courage and their devotion to the Communist cause. They for their part regarded him with admiration and affection. *"Stari,"* they called him—"The Old Man." He was just forty-five.

The only remaining member of the old Central Committee besides Broz himself was Sretan Žujović, a tall, dark, cadaverous Serb of forty or so, known in the party as *Crni* or "Black." Crni had, on Comintern instructions, been purged for "fractionalism" with the rest of his colleagues, but had subsequently been reinstated at Broz's request. He was a man of considerable ability and relatively wide experience and culture. During the Great War he had fought in the French Foreign Legion and spoke fluent French, German and Russian.

With his new general staff to help him, Broz infused new life into the party. He himself possessed in a high degree that energy of feeling, that personal quality of conviction, that make the true leader of men. Nothing could shake his own faith in the rightness of his cause or his certainty that in the end that cause must triumph. And in those around him he could inspire the same faith and the same certainty. In his underground army, he made new appointments, allotted new tasks and established a new discipline. In true Communist fashion he purged all dissident elements. He changed the methods of recruiting, organizing and indoctrinating party members, bringing to this task a lighter touch and a greater understanding of human nature. His aim was not only to expand the membership of the party but to recruit key men of outstanding character and ability in a wide range of trades and professions. In other words he sought to form cadres of active revolutionaries whose influence would be out of all proportion to their numbers. At the same time, from his head-quarters in Zagreb, he extended the activities of the party to the whole of Jugoslavia, and before long branches had been set up in areas such as Bosnia and Macedonia where before there had been no proper organization. Henceforward he refused all outside financial assistance in the belief that it was better for the party to raise its own funds and depend on its own resources. He also improved the party's security system and increased the efficiency of its underground network. Finally, as proof, had proof been needed, that the time he had spent in Moscow had not been wasted, he orientated the party's propaganda more strongly than ever toward the Soviet Union. Everything was done to make Russia and the Russians more popular in Jugoslavia. "It was," he wrote afterward, "our principal activity; it commanded the bulk of our funds."[2]

Broz made Zagreb his headquarters, as being the best center for communications with the rest of the country. At first he lived under the name of Ivan Kostanjsek, an engineer working for the Ministry of Forests and Mines. Sometimes, too, he was known as Tomanek. Lated he provided himself with a new set of papers in the name of Engineer Slavko Babić. Under one or other of these names he rented various flats and houses and bought a Ford car so as to be more mobile. He would meet Kardelj and the others surreptitiously at a café in the Ilica. His neighbors never for a moment suspected that he was anything but what he said he was—a prosperous engineer. He was always smartly dressed and his naturally good manners and distinguished appearance made it easy for him to pass as a member of the bourgeoisie. On his finger he wore a handsome diamond ring which he had bought with the fee he had received in Moscow for translating the official *History of the Communist Party* into Serbo-Croat. Apart from further enhancing his already distinguished appearance, this constituted a useful financial reserve in case he should at any time run short of funds. When he went by train he always traveled first class and often he would fly. The gendarmes at the stations or airport would touch their hats deferentially to the distinguished-looking passenger with the flashing diamond on his finger and offer to help him with his luggage. He was thus able to move freely about the country under the noses of the Royal Police, who still clung somewhat naïvely to the belief that all revolutionaries were shabby, wild-eyed and unshaven. In the party he was now known as "Tito." For some time past he had used this, among others, as a conspiratorial name. Henceforward he was to use it exclusively. Soon it grew to be more than a nickname, it became a rallying cry, a call to revolt.*

From now onward the party membership increased rapidly, rising from four to twelve thousand in less than three years. In addition to the urban proletariat marked progress was made in the rural areas and among the peasants. But, more important than any purely numerical increase, carefully picked cadres were built up of hardened revolutionaries, completely reliable men who could be counted on to act promptly and correctly in any emergency and whose influence on their fellows was out of all proportion to their numbers. It was the practical application of Lenin's old theory of the revolutionary élite. At the same time, particular attention was paid to the infiltration of the armed forces, and a section of the party machine devoted specially to this work. Propaganda, too, of all kinds, was intensified and *Proleter,* the party newspaper, which hitherto had appeared abroad, was now clandestinely printed and distributed in Jugoslavia.

Tito paid short visits to Moscow in 1938 and again early in 1939. At Comintern Headquarters, where he saw Dimitrov, he found that the Jugoslav party was still not very popular. Lunching with him at the Hotel Lux, Veljko Vlahović, the new Jugoslav representative with the Comintern, observed gloomily that no one seemed to want to sit at their table. Tito's reply was typical and, as it happened, prophetic. "It is of no importance," he said, "one day they will be falling over each other to sit with us."[3]

In a sense the Soviet Union, the Country of the Revolution, was for him, the professional revolutionary, living illegally, permanently wanted by the police, a sanctuary, a haven of security. Having reached it, he was safe. But safe in one sense only. In another he was very far from safe. The great purge was still in progress and he was still very much on test. "When I went to Moscow," he said many years later, "I

---

* According to one widely current version, Tito was so called because he was always sending for people and telling them what to do. "You," he would say, "do this; and you that," in Serbo-Croat *"Ti to; ti to."* I have always liked this story. But I am assured by Tito himself, who I suppose should know, that it is apocryphal.

never knew whether I should come back alive. And while I was there never knew that I would not wake in the middle of the night to hear the fatal knocking at my door."[4]

That, in itself, was unsettling. So might have been a great many of the changes which had taken place in Russia since Stalin had gained control: the increasingly repressive and reactionary character of the Soviet regime, the increasingly blatant opportunism of Soviet policy, the jettisoning, one after the other, of so many basic Marxist principles, the increasing subordination of all else to the narrowest personal interests of the *Vozhd* himself.

But Tito was too good a Communist to let himself be disturbed by doubts or dangerous thoughts. Neither the danger of liquidation nor the fate of his predecessor could deter him; they were risks to be taken in the ordinary course of revolutionary business. There was much in the Soviet Union that was hard to understand; there was much, even, that was profoundly disillusioning. But the Soviet Union was the Country of the Revolution, the only country in which Socialism had triumphed, the country which eventually would secure its triumph throughout the whole world. "It was," he wrote later, "my revolutionary duty not to criticize and not to help alien propaganda against that country, for it was then the only country where the revolution had succeeded and where Socialism was being built. . . . Many of us had but one thought at that time: to do nothing to harm the further development of the international movement."[5]

On his way back from the Soviet Union in March, 1939, Tito, using a forged Swedish passport, traveled by sea to Le Havre, thence by rail through Switzerland to Venice and from Venice by sea again to the Jugoslav port of Sušak.

Over the Europe across which he traveled on his journeys back and forth to Moscow, the storm clouds were gathering fast. March, 1938 had seen the *Anschluss* and Hitler's entry into Austria. By the summer the Czech crisis had reached its height. The autumn brought Munich and the capitulation of the Western powers. In Spain, Franco's victory was now assured. Hitler had triumphed all along the line. Where would he strike next? His entry into Prague in March, 1939 gave the answer. Simultaneously German propaganda attacks on Poland were intensified. In April, Mussolini, following the *Führer's* example and wishing to strengthen his position in the Adriatic, annexed Albania. Meanwhile, on instructions from Moscow, the Soviet Ambassador in Berlin had let it be known at the Wilhelmstrasse that his government saw no reason why relations between the countries might not be normal, "and from normal might become better and better."[6] Nor, thanks to the German General Staff's fear of a war on two fronts, had the response proved as unfavorable as might have been expected. The preliminary talks between Germany and Russia were already well advanced.

On August 23 Ribbentrop arrived in Moscow for the signature of a Soviet-German Nonaggression Pact. The Pact was signed the same evening, and with it a secret protocol providing, in effect, for the partition of Poland and the Baltic States. That night there was a banquet in the Kremlin at which Stalin proposed Hitler's health. "I know how much the German nation loves its *Führer*," said the *Vozhd*, "I should therefore like to drink his health." On September 1, the Germans, having thus secured their rear, marched into Poland. The Second World War had begun.

At one time or another in its long and devious history the party line had undergone some pretty abrupt and pretty drastic chops and changes. But for complete and utter opportunism none of them could compare with this latest *volte-face*. The sudden announcement of an alliance with a country and a regime which until a few weeks before had been freely denounced, not only as an enemy and an aggressor, but as the embodiment of all evil, was strong meat even for Soviet opinion. It would take still more explaining, in all its implications, to "progressive" opinion abroad.*

Tito, for his part, saw nothing to worry about in the new situation. "We accepted the Pact," he wrote later, "like disciplined Communists considering it necessary for the Soviet Union, at that time the only Socialist state in the world."[7] Had he felt any doubts, he would have had ample opportunity of allaying them, for in the autumn of 1939 he was once more summoned to the Soviet Union, to be initiated on the spot in this latest manifestation of Soviet truth and to

* The danger that even seasoned Communists might fail to grasp all the implications of what had happened was demonstrated in spectacular fashion by the Communist party of Great Britain, who, until their mistake was abruptly pointed out to them by Moscow, persisted in regarding the war in which their country was involved as a struggle against Fascism meriting the support of the workers and not as a "Second Imperialist War" of no concern to the working class.

receive fresh directives. After spending some weeks in Moscow, where he gained the impression that the Jugoslav party were regarded with rather more favor than they had been twelve months earlier, he set out for home in December, 1939.

With Europe at war and the police everywhere on the lookout for illicit travelers, the journey was a difficult one.[8] In Belgrade the party leaders waited anxiously for news of the Old Man. Equipped with a Canadian passport made out in the name of Spiridon Mekas, whom it described as "a naturalized British subject of Croat origin," Tito traveled by Soviet freighter from Odessa to Stambul. On landing there he found himself, to his dismay, besieged by journalists. A foreigner freshly arrived from the Soviet Union was a rarity. The newspapermen wanted his impressions of the country and people. Tito did his best to fend them off. He had, he said, been working in Russia as an engineer. He had been well paid and had taken no interest in politics or in anything else except his work. He had noticed nothing and heard nothing. The newspapermen went away disappointed.

The next step, the appropriate department of the Comintern having apparently overlooked this important detail, was to provide himself with a visa for Jugoslavia. He communicated secretly with Zagreb and in due course received the reply that a courier would be sent to him with the necessary forged documents. There was nothing for it but to wait. A neat, impatient figure, he spent his time surveying the splendors of Stambul: Saint Sofia, the Mosque of Sultan Ahmed, the muddy waters of the Golden Horn, glittering palely under the wintry sun; and, after dark, the lights twinkling on the far shore of the Bosporus, in Asia. Methodically, guidebook in hand, for he believed in doing everything in an orderly fashion, he visited all the principal sights. He took a steamer to Scutari and looked back at the city from the sea. He inspected the smart shops in the Rue de Pera and he observed the dirt and squalor in the little side alleys running down to the water's edge. He noticed that, to look at, it all seemed much less Turkish than Macedonia or Bosnia, where the men still wore the fez and the women the veil. In the evenings he went back to his room at the Park Hotel with its little balcony overlooking the Bosporus. It was a comfortable hotel and a good address but it was also extremely expensive and his funds were beginning to run short.

Finally, the courier arrived from Jugoslavia. He turned out to be a young man called Vladko Velebit. Like other young men and women from all walks of life, Velebit had become a Communist partly from a feeling of disgust at the existing state of affairs in Jugoslavia and partly because Communism seemed to him the only solution to the manifold problems which beset his country and humanity at large. He was a useful acquisition to the party. Tall, dark and good-looking, with pleasant manners and considerable personal charm, he was much sought after in Zagreb where, in the intervals of practicing, not unsuccessfully, at the bar, he led the life of a fashionable man about town—a playboy, one might almost say. His father, who came of a distinguished Serbian military family, was a general in the Jugoslav Army. His grandfather and great grandfather had been generals in the Austrian Army. He had plenty of money and a good brain. He was excellent company and a first-class shot. Every door was open to him: everyone talked freely to him. And no one would think anything of it, were he suddenly to decide to take a trip to Stambul or anywhere else; he had so many connections and so many interests. On his arrival in Stambul, Tito, who had never met him before, took to him at once.

But the forged documents he had brought with him proved a disappointment. On examining them carefully, the two of them agreed that they would take in no one. There was nothing for it but to send a further message back to Jugoslavia asking for another courier to be sent to Stambul with another and better forged passport. This time the courier was a young Slovenian girl. But once again the work of the *Technika*, as the appropriate branch of the party was known, was not up to standard. The passport she brought with her would, they decided, never pass muster. Tito meanwhile was in a hurry to be off. He had important work ahead of him and here in Istanbul things were getting difficult. Money was short; he had already had to leave the Park for a cheaper hotel. And it looked as though the Turkish police had got on his tracks: there was one man in particular who said he was a "tourist guide," and was suspiciously assiduous in his attentions. They decided to try a little forgery themselves. The Slovene girl who had brought the second passport was a student of architecture, and with the help of her skilled draftsmanship, the passport of Spiridon Mekas was provided with a neatly drawn Jugoslav transit visa which they hoped would pass muster. Tito now booked, in the name of Spiridon Mekas, a passage to America on the Italian S.S. *Conte di Savoia*, sailing from Genoa, and a railway ticket from Salonika to Genoa, via Jugoslavia. Thus equipped he left Stambul in a British ship bound for Salonika.

At Djevdjevlje on the Greek-Jugoslav frontier the passports of the passengers in the Orient Express were duly collected by the police. And duly returned to them—expect for the passport of Spiridon Mekas. Its owner had a moment of uneasiness. Then two gendarmes appeared. Where, they inquired, was Spiridon Mekas? They wanted to ask him some questions. Tito's heart sank. What, they asked, had he been doing in the Soviet Union? At the mere mention of the Soviet Union, a Jugoslav officer, who was sitting next to him, looked at him uneasily and edged away. Tito told the story that went with his passport. He said that he had been working under contract in Russia as an engineer and was now on his way home. He showed his train and steamship tickets. He added that he was only passing through the country of his birth on his way back to Canada. The gendarmes listened to what he had to say and in the end grudgingly handed him back his passport. As they left the compartment, he heard one say to the other: "It's a pity he's a British subject. Otherwise we could have run him in." Settling back in his seat, Tito breathed a sigh of relief. His stratagem had succeeded. From now onward the journey was plain sailing. When, two days later, the train reached Zagreb, he slipped off it and disappeared among the crowd on the platform. After a few months' absence from his usual haunts, Engineer Ivan Kostanjsek, that much-respected citizen, had returned home.

Among those who had anxiously awaited Tito's return was Herta, a pretty, fresh-looking young Slovene girl who had become his second wife. Some months afterward a son was born to them, Aleksander, or Miško as Tito called him. But Tito had little time now for family life.

Henceforward he stayed in Jugoslavia. Much remained to be done. There was the purge to be completed and the party organization to be built up. The purge, in particular, was long and arduous. There were all sorts of complications. It was, for instance, as Tito himself put it, "especially difficult to effect a purge of those who were in prison," such as Petko Miletić, "the well-known fractionalist," who, safely out of reach of the purgers, was busily instilling his particular heresy in the minds of his fellow prisoners. In Dalmatia, the party organization had got into the hands of "sectarians" and "nepotists." In Zagreb, "nationalists" and "right-wing opportunists" had been at work. But, by one means or another, he was to overcome most, if not all of these difficulties.[9]

In the late autumn of 1940 the Fifth Party Conference was held in a house on the outskirts of Zagreb. It was attended by over a hundred delegates who had come together secretly from all over Jugoslavia. Such were the precautions taken to ensure secrecy that, until the very last moment, even the delegates themselves were not told their destination, while, once inside the house, which had been specially rented for the occasion, they were not allowed to leave it until the end of the proceedings three days later. During this period the party provided food for all those taking part. Guards were posted all round the house. In the event, all went well except that an overzealous lookout man opened fire on the Montenegrin delegation, who, with the careless enthusiasm of their race, had mislaid their instructions.

But the problems which confronted Tito on this occasion were by no means purely administrative. There were, as usual, deviationists to be disciplined. There was the new line to be put across. With the conclusion of the Soviet-German Pact, the era of the Popular Front against Fascism, or limited Soviet co-operation with the Western democracies, had come to an abrupt end. For Communists, the war was not a War of Democracy against Fascism, but "the Second Imperialist War," fought between rival groups of imperialist powers, and of no concern to the workers, whose duty it thus became to sabotage the war effort of their respective countries. Such, at any rate, was the line dictated by Moscow for use by Communists in Great Britain, France and the United States, a line which, though nominally neutral, in practice worked out rather to the advantage of the Axis. The party line in the Balkans, on the other hand, seems to have been slightly different, or at any rate to have become so by the end of 1940.

The Russians had lost no time in exacting the pound of flesh allotted to them under the Soviet-German Pact. Eastern Poland, the Baltic States, Bessarabia, had disappeared one after another into the Soviet maw. So far everything had gone according to plan. The first serious hitch in their program was the fall of France. They had not expected such an overwhelming German victory, and they had not expected it so soon. This was not the long-drawn-out, evenly balanced, exhausting struggle they had hoped for. Their next unpleasant surprise, though it is hard to see why it should have been one, was the discovery that Germany had active designs on South-

eastern Europe and the Balkans. They still apparently refused
to believe the stories of an impending German attack on the
Soviet Union, but they could nevertheless scarcely regard
with pleasure the prospect of an extension of Hitler's rule to
what was, after all, historically a Russian preserve.

In the course of 1940 there were signs that the Soviet
Government were themselves taking a more active interest
than hitherto in the Balkans and especially in Jugoslavia.
After an interruption of more than twenty years, trade and,
shortly afterward, diplomatic relations had been resumed between the two countries.

The sudden solicitude of the Soviet Government for the
welfare of Jugoslavia was, needless to say, reflected in the
party line of the Jugoslav Communists. This now prescribed
that Jugoslavia must on no account be weakened and must
at all costs be kept out of the war. Moreover, since the threat
to her security came from the Axis, the line, though favorable
to neither, was slightly more unfavorable to the Axis than to
the democracies. As early as the summer of 1940, soon after
the fall of France, British Intelligence Officers, in search of
potential elements of resistance in case of a German invasion
of the Balkans, had been surprised to find Yugoslav and other
Balkan Communists ready to co-operate with them. A further
indication of the attitude of the Jugoslav Communist party at
this time is furnished, for what it is worth, by the German
Foreign Minister, Herr von Ribbentrop who, in a speech delivered on June 22, 1941, explaining the reasons for Germany's attack on the Soviet Union, claimed that the Jugoslav
Communists had taken a consistently anti-Axis line from the
summer of 1940 onward and quoted Communist pamphlets in
support of this. Certainly, a perusal of Jugoslav Communist
publications for the first eighteen months of the war shows
that, while criticizing the democracies, they continued to attack the Axis powers with at least equal vigor.

The theme of the Fifth Conference was neutrality. The
party was to do everything in its power to prevent Jugoslavia
from becoming involved in the war and, in particular, to press
for the conclusion of a mutual assistance pact with the Soviet
Union. It was also to "do everything in its power to prevent
Jugoslavia from being turned, with the help of Axis agents
inside and outside the government, into a colonial base for
the further prosecution of the war by the Axis powers." At
the same time, it was to agitate for better social and enconomic
conditions and for equal rights for the various nationalities

and to continue its work in the trade unions, among the peasants, and among women and young people.[10]

Whatever shortcomings still remained, Tito could congratulate himself on one very important achievement: during his three years of office as Secretary General he had, to all intents and purposes, put an end to "fractionalism." When the Conference was over and the delegates had dispersed, he dispatched to Dimitrov in Moscow a message, signed Walter, proudly announcing that "complete unanimity" had been achieved.[11] The purge had had its effect; the new broom had swept clean; the Jugoslav party, like its Soviet counterpart, had become "monolithic." The decks were cleared for whatever an uncertain future might hold in store.

That this would in fact be neutrality seemed, on the face of it, highly improbable. By now the "phony" war had come to an end. Norway, Denmark and the Low Countries had been overrun. France had collapsed. The Italians, already established in Albania, had invaded Greece. Hungary, Rumania and Bulgaria were, practically speaking, Axis satellites. Meanwhile, the position of Jugoslavia was becoming daily more precarious.

Under the regency of Prince Paul there had been a certain relaxation in the character of the regime and a return to a modified form of constitutional government. But the Croat problem, the central cause of tension, still remained unsolved. Now, as the danger of war grew greater, the need for some kind of settlement with the Croats became imperative. It was common knowledge that not only the Ustaše, but important elements in the Croat Peasant party strongly favored the idea of an independent Croatia under Italian protection —an idea which the Italians, needless to say did nothing to discourage. It was all too clear that, without a settlement, her involvement in war or indeed in any serious crisis, might well lead to the final disintegration of Jugoslavia. Accordingly, Prince Paul had in April, 1939 instructed his Prime Minister, Dragiša Cvetković, to open negotiations with Dr. Vladimir Maček, who had succeeded Stjepan Radić as leader of the Croat Peasant party. These negotiations, after various vicissitudes, had led to the conclusion in the following August of an agreement, known as the *Sporazum,* granting Croatia a certain measure of autonomy and providing for Dr. Maček's entry into a coalition government. But it was already too late; the harm had been done. The agreement was only grudgingly accepted by large sections of Dr. Maček's own party, over which his control was by now of the loosest. Scarcely had it been concluded and the new government formed, than fresh disputes broke out between Serbs and Croats, the Serbs complaining that it went too far to meet the demands of the Croats, while the Croats complained that it did not go far enough. The feelings of bitterness and resentment lingered on. The peoples of Jugoslavia, it seemed, irretrievably divided among themselves. Their country, meanwhile, stood in mortal peril.

Internationally, the years which followed the death of King Alexander had been marked by a gradual increase in German and Italian pressure and by a gradual shifting in the position of Jugoslavia away from the Western democracies and closer to the Axis powers. From first to last King Alexander's foreign policy had been firmly founded on membership of the Little Entente and on friendship with France and Great Britain. Prince Paul, on the other hand, though personally well disposed toward the Western Allies, felt bound to reinsure with Germany and Italy in the hope that by so doing he would keep his country out of war. Visits had been exchanged and contacts made. Marshal Goering and Count Ciano had come to Belgrade, where the latter had in March, 1937 signed a political agreement. The Jugoslav Prime Minister, Milan Stojadinović, had gone to Rome and Prince Paul himself had visited the *Fuhrer* at Berchtesgaden and the *Duce* in Rome. "Prince Paul's attitude," wrote the British Prime Minister on January 14, 1941, "looks like that of an unfortunate man in a cage with a tiger, hoping not to provoke him, while steadily dinnertime approaches."[12]

Initiated under the government of Milan Stojadinović, this "realistic policy" had been continued under that of Dragiša Cvetković, who succeeded him as prime minister early in 1939. It was brought to its logical conclusion when on February 14, 1941 Cvetković and his corpulent Foreign Minister, Aleksandar Cincar-Marković, were abruptly summoned by Hitler to Berchtesgaden and called upon to accede to the Tripartite Pact linking Germany, Italy and Japan—in other words, to throw in their lot with the Axis. On March 4 and again on the seventeenth Prince Paul himself secretly visited Hitler at Berchtesgaden and there that "amiable, artistic personage," as Sir Winston Churchill has called him, was subjected to the same pressure. By now he and his ministers were resigned to what they had come to regard as the inevitable. On March 25, at the Belvedere Palace in Vienna, Cvetković and Cincar-

Marković, on instructions from the Regent, formally signed the Tripartite Pact.

But Prince Paul and his ministers had reckoned without the people of Jugoslavia and in particular of Serbia, who, for their part, remained overwhelmingly hostile to the Axis and friendly to the Western powers. The popular reaction was immediate and characteristically violent. As soon as it became known what had happened, there were violent demonstrations in Belgrade and elsewhere. *"Bolje rat,"* the crowds shouted, *"nego pakt—Bolje grob nego rob,"* "Better war than the Pact. Better death than slavery." The Jugoslav nation had, in the words of the British Prime Minister, found its soul. On March 27 Prince Paul and Cvetković were placed under restraint by a group of Air Force officers; the young King's majority was proclaimed six months early, and a National Government was formed by an Air Force General named Simović with Dr. Maček as Vice-Premier. In the Orthodox cathedral at Belgrade a solemn Te Deum was sung to celebrate the occasion.

General Simović's government had been swept into power on the wave of popular indignation which had swept away their predecessors in protest against the signature of the Tripartite Pact. It may, therefore, at first sight seem a little surprising that almost the first action of the new government on taking office was to inform the governments of Germany and Italy that they recognized all Jugoslavia's international commitments, including her adherence to the Tripartite Pact. They also rejected out of hand the offers of immediate co-operation made to them by the British Government.

But these last-minute attempts at appeasement were of no avail. Hitler's mind was already made up. On being told early on March 27 of what had happened in Belgrade, the *Führer* had at first refused to believe the news—"I thought," he said later, "that it was a joke." Then, on being convinced that it was not, he had at once summoned his leading military and political advisers and given orders for the immediate destruction of Jugoslavia. "The *Führer* is determined," ran the minutes of this meeting, "without waiting for possible declarations of loyalty from the new government, to make all preparations in order to destroy Jugoslavia militarily and as a national unit. No diplomatic inquiries will be made nor ultimatums presented. Assurances of the Jugoslav Government, which in future cannot in any case be trusted, will be 'taken note of.' The attack will start as soon as the means and troops needed for it are ready."[13]

The necessary preparations did not take long. Ten days later, at 5 A.M. on Palm Sunday, April 6, a fine sunlit morning, a message from Hitler went out over the air announcing that German troops had already entered Jugoslavia, and two hours after that wave after wave of German bombers were systematically obliterating Belgrade. "Operation Punishment," as it was called, had begun.

The campaign lasted only a few days. "Politically," the *Führer* had decreed, it is especially important that the blow against Jugoslavia should be carried out with unmerciful harshness and the military destruction done in lightning-like fashion." Jugoslavia was not prepared for war. The Jugoslav Army was inadequately armed and equipped and insufficiently supplied with ammunition; communications were bad; mobilization had been too late; sabotage and treachery were rife. In some parts of the country, notably Croatia, the enemy were helped by an active and numerous fifth column. The main German attack, coming through Bulgaria, took the High Command by surprise. Their communications with the government, with the troops in the field and with the rest of the country, broke down completely. Fresh German armies, with Bulgarian, Hungarian and Italian support, invaded from all sides. Skoplje fell on April 9, Zagreb on the tenth, Ljubljana on the eleventh and Belgrade on the twelfth. On the sixteenth the young King and his government left the country by air. On the seventeenth the High Command capitulated.

Not only was the *Führer* determined to defeat Jugoslavia by force of arms. He had also now resolved to make an end once and for all of the Jugoslav State as such: "to destroy Jugoslavia militarily and as a national unit." Had it proved possible to make a reliable satellite of Jugoslavia, she might well have been incorporated as she stood in Hitler's New Order. But the events of March 27 had been enough for the *Führer*. Jugoslavia, he decided, should cease to exist. Her place on the map would in future be taken by a large, nominally independent Croatia, closely linked to the Axis, by a separate and much diminished Serbia under German occupation and by a puppet state of Montenegro under Italian control; her remaining territories would be distributed piecemeal among her neighbors.

On April 15, two days before the final capitulation of the Jugoslav High Command, Dr. Pavelić made his triumphal entry into Zagreb amid the acclamations of the assembled multitude. With him from Trieste in a fleet of hastily requisitioned motor busses had come the few hundred Ustaše who had shared his exile, hurriedly brought together from their various internment camps and arrayed in borrowed Italian uniforms.

He had been accepted first by the Italians and now by the Germans as *Polglavnik* or Leader of the new Croat State. But the price which he had paid for recognition was a heavy one. A more skillful statesman might conceivably have succeeded in playing off his rival protectors against each other to his own advantage. The tension between them had not escaped him. "They fight," he said to one of his companions, "like cat and dog." But diplomacy was not the *Poglavnik's* strongest suit. He somehow managed to get the worst of both worlds. By surrendering large areas of Dalmatia to Italy and handing over the remainder to Italian administration, he deprived himself of many potential supporters throughout Croatia; and, if Mussolini was disappointed in his hopes of establishing a protectorate over the rest of Croatia, it was only because, despite the Rome Agreements, the Independent State was from the first moment of its existence irretrievably tied to the chariot wheels of his German ally. "There is no longer a Croat-Italian problem," Ciano wrote in his diary six months later, "but a German-Italian problem in relation to Croatia."[14]

But, if the frontiers of the new kingdom did not fulfill the expectations of all its citizens and if its independence was no more than a polite fiction, in one respect at any rate Dr. Pavelić was to surpass the hopes of the most passionate devotees of Croat culture. The Independent State of Croatia might not be independent; it might not, strictly speaking, be a state; but it was at all costs going to be thoroughly Croat. Dr. Pavelić's racial theories went even further than those of Hitler himself. Croatia, he decreed, must be purged, not only of Jews and gypsies, but of Serbs, who, in the new state, amounted numerically to approximately one-third of the population. "The Serbs," he proclaimed, "are alien elements on Croat territory. They are by their nature irreconcilable enemies of the Croat State. They are rebels and as rebels they must be treated."*[15] His Minister of Education and Religion, Dr. Mile Budak, was even more explicit. "We shall kill some of the Serbs," he announced at a banquet at Gospic on June 6, "we shall expel others, and the remainder will be forced to embrace the Roman Catholic Faith. These last will in due course be absorbed by the Croat part of the population." Asked by a journalist what the government's policy would be in regard to the non-Croat racial and religious minorities, "For them," Dr. Budak replied, "we have three million bullets."[16]

As a first step toward the execution of this ambitious program, Dr. Pavelić now set up without loss of time a totalitarian dictatorship on the Nazi or Fascist model. Nominally, the new state was a kingdom, but the Duke of Spoleto, a cousin of the King of Italy, who at the instance of Mussolini had been chosen king under the somewhat fanciful name and style of King Tomislav II, showed no inclination either now or later to take up his appointment, wisely preferring to remain in his own country. As *Poglavnik* or leader, Dr. Pavelić himself wielded the supreme power; his faithful Ustaše became the single party in a one-party state, while special Ustaše shock units played the part of a Praetorian guard. "He has," wrote Ciano, who saw a lot of him at this time and knew a dictator when he saw one, "assumed the tone and manner of a dictator."[17]

Although Pavelić and his followers had returned in the baggage train of the invading German armies, and although the character of their regime was soon to alienate large sections of the population, it should not be assumed that the establishment of an Independent Croat State was at the outset unpopular with the people of Croatia as a whole. Many Croats, including the majority of the Croat Peasant party, had long grown exasperated with Serb hegemony, indeed with the whole concept of Jugoslavia. During the fighting a number of Croat regiments had deserted wholesale to the enemy and Pavelić's henchman, Colonel Kvaternik, had publicly proclaimed Croatia's independence amid scenes of genuine enthusiasm some hours before the first German troops actually entered Zagreb. In particular the change had been welcomed by many of the Catholic clergy, whose attitude had always reflected the Vatican's traditional dislike for Belgrade and who now looked forward to enjoying a privileged position in a Catholic country,

---

* Dr. Pavelic also regarded it as his mission to clear his new state of Jews. By December, 1941, according to the figures which he himself gave Count Ciano, the total number of Jews in Croatia had been reduced from 35,000 to 12,000. This was only a start (Ciano, *L'Europa verso la Catastrofe,* p. 703).

freed forever from the influence of their hated Orthodox rivals. Among the first to pay his respects to the *Poglavnik* after his return from exile was Monsignor Stepinac, the Catholic Archbishop of Zagreb and Metropolitan of Croatia. In a circular letter of April 26 the Archbishop formally called upon the clergy to render loyal service to their new rulers. "These are events," he wrote, "which fulfill the long dreamed of and desired ideal of our people. . . . Respond readily to my call to join in the noble task of working for the safety and well-being of the Independent State of Croatia."[18]

While Croatia was thus strengthened and exalted, the Germans did everything in their power to abase and weaken Serbia. What remained of it was placed under direct German military control, a puppet government of halfhearted Serbian quislings under General Milan Nedić being later formed for administrative purposes. Meanwhile, the remainder of Jugoslavia was portioned out between the victors and their jackals. Slovenia was divided between Germany and Italy. The Italians occupied Montenegro and part of Dalmatia and, to the disgust of the Ustaše, undertook the administration of what was known as the Second Zone of Croatia. The Bačka went to Hungary, Macedonia to Bulgaria, and the historic plain of Kosovo, with the adjacent areas, to Albania. On paper, at any rate, Jugoslavia had ceased to exist.

Where, it may be asked, were Tito and his friends, while these dramatic events were taking place, and what part, if any, did they play in them?

The claim has since been advanced on behalf of the Jugoslav Communist party that on March 25, 1941, they issued a proclamation vigorously condemning the government's adherence to the Three Power Pact and that the ensuing demonstrations were led and inspired by them.[19] The exact truth of the matter may never be known. In view of the dissensions known to have existed in the party up to a short time before, it is even possible that different sections of it may have taken different lines. At the same time, it is hard not to discern in these latter-day versions traces of a certain ideological *esprit d'escalier* and it seems safe to assume that the more extravagant claims of the Jugoslav Communists concerning their part in these important events are at any rate exaggerated.

But, though there is no valid reason to suppose that the Communists in fact played the decisive part in the *coup d'état* of March 27, there are numerous indications that, once it had taken place, the Kremlin decided that there were certain very definite advantages to be derived from it. While denying the story that the Soviet Government had officially congratulated the new Jugoslav Government on their attitude, *Pravda,* the official organ of the Soviet Communist party, went so far as to say that the Jugoslav people were worthy of their glorious past and deserved congratulations, and these sentiments were echoed by the Communist press elsewhere. Finally, on the night of April 5, a few hours before the German invasion of Jugoslavia, a Pact of Friendship and Nonaggression with General Simović's Government was signed in Moscow by Molotov in the presence of Stalin himself.

The most probable explanation of this "amicable grimace," as Mr. Churchill later called it, is that, disturbed by the latest turn of events, the Russians were belatedly attempting to deter the Germans or at least to bolster up Jugoslav resistance. It was, moreover, only logical that a corresponding change should take place in the attitude of the Jugoslav Communist party. And indeed such records as are available of their attitude during the immediately following period display a spirit of robust resistance to Axis aggression.

Tito himself, it appears, was in Zagreb on March 27, but hurried to Belgrade on the following day. "We are heading for war," he said to a friend, "we must be prepared."[20] April 6 found him back in Zagreb. According to his official biographer, on learning of the German attack, he at once sent a "delegation of leading Zagreb workers" to General Orlović, Chief of Staff of the Fourth Jugoslav Army, asking that arms should be issued to the workers of Zagreb in order that they should help defend the city.[21] In view of its origin, this request was not unnaturally rejected. Three days later Zagreb was occupied by the Germans. On April 10 Tito, again according to his official biographer, issued a proclamation to the peoples of Jugoslavia calling on them to close their ranks and not to lose heart or be bowed down, [22] and on April 15 yet another proclamation appears to have been issued by the General Committee of the party, declaring that, despite momentary defeat, ultimate victory was certain.[23]

One might be inclined to regard these stirring statements as yet further examples of the retoucher's art, were it not for the fact that they correspond, by and large, to the line taken by Moscow at that time. There thus seems no especial reason to doubt their genuineness. Rather less clear is the attitude of the Jugoslav Communists after the middle of April.

Once the Jugoslav Army had finally surrendered and the King and government had fled abroad, the Soviet Government with their usual realism and adaptability, appear once again to have reconsidered their position. It is proverbially no good flogging a dead horse and to the Russians this particular horse must have seemed irremediably dead. So long as there was something there to bolster up, they had, rather halfheartedly, bolstered it up. Now there could clearly be no advantage in gratuitously offending Hitler out of regard for an exiled king and government. Recognition was promptly withdrawn from the Jugoslav Communists after the middle of April.
sador in Moscow, with whom Molotov had a few weeks earlier signed the Pact of Friendship and Nonaggression, was invited to leave the Soviet Union without delay. In the Soviet press a discreet silence descended on the whole unwelcome subject of Jugoslavia.

Where did Tito stand now? The available documentary evidence, for what it is worth, suggests that, as far as propaganda was concerned, he prudently concentrated on blaming the Serb ruling class for what had happened. This "terrible disaster," said the party's May Day Manifesto, was due to "the criminal policy of the Belgrade rulers who while in power had cared for nothing save their own capitalist interests," had neglected the country's defenses, had "tied themselves to the Axis bandits" and had failed "to conclude in time a pact of mutual aid with the great and strong Soviet Union in the interest of peace and of the independence of the peoples of Jugoslavia."[24] For the rest, his attitude seems to have been one of vigilance and preparation, as well it might in so uncertain a situation.

It has since been claimed by certain of his followers that during the weeks that followed the Communists engaged in active resistance to the Axis forces of occupation. It is true that in many places the acts of terror perpetrated by the occupying forces and by native quislings provoked a spontaneous reaction on the part of the local populations, and it may be that here and there the Communists, whom the Germans were now hunting down quite as relentlessly as the Royal Police had ever done, joined in these local revolts. But for the first two months and more after the German invasion there is no convincing evidence of any organized Communist resistance movement. Tito himself has described this period as having been used by the party "for final preparations for an uprising, for diversions, for gathering arms and so on."[25] The decision to take these measures was, we are told, reached at a plenary meeting of the Central Committee of the party held in a flat in Zagreb at the end of April.[26]

But, whatever ambiguities may obscure the attitude of the Jugoslav Communist party before the German attack and during the two months which followed it, this question was soon to be cleared up once and for all. Hitler's sudden invasion of the Soviet Union—of the Country of the Revolution—on June 22, 1941, left no doubt whatever where they or any other Communists stood. Overnight, for all of them, wherever they were, the Second Imperialist War had become the Fatherland War, the People's War for Freedom and Democracy.*

As soon as he heard the news, Tito, who had moved to Belgrade early in May, at once called together the Politburo in order to discuss this "new situation" and the new measures for which it called. After the meeting, a proclamation was issued, reminding the people of Jugoslavia that the struggle of the Soviet Union was their struggle and calling upon them to rise and take arms, under Communist leadership, against the Fascist invaders "who, like mad dogs, are attacking the Soviet Union, our dear Socialist fatherland, our hope and beacon." "This," said Tito later, "was our party's war cry, its call to arms and to revolt."[27]

---

* Djilas made this clear in a speech delivered on November 6, 1943. "We Communists," he said, "are often reproached with not having called the people to arms until Hitler attacked the Soviet Union. . . . After the occupation of our country the party organized mass political resistance to the enemy forces and the Central Committee, for its part, made serious preparations for military action. But the time for armed revolt had not yet come. It could only come when Hitler's troops were engaged on some other front, when it had become clear to the mass of the people that a struggle was possible, that it had some prospect of success and that they themselves would stand to gain by it. And this was only so once Hitler had attacked the Soviet Union. The participation of the Soviet Union in the war was a guarantee that it would really be a war of national liberation and not just a war to serve the interests of those foreign reactionaries on whom the repulsive former

rulers of this country had pinned their faith" (V. Dedijer, *Dnevnik*, Belgrade, 1946, Vol. II, p. 582).

It may also be observed that July 7 has since been regularly celebrated as the anniversary of the rising in Serbia (Tito, *Borba za Oslobodjenje Jugoslavije*, Belgrade, 1947, pp. 68 and 73).

part two

★⧖⧖⧖⧖⧖⧖⧖⧖⧖⧖⧖⧖⧖⧖⧖⧖⧖⧖⧖⧖⧖⧖⧖⧖⧖★

IN THE WOODS

Leninism recognizes the latent revolutionary
potentialities of the national liberation movement.
STALIN, *Foundations of Leninism*

V ꙅꙅꙅꙅ SERBIAN RISING

"WHAT struck me most," an old friend said later of a conversation which he had with Tito in 1937, "was his calm assurance that there was going to be a war; that the old regime would collapse; that the Communist party would lead a tremendous fight, would win and would govern the country. . . . He had no doubts—to him it was all clear cut and his confidence was absolute."[1]

Ever since he had returned home from Russia in 1920 Josip Broz's chief ambition, his dearest wish, had been to see a Communist regime set up in Jugoslavia. All his efforts, all his endeavors had been directed to that end. Two or three times during the past twenty years there had been brief moments when civic disorders or economic stress had made it seem possible that a revolutionary situation might arise and that his dream might somehow be fulfilled. There had been the early days of unrest in 1920 and 1921. There had been the riots in 1928. There had been King Alexander's murder in 1934. But each time the forces of law and order had triumphed, his hopes had been dashed, and he had gone back to the wearisome business of dodging the police, fighting fractionalism and following and interpreting the intricate convolutions of the party line.

Now, at long last, after all those years of waiting, the hour had struck when he and his comrades could finally pass from underground conspiracy and intrigue to revolutionary war. The old Jugoslavia had ceased to exist; it was for them to put a new Jugoslavia, a Communist Jugoslavia, in its place. It was an opportunity, an opportunity which they must grasp with both hands.

Tito was not slow to grasp it. This was the supreme test of his devotion and organizing ability. "Organize," Grandpapa* had signaled, "partisan detachments without a moment's delay. Start a partisan war in the enemy's rear."[2] And indeed, within two or three weeks of Hitler's attack on the Soviet Union and

---

* The code name for the Comintern.

of the party's call to arms, a number of guerrilla bands were operating in Serbia and elsewhere under Communist command. They consisted of small groups of determined men and women, mostly party members, who, at a word from party headquarters, had taken to the woods and forests, equipped with such arms as they had been able to collect, with cudgels and axes, with old sporting guns and with anything else they could lay hands on. For further supplies they depended on what they could capture from the enemy and on what the country people would give them. They wore as their badge a five-pointed red star. They were known as Partisans. Early in July news began to reach Belgrade of their achievements: of ambushed German convoys and of surprise attacks on enemy units and outposts. At the same time their comrades in the towns carried out acts of sabotage: petrol dumps were fired, German soldiers set upon and killed, and vehicles and machinery destroyed.

The immediate aim of all these operations, whether in town or country, was to harass the enemy, to destroy his communications, to disrupt his administration, to shatter the morale of his troops, and so in some small degree to relieve the pressure which he was now exerting on the Russian front. Their ultimate aim was the creation of a Communist Jugoslavia.. The time, in Tito's own words, had come for the party "to prepare to seize power and to seize it in such a way that the bourgeoisie would never regain it."[3] The rising against the invader must, he had said at a meeting of the Central Committee, be no bourgeois revolution; it must lead to the establishment of the dictatorship of the proletariat. To some of his more optimistic followers this happy event seemed so close, now that Russia had entered the war, that they actually sat down to plan the immediate administrative measures which would be necessary when they assumed power, and were only induced to take a more realistic view of the situation by the increasingly depressing news arriving from the Eastern front.

At first Tito conducted operations from Belgrade. He had gone there from Zagreb in May, traveling as usual on forged documents and accompanied by a Communist girl "courier" whose duty it was to go through the check posts ahead of him in order to make sure that the Germans had made no change in the documents and passes required. Soon after reaching Belgrade he installed himself in a villa in the fashionable garden suburb of Dedinje only a few hundred yards away from the official residence of the German Commander-in-

Chief. From his bathroom a secret door in a cupboard behind the washbasin led to a specially contrived hiding place under the roof, where he kept, in case of need, two revolvers and sixteen hand grenades.

Also now in Belgrade were Djilas, Marko Ranković, Ribar, Black Žojovic and other members of the little group of picked men he had formed round him during the past four or five years. Kardelj had already left for his native Slovenia, to organize resistance there. The party was on a war footing. Some months earlier, in Zagreb, a Military Committee had been set up with Tito at its head. Then, at a meeting of the Central Committee held on June 27, it had been decided to appoint Tito military commander of all Partisan detachments and to form from the members of the Politburo a General Headquarters of National Liberation Partisan Detachments.

Outwardly Tito was still that well-dressed, well-fed and generally respected citizen, Engineer Slavko Babić, now a man of property, for he had recently bought himself a vineyard near Zagreb. He and his friends spent much of their time in the nearby villa of Vladislav Ribnikar, a rich Belgrade newspaper proprietor who was also a secret member of the Communist party. Those who met Engineer Babić in Madame Ribnikar's elegantly furnished salon could not help being struck by the good looks, polished maners and fashionable appearance of this new recruit to Belgrade society and would ask their attractive little hostess to tell them more about him. They would have been astonished and perhaps some of them would have been a little shocked had they been able to see him in the same room an hour or two earlier, presiding over a meeting of the Partisan General Staff, dispatching couriers to outlying detachments, planning sabotage operations on the railways, while the Ribnikars kept watch outside. At other times, in the stifling July heat, he would sit out in the garden under a vine arbor, working all day long, with his usual efficiency and attention to detail, on plans and operation orders. Meanwhile, by means of secret couriers and of a wireless set, hidden under the staircase of a house in Zagreb occupied by Vladko Velebit, he continued to maintain regular contact with Moscow.

On July 4, a fortnight after issuing his first call to arms, Tito held at the Ribnikars' villa a meeting of the Politburo which lasted all day and at which detailed plans were made for the prosecution of the revolt. He himself arrived first, followed at carefully spaced intervals by Marko Ranković, the journeyman tailor from central Serbia who since 1937 had become one of his closest associates, Black Žujovic, and Tempo Vukmanović, an energetic young Montenegrin with a long and successful record as a conspirator and organizer. Djilas and Ivo Ribar were already there for they were both staying in the house. Outside in the garden, Vlada Ribnikar and his wife kept watch, successfully fending off two itinerant black-market firewood vendors who they thought might be police spies.

It was decided at this meeting that the revolt should be extended and intensified; that there should be more sabotage in the towns; that stronger and more numerous Partisan detachments should be formed in the country areas, each with its own political commissar; and that in the place of isolated guerrilla actions there should be nation-wide resistance, centrally co-ordinated. At the same time, it was decided that wherever possible what remained of the old administrative machinery should be destroyed and new Partisan authorities set up in its place. For were they not engaged in a revolution as well as a war?

Immediately after the meeting Djilas left to take command in his native Montenegro, while Tempo Vukmanović, dark, lean and decisive-looking, was sent off to raise the standard of revolt in neighboring Bosnia and Herzegovina. Kardelj was already in Slovenia. Tito himself, Marko Ranković and Black Žujovic assumed responsibility for operations in Sibera.

Up to now Belgrade, despite the German occupation, had possessed numerous advantages as a site for the Communists' secret headquarters. It was central and possessed good communications with the rest of the country. As yet the underground system of contacts and hideouts, the whole intelligence network which they had built up over the past twenty years to help them evade the vigilance of the Royal Police, was still very largely intact. But as the Gestapo's hold on the city tightened, their existence became more and more precarious. Since Russia's entry into the war the Germans, with the active help of the Belgrade police, were methodically hunting down Communists. Anyone who had been in jail before the war and whose appearance was familiar to the police was in constant danger of being recognized and caught. It became increasingly dangerous for Tito and his friends to show themselves in the main streets of the town. Every day that went by brought depressing news of fresh arrests and executions of party members; some were hanged in public in the main square of Belgrade and their bodies left dangling from the lamp posts as a warning. On July 1 Djilas's wife, Mitra Mitrović, one of the leading women Communists, had been arrested in the street by a police agent who knew her by sight and taken off to prison. On July 11 came the news that three more leading Communists had been arrested and shot in Zagreb. On July 17 Radio Belgrade broadcast a long list of party members who had been caught and executed, while another long list was published in *Novo Vreme* of July 19. Then on the night of July 27 a message reached Tito to say that Marko Ranković had been taken.

Marko had gone earlier that evening to meet some wireless technicians with whom he was plotting to blow up Radio Belgrade. But at the last moment one of them had, it seemed, betrayed him to the Germans. When he reached the rendezvous, eight Gestapo men jumped out on him and knocked him down. The identity card which he was carrying bore the name of Perisić and the Germans did not know whom they had caught, though they suspected that it was someone of importance. In their anxiety to find out more about him, they beat their prisoner senseless. When he came to, he found himself in bed in the prison hospital. His first thought was that, if he could feign unconsciousness for long enough, the party might have time to rescue him before he was again interrogated, tortured and finally executed. He accordingly lay inert, vomited up the tea that the nurse poured down his throat and in due course had the satisfaction of hearing the doctor who had come to examine him say to the Gestapo man with him, *"Fünf Tage"*—"Another five days."

Marko's faith in the party was justified. On learning of his arrest, Tito had at once given orders that he must at all costs be rescued. The difficulty was to find out where he had been taken. But Mitra Mitrović, who had been arrested three weeks earlier, happened by chance to be in another ward of the same hospital and, on learning of his arrival, succeeded in smuggling out a message describing his exact whereabouts. On the morning of July 29, barely thirty-six hours after his capture, the hospital was unobtrusively surrounded by forty nondescript-looking men, all Partisans, and all armed with revolvers and hand grenades. As soon as these had taken up their positions, ten more Partisans, pretending to be detectives escorting a prisoner in handcuffs, pushed past the guards at the gate and forced their way into the hospital. A police sergeant who tried to stop them was shot dead. While five of the party covered their withdrawal, the others burst into the room where Marko was lying, dragged him out of bed, along the passage, out of the building, and, with a stupendous effort on his part, over a wall and into the street. In the street two Gestapo men opened fire on them, but were at once shot down. From the hospital came shouts and the sound of more shooting. While the Partisans surrounding the building held off the pursuit, Marko was taken to a near-by house where he changed his clothes and tidied himself up; after which he was bundled into a peasant's waiting cart near by and driven to a secret hiding place on the outskirts of the city. To the last, the Germans never discovered their prisoner's identity, though they must have felt surer than ever that he was someone of considerable significance. It must also have become clear to them by now, if they had not realized it before, that there existed in their midst an extremely formidable and capably led underground organization.

More and more recruits were now joining the Partisans and in Serbia the revolt was spreading through the countryside like wildfire. Having recovered from his injuries, Marko Ranković was once more in charge and his daily reports to Tito told of widespread guerrilla operations on an ever-increasing scale. Every day petrol and ammunition dumps were blown up, convoys ambushed, trains derailed, enemy outposts raided and more and more arms and ammunition captured. Soon large areas of the country were in the hands of the insurgents, while in the towns the German garrisons lived in constant fear of attack. From Djilas in Montenegro came news of a spectacularly successful rising against the Italians, while couriers brought reports of Partisan activity on varying scales in other regions. Not all the news was good. From Bosnia Tempo Vukmanović reported heavy casualties among the party leaders and resulting disorganization. In Croatia and Slovenia Kardelj had found much that was satisfactory, but much also that was unsatisfactory.

In Belgrade Tito considered these reports and sent out in reply his own comments and instructions, calling for better organization, for stronger leadership, for the elimination of unsatisfactory elements and, above all, for constant action against the enemy. "From your report," he wrote to the Partisan leaders in Croatia on August 17, "it appears that the revolt in your area has now attained considerable proportions. But it also appears that the organization and leadership of the party and staff is inadequate. Do everything in your power to see that in future the conduct of operations is well organized and centralized under strong leadership. Form strong Partisan formations and see that they are constantly in action."[4]

At the same time, in a series of messages signed "Walter" and sent by courier to Zagreb for dispatch over Vladko Velebit's secret wireless transmitter, Tito kept Moscow informed of the achievements of his Partisans. "Partisan operations in Serbia," he signaled on August 23, "are assuming to an ever greater extent the character of a national uprising. The Germans are only holding the larger towns while the villages and hamlets are in the hands of the Partisans. All headquarters and commanders of Partisan detachments throughout Jugoslavia are in direct touch with Partisan G.H.Q. under Walter." The message concluded with an appeal for help. "Our great need," Tito signaled, "is for arms. Please let us know if you can supply us with arms. We will tell you where and when to drop them."[5] But the Russians, it seemed, were at this stage of the war too preoccupied with their own supply problems to spare anything for Tito.

Another report dispatched from Belgrade at about this time gave an account of the situation from a different angle—from that of the Germans. "All our attempts," wrote Staatsrat Dr. Thurner in a dispatch to Berlin,

> to canalize these people in a constructive direction and separate them from the Communists have failed and had to be abandoned. We have argued with them, conferred with them, cajoled them and threatened them, but all to no purpose. We do not believe that it is possible to achieve anything in this country on the basis of authority. The people just do not recognize authority. A minority question cannot be created among the Serbs as it was with such success among the Croats. Practically nobody is interested in the old political parties. They do not believe in anyone any more and they follow the Communist bandits blindly. With their slogans the Communists have succeeded in rallying round them elements who in the past would never have dreamt of co-operating with them. Some go so far as to prefer Bolshevism to occupation by our troops—and these are people on whose co-operation we were counting. Only one means is left: armed force. It is difficult to get any sense out of the Militia. The Italians are worse. Our intensified pro-

paganda to the effect that things are going badly for the
Bolsheviks at the front has proved useless. My impression
is that even the news of the capitulation of the Soviet
Union would not cause these bandits to capitulate. They
are tougher than anything you can imagine. What is
more, their organization is excellent. It might serve as the
classical example of a perfect secret organization.[6]

Toward the end of August Tito decided that the moment
had come for him to leave Belgrade and join his troops in
the field. It was a journey which called for careful preparation. Among Vladislav Ribnikar's many friends and acquain-
tances was a certain Pop Milutinović, an Orthodox priest
with wide official and unofficial contacts in western Serbia,
whose sympathies were known to be wholeheartedly with the
resistance and who might, it was felt, be of help in this
particular contingency. It was accordingly arranged that he
should meet Tito at luncheon at the Ribnikars'. Although the
actual identity of Engineer Slavko Babic was not revealed to
him, he was given a shrewd idea of the nature of the business
which was shortly to take the latter and some of his friends
out of Belgrade and by the end of luncheon had not only
agreed to provide him with the necessary documents but had
announced his intention of accompanying him himself.[7]

A few days later an oddly assorted little party assembled at
Belgrade railway station, some with genuine and some with
forged or partly forged travel documents, and all bent on
business which, should its nature be discovered, would render
them liable to immediate execution. There was Tito, as elegant
as ever, with yet another false identity card. There was Pop
Milutinović with his beard and flowing robes and, concealed
in one boot, a stolen official rubber stamp for use in
emergencies. There was a *Volksdeutscher* called Reiter, a
reliable party member, with a complete set of German identity
papers. And, in order still further to confuse the mind of the
inquisitive onlooker, there were three nondescript young
women, all in fact active party members.

The six of them took tickets to Požega, a small town in
central Serbia at the end of the western Morava Valley a
hundred miles or so south of Belgrade. Sitting in the railway
carriage, Tito and Reiter conversed ostentatiously in German.
Tito was in the best of humors and laughed and joked all the
way. Just before reaching Kraljevo, where the railway crosses
the western Morava, the train stopped and they were invited

to get out. On asking the reason for this, they were told that the train could go on no farther as the bridge had been blown up by Communist bandits. Loudly proclaiming their disgust at this abominable outrage, they made their way on foot to the other side, where they waited for another train. Farther on, at Čačak, they had a narrow escape from some police agents who knew one of the girls by sight. Finally they reached Požega, whence they set out northwestward in a horse cab in the direction of Krupanj, a small town some thirty miles west of Valjevo which had recently been captured by the Partisans. The cabman, as they drove along, kept telling them how dangerous it was with the woods full of bandits and asking for more money. "I suppose you aren't going to join the Partisans?" he asked all of a sudden. "Is it likely—in these clothes?" Tito replied, pointing proudly to his city suit. And the driver apologized.

Some time before getting to Krupanj, they came upon the first outposts of the Valjevo Partisan detachment and Tito was challenged and stopped by his own sentries. A little farther on they met Marko Ranković, who had arrived a few days earlier. It was four in the morning when Tito reached his headquarters, and they had been traveling solidly for two days and two nights. But despite the late hour he at once started work, clearing up problems which had been awaiting his arrival.

Already during July and August the character of the Partisan Movement in Serbia had undergone a marked change. The Partisans were fast becoming more than armed raiders. The size of their bands and the scope of their operations were increasing. A number of small towns and villages had fallen into their hands. In the districts under their control the Partisans were in a rough and ready way taking over the civil administration. New recruits, including many non-Communists, were flocking to their standards. From a few hundreds, their numbers had increased to several thousands. In central and western Serbia they were driving the enemy from ever larger areas and back onto the big towns, where his troops, harassed from all sides and with their communications disrupted, were being forced more and more into the position of beleaguered garrisons.

Militarily the situation in Jugoslavia favored guerrilla operations. Although strategically on the offensive, the enemy was tactically and locally on the defensive, being obliged to guard with inadequate forces greatly extended lines of communication and dangerously isolated garrisons and installations. The terrain, too, favored the guerrillas. In their native forests and mountains the Partisans possessed a background for their operations which served them at will as a base, a jumping-off point, a space in which to maneuver, a place in which to hide. It was an element as essential to their kind of warfare as the sea is to naval warfare. By suddenly emerging from it, they could achieve the surprise which is the essence of irregular operations. By fading swiftly back into it, they could at the critical moment deny the enemy a target against which to strike back. They also enjoyed the support of a civilian population deeply imbued with the tradition of resistance. But perhaps their greatest strength was the idea which inspired them. In guerrilla war ideas matter more than material resources. Few ideas equal revolutionary Communism in its strength, its persistence and its power over the individual. Communism gave the Partisans a singleness of purpose, a ruthless determination, a merciless discipline, without which they could not have survived, let alone succeeded in their object. It helped them to overcome their old national feuds and divergencies. It inspired in them an absolute devotion to their cause which led them to count as nothing their own lives or the lives of others. It brought them a ready-made intelligence system, a well-tried, widespread underground network. It endowed them with an oracle: the party line. To what had begun as a war it gave the character of a revolution.

By the beginning of September the Partisans had gained control of a large area of hill country between Sabac and Užice and it was here in the little mountain hamlet of Stolice that Tito, having exchanged his smart city suit for a more serviceable jacket and breeches with a revolver at his belt, set up his combined political and military High Command.

Shortly before leaving Belgrade he had issued his first order of the day as Commander-in-Chief. This enumerated Partisan successes up-to-date—trains and bridges blown up, convoys ambushed, petrol dumps set on fire. It also laid down a general political directive concerning the general character of the detachments. "These," it said,

> are called National Liberation Partisan Detachments, for the reason that they are not the fighting formations of any political party or group—not even the Communist party, though Communists are fighting in their front ranks. They are the armed detachments of the peoples of

Jugoslavia which all patriots capable of fighting the
enemy against the invader should join, whatever their
political convictions.

Experience hitherto has shown that insufficient attention has been paid to the concept of a general uprising
of the people. This mistake must be rectified without
delay. There is a danger that otherwise the Partisans
may lose touch with the masses who are ready to fight for
the just cause. The political line of the Partisan Detachments lay down that there must be a National Liberation
Anti-Fascist Front of all the peoples of Jugoslavia regardless of party or religion. In forming Partisan Detachments it is essential not to be narrow-minded but to give
wide scope to initiative and enterprise of every kind.[8]

Tito and the members of his Politburo had received their
most intensive political training in the 1930's, in the days of
the "Popular Front against Fascisim." Now that Fascism
was again the archenemy, they easily reverted to the old line
once more, seeking, at Moscow's behest, to give the movement they were launching a national rather than a purely party
character. As it happened, it was a line which in present circumstances presented considerable possibilities—possibilities
which did not escape Tito either now or later. Meanwhile
control, both military and political, remained firmly rooted in
the Communist party.

When the Partisans first entered the field in Serbia in the
summer of 1941, they found another resistance movement
already in existence: the Cetniks of Colonel Draža Mihajlović.
Before the war, Colonel Mihajlović, a regular officer who had
served with distinction in the Serbian Army in the First World
War and had since held a variety of regimental and staff appointments, had been associated with the official Cetnik
Organization. This was a patriotic body of strongly Serb affili-
ations founded to carry on the tradition of the Serb *ceti* or
armed bands who had kept alive the spirit of Serb independence in the days of Turkish domination. It was sponsored
by the General Staff, the key posts in it were held by serving
officers and the intention was that, in case of war, its members should conduct guerrilla activities on territory occupied
by the enemy.*

* In the event, Kosta Pecanac, the *Vojvoda* or Commander of the
official Cetnik organization, took an early opportunity of coming

After the capitulation of the Jugoslav Army in April, Colonel Mihajlović had managed to avoid capture and, accompanied by twenty-six other like-minded officers, noncommissioned officers and men, had made his way through Bosnia to the thickly wooded hill country of western Serbia. On May 11 he reached the plateau of Ravna Gora in the Sumadija, an inaccessible region of forests and hills, where he made his headquarters. Once established on Ravna Gora he set about recruiting more volunteers, drawn in the main from the conservative elements of the Serbian population, organizing them under local leaders on a largely territorial basis. With the Cetniks, tradition and local connections counted for a lot. They cultivated, for example, a highly traditional appearance, wearing long hair and flowing beards, tall sheepskin caps bearing the royal arms or a skull and crossbones badge, and a regular arsenal of daggers, fancy firearms and bandoliers which would have done credit to their forebears who fought the Turks. The Cetniks attached particular importance to the wearing of beards. "The beard," wrote Mihajlović, "is for the Cetnik a symbol of heroism. It also strikes fear into the hearts of our enemies." But if their appearance was warlike, their conduct was less so. For the time being, their leader concentrated on building up his organization and did not encourage the idea of a general rising or of active operations against the enemy.

Mihajlović's caution was understandable. He knew that any guerrilla action would inevitably provoke immediate and savage reprisals by the enemy against the civilian population. It had done so in the first war and would do so again. And this he wanted to avoid. His object was not to destroy, but to preserve, to keep in being in Serbia something that could serve as a nucleus from which to rebuild some day the old order that was so dear to him: the monarchy, the church, the army, the Serb way of life. At present his resources were limited. Nor could he hope for any outside help. In August he had managed to establish wireless contact with the British, but they had just been thrown out of Greece

---

to terms with General Nedic, the head of the puppet government which the Germans set up in Belgrade, and through him, with the Germans. His followers were recognized as "legal Cetniks" and later incorporated in the Serbian State Guard, a purely quisling force. Thereafter the term "Cetnik" was chiefly used to denote the followers of Mihajlovic.

and now they had their hands full elsewhere. In time, perhaps, if all went well, the Allies would reinvade the Balkans. Then would be the time for a general rising. In the meantime his aim must be to keep something in being in Serbia.

Tito's aim was almost exactly the opposite. He was a revolutionary. He had no wish to see the old order restored. He had been fighting against it all his life and rejoiced at its downfall. He welcomed the opportunity of destroying what remained of it. He was determined to set up a new order in its place, a revolutionary order. That aim bulked at least as large in his plans as the defeat of the enemy. He refused to let himself be deterred by the enemy's reprisals against the civilian population. This after all was a People's War. The whole population was in the firing line, with the same chance of a hero's death as the Partisans themselves. If, in the course of the war, towns and villages were burned and property destroyed, might this not help on the work of the Revolution? If hostages were shot and men and women bereaved and driven from their homes, would this not serve to swell the ranks of the revolutionaries? His Partisans, in contrast to the Cetniks, were largely drawn from elements of the population without strong local attachments, industrial workers from the towns and uprooted peasants, men ready to go anywhere and fight anyone without fear of the consequences for their homes and families. His immediate task was clear: to harass the enemy—his enemy and that of the Soviet Union—by all the means in his power and not to count the cost. He was sustained in this task by his own energy and strength of character and by the devotion, efficiency and disciplined fervor of the little band of party members who, under his guidance, had assumed the direction and leadership of the revolt. He was sustained, too, by the turbulent and indomitable spirit of the Jugoslav people.

The rising which took part in Serbia in the late summer and early autumn of 1941 was due in part to the organized activities of the Partisans and Cetniks. It was, also, to a very large degree, a spontaneous national rising. At first the Serbs had been dazed by the suddenness of the German onslaught. Now, when the first shock had passed, there returned to them the fierce will to resist for which they have been famous throughout history. Many of the individual Cetnik leaders, disregarding Mihajlović's appeals for caution, joined vigorously in the rising. In the battles which ensued, Cetniks and Partisans fought side by side against the common foe. They

were astonishingly successful. The Germans had let themselves be taken by surprise. The greater part of the troops
which had been used for the original invasion of Jugoslavia
had by now been moved elsewhere, leaving behind only relatively small forces for garrison and guard duties. Large areas
of territory and a number of important towns were now
liberated. More and more prisoners were taken and ever
larger quantities of arms and ammunition fell into the hands
of the insurgents. Soon, the greater part of Serbia was free.
Some areas were under Partisan and some under Cetnik control. Everywhere the peasants flocked to join the resistance.
A united command and a united effort against the invader
seemed possible, indeed probable.

It was in these circumstances that in mid-September a
meeting between Tito and Mihajlović took place at Tito's
request on Cetnik territory in the village of Struganik at the
foot of Ravan Gora, some forty miles southeast of Tito's own
heaquarters at Stolice. Earlier discussions between Partisan
and Cetnik representatives had proved inconclusive and it
had accordingly been decided that the two leaders should
meet in person. Tito now set out from Stolice on horseback
with an escort of fifteen young Partisans. A mile or two from
Struganik they were met by a resplendent mounted guard of
honor sent out by Mihajlović to welcome them and bring
them in. Looking at the well-nourished, well-mounted Cetniks
with their long hair, impressive beards and high sheepskin
hats, Tito could not help contrasting them with the hungry,
half-grown youths who trudged in the dust beside his horse.
Mihajlović himself was waiting to receive him in a house in
the village. He was slightly built and of medium height and
was wearing uniform. He had let his beard grow and wore
steel-rimmed spectacles through which he peered benignly and
inquisitively at his guest. His thick thatch of hair was turning
gray. His voice, when he spoke, was curiously soft and gentle.
He was inclined to stoop. Tito's first impression of him was
not unfavorable. "He struck me," he said long afterward, "as a
nice, pleasant-mannered sort of man—a typical regular officer."[9]

After they had had something to eat and drunk some
Turkish coffee, they began their discussions. The general tone
of these was friendly enough. But, although for the time being
circumstances had made them allies or at any rate potential
allies, both parties were very much on their guard. Tito, who
for so many years had been wanted by the Royal Police, could

not but feel it strange that he should have dealings with a representative of the Royal Government. Mihajlović, very much the professional staff officer, scarcely knew what to make of this Communist agitator turned guerrilla leader, whom he half believed to be a Russian. At the same time, each felt that the other perhaps had something to offer that might be worth having. When they came to discuss future operations, Mihajlović, cautious as ever, refused to commit himself to any large-scale action against the Germans, objecting that the time was not yet ripe. The Partisans, he warned Tito, were heading for disaster with their shock tactics. They themselves would be wiped out and they would bring terrible suffering on the people of Serbia. By the end of the interview Tito had begun to suspect that, as far as fighting the Germans was concerned, Mihajlović did not really mean business. He was also quite certain that such a man could never have any sympathy for the basically revolutionary policies of the Partisans. In the end a provisional arrangement for a measure of co-operation was arrived at. But it proved impossible to reach agreement on the unified command at which Tito was aiming, in the hope, no doubt, of ultimately absorbing Mihajlović's whole movement into his National Liberation Front.

Meanwhile events in Serbia were moving fast, and in a direction far from reassuring for Mihajlović. Ever larger areas were falling into the hands of the insurgents, and, as a result of their superior leadership and organization, and of their more active policy, control was passing more and more to the Partisans. During September several Cetnik leaders, tiring of Mihajlović's inactivity, went over to Tito, taking their followers with them. Among these was Pop Vlado Zečević, the red-bearded Orthodox parish priest of Krupanj, who had taken an active part in the fighting against the Germans in August and had thereby quickly incurred Mihajlović's displeasure. Even after he had joined the Partisans, Pop Vlado clung to the Cetnik custom of carrying on his person a large and varied collection of arms and ammunition. With his flaming red beard and hair surmounted by an army cap on which, in addition to the red star of the Partisans, he wore a small metal cross to denote his holy calling, he presented an unusual and formidable appearance.

On September 26, a few days after his meeting with Mihajlović, Tito held at his headquarters at Stolice a conference of Partisan commanders from all over Jugoslavia. The tiny

three-roomed cottage in which he was living stood at the head
of a narrow mountain valley. Immediately below it lay the rest
of the village: a dozen more houses, whitewashed and red-
roofed, with their orchards of heavily laden fruit trees and
their patches of maize ripening in the autumn sun. From
the window you looked down the valley toward a wider prospect of distant blue hills stretching away, range upon range,
to the horizon. A steep track, which followed the course of
a little mountain stream, led up the valley from Krupanj. It
was along this that the Partisan commanders arriving for the
conference had made their way.

There were ten or twelve of them. Some came from nearby.
Others had traveled long distances across country on foot or
on horseback, dodging the enemy's patrols. Those from
Slovenia and Croatia, using one disguise or another, had
traveled most of the way by train. Marko Ranković was there,
and Black Žujović and Ivo Ribar. Tempo Vukmanović had
come from Bosnia. Djilas was still in Montenegro. Kardelj,
too, was missing when the conference opened. He had traveled
by train from Ljubljana to Zagreb and thence to Belgrade,
disguised as a representative of the International Red Cross.
But in Belgrade he had found that the contact who was to
send him on his way had already been caught by the Gestapo
and he had been obliged to go round knocking on the doors
of houses where he believed members of the Communist underground to be living, looking for a friend to help him. In
the end he had had to go the whole way back to Zagreb to
get some more forged papers. It had been a long and nerve-
racking business and when he finally reached Stolice, the
conference had already been in progress for two days.

All the men who assembled at Stolice were experienced
revolutionaries, trusted party members who had worked underground with Tito before the war. Several had fought in
Spain—Koča Popović, for example, the son of a Belgrade
millionaire. Small, dark and vital, with glittering eyes and a
fierce black mustache, he had caused a sensation in intellectual circles before the war as a surrealist poet and philosopher
and had made himself a reputation as a guerrilla leader in
Spain to which he was now adding by his exploits in Serbia.
To look at, they were a motley crowd, from all walks of life
and from all parts of the country, peasants, soldiers, intellectuals and industrial workers. Some wore uniforms of one
kind or another and some civilian clothes, slung about with
revolvers, submachine guns and hand grenades. But their re-

ports showed that, in addition to what had been achieved in Serbia, active resistance movements under Communist leadership were now in existence in Slovenia, Croatia, Bosnia, Herzegovina and Montenegro, in fact throughout the whole country. Unlike Colonel Mihajlović's Cetniks, who were predominantly Serb, the Partisans were not confined to any single area or nationality. Their activities extended over the whole of Jugoslavia. The ideological bonds which united them were stronger than any local patriotism, and so, by an odd paradox, these declared internationalists formed the nucleus of what was already becoming a movement of national resistance.

At Stolice it was decided to set up a separate command in each different region under the over-all control of Tito's Supreme Headquarters and to aim wherever possible at establishing "liberated areas" as had been done in Serbia. The decision was also taken to set up on liberated territory National Liberation Councils whose members would be "bearers of the people's authority" and would be responsible for the administration and for the maintenance of order. These councils would supersede what remained of the old local administration. Though nominally "not the organs of any party or separate organization," there could be no doubt that they would be under Communist control and, though much more carefully selected than their prototypes, would approximately correspond to the Soviets' setup in Russia during the Revolution.

At the same time the Partisan leaders reviewed their military strategy in the light of their experience up-to-date. They agreed that, while hitting the enemy as hard as possible, they must at all costs deny him a target at which to strike back. Manpower was precious. Pitched battles against a stronger and better-equipped enemy must be avoided. Use must be made of a large number of small, highly mobile detachments. These would be closely linked and so be capable of combining to form larger units of battalion strength which could be used as shock troops in an emergency and then split up again into their component parts.[10]

As usual, the political and the military went hand in hand. The establishment of "liberated areas," the liquidation of what remained of the old political and administrative system, and the substitution of new "People's Authorities" were an essential part of the Movement of National Liberation. It was the Revolution in action. But the conference left one problem unanswered. How was the political decision to establish "liberated areas" to be reconciled with the classical guerrilla principles of surprise and mobility, of denying wherever possible a target to the enemy? It was a problem to which, in the months and years that followed, the Partisans were to find the answer the hard way, by a painful but effective process of trial and error.

At the end of September Tito moved his headquarters farther south to Užice, now in Partisan hands. Užice, a flourishing little market town of about fourteen thousand inhabitants, lay up in the hills at the end of the strategically important western Morava Valley and dominated the main road and rail communications of western Serbia. The Partisans also held Čačak, farther up the valley. Požega, in between the two, was in Cetnik hands. On the far side of Čačak, the key town of Kraljevo, situated at the junction of the Ibar and western Morava valleys and comamnding the main north-south and east-west road and rail communications of the whole area, was still held by the Germans, but was strongly invested by both Partisans and Cetniks. Meanwhile enemy road and rail traffic was at a standstill and the economic life of the country completely disrupted.

Užice was a valuable prize. The local branch of the National Bank yielded nearly fifty million dinars and the various government offices twenty million more. The Partisans also found three hundred thousand kilograms of tobacco and twenty-three truckloads of cigarette paper and were already producing their own brand of Red Star cigarettes. Best of all, Užice contained a small-arms and munition factory, where they were soon turning out over four hundred rifles a day, each stamped with a red star on the butt. Altogether, the red star was very much in evidence at Užice. The Partisans wore it in their caps—as their only distinguishing badge. It was scrawled all over the walls, together the Partisan slogan: *"Smrt Fašismu—Sloboda Narodu"*—"Death to Fascism—Liberty to the People." It was superimposed on the Jugoslav tricolor which hung from the windows. At night, an electrically illuminated version of it blazed out, ruby red, from the large modern bank building which housed the Partisan General Staff and where Tito, Ranković and Kardelj were now installed in handsome first-floor offices complete with desks and telephones.

Since the arrival of the Partisans the town had, in Tito's words, become the scene of "intense political activity."[11]

Borba, the official organ of the party, was being published every second day and distributed free at the newspaper kiosks. A People's Court was trying "traitors" and "collaborators," terms which were given a wide interpretation. National Liberation Councils were being set up everywhere within reach. Every sign of the old order had been swept away. The Revolution was in full swing.

Meanwhile, despite occasional clashes and mutual accusations of ill faith, the uneasy alliance between Cetniks and Partisans continued in being. The Stolice conference had approved Tito's attempts to reach an understanding with the Cetniks and authorized him to continue them, and on October 26 a further meeting took place between the two leaders in the village of Brajići not far from Ravna Gora, in the heart of the Cetnik country.

The meeting was held round a table in a large house in the village. Tito, who this time arrived by car, was accompanied by Black Žujović and his personal adjutant, Mitar Bakić, and by a bodyguard of eight Partisans carrying submachine guns. Mihajlović had with him his second-in-command, Colonel Pavlović, and his political adviser, Dragiša Vasić. He too had a bodyguard. While the negotiations were in progress the rival bodyguards stood behind their masters, the Partisans clean-shaven and businesslike, the Cetniks heavily bearded, heavily armed and festooned with bandoliers. From time to time one or other of these formidable onlookers would lean over and join vigorously in the conversation.

By now a new character had appeared on the scene, Captain William Hudson, Mihajlović's British liaison officer. Hudson, a mining engineer with a good knowledge of Jugoslavia, had been landed some weeks before by submarine on the coast of Montenegro together with two officers of the Royal Jugoslav Army, Major Ostojić and Major Lalatović, and had made his way through Partisan-occupied territory to Ravna Gora. His mission was an outward and visible sign of the recognition accorded to Mihajlović both by the British Government and by the Royal Jugoslav Government, who, with young King Peter, were now installed in London. From the moment when they first established wireless contact with the British authorities in August, the story of Mihajlović and his Cetniks had spread through the free world like wildfire, growing as it spread, until it soon came to bear but little relation to the real facts. It had naturally been greeted with enthusiasm by the Jugoslav Government in exile, who in due course responded by promoting Colonel Mihajlović to general and appointing him Minister of War and Commander-in-Chief of the Royal Jugoslav Army in the Fatherland. For the time being, the British Government, through Captain Hudson, did no more than promise the Cetniks their support for the future. For the present their advice to him seems to have been to lie low in the hope of better times ahead, and husband his resources— advice which he was only too glad to follow. Mihajlović had brought Hudson with him to Brajići, but would not agree to Tito's suggestion that he should attend the negotiations, which he maintained were a purely Jugoslav affair. Hudson accordingly remained in another room while the talks were in progress, only joining the others at supper.

On this occasion, the basis for negotiations was a letter which Tito had sent to Mihajlović a few days before, putting forward definite proposals for an understanding. Of these the most important were: the retention of separate high commands, with close liaison between them; joint or closely linked local commands; joint equipment and supply; voluntary and not compulsory mobilization; a joint operational staff and joint operations against the enemy; joint sharing of booty; the substitution of National Liberation Councils for the existing machinery of government in the liberated areas.[12]

But once again the meeting broke up without a comprehensive understanding having been arrived at. Needless to say, the idea of National Liberation Councils did not appeal to Mihajlović; nor did he feel able to accept joint operations, joint equipment and supply or voluntary recruitment, all of which, the last in particular, would have facilitated Communist infiltration of his forces. Of recent weeks his uneasiness as to the political intentions of the Partisans had if anything increased, while the unwisdom of their military operations had in his eyes been abundantly confirmed by the massacre by the Germans a week earlier of the entire male population of the neighboring town of Kragujevac—some five thousand all told —in retaliation for the activities of the Partisans. Finally, the arrival of Captain Hudson and his two companions had increased Mihajlović's self-confidence and made him less anxious to come to terms with the Communists. Hudson's own reports make this clear. "The British promise of support," he wrote, "had the effect of worsening Cetnik-Partisan relations. When I first arrived at Ravna Gora and Užice, at the end of October, 1941, before Cetnik-Partisan hostilities, Mihajlović already knew by telegram that he would get British support. He felt rightly that no one outside the country knew about the Partisans or that he alone was not responsible for the revolt."[13] In the circumstances, it is not surprising that the Brajići negotiations were no more successful than those at Struganik. Agreement was reached on secondary points only. For the rest, relations between Cetniks and Partisans were left to follow the same haphazard course as before.

It was not long before they took a sharp turn for the worse. For some time past there had been constant minor incidents and clashes. Now, on the night of November 1, a major engagement between Partisans and Cetniks took place between Užice and Požega which ended in the defeat of the Cetniks and the capture of Požega by the Partisans. According to the Partisans their move against the Cetniks was made to avert a Cetnik attack on Užice. This is borne out by Captain Hudson, who writes: "Mihajlović, grossly underestimating the Partisans hold on their followers, unsuccessfully attacked Užice.[14] Meanwhile the attack on Kraljevo, the key town of the Ibar Valley, still held by the Germans and jointly invested by Cetniks and Partisans, came to nothing. "The respective commanders," writes another British eyewitness, "received orders to stop fighting the Germans and to fight each other. But they were so intermingled and friendships and loyalties were so mixed that the orders were not obeyed. The attack just disintegrated. Those who happened to find themselves with the Partisans went one way, and those with Draža Mihajlović's leaders went the other. But all who could merely went home."[15]

Once again Tito and Mihajlović communicated with each other, this time by telephone, and a joint commission was set up to settle the dispute. Agreement of a sort was reached. But by now it was too late. Other clashes ensued. By the end of November any real prospect of reconciliation had vanished. Simultaneously with the war of resistance a civil war was in progress. Henceforward, the elimination of their rivals and their own ultimate accession to power was an objective which neither faction ever for one moment let out of sight.

For the time being, the only people to benefit from this state of affairs were the Germans. Since the middle of September they had been hurriedly bringing up reinforcements with the object of clearing the countryside of insurgents, freeing their lines of communication and forcing a way through to the towns where their garrisons were held besieged by the Partisans and Cetniks. The 342nd German Division had been

moved to Jugoslavia from France, then the 125th Regiment
from Greece, and then, despite the heavy fighting in progress
there, another division—the 113th—from the Russian front.
At the same time increasingly savage measures of retaliation
were taken against the civilian population. By the end of
September a strong German column had, after heavy fighting
against the Partisans in western Serbia, broken through to
Valjevo and joined up with the German garrison there. By
the end of October the Partisans had been dislodged from
Stolice and Krupanj. Using armor, artillery and aircraft, the
Germans now made a determined attack on the areas held by
the Partisans and Cetniks in the western Morava Valley, blast-
ing their way along the main lines of communication, while
carrying out encircling movements with their infantry against
the Partisan positions in the hills.

Divided among themselves, faced with an overwhelmingly
superior enemy and completely unprotected against air attack,
the insurgents found themselves at a hopeless disadvantage.
By November 28 Tito's position in Užice had become un-
tenable. The Germans had broken out of Kraljevo. Čačak
and Požega were seriously threatened and strong German
forces were rapidly advancing up the western Morava Valley
toward Užice. A second German column was advancing on
Užice Valjevo, while a third force was closing in from the
northwest along the Drina Valley. In Užice itself there was
pandemonium. Fugitives and wounded were pouring in from
all sides, while the town and its approaches were under
constant and heavy air bombardment.

In these circumstances Tito gave the order for the evacuation of Užice and for a general withdrawal of all Partisan
forces in the area southward across the Zlatibor Range into the
Sandžak, the wild, mountainous region on the borders of
Serbia and eastern Bosnia. He himself and two or three others
remained with the little force of Partisans who had been left
to cover their comrades' retreat. An attempt had been made
to mine the bridges on the main road. "Now we shall see
them blow up," said Tito hopefully to a companion, as they
watched the first German tanks come rumbling down the
road. But the charges had been removed or failed to explode.
Nothing happened, and the tanks and motorized infantry came
straight on through the town and out the other side in hot
pursuit of the Partisan rear guard. Taken by surprise, Tito
himself and those with him were soon under heavy machine-
gun fire and were almost overrun by a flying column of

German infantry before before they finally made good their escape into the hills. It was not until late the following night, after marching twenty miles through the mountains, that Tito, accompanied by his personal bodyguard and by Captain Hud-

son, who had temporarily left the Cetniks, joined up with Djilas and Kardelj, who had begun to despair of ever seeing him again. Not long after, the door of the peasant's hut in which they were sitting opened and Marko Rankovic came in. Black Žujović, who had been shot in the stomach, was lying in a corner. The High Command had reassembled. An hour later it was daylight and they were on the move once more. From farther down the road came the ominous rumble of tanks.

By the beginning of December the First Enemy Offensive, as it was afterward to be known to the Partisans, had achieved its objectives. The Partisans and Cetniks had been dispersed and put to flight and the "liberated areas" reoccupied. While the surviving guerrillas licked their wounds in the forests and mountains, savage reprisals were inflicted on the civilian population. The towns and villages of the plain were burned and devastated and thousands of men, women and children taken out and shot. The revolt in Serbia had, for the time being, been quelled.

"When the battle was over and you heroes retired to your mountain fastnesses," a Jugoslav woman doctor said later to a British officer, "the Germans . . . shot nine thousand hostages —three hundred for every German you killed. They burned to the ground seventeen villages. In Kraljevo there is not a family which has not lost one of its members, and all the refugees from the north were shot. Your military objectives may, of course, have been worth all this, but I cannot know anything about that. All that I see is suffering among the people—my people."[16]

Mihajlović, for his part, had withdrawn to the wilds of Ravna Gora. As he had foretold, the aggressive tactics of the Partisans had brought down a terrible retribution on all concerned. But at least this had led to the withdrawal of the main Partisan force from Serbia, a result which he welcomed and to which he had himself to some extent contributed, not by direct collaboration with the enemy, but by what might be termed "parallel action." There had, it is true, been contact of a kind between Mihajlović and the Germans. On November 10, Mihajlović, fearing that a large Cetnik force was about to be wiped out, had secretly met Dr. Matel of the German Intelligence Service at the village of Divca near Valjevo. But the Germans, who were as suspicious of him as he was of them, had simply demanded his surrender and that of the forces under his command, and this he had indignantly refused.[17]

Mihajlović's next task, now that the Partisans were out of the way, was to consolidate his own position, if possible without doing anything that would further antagonize the Germans. It was now that he hit on, or perhaps it would be fairer to say, drifted into, an arrangement which, from his point of view, had much to commend it. General Nedić, who in August had become the puppet prime minister of what was left of Serbia, had been authorized by the Germans to raise certain forces, notably the Serb Volunteer Corps, for the purpose of fighting the Communists. By temporarily allowing his men to work in with these forces, Mihajlović could secure for them a badly needed respite, arms and supplies, of which he was desperately short, and, finally, the opportunity of continuing their struggle against the Partisans under more favorable conditions. He could also hope to keep in being something which under happier circumstances might someday be converted into an active resistance movement. Nedić, he knew, would raise no objection, for, although at present under German orders, he would be glad to have a foot in the other camp in case the Allies should ultimately prove victorious. It was thus that during the months that followed, a number of Cetnik leaders, with or without Mihajlović's express consent, established more or less close liaison with the Nedić forces and received in return freedom from interference and in some cases material assistance in the shape of arms and supplies. Returning to Ravna Gora at this time, Captain Hudson "found no remains of Mihajlović's men except himself and a few officers, everyone else having converted himself into Nedić's men and departed to the complete frustration of the Germans."[18]

But, whatever their initial reaction may have been, the Germans, like Nedić, soon came to realize the advantages, from their point of view, of such an accommodation. Mihajlović was on a slippery slope. As time went on, resistance to the Axis came to mean less and less to the Cetniks and their struggle against the Communists more and more. The Partisans, rather than the Germans, became the real enemy. The prospect of any "general uprising" grew increasingly remote. Nor were they encouraged to think otherwise by London. "Speaking as Jugoslav Prime Minister," said Slobodan Jovanović in a broadcast, "I call upon you not to start an armed struggle against the enemy forces of occupation, for you would bring upon yourselves severe losses and reprisals and your struggle would not help our Allies. When the right moment for an armed fight comes, you may be sure that we shall call upon you to rise through the supreme commander in our country, the Chief of Staff of the Supreme Command, Dragoljub Mihajlović, who will lead you on the road to glory and victory. . . ."

And so indirect liaison with Nedić was followed by indirect liaision with the Germans, while some of Mihajlović's commanders, over many of whom he had very little control, went further still and concluded formal agreements with the enemy. What had begun as "parallel action" gradually developed into what could only be described as collaboration.

On this basis, the Cetniks prospered. Henceforward, avoiding military action against the Germans, they concentrated on hunting down such Partisan bands as still remained in Serbia. While the effective control of the towns remained in the hands of the Nedić authorities, large areas of the countryside were left under Cetnik domination. Neither Nedić nor the Germans, upon both of whom the Cetniks were becoming increasingly dependent, made any great effort to disturb this, from their point of view, not unsatisfactory state of affairs. "Why," in the words of one British liaison officer, "should they? The Cetniks were, from the German point of view, doing a useful job of work." [19]

Who, in this typically Balkan situation, was being fooled and who was getting the best of it? The Germans, who had succeeded in neutralizing what had started as a resistance movement? Or the Cetniks, who in effect were being armed by an enemy against whom they hoped one day to rise? Time alone would show.

VI 〰〰 UNTO THE HILLS

THE "liberated areas" so proudly established by the Partisans
a few weeks earlier had quickly melted away before the German onslaught. Any Partisan sympathizers who were unlucky
enough to fall into the hands of the enemy had been ruthlessly put to death. Such Partisan bands as still remained in
Serbia lurked in the forests and hills and, for the time being,
lay low. But, if the enemy's offensive had temporarily quelled
resistance in one part of the country, it served indirectly to
give it fresh impetus in another.

Harassed by the enemy as he went, Tito had succeeded in
bringing his main force of nine detachments through the
Sandžak into the snow-clad uplands of eastern Bosnia, arriving on December 24 at Rogatica, a battered little Moslem
town in the hills some forty miles east of Sarajevo. It had
not been an easy march. Snow was falling as they reached the
mountains. It was bitterly cold. Morale was low. The country
was wild and mountainous. They were short of food and
sleep. There was nothing to eat in the villages. The enemy
was pressing after them and continuing to attack them from
the air. The wounded, in particular, presented an anxious
problem. There were several hundred of them, many of whom
could not walk. On the second day out from Užice the Germans had caught up with a Partisan field hospital. Sixty of
the wounded, some of whom had lost arms or legs, had managed to crawl away into the fields, but the Germans had found
them and driven their tanks backward and forward over them
until they were all dead. No sooner had the Partisans shaken
off the German pursuit from Serbia than they encountered
the Italians. These they found less formidable foes and, having captured from them the little town of Nova Varoš, they
gained a brief respite on the slopes of Mount Zlatar. Then
they pushed on northwestward into Bosnia, fighting as they
went.

Though cold, hungry, weary and sadly diminished, Tito's
main force was still in existence. So was the idea behind it:
the spirit of resistance, the spirit, above all, of revolution.

The Partisans had even brought with them, in twelve oxcarts, their printing press and five thousand newly printed copies of *The Short History of the Communist Party,* translated from the Russian. On occasions like these ideological uplift combined with strict discipline was more necessary than ever. If now and then some of the weaker brethren were inclined to falter, the old hands were always there to bring them back into line. As one observer put it at the time: "Units had got slack, morale was low but the firm hand of the party has put all that right."[1] And again: "A meeting of the party cell of No. 1 Company. How purified one feels after such a meeting!"[2]

Just before reaching Rogatica, on Stalin's birthday, December 21, Tito had formed from among the troops he had brought with him from Serbia a special shock unit, the First Proletarian Brigade, who wore, superimposed on the red star in their caps, a golden hammer and sickle. To command it, he appointed Koca Popovic, the brisk little Communist millionaire philosopher-poet, who in Serbia had more than fulfilled the promise he had shown in Spain.

Thus Tito and his comrades gave practical effect to the revolutionary theories, to the theory of "leadership for action," which they had learned in Moscow and elsewhere and which they now at last had a chance of applying. And thus they formed the nucleus of an armed and disciplined force which would fight, not just in defense of its own village or strip of country, but in any part of Jugoslavia whatsoever. In Tito's own words, "every setback we suffered had to be followed by a bigger victory. That is the law of revolutionary strategy and tactics. Revolutionary tactics demand constant offensive action. Offensive action can alone inspire those who are already fighting and those who are about to go into battle with the necessary fighting spirit."

Having made contact with the Bosnian Partisans, Tito now set out to fan the flames of rebellion in Bosnia as he had in Serbia, to raise more Partisan detachments, to establish "liberated areas" and to install People's Authorities.

His task was facilitated by a variety of circumstances. Having reached Bosnia, he was on the territory of the Independent State of Croatia. But, although, under the new dispensation, Bosnia had been given to Croatia, its population was not even predominantly Croat. For centuries, a disputed frontier land, it contained a mixed population of Serbs, Croats and Moslems, in which Orthodox Serbs outnumbered the Catholic Croats by more than two to one. In the eyes of Dr. Pavelić this was an anomaly requiring immediate attention. From the moment he came to power, he regarded it as his mission to clear Bosnia of Serbs.

The *Poglavnik* had spent the first few weeks after his accession to power in a round of visits. He had gone to Rome to settle with Mussolini, to offer the crown of Croatia formally to its new monarch, the Duke of Spoleto, and, as a devout son of the Church, to be received in special audience by the Pope. He had gone to Germany to see Hitler, now rapidly replacing Mussolini as his principal protector. He had gone to Venice to sign the Tripartite Pact with Ciano and Ribbentrop. In between these visits he lived quietly in Zagreb with his children and his plump, dowdy wife, hearing Mass daily in his private chapel, for he was a devoted husband and father and intensely religious.

On his return from Venice in June, he had got down to work. In his faithful Ustaše, trained for the last ten years as terrorists in the special camps of Italy and Hungary, embittered by their long exile and by a multitude of real and imaginary wrongs, he had an abundance of ready helpers. They were now joined by numbers of other Ustaše, some of long standing and others of more recent vintage. Every evening he would hear the reports of their activities. They left nothing to be desired.

The massacres began in earnest at the end of June and continued throughout the summer, growing in scope and intensity until in August the terror reached its height. The whole of Bosnia ran with blood. Bands of Ustaše roamed the countryside with knives, bludgeons and machine guns, slaughtering Serbian men, women and little children, desecrating Serbian churches, murdering Serbian priests, laying waste Serbian villages, torturing, raping, burning, drowning. Killing became a cult, an obsession. The Ustaše vied to outdo each other, boasting of the numbers of their victims and of their own particular methods of dispatching them. The aged Orthodox Bishop of Plaški was garroted by his assassins. Bishop Platon of Banjaluka was prodded to death in a pond. Some Ustaše collected the eyes of the Serbs they had killed, sending them, when they had enough, to the *Poglavnik* for his inspection or proudly displaying them and other human organs in the cafés of Zagreb. Even their German and Italian allies were dismayed by their excesses.

Pavelić, who saw Croatia again in its historic role of *Ante-murale Christianitatis* and himself as the defender of Western civilization in the struggle against Eastern barbarism, attached considerable importance to obtaining the open and official support of the Catholic Church for his policy of racial and religious *Gleichschaltung*. But in this he does not seem to have been as successful as he had hoped. The rank and file of the Catholic clergy in Croatia were, he confided to Ciano in December, 1941, "very favorable" to his regime; the higher ecclesiastical authorities considerably less so—indeed some of the bishops were "definitely hostile."[3]

As we have seen, the Metropolitan, Archbishop Stepinac, had, in a pastoral letter issued in April, 1941, welcomed the establishment of the Independent State of Croatia and called upon the clergy to serve it loyally. But, as time went on, his initial enthusiasm seems to have given way to a sense of serious misgiving. No one was more anxious than he was to see the Orthodox population of Croatia converted to Catholicism and the last traces of "Byzantium" removed from Croat soil. "The Schismatics," he had written some months earlier, "are the curse of Europe—almost worse than the Protestants."[4] But the means by which the new regime was seeking to achieve these ends could scarcely command his approval.

The Ustaše's favorite method of religious unification was, as we have seen, the wholesale massacre of the Orthodox population. But, in their more merciful moments, they would sometimes offer their victims immediate conversion to Catholicism as an alternative to annihilation. A priest would be produced and, while armed Ustaše looked on, whole villages would be received into the Church simultaneously.[5] Soon, throughout the country, Catholic priests were besieged by crowds of panic-stricken men, women and children, clamoring for admission to the Church of Rome, in the hope that they might thus succeed in saving their lives.

This presented Archbishop Stepinac with a decidedly awkward problem. Canon law expressly forbade the admission to the Church of anyone who had not been duly instructed in its doctrines or whose motives for wishing to enter it seemed dictated by self-interest or were otherwise open to suspicion. These conditions were quite clearly not being fulfilled. What is more, the officiating priests were in many cases acting without proper authority from their ecclesiastical superiors. Taking a long view (and the Church has always taken a long view), there was a serious risk that what was happening might do the Church more harm than good, a risk that its reputation might suffer, a risk that under changed circumstances (and circumstances might always change) the mass conversions might be followed by mass backslidings. These and other dangers were all too evident from the reports which he was now receiving from all over Bosnia and Herzegovina.

"I had hoped," the Bishop of Mostar wrote on November 7, 1941,

> that large numbers of Schismatics would enter the Catholic Church. But the *Stožerniks and Logorniks* [Ustaše officials] have abused their position, exploiting the worst instincts of the crowd and playing on the weaker side of human nature. The results have been horrifying. Human beings have been hunted down and caught like animals; they have ben slaughtered; they have been thrown alive over precipices. The Deputy Mayor of Mostar, Balic, a Moslem, said out loud (he would do better to keep quiet and not say such things) that at Ljubinj in one day seven hundred Schismatics were thrown into a pit. From Mostar and from Capljina six railway truckloads of women, girls and children under eighteen were taken to Surmnaci. There they were all made to get out. They were taken into the mountains and mothers and children alike were thrown over a precipice. In this way they were all killed. In the parish of Klpeci seven hundred Schismatics from the surrounding villages were killed. It would take too long to give you any more figures. In Mostar itself hundreds and hundreds of Schismatics have been bound and taken out of the town and slaughtered like animals.

In the end, the Bishop continued, the Italians had intervened and had shown themselves friendly toward the Serbs and hostile to the Catholics, with the result that "the Schismatic churches at once came back to life and the Orthodox priests who up to then had been in hiding now showed themselves quite freely. . . . Small wonder," he concluded,

> if for these reasons the conversion of the Orthodox to Catholicism has been a complete failure. The ferocity of the *Stožerniks* and *Logorniks*, the brutality of certain individuals, the lack of understanding shown by the higher authorities has done grave harm not only to the

cause of religion but also to the state itself. If the Lord
had granted the competent authorities more understanding and the common sense to carry out the conversions
with more tact and less violence, the number of Catholics
would have increased by at least five hundred thousand
and the Catholics in Bosnia and Herzegovina would thus
have risen from seven hundred thousand to one million
three hundred thousand. . . .[6]

There were cases, too, where not only heretics but actual
converts to Catholicism were done to death. To quote from
another report from the Bishop of Mostar:

They go to Mass; they learn the Catholic catechism;
they have their children baptized. And then outsiders in-
trude and start giving orders. While the new converts are
in church attending Mass, they seize them, young and
old, men and women, drag them outside and . . . send
them to eternity in droves. That sort of thing does no
good to the holy cause of Catholicism nor to that of
Croatia. In a few years' time everyone will condemn
these thoughtless actions. In the meantime we are losing
a splendid opportunity of furthering the Croat and the
holy Catholic cause and of becoming a majority instead
of a minority in Bosnia and Herzegovina.[7]

From the Bishop of Banjaluka came reports of the "bestial
cruelties," of the "indescribable acts of ferocity" committed
by the Moslems and, worse still, of forced conversions to Is-
lam.[8] Even Archbishop Sarić of Sarajevo, an enthusiastic
supporter of the Ustaša movement and the author of a number of ecstatic odes to the *Poglavnik,* was not altogether satisfied. But his complaint was that the conversions were not
going fast enough. "The policy of the authorities is to convert as many Orthodox as possible, but unfortunately they are
not setting about it in the right way. From several quarters
we have received complaints that the civil authorities, in cases
where posts are held by Moslems, do not give effect to Orthodox requests for admission to the Catholic Church. In other
places they impose taxes on conversions that are too high,
taxes which the poor cannot pay. . . . It is easy to see that
such a line of conduct acts as a serious hindrance to conversions . . ." and the Archbishop went on to expatiate on the

danger that the Protestants might exploit the situation to their own ends.[9]

The Bishop of Kotor, for his part, expressed the fear that the use of force for religious ends might "react unfavorably on the reputation of the Catholic Church" and that the Serbs might, "out of sheer capriciousness, turn Mohammedan en masse." The task of conversion should, he wrote, in future only be entrusted to the most carefully chosen missionaries and not to "priests lacking all moderation and better suited to handle a pistol than a crucifix."[10]

After receiving and pondering these and other reports and talking things over with the rest of the Catholic hierarchy at their annual conference, Archbishop Stepinac decided to address a formal communication to the *Poglavnik* on the subject of the conversions. In a letter dated November 20, he informed him officially of the conclusions reached by the conference, notably: that questions appertaining to conversions to Catholicism were a matter for decision by the Roman Catholic hierarchy and by no one else; that only the Roman Catholic hierarchy might appoint "missionaries" to preside over conversions; and that only those might enter the Church who did so from genuine conviction and of their own free will. It was, he continued, impossible to deny that horrible acts of cruelty and violence had been committed. The reports which he had received from his bishops were sufficient proof of that. "It is," he wrote, "essential to take a strictly realistic view. Even the Orthodox Church has its genuine adherents, who cannot automatically change their views or their nature overnight. A purely mechanical procedure is for this reason apt to have unfortunate results. . . . In this manner houses are built on sand, and not on rock, and when the rain descends and the wind blows nothing is left of them but ruins."

He did not, he wrote, blame the government for what had happened, regarding it rather as the work of irresponsible elements who did not realize how much harm they were doing. The *Poglavnik's* decision to establish peace and justice merited the gratitude of all. But the Church, for its part, was bound to condemn the crimes and excesses which had been committed and "to demand the fullest respect for the individual, regardless of status, sex, religion, nationality or race. . . . We are sure," he concluded, "that you share our view and that you will do everything in your power to check the violence of isolated individuals and to ensure that control is vested in the responsible authorities. Should this not be the case, any attempts to convert the Schismatics will be in vain."[11]

The tone of the Archbishop's letter was studiously moderate. He was careful, in particular, not to hold the *Poglavnik* responsible for the misdeeds of his henchmen. But, for all that, it was not the sort of letter that was calculated to please a man of Pavelić's temperament, already irritated by the numerous appeals and protests which Monsignor Stepinac had from time to time addressed to him: begging him to spare the lives of hostages and to put a stop to mass executions; criticizing his new racial laws, and asking him to grant special treatment to Serbs and Jews who had entered the Catholic Church and to excuse the latter from wearing yellow armbands. His sermons, too, had contained a number of pointed allusions to "those who, while glorifying in being Catholics or even possessing a spiritual vocation, nevertheless abandon themselves to passion and hatred and forget the essential Christian rule of love and charity."[12] In fact it was not long before Dr. Pavelić had conceived a hearty dislike for the tall, thin, stubborn, ascetic-looking prelate in his massive palace next to the cathedral. "That sniveler," the *Poglavnik* was heard to exclaim a few weeks later, after hearing Stepinac preach at St. Mark's Church on the occasion of the opening of the new Croat Assembly, "that sniveler is trying to give me a lesson in politics."[13]

Nor indeed was the Vatican quite as forthcoming as had at one time seemed likely. The Pope, it is true, had received the *Poglavnik* in May in the most amiable manner. He had also received the Duke of Spoleto—now, in theory, King Tomislav II. Finally he had sent to Zagreb as papal legate Monsignor Marcone, a robust-looking Benedictine, who joined with gusto in the official life of the new capital. But, for all this, he had not yet granted *de jure* recognition to the new Croat State, and the Vatican authorities, when approached on this subject by Pavelić's representatives, though friendly and sympathetic, were inclined to be evasive and to talk at length of the Vatican's neutral status.

There were also signs that some, at any rate, of the cardinals had received unfavorable reports of what was happening in Croatia. Cardinal Maglione, the Cardinal Secretary of State, spoke of "not very nice stories."[14] And Cardinal Tisserant, the heavily bearded Cardinal Secretary for the Eastern Congregation, had, in conversation with Pavelić's diplomatic representative in Rome, made some very wounding remarks about the alleged "independence" of the Independent State of Croatia and about Croats generally, and had gone on to comment most unfavorably on the atrocities committed by the Ustaše. Indeed, the tone of his remarks had been so critical and so ironical that Lorković, the Ustaša Minister of Foreign Affairs, had been moved to scrawl the words *"Oprez! Neprijatelj!"* "Look out! An enemy!" across the foot of the dispatch reporting them.[15]

But, despite the reserved and at times even disapproving attitude of Archbishop Stepinac and of the Vatican, a certain number of the Croat clergy continued to give the Ustaša regime their enthusiastic support. Nor were they confined to the "rank and file" of whose loyalty Pavelić had boasted to Ciano. Archbishop Sarić of Sarajevo lost no opportunity of ingratiating himself with Pavelić and celebrated Christmas, 1941 by publishing yet another exceptionally fulsome ode to the *Poglavnik* which made up in warmth of feeling what it lacked in literary merit. Other lesser clerical lights went further still, allowing their enthusiasm for the regime to lead them into activities which in the words of Cardinal Tisserant were "unworthy of a civilized human being, let alone a priest."[16] As one enthusiastic parish priest put it: "Until now we have worked for the Catholic faith with missal and crucifix. Now the time has come for us to go to work with rifle and revolver."[17]

But the *Poglavnik* did not rely exclusively on his own coreligionaries to help him fulfill his misson. As has been seen, he also found ready allies among the Bosnian Moslems, always glad of a pretext for massacring Christians, whatever their denomination. In order to endear himself still further to the Moslem community, he now made them a present of a handsome new mosque in the center of Zagreb and also raised a special Moslem Ustaša formation, which soon became notorious for its atrocities.

And so the massacres and the "conversions" continued and the candidates for admission to the Catholic faith multiplied. Indeed cases came to the notice of Monsignor Stepinac of priests being actually threatened with physical violence by the panic-stricken crowds who besieged their presbyteries because they would not admit them fast enough to the Church. This presented the Archbishop with yet another problem: whatever the exact provisions of canon law, could he, in all conscience, condemn these unfortunates to almost certain death by refusing them admission to the Church? In a circular dated March 2, 1942, he gave his clergy discretion to overlook "secondary motives" for wishing to enter the Church, providing the essential motive was also present in the candidates, namely, a genuine belief in the Catholic faith or at any rate "genuine good will." And even where these conditions did not appear to be fulfilled, the priest was authorized to "pursue the matter further."[18] Thus, mainly from humanitarian motives, the door was opened a little wider than a strict interpretation of canon law would perhaps have permitted and the number of conversions to Catholicism multiplied still further.

Meanwhile the excesses of the Ustase had had a consequence which Pavelić had not foreseen. Before the end of the summer what was left of the Serb population of Bosnia had risen almost to a man and taken to the hills, determined to sell their lives dearly. They were joined by a number of Croats, more and more of whom had come to detest the new regime. Once on the hills, the insurgents, who called themselves Cetniks or Partisans according to taste, set up a joint Partisan-Cetnik headquarters, under whose command they were now prosecuting the struggle against both Ustaše and Germans with vigor and determination. The leading part in organizing the revolt and directing subsequent operations was played by Tempo Vukmanović whom Tito had sent to Bosnia for this purpose from Belgrade in July, 1941 and who, after some initial setbacks had succeeded in building up in the wild mountainous country round Sarajevo an effective network of Partisan detachments. Such was the not unpromising nucleus of rebellion which Tito and his staff found on reaching eastern Bosnia at the end of December, 1941.

The arrival of Tito in person at the head of the First Proletarian Brigade still further strengthened and stimulated the Bosnian insurgents. It was not long, however, before the news of this link-up provoked a vigorous reaction on the part of the enemy. The weather was bitterly cold and the deep snow in the mountains did not favor military operations. But toward the middle of January, 1942, two or three weeks after Tito's arrival in Bosnia, the Germans and Ustaše, using ski troops, launched a strong attack against the Partisan positions in the east Bosnian hills from bases at Sarajevo, Zvornik and Višegrad and from the Sarajevo-Višegrad railway. At the same time the Italians were asked to use their four divisions in Montenegro to prevent the Partisans from breaking out of this encirclement to the south. But Tito, taking part of the First Proletarian Brigade with him, managed by a skillful maneuver to slip through the enemy's lines, cross the Sarajevo-Višegrad railway and reach the Jahorina Mountains in the south. Here he was joined by the remainder of his force, who, having been cut off, had ventured boldly across the open plain to the west of Sarajevo and then crossed the frozen heights of Mount Igman with the temperature at twenty degrees below zero. Though short of food and ammunition and suffering severely from cold and frostbite, the Partisans had nevertheless successfully extricated themselves from yet another dangerous situation.

By the beginning of February, the fury of the enemy's attack—to be known by the Partisans as the Second Offensive—had considerably abated, leaving Tito in control of a sizable area of wild mountain country to the south of the Sarajevo-Višegrad railway. He now established his headquarters in the little east Bosnian town of Foča on the upper reaches of the Drina, where he and his General Staff were installed in the Hotel Gerstl, a small modern hotel frequented in peacetime by tourists, commercial travelers and itinerant officials. In his own office a large-scale map of Jugoslavia, captured from the enemy, lay spread out over two tables placed side by side. Here he would go through the messages and signals, brought in by couriers or received over the Partisans' growing wireless network, which reached him from neighboring or more remote units and formations. And here he would confer with his commanders and with the little group of men who with him presided over the military and political fortunes of the Movement of National Liberation, and, in consultation with them, issue decrees and operation orders.

Winter, with food short in the countryside and no leaves on the trees to give cover, is not a good season for guerrillas. That winter the news which the couriers brought or which came in by wireless was very often bad. There was bad news, for example, from Serbia, and bad news from nearer by, from Bosnia and Montenegro. Hardly a day passed without news of some close friend who had been killed in action or caught and executed by the enemy. The few thousands of original party members who had so readily responded to Tito's call to arms in June were dwindling fast. Most of them had been personally known to each other and most of them were friends. As one of them wrote at the time: "It is not easy to

bear. More and more of us are going. Less and less of the old
lot are left."[19]

It fell to Djilas to break to Marko Ranković the news that
his wife Andja had been killed in action. "My dear Leko," he
wrote on a sheet of paper torn from a child's exercise book,

> I have had news for you, the worst there could be. It
> is hard for me to tell you, because I am, I think, closest
> to you. But because I am so close to you, it is only right
> that I should tell you. Your true faithful comrade,
> Andja, who loved you so dearly and whom we all loved,
> has been killed in action. . . . Many other comrades of
> ours were killed with her. I do not hope to console you.
> You are not a man to be consoled. Nor are these times
> for consolation. You will, I know, bear this blow, the
> worst of all, as you have borne others, calmly and bravely.
> Andja deserved that you should grieve for her forever.
> Perhaps you will find another companion in life, and
> perhaps you will be happy with her. Do not think that
> impossible. But you will never find another Andja, so
> completely, so devotedly yours. For all that, bear your
> loss bravely and steadfastly. Do not forget that what you
> lose the party loses and that it shares your sorrow with
> you. My dear Leko, there is nothing more I can say. If
> true comradeship and love could help you to bear this
> blow, mine would—ours would. The greater your loss,
> the stronger is my friendship for you.[20]

And yet, the mere fact that news came, that couriers arrived, was, in itself, an encouragement, was proof that all over
the country fighting was in progress, proof that resistance was
spreading. And if the couriers, slipping through the enemy's
lines, covering enormous distances on foot, enduring every
kind of hazard and hardship, brought tidings of the death of
old comrades, did they not also tell of new recruits who all
over the country, singly and in groups, were flocking to join
the Partisans?

At Foča, where he was to remain undisturbed for more
than three months, Tito settled down to the task of re-forming
and building up his main force. On March 1 a Second Proletarian Brigade was formed and this was quickly followed by
three more. Meanwhile, unceasingly, the work of "political
education" went on: political education of new recruits, polit-

ical education of women and young people, political education of the civilian population.

It was not always an easy task. In these remote east Bosnian highlands the peasants, largely Moslem, were anything but receptive of new, let alone revolutionary, ideas. They were, moreover, bitterly divided among themselves. The country round Foča had witnessed some of Ustaše's most unspeakable atrocities. Bands of Moslem Ustaše had murdered thousands of Orthodox Serbs. The Serbs, in particular the Cetniks, had retaliated as soon as they got the chance by massacring all the Moslems they could lay hands on. When the Partisans occupied Foča itself, they found the river bed filled with freshly murdered Moslem corpses. Against this background of terror and bloodshed, it was not easy to persuade Serbs and Moslems that they must forthwith forget their differences and unite in the name of national liberation and dialectical materialism. "I should like to kill every Turk there is," said one Serbian girl whose aunt and three cousins had been raped and then murdered by the Moslems. "We asked her," wrote a Partisan, "what harm there was in innocent Moslem children, but it is hard for her to understand." And again: "It is hard to convince the Serbs that all the Moslems should not be killed."[21]

It was uphill work. But the Partisans did their best. "Here," said Tito in a speech to the Fourth Brigade, "are five brigades from almost every part of Jugoslavia. Between them there must be brotherhood and comradeship and friendly competition in battle and at work. May you be united by unbreakable bonds of brotherhood and love, for you are the Army of the Nation. In this our war of liberation we are for the first time in the history of Jugoslavia uniting all her peoples under arms. Fifth columnists have sought to sow discord between them. We will join them together in brotherhood."[22] And certainly in the Partisan ranks, fighting side by side against a common enemy, there was gradually growing up between Serbs and Croats, Bosnians and Croats, Slovenes and Montenegrins, a new comradeship at arms, a fellow feeling which had never existed before.

The Partisans, for their part, were at pains not to alienate the civilian population and to live down the reputation of bloodthirsty Bolsheviks which their enemies sought to fasten on them. "The people are the water. The Partisan is a fish. A fish cannot live without water. That goes for us too," said one of them, quoting a Chinese saying.[23] Looting was punishable

(and punished) by death. The theft of a few onions or pota-
toes would often cost the hungry man who had stolen them his
life. Where food was commandeered from the peasants it was
in general paid for and care was taken to see that the burden
was not inequitably distributed. The Partisans showed themselves ruthless in many respects, and they had a short way with
any enemies who fell into their hands. But they did not kill
for the sake of killing, and it is safe to say that, by comparison
with the Ustaše or indeed with any of the other armed forces
who roamed through Jugoslavia during these years, their
record, though by no means unblemished, was relatively good.
Nor did they, as a general rule, seek to put into practice any
of their more extreme political theories. That could wait.
The party line called at present for a broad front. "We must
not," said Djilas at a party meeting at this time, "let ourselves
be pushed into a class war. That is what the invader would
like to see. He would like to see us isolated."[24]

Looking southward from the hills round Foča, the Partisans
guarding Tito's Headquarters could see the snowy peaks of
Mount Durmitor towering above the other ranges thirty miles
away in Montenegro. Tito was now in direct touch with the
Montenegrin Partisans. Soon after his arrival in east Bosnia
their leaders had come to report to him in person. There was
Arso Jovanović, a tall, gaunt, rather bleak-looking regular
officer who before the war had worked under Mihajlović at
the Staff College. And Peko Dapčević, a peasant's son with
strong, clearly defined features and a look of exceptional determination, who had fought with the International Brigade in
Spain. Finally there was Moša Pijade, Tito's former cellmate
at Lepoglava who, like Djilas, had been sent to Montenegro
on a special mission.

In Montenegro events had taken a course no less dramatic
than in Serbia or Bosnia. The Montenegrins are by tradition
warriors and heroes. They have a Homeric quality. In them
the fighting spirit of the South Slavs, their pride, arrogance
and violence of temperament occur in a concentrated, an extreme form. In their eyes a warrior's calling is the only honor-
able one; manual labor, tilling the soil or watching the flocks
and herds, are tasks better left to women and children. The
history of their wild, mountainous country, Crna Gora—"the
Black Mountain"—has been one long chronicle of war, rebellion and strife. While their neighbors succumbed one after
another to Turkish domination, they in their mountain fastnesses alone maintained their independence throughout the

centuries. And, now that their freedom was once more at stake, they once more showed themselves worthy of their national traditions.

On July 12, 1941, the Italians, to whom Montenegro had been allotted under the partition of Jugoslavia, were imprudent enough to proclaim it a puppet principality. On the following day there broke out a national uprising of such proportions and such violence that it all but swept the invaders into the sea.*

Djilas had arrived clandestinely from Belgrade a few days earlier and made contact with the local party organization. He had found them well provided with weapons. The Montenegrins have always had a passionate love of firearms and, on the capitulation of the old Jugoslav Army in April, large quantities of arms and ammunition had been hidden away for future use. Each party group had its own secret store; one had a whole battery of field guns buried somewhere in the hills. On the morning of July 12 the word was passed to leaders of local party groups to form their members into detachments, arm them and go into action against the Italians next day. Meanwhile contact had also been established with the local Cetnik leaders and other patriotic organizations. Plans were made simultaneously for concerted action on their part and a joint headquarters set up. Next day, on July 13, all over Montenegro, Italian garrisons were attacked, convoys ambushed and outposts stormed. No Montenegrin can resist a fight. All carry weapons as a matter of course. As soon as they saw what was afoot, even those who had been left out of the original plot joined in enthusiastically. In the mountains (and Montenegro consists almost entirely of mountains) the population rose to a man.

A leading part in these events was played by Djilas himself, by the former staff captain, Arso Jovanović, and by the Spanish veteran, Peko Dapčević. The latter, after spending some years following the end of the Spanish War in a French concentration camp, had, after the fall of France, been sent by the Germans to a forced labor camp in Austria. Thence he had in due course escaped across the frontier into Slovenia and so made his way back to his native Montenegro, arriving there on July 11 to find to his delight that he was just in time

---

* In fact, no prince or king was ever found to take on the job and the Italians were eventually obliged to appoint a high commissioner, Signor Mazzolini.

for the rising. Politically the tone of the rebellion was set by old Moša Pijade, who had even assumed Montenegrin national dress for the occasion.

The Italians were taken completely by surprise. Large numbers were killed, but even larger numbers surrendered with conciliatory cries of *"Viva Stalin!"* while others hopefully reminded their captors that the Queen of Italy was a Montenegrin too. The remainder fell back in confusion on the three main towns, Nikšić, Cetinje and Podgorcia, where they barricaded themselves in and held out as best they could. Within a week the rest of Montenegro was free. "In Montenegro," wrote Count Ciano on July 15, "things are going pretty badly. The capital has been cut off and all the approaches to it are blocked by the insurgents." "If it were not deeply and bitterly significant," he added two days later, "it would be grotesque."[25]

But these initial Partisan successes were to be of but brief duration. The Montenegrin Partisans were lacking both in discipline and in organization. Their operations were uncoordinated. Their central headquarters had little control over individual units which were organized on a local territorial basis. Politically, too, they showed more enthusiasm than judgment and by their excesses lost the sympathy of large sections of the population. The Italians now collected themselves. Strong reinforcements were brought in from Albania and a determined effort was made to put down the revolt. Village after village was subjected to intensive and methodical air bombardment. The main lines of communication were cleared and strong armored and motorized columns were sent out into the countryside to kill and to burn. By the end of the summer a considerable part of Montenegro had been reoccupied and the insurgents had been driven back into the mountains.

Here, undeterred by their misfortunes, the Partisans set about reorganizing themselves on a more orderly basis. Larger, better-organized units were formed and a proper chain of command instituted. The operations which they now undertook, though less ambitious in scope, formed part of a central, well-thought-out plan. During the winter of 1941, encouraged by the news of Tito's arrival in eastern Bosnia, they succeeded in fighting their way back into many of the areas from which they had been expelled and regaining much of the ground which they had lost.

But, if the Montenegrin Partisans had learnt by their military mistakes, they showed no signs of mending their ways politically. With typical Montenegrin exuberance and with but little regard for the deliberately moderate line laid down by Tito, they established in the areas under their control a Communist regime of the most extreme kind. Political opponents were ruthlessly liquidated and in February a conference of sympathizers and notables actually proclaimed Montenegro an integral part of the Soviet Union.

As Tito himself put it at the time, the Partisans were to "pay dearly for the mistakes made by some of our people."[26] Not only did they alienate public opinion; they played right into the hands of the enemy, always ready to take advantage of divisions and dissensions in the insurgent camp.*

Since the end of the summer relations between the Montenegrin Partisans and their Cetnik and Nationalist allies had become increasingly strained. Here, as in Serbia, the savage enemy reprisals which followed their early operations had made the Cetniks hesitate to undertake any more. At the same time the blatantly Communist policy of the Montenegrin Partisans had aroused in the minds of the Cetniks serious doubts as to the desirability of further collaboration with them and these doubts had been further strengthened by the arrival in the autumn of emissaries from General Mihajlović. In their propaganda the Italians lost no opportunity of drawing attention to the Communist danger or of emphasizing the need for a common front to combat it. Meanwhile, through devious channels feelers were put out and contacts made.

In the autumn of 1941 Colonel Bajo Stanišić, one of the leading Montenegrin Cetniks, withdrew on grounds of ill health from the joint Partisan-Cetnik Headquarters. Cetnik operations against the enemy now became rarer while Cetnik-Partisan clashes became more and more frequent. Then at the beginning of March, 1942 Colonel Stanišić went a step further and concluded a formal written agreement with the Italian High Command, providing for substantial Italian help to the Cetniks and for combined action against the Communists. Another Cetnik leader in Montenegro who at this time contrived to establish cordial relations with the Italians

* Tito was again to refer to "the serious blunders made in Montenegro" in his report after the war to the Fifth Party Congress in which he spoke of the "harsh, sectarian and incorrect attitude" of the Montenegrin leaders.

was Major Pavle Djurišić, a close personal friend of Mihaj-lović.[27]

Much the same thing was happening in Bosnia. Here, too, there had been a considerable measure of co-operation between Cetniks and Partisans. Here, too, the deterrent effect of enemy reprisals and the realization that their ultimate aims and those of the Partisans were almost diametrically opposed had caused a change of attitude on the part of the Cetniks. Here, too, a feeling that the Communists were really the greater danger had led them to reach accommodations with the enemy for common action against the Partisans. In April, 1942 the first formal agreements were concluded between the local Cetnik commanders, notably Uroš Drenović and Rado-slav Radić on the one hand, and the Germans and Ustaše on the other. They provided for a mutually satisfactory *modus vivendi* between the two parties and for joint operations against the Communists. For Pavelić formally to accept the presence of Serbs within the frontiers of Croatia must have been a bitter pill to swallow. Nor, as good Serbs, can it have been easy for the Cetniks to put out of their minds the memory of the Ustaše massacres of the previous summer. No doubt the agreement, like most agreements in the Balkans, was concluded with mental reservations on both sides. But for the time being the need to combat the menace of Communism outweighed for both all other considerations.[28]

That Mihajlović accepted the agreements reached by his Montenegrin commanders with the Italians seems certain. His attitude in the matter was thus described by Captain Hudson, who wrote of Djurišić: "The latter is loyal to Mihajlović, as the latter backs him as the most important Cetnik leader in Montenegro. Nor does Mihajlović interfere but accepts the Montenegrin Cetniks' compromise with the Italians.[29] Indeed, when, early in 1942, Mihajlović transferred his own head-quarters to Montenegro, Djurišić used his good offices with the Italians to ensure that he would not be disturbed there.[30] Whether he gave his consent to the arrangements in Bosnia is less clear, but, insofar as they provided for vigorous action against the Partisans and a passive attitude in all other respects, they were certainly in line with his general policy. The Italians, for their part, had a further reason for wishing to build up the Cetniks, particularly in Dalmatia; they saw them as a counterweight to the Ustaše, whom they hoped ultimately to dislodge from the coastal areas altogether.

Throughout the winter Tito had continued to keep Moscow informed as best he could of the course of operations. He had told in his signals of the first and second enemy offensives, of the hardships endured by the Partisans, of their successful withdrawal into eastern Bosnia and of the formation of the First Proletarian Brigade. He had also dwelt at length on the behavior of the Cetniks and had expressed himself with some asperity concerning the "shocking nonsense" broadcast by Radio Moscow, which in spite of everything still referred to Mihajlović as the leader of the forces of resistance.[31] Finally, he had continued to press for the early dispatch of airborne supplies, emphasizing his need for them and the encouraging effect that they would have on the morale of the Partisans. "We await your aircraft day and night," he signaled on December 29, 1941.[32] But his messages, carried precariously by courier across the mountains and through the enemy lines to Zagreb, whence they were dispatched over Vladko Velebit's secret wireless link, took a long time to reach their destination and in the meantime there were no signs of any practical response to his repeated requests for help.

Early in February, 1942, shortly before they reached Foca, a lull in the fighting enabled Tito's Headquarters to establish direct wireless contact with Moscow, making possible a daily exchange of messages. The signals which now came pouring in from the Comintern asked anxiously for information on a variety of subjects, in particular the Partisans' propaganda and the political line they were taking. But in their present position, short of food, short of ammunition and hemmed in by enemies on all sides, the Partisans were at least as interested in obtaining material aid as they were in receiving ideological guidance, and Tito, for his part, continued to urge that the Russians should try to supply them by air. There was, he explained in a signal dated February 17, a safe site near Zabljak at the foot of Mount Durmitor in Montenegro, where men and supplies could be dropped by parachute immediately and where it might later be possible for aircraft to land. They were in urgent need of automatic weapons, ammunition, medical supplies, signal stores, boots, clothing and explosives. And he gave map references and recognition signals. "If you send us sufficient military equipment," he signaled, "we can mobilize one hundred thousand more men." He also urged the dispatch of Soviet parachutists whose arrival would, he said, have "enormous moral and political effect." "They would," he added reassuringly, "be completely protected."[33]

The Russians replied that they would see what they could do, and every night from February 23 onward the Partisans awaited the arrival of the Soviet aircraft. Tito had sent no less a person than Moša Pijade to supervise the arrangements for their reception. The appointed place was a bleak wind-swept plateau four miles from Zabljak on the slopes of Mount Durmitor, five thousand feet up and now under six feet of snow. There they deposited four piles of straw, to be set alight when they heard the sound of aircraft approaching. And there Moša and his little party assembled each evening and waited in the snow until dawn, getting colder and colder as the wind howled round them. Then they trudged back to Zabljak.

After doing this every night for a fortnight, even Moša, the most fanatical Communist of them all, who before the war had spent fourteen years in prison for his political convictions, began to get a little restive, and on March 5 Tito thought it necessary to send him up a letter counseling patience. "I believe you," he wrote, "when you speak of your impatience at waiting in vain like this, but you had better resign yourself to much more waiting. Things do not go so simply. Today I sent a signal to Grandpapa, stressing the urgency of it and hope soon to have a favorable reply. . . . Don't get worried at having to go on waiting." And on March 14 he wrote again: "Be patient for just a little longer, for I still count on the visit coming off."[34]

Meanwhile there was no dearth of signals from Moscow. They came pouring in, keeping the Partisan operators up half the night receiving and deciphering them. But they hardly mentioned the question of supplies; they dealt in the main with political issues. And to the Partisans, cold, hungry and hard-pressed by the enemy, neither their tone nor their contents brought any comfort at all.

In reply to Moscow's inquiries about their ideological attitude, the Partisans had given vent to a series of passionate outbursts concerning Mihajlović, the Cetniks, and their sponsors, the Royal Jugoslav Government in London, a subject on which by now they felt very strongly. They had also described with uninhibited fervor the heroic exploits of their own new Proletarian Shock Brigades. Their messages were fairly bursting with the spirit of 1917.

This did not please the Soviet authorities, who at this stage of the war were primarily interested in the problem of their own survival and were particularly anxious that nothing should be done by a bunch of Balkan hotheads which could possibly upset their alliance with Great Britain and America or make their new-found allies in any way suspicious as to the purity of their ultimate intentions. World revolution and militant international Communism might be all very well in their proper time and place, but this was one of the moments when the less that was said about them in public the better. What mattered just now was to keep on friendly terms with the British and Americans and extract from them all possible material assistance for the Soviet Fatherland in its hour of peril. Thus we find the Comintern, Lenin's great instrument of world revolution, being used, no longer to fan the flames, but rather as an extinguisher of revolutionary ardor.

"Study of all the information you give," wrote Grandpapa to Tito in a signal dated March 5, 1942,

> gives the impression that the adherents of Great Britain and the Jugoslav Government have some [? justification] in suspecting the Partisan movement of acquiring a Communist character, and aiming at the Sovietization of Jugoslavia. Why, for example, did you need to form a special Proletarian Brigade? Surely at the moment the basic, immediate task is to unite all anti-Nazi movements, smash the invaders and achieve national liberation. How is one to explain the fact that supporters of Great Britain are succeeding in forming armed units against the Partisan Detachments? Are there really no other Jugoslav patriots—apart from Communists and Communist sympathizers—with whom you could join in a common struggle against the invaders? It is difficult to agree that London and the Jugoslav Government are siding with the invaders. There must be some great misunderstanding here. We earnestly request you to give serious thought to your tactics in general and to your actions, and to make sure that you on your side have really done all you can to achieve a true united national front of all enemies of Hitler and Mussolini in Jugoslavia, in order to attain the common aim—the expulsion of the invader and would-be conquerors. If you have not already done so, you should urgently take the necessary measures and inform us.[35]

In another signal of about the same date Grandpapa was even more explicit. "Defeat of the fascist bandits," he wrote, and liberation from the invader today constitute the main task, the task which stands above all other tasks. Take into account that the Soviet Union has treaty relations with the Jugoslav King and Government and that taking an open stand against these would create new difficulties in the joint war efforts and the relations between the Soviet on the one hand and Great Britain and America on the other. Do not view the issues of your fight only from your own, national standpoint, but also from the international standpoint of the British-American-Soviet coalition. While doing all you can to consolidate positions won in the national liberation struggle, at the same time try to show political elasticity and some ability to manoeuvre.[36]

It is easy to see how even someone of a more placid disposition than Tito might have been annoyed by such communications. Certainly a note of irritation is discernible in the long chatty letter which he sent to Žabljak to cheer up the unfortunate Moša Pijade. "A day or two ago," he wrote on March 11,

I got an immensely long signal from Grandpapa in which he says that our reports give him the impression that the Partisan movement is getting deeper and deeper into Communist waters. Otherwise, he asks, how would it be possible for supporters of the London Government to organize the Cetniks against us? He further asks why it was necessary to form a special Proletarian Brigade. He wants us to revise our policy and create a broad national liberation front. To this I have replied, briefly and clearly, that he has drawn the wrong conclusions from our reports, that we have already got a broad national liberation front, not in common with fifth-columnists, but with the great majority of true patriots; that the supporters of London are not working with the label London, but that of the occupying forces, i.e., the Nedic label, in their struggle against us; that we have sufficient documentary proofs of this; that the setting up of Proletarian Brigades was an indispensable step, when the Partisan movement was in danger of being broken up by fifth-columnists, and that the proletarian Brigades are not fighting for Sovietization, but by their heroic example are showing our people how to fight for freedom and independence.[37]

Time passed and still there was no sign of the Soviet aircraft. On March 9 Tito sent the following signal to Moscow: "We need arms and munitions. That is the best way of creating a national liberation front. In this country we have huge numbers of people anxious to fight the invaders, but without weapons." On March 19 he sent another: "We are in a critical situation owing to lack of ammunition. Please do all possible to send us ammunition and military supplies. Tell us if we can expect anything, and when." Ten days later he received the following reply: "All possible efforts are being made to help you with arms. But the technical difficulties are enormous. You should alas not count on our overcoming them in the near future. Please bear that in mind. Do all you can to try to get arms from the enemy and to make the most economical use of what armament you have."[38]

Technical difficulties . . . In Tito's mind doubts were beginning to arise as to whether the difficulties were not perhaps in reality of a political rather than of a technical nature. There had been the question of the proclamation which it had at one time been suggested that the Partisan High Command should address to the peoples of Europe. Endless signals had passed to and fro, amending and re-amending the proposed draft until it contained nothing that could possibly have shocked the most convinced conservative. The Comintern had even objected to Tito calling himself Tito. Why, they asked, could he not use his real name? And then on March 22 had come quite a short personal telegram from Moscow shelving the whole project "until certain matters in the relations between the Soviet Government and the Jugoslav Government in London have been settled."[39]

It was obvious, too, that Russians were afraid of calling a spade a spade. Tito's war was essentially a revolutionary war, waged not only against the invader but against his own political opponents, and, to do him justice, he made no bones about it. But the Russians were always wanting to wrap things up. "It is not opportune," they telegraphed, "to emphasize that the struggle is mainly against the Cetniks. World public opinion must first and foremost be mobilized against the invaders; mentioning or unmasking the Cetniks is secondary. That, of course, at the present juncture. . . ."[40]

It was infuriating. Tito communicated his impressions to Moša in a letter dated March 26. "I have not," he wrote,

> made much attempt to argue it out with Grandpapa. I have, however, told him that he has drawn the wrong conclusions from my reports, for the situation is quite different from what he imagines it to be. Concerning the Brigades [i.e., the Proletarian Brigades], I have told him the they were necessary, and have already played a great part in the people's struggle for liberation. I have told him that the fifth-columnists united to fight us long before we even thought of setting up the Brigades, and that that was what prompted us to do so. . . . You ought to know that long before Grandpapa's telegram I outlined our attitude to be that we should not attack the pro-British as such, but as servants of the invader, and that we should not allow the fifth-column to divert us from the line of a struggle for national liberation to a class struggle. Since my explanation, Grandpapa has stopped bothering about the subject. There is, however, something else at the bottom of our not getting any visits. Yesterday I got a telegram from Grandpapa, in which he informs us that we are to hold up publication of our proclamation to the peoples of Europe until the relations between the Soviet Government and the Jugoslav Government in London have been settled. From which one can see that the Jugoslav Government and not our policy is the main obstacle to our obtaining assistance. But hold on a little longer. We must see what comes of these talks between the Soviet and Jugoslav Governments.[41]

Three days later Tito decided to recall Moša and his men from Žabljak. "For the present," he wrote on March 29, "you need do no more night duty. I leave you to decide how to explain it to the men." Moša did his best, but the men, he recorded, did not seem particularly convinced. Some even wept. They had spent altogether thirty-seven nights waiting on the snow-swept plateau for help from Grandpapa which never came.[42]

Meanwhile, with the active support of their Cetnik allies, the Italians had launched a strong attack against the Partisans in Montenegro, while the Germans and Ustaše, with Italian support, intensified the pressure which they had maintained all winter on Tito's main force in eastern Bosnia. This offensive—the third by Partisan reckoning—lasted until June and was largely successful. The Montenegrin Partisans were forced back toward Bosnia and Herzegovina and a kind of Cetnik-Italian condominium was established throughout most of Montenegro, the Italians occupying the towns and the Cetniks the country. Having thus established their supremacy, the Montenegrin Cetniks now proceeded to hunt down and exterminate any Partisan sympathizers they could find with the same relentless ferocity that the Partisans themselves had shown in their own hour of victory. From his headquarters, Mihajlović urged on his followers, warning them against tenderheartedness and "Kerenskyism." "We must," he wrote to Stanišić, "mercilessly destroy these bloodthirsty men as they would destroy us." In Montenegro nothing is done by half-measures.[43]

The Third Offensive found Tito still at Foča. By now he had under his immediate command no less than five brigades of roughly one thousand men each. He had, moreover, reorganized his headquarters to meet the increased scope and complexity of the military problems which now confronted him. From Montenegro he had brought Arso Jovanović, a trained staff officer, to be his Chief of Staff. Arso's place in Montenegro had been taken by Peko Dapčević, the Spanish veteran. The Partisans were, however, still desperately short of ammunition. From time to time Tito made fresh appeals to Moscow for help. "Can we hope for munitions soon?" he signaled on April 23. But the replies he received were uniformly discouraging. "As we informed you earlier," came the answer, "for reasons which you understand, you unfortunately cannot expect to receive from us either ammunition or automatic weapons in the immediate future. The chief reason is the impossibility of getting them to you." And Grandpapa, adding insult to injury, went on to advise Tito to make a "general approach" to the Royal Jugoslav Government in London.[44]

Tito remained in Foča until early May. Then, as the pressure from the north grew greater and the news from the Montenegrin front became increasingly disturbing, he moved southward into Montenegro to assume command there personally, taking with him the First and Second Proletarian Brigades. From Montenegro he signaled to Moscow as follows on May 24:

Since May 20th I have been . . . on the Montenegrin

sector of the front. The situation here is critical . . .
Incessant fighting has left our Partisans exhausted. Apart
from that, there is no more ammunition. We shall have
to withdraw most of our battalions from Montenegro,
if they are not to be wiped out. The whole people curse
the Jugoslav Government in London which through Draža
Mihajlovic is aiding the invader. On all sides both soldiers
and civilians are asking why the Soviet Union does not
send us aid, were it only automatic weapons and ammunition. Our Partisans are fighting with unprecedented heroism. . . . For us the question of help is extremely serious.
On behalf of our High Command please pass on to the
High Command of the Red Army our request for assistance. The enemy is making every effort to annihilate us.[45]

But still there was no response and when, after a month's
hard fighting against the combined and well-equipped forces
of the Italians and Cetniks, it became clear that the Montenegrin Partisans were facing overwhelming odds, Tito, elud-
ing the enemy's attempts at encirclement, withdrew them into
the highlands of eastern Bosnia where he incorporated them
in his main force, now situated in the remote Sutjeska Valley,
between the mountain ranges of Maglić and Zelengora.

In the meantime Tito had decided on a bold new course
of action. Lack of food made it impossible for the Partisans
to stay any longer in a barren, mountainous region where the
peasants had barely enough to feed themselves. Likewise their
only hope of replenishing their dangerously depleted supplies
of ammunition was to resume the initiative. There was also,
constantly before his mind, the fundamental necessity of
"spreading the revolt," of extending its scope, of bringing its
message to ever wider areas and ever larger sections of the
population. Even in the mountains spring had come at last.
The leaves on the trees favored guerrilla operations. For some
time past he had been receiving encouraging reports from
Partisan commanders operating in Croatia and in west and
central Bosnia, reports of Partisan successes and of growing
popular discontent at the excesses of the Ustaša regime. On
the strength of these reports, he now determined to go over
to the offensive and, breaking through the enemy encirclement, push northwestward with all the forces at his disposal
in an attempt to form a new "liberated area" in the very heart
of Pavelić's Independent Kingdom of Croatia.

VII 𝔰𝔰𝔰 MARCHING THROUGH BOSNIA

THE order to move was issued on June 22, 1942, the first anniversary of Hitler's attack on the Soviet Union. In the dense beech forest above Vrbnica, where Tito and his Headquarters Staff had been encamped for the last few days, it was cold and wet. Every one of them was crawling with lice. Food and ammunition were short and the rough shelters of branches they had built themselves did not keep out the rain which soaked in everywhere. But they forgot all these miseries in their excitement at what lay before them. Two days later they were on their way. In the hope that they might be able to slip through before the enemy commanders had decided whose responsibility it was to stop them, they took a route which followed as nearly as possible the boundary between the German and Italian zones of occupation. Their immediate objective was to attack and put out of action the railway line linking Sarajevo with Mostar and the Adriatic.

For the first few days the going in the mountains was hard; the weather was bad and prolonged lack of food was beginning to tell. The men, their strength already sapped, were nearing starvation. They were short of pack ponies—many had already been killed for food. The long steep climb strained them to the utmost. There was no food in the villages.

Then, on the tenth day out, emerging from the woods, they came to the outskirts of Bradina, a village built round a railway station near the mouth of a tunnel on the Sarajevo-Mostar line, and the birthplace, as it happened, of Dr. Pavelić. At nightfall, while other units attacked at other points along the line, Tito himself with one battalion attacked Bradina. The thickly wooded mountainside sloping steeply down to the village offered excellent cover and the Partisans were able to approach it without being seen. The garrison of Ustaše were taken by surprise and the attack was successful. In the station the Partisans found a goods train, with steam up, just moving off. Two of them managed to jump onto the engine. There was a shot and the train stopped. It was a rich prize: thirty-three truckloads of food and other welcome supplies, and

145

more in the station warehouses. "Here's a truck full of apricots!" shouted one Partisan. "Here's some honey," shouted another. "Carbide!" "Linen!" "Motor bicycles!" yelled others, as they ransacked the train and the buildings. Among other things, they captured four tons of flour, three tons of maize, a ton of beans, half a ton of bacon, a large quantity of oil, fruit, honey and—best of all—nearly half a ton of dynamite. For the time being, their supply problem had been solved. Somebody had found a fiddle and was sitting in a corner playing it with more vigor than skill. Others were singing. Before leaving they utterly destroyed the station and as much as they could of the line. The bridges were dynamited, the tunnel blocked, the rails ripped up, the turntable destroyed, and at dawn a train made up of two locomotives and the thirty-three empty trucks was set on fire and sent blazing round the bend and over a precipice to destruction. "This," said the guard of the train philosophically, as he watched the proceedings and smoked a cigarette, "is the sixth time the Partisans have taken me off a train, but I have never seen them make such a mess of the line before."[1]

After a brief rest and a memorable meal of bean stew and bacon prepared under the direction of Moša Pijade, they set out again, much refreshed. A few days later the Partisans attacked and stormed Konjic, another important railway center, and then the little hill town of Prozor. Still they advanced. But it was not all such easy going. Repeated attacks on Bugojno and the neighboring village of Kupres were repulsed with heavy losses by the Ustaše garrisons. At about this time, too, the enemy launched a concerted attack against the Kozara region in central Bosnia. Here a number of Partisan units as well as some fifty thousand women, children and old people were surrounded in strength and it was only after several weeks of heavy fighting that the Partisans managed to break out, taking with them such civilians as they could. But there were severe casualties and many women and children fell into the hands of the enemy. Meanwhile, during the last days of July a fierce battle had begun for the possession of Livno, another Ustaša stronghold, the enemy bringing up tanks and aircraft in an attempt to relieve the mixed garrison of Germans and Ustaše. But on the morning of August 7 the garrison, two hundred strong, sent out a flag of truce and surrendered, leaving the Partisans in possession of the little town, with its cattle market, its mosque and its monastery, and of most of the surrounding plain.

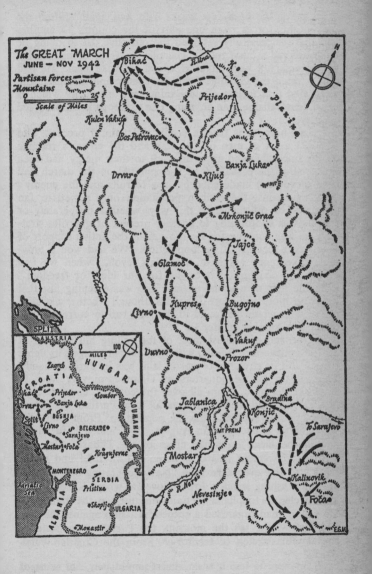

The GREAT MARCH
JUNE — NOV 1942

Partisan Forces
Mountains
0   25
Scale of Miles

Bihać
R.Una
Kozara Planina
Prijedor
Kulen Vakufa
Bos Petrovac
Banja Luka
Drvar
Ključ
Mrkonjić Grad
Jajce
Glamoč
R.Cetina
Kupres
Bugojno
Livno
Vakuf
Duvno
Prozor
Bradina
SPLIT
AUSTRIA
Tablanica
Konjić
To Sarajevo
HUNGARY
0   MILES   100
Zagreb
CROATIA
Prijedor
Sombor
ROUMANIA
Bihać
Drvar
Banja Luka
BOSNIA
Split
Livno
BELGRADE
Mostar
MT PRENJ
Mostar
Sarajevo
Kalinovik
Foča
SAVA
Kragujevac
Kalinovik
MONTENEGRO
SERBIA
Foča
Pristina
R.Neretva
Nevesinje
Adriatic
Sea
ALBANIA
Shoplje
Monastir
BULGARIA
E.G.M.

In the space of a few weeks Tito had again shifted the bulk of his forces from one part of the country to another and there successfully resumed the offensive. In so doing he had observed a basic rule of guerrilla warfare: he had denied his adversary a firm target at which to strike back. He had also wrested the initiative from the enemy and increased and intensified that feeling of uncertainty and insecurity which is more demoralizing than anything else to troops in an occupied country.

It had been, it is true, a costly and painful process. Tito had lost a lot of men on the way and the enemy's revenge on the once liberated areas now left to their mercy had been savage. But the casualties he had suffered on the march had been more than made good by new recruits and the enemy's reprisals against the civilian population only served to fan the flame of resistance. In this way, whether deliberately or not, he was conforming to another precept of guerrilla strategy: he was winning for his movement the active support of ever larger sections of the population. "We had won a province," Lawrence wrote of the Arab revolt, "when we had taught the civilians in it to die for our ideal of freedom." With the help of a brutal enemy, Tito was teaching just that lesson to more and more Jugoslavs, though whether his ideal of freedom would be found in the long run to correspond to theirs was another matter.

By the end of August most of the rolling hill country of central and western Bosnia, with its mountain ranges, its dense forests and its stretches of open plain, was in Partisan hands. Tito set up his headquarters at Glamoč, moving later to Bosanski Petrovac. From all over the country, couriers were now arriving with news of successful local Partisan operations and increasing support from the population. From Dalmatia, where, after a bad start in August, 1941 and a hard winter among the bleak limestone crags of the Dinaric Alps, the Partisan movement had now taken a firm hold and where there was now even a Partisan "Navy" operating off the coast in armed fishing smacks. From Slovenia, where Kardelj, having traveled to Ljubljana by train, disguised as the fireman of the engine, had organized a successful rising against the Italians and where, for the moment, the Partisans controlled a considerable stretch of territory.* From the Croatian Parti-

* They were to lose it again almost immediately, but managed to keep their forces, their armament and their organization intact.

sans, whose Chief of Staff, Ivo Rukavina, a pale, slightly
built young man with fair hair and blue eyes, had arrived in
person to report to Tito. From eastern Bosnia, where Tempo
Vukmanović had stayed behind to conduct operations after the
main body had left. From Slavonia, where one Partisan demolition expert alone had wrecked seventy trains on the Zagreb-
Belgrade line. From Serbia, even, where, after last year's
setback, Partisan detachments were now once again in action.
The rising was fast spreading over the whole country. As soon
as the Germans and their allies thought that they had put it
down in one place, it flared up in another.

Tito was also in touch with his underground organization
in the big towns. Kardelj was in Ljubljana, where he lived
underground in a specially built cellar with a wireless set and
a red light to warn him of the approach of the police. Tempo
Vukmanović spent much of his time in Sarajevo, plotting with
Moslem Communists in a tall, rather shabby house in a side
street. In April, while Partisan Headquarters were still at Foča,
Vladko Velebit had arrived from Zagreb, where for the past
year he had been continuing to practice as a lawyer, while
at the same time operating the Partisans' secret wireless link
with Moscow. Now that direct wireless contact had been established between Partisan Headquarters and Moscow this
was no longer needed. In order to avoid trouble with the
Ustaše, Velebit had taken the very necessary precaution of
entering the Catholic Church, but even so, life under Pavelič
had been nerve-wracking and after the long months of nervous
tension ordinary Partisan life in the woods seemed like a rest
cure. Only a few weeks before, in February, Andrija Hebrang, a high party functionary living clandestinely in Zagreb,
had been caught by the Ustase and, it was believed, terribly
tortured.

With Velebit came Ivo Ribar, who had also been working
underground in Zagreb since January. The two of them had
traveled quite openly by train from Zagreb to Sarajevo, and
then, in order to fool the police, had walked out into the
country, each carrying an empty bottle, as if in search of
milk. Two miles outside the town they had met the first Partisan patrol. Velebit now stayed with the Partisans "in the
woods," but in June Ribar made his way back to Zagreb for
another spell "in civilization," as they called it. Now Djilas
was to go to Belgrade and was already growing a large black
mustache to alter his appearance. He would shortly be followed by Tempo Vukmanović, who, having completed his

mission in Bosnia, was setting out this time for Macedonia, where the local party had gone badly off the rails and where, consequently, little progress had hitherto been made in organizing resistance. To save time, Tempo, an old hand at this sort of thing, would disguise himself and travel by train via Sarajevo, Zagreb and Belgrade to Leskovac in southern Serbia. There he would make contact with the nearest Partisan detachment and so make his way across country to Macedonia.

Nothing succeeds like success. The situation was full of possibilities. Volunteers came flocking in from all sides. All that was needed were the arms to equip them. Again Tito turned hopefully to Moscow. "The High Command," he signaled on August 26, breaking into the third person, "requests the General Staff of the Red Army to help us with military equipment, particularly arms. We have great opportunities of mobilizing men for a Partisan and volunteer army. Through lack of arms we are unable to accept thousands of volunteers. . . ." And on September 8: "Hundreds come to volunteer every day, but we have not enough weapons." But again there was no response.[2]

Nor were the Russians any more helpful politically. Radio Moscow, so eagerly listened for by the Partisans, said little or nothing about them and, when it did mention Jugoslavia, tended to talk in flattering terms of Mihajlović and his Cetniks. It was bad enough that the B.B.C. should pretend the Partisans did not exist. That Moscow should also ignore their heroic exploits was the last straw. And then, at the beginning of August, came the news that the Soviet Government had raised their legation with the Royal Jugoslav Government in exile to an embassy and vice versa. This was too much for Tito. On August 11 he gave vent to his feelings in an angry telegram to Grandpapa. "The raising," he wrote,

of the representation of the Jugoslav Government in Moscow to the rank of Embassy has made a most unfavorable impression on all patriots of Jugoslavia, particularly on those in the ranks of our Army, all the more so since this has come at a moment when the treacherous Government of Jugoslavia is openly collaborating with the invaders, decorating every bloody-handed executioner against whom we are waging a life and death struggle, just as we are against the invaders. Yesterday the Jugoslav Government demonstratively and openly decorated Pop Perisic, Djuic and many other Cetnik executioners. This has made our struggle for national liberation much more difficult. All waverers and open enemies of our fight quote it, not as recognition by the Soviet Government of our national struggle, but as recognition of the policy of the Jugoslav Government in London. Can nothing be done to ensure that the Soviet Government is better informed concerning the treacherous role of the Jugoslav Government and the superhuman sufferings and difficulties of our people who are fighting the invaders, the Cetniks, the Ustaše and the rest of them? Do you really not believe our daily reports? We are asked on all sides what it all means. How are we to explain it? There is already a lack of spirit showing in our ranks. This may have terrible consequences for our struggle. We repeat: the Jugoslav Government are openly collaborating with the Italians, and, clandestinely, with the Germans as well. They are betraying our people and the Soviet Union. We are also quite sure that the Intelligence Service is supporting this policy . . . .[3]

But all he got in return was a brief message suggesting that the documents on which he based his claim that the Cetniks were collaborating with the enemy might be fakes. This and the persistently noncommittal attitude of Radio Moscow made Tito angrier than ever. "Why," he signalled on September 9, "does Radio Moscow in its Serbo-Croat programme make no mention of the Cetnik atrocities? Why does it give no publicity to our struggle? That is what a lot of people here are asking. They demand, with some reason, that they should at least be given moral support. Many of them are dissatisfied with Radio Moscow's Serbo-Croat programmes."[4]

Meanwhile, with no outside help at all, Tito and his main force were continuing their victorious progress northward through western Bosnia. By the end of September a score of towns and villages had been taken and the "liberated area" still further extended. On September 25, after a fierce battle, the Partisans captured Jajce, a town of considerable strategic importance, only to lose it again to the enemy ten days later. By now the Germans, thoroughly alarmed, had brought up heavy reinforcements, supported by tanks, artillery and aircraft, while the Italians and Cetniks were threatening Partisan territory from Dalmatia. But, although individual towns and villages changed hands constantly (and suffered severely in the process), the bulk of western Bosnia was now controlled by the Partisans.

In the areas under their control the Partisans found plenty to occupy them. National Liberation Committees had to be set up and some sort of local administration established. Supplies of all kinds had to be brought or requisitioned. Where there were workshops or factories or power stations an attempt had to be made to get them going again. Generally somebody could be found with the necessary knowledge or skill. Butchers, bakers, electricians, engineers, all came in useful sooner or later. Postmen, too, for, of recent weeks, the Partisans had started their own postal service, overprinting a red star on the stamps of the Independent State of Croatia. And engine drivers were needed to drive the one sound railway locomotive they had managed to piece together out of parts taken from half a dozen derelict ones. There was even work for Pop Vlado Zečević and for the other Orthodox priests who were with the Partisans: Orthodox churches which had been desecrated by the Ustaše to reconsecrate, babies to christen in Orthodox villages whose priests had been murdered—216 babies in one village. Finally, there was the need for a final reckoning with any Ustaše who were unlucky enough to fall into Partisan hands, a task complicated as often as not by the difficulty of preventing the local population from tearing the prisoners limb from limb before the firing squad could do their work. An eyewitness has described one such scene: "As the Ustaše were being led off to execution, a peasant woman rushed into the middle of them and began scratching and hitting at them, screaming all the time. The Partisans had difficulty in pulling her off them. Then the shots rang out and she again rushed forward, this time among the corpses, dancing in the blood. 'A-ah!' she gasped, dripping with sweat and blood. It seemed that the Ustaše had slaughtered all her sons."[5]

Up to now a constant source of irritation to the Partisans had been the enemy garrison at Bihać, a town of some twelve thousand inhabitants on the River Una near the borders of Bosnia and Croatia and the scene incidentally of some of the Ustaše's worst atrocities. Operating from this base, the enemy had been able to drive a wedge into Partisan territory and also to interrupt communications between Tito's main force and the Partisans in Croatia. The capture of Bihać, which took place on November 5 after a fierce battle lasting two days, was the final triumph of Tito's long march. Despite all the enemy's efforts to dislodge him, he now controlled the greater part of Bosnia. His forces had won back the position in eastern Bosnia which they had lost earlier in the year. They had established a firm hold on northern and central Bosnia. And in western Bosnia they now had a firm base on the borders of Croatia.

Four months earlier the Partisans had been on the run, without a secure base; they had suffered heavy losses; they had been hungry and exhausted and short of rifles and ammunition. Now, all this had changed. They had covered a distance of some two hundred miles, fighting as they went. Though they had had no help from outside, they had captured from the enemy large quantities of arms and ammunition. Everywhere fresh volunteers were flocking to join them. Their detachments had grown into formations. Their numbers were rapidly increasing. From mere guerrilla bands, they had become an army in their own right, an army, they claimed, of 150,000 men.

Tito took advantage of this period of relative security to give formal recognition to these changes. Since January, 1942 the forces under his command had been divided up into "brigades." Now, by a series of decrees issued during the course of November, eight "divisions" and two "corps" were formed, the whole constituting the "National Army of Liberation and Partisan Detachments of Jugoslavia." Tito's new corps and divisions did not bear any very close resemblance, either in size or organization, to the corresponding formations in any ordinary army, the average strength of a Partisan division being about 3,500. But they were now better armed than ever before—the First Division alone possessed nearly 4,000 rifles and 150 rounds of ammunition per man. In addition to small arms, they were equipped with a certain number of captured antitank and other light guns. They possessed a supply system, a sytem of communications and a chain of command. And finally they fought, as they had always fought, extraordinarily well.

Just as the increase which there had been in the size of his military forces had made it necessary to overhaul their organization, so the greatly widened scope of the civil problems now confronting Tito necessitated a revision and extension of his political and administrative arrangements. On November 12 he informed Moscow of what he had achieved up to date and of what he now had in mind. "So far," he signaled,

we have formed eight divisions of three brigades each,

on the territory of Bosnia, Croatia and Dalmatia. In the rest of Jugoslavia we have begun the formation of brigades from the stronger Partisan detachments. Numerous Partisan detachments and battalions, with their staffs, remain for Partisan action. All these divisions are well armed, inclusive of artillery, with arms captured in engagements with the enemy. These divisions are no longer called Partisan Detachments but Shock Divisions of the Jugoslav Army of National Liberation. We shall now set up something like a government, which is to be called the National Liberation Committee of Jugoslavia. This Committee will include representatives of all the nationalities of Jugoslavia, drawn from the various former political parties.

As usual the reply he received was fussy and discouraging. "Do not fail," wrote Grandpapa,

to give your Committee an all-national Jugoslav and all-party anti-fascist character, both in its composition and in its programme. Do not look upon the Committee as a sort of government, but as the political arm of the struggle for national liberation. Do not put it in opposition to the Jugoslav Government in London. Do not at the present state raise the question of abolition of the monarchy. Do not make any mention of a republic.* [6]

Having reluctantly noted these somewhat negative instructions, Tito went ahead with his preparations for the first meeting of AVNOJ, the Anti-Fascist National Liberation

---

* One of the reasons for the cautious attitude of the Soviet Government was that they were at this moment endeavoring to persuade the Royal Jugoslav Government to let them send a military mission to Mihajlovic. A condition made by the Royal Government was that the Partisans (whom they regarded as being under Soviet control) should stop fighting the Cetniks and place themselves under Mihajlovic's command. Although in the end nothing came of this scheme, Molotov mentioned it as a possibility to Mr. Eden as late as October, 1943. What lay behind it was not altogether clear. It is possible that the Russians attributed to Mihajlovic greater political and military importance than he in fact possessed. It is also possible that they had doubts about Tito and were looking round for a second string. (See Moša Pijade, *About the Legend That the Jugoslav Uprising Owed Its Existence to Soviet Assistance,* pp. 18 and 19.)

Committee of Jugoslavia, as the new body was to be called. This took place at Bihać on November 26 and was attended by delegates from all over Jugoslavia.

The delegates started arriving at Bihać a day or two before the date fixed for the meeting of the council. Some had traveled great distances. There was snow on the hills all round, but none in the town itself, and the valley of the Una in which it lay was green and smiling in the pale winter sunshine. To the southwest the snow-clad peaks of the Plješevica Range rose like a wall above the mists. Most of the houses on the outskirts of the little town had been shattered or burned out in the recent fighting. Here and there were strong points where little bands of Ustaše had made a last stand—some barracks, the old castle, a confectioner's shop, some houses commanding the bridge over the Una. Everywhere the walls were scored and pitted by bullets and shrapnel. Near what was left of an Ustaša machine-gun nest children were playing, knee-deep in old cartridge cases. The mosques and the Catholic church with its square towers were still standing, but the Orthodox church had been razed to the ground by the Ustaše and even the foundations removed. In the park, the trees were gashed and scarred by machine-gun fire. The delegates were quartered in the Hotel Bosna. To some of them, who had not been in a town for many months, it seemed strange to see men wearing collars and ties and hats again, and women with silk stockings and make-up.

Before leaving Montenegro in June, Tito had made a speech to his men, giving them the general wartime party line. "This," he had said, "is not the time to speak of what will come after the war. Today all of us, regardless of class, religion or political beliefs, are involved in a struggle for national liberation. That is our chief and most urgent concern. We must seek to rally to our ranks all good patriots. That means that we have got to take a broad, liberal view of things. . . . The path of national liberation must be kept straight but wide."[7]

At Bihać, five months later, the line was still the same. It was the old line, Moscow's line, the line of the "Popular Front Against Fascism." It was most important that there should be no repetition of the blunders, the deplorable blunders, which through excess of zeal, through deviations to the left, had been committed in Montenegro. They were the sort of thing that alienated public opinion and gave the enemy material for propaganda. They were also the sort of thing that upset

Moscow. And, however irritating Grandpapa might be, that was something which Tito had no wish to do. One of the purposes of the Bihać assembly was to counteract what had gone before, to correct the impression that the Partisans were bloodthirsty Bolsheviks, to give, on the contrary, the impression that they were patriotic, public-spirited democrats and thus to gain for the Movement of National Liberation the widest possible measure of popular support. For that was essential to Tito if he was to achieve his twin aims: the liberation of his country from the Germans and the ultimate establishment of himself and his party as the decisive political force. What would happen after was another matter. As he himself had so shrewdly remarked five months earlier, "This is not the time to talk of what will come after the war."

On November 26, just a year after being driven out of Užice, Tito opened the proceedings in his new capital. The little hall in which the council met was hung with Bosnian carpets and decorated with large roughly drawn pictures, not only of Stalin, but of Churchill and Roosevelt, and with the flags of the Allies, also homemade. In his opening speech, he explained the purposes for which they were meeting. "This is not the moment, Comrades," he said, remembering his instructions, "for us to form a new government in the full sense of the word. The international situation is not yet ripe for that. But we have at least the right in these grim days to form a political body which will rally the people and lead them, together with our heroic army, into battle—into the many fierce battles which lie before us. We do not recognize the puppet governments. No legal form of government exists on our liberated territory, save the People's Committee which the people themselves have formed. So long as our army was small, and our Partisan detachments few in number, we needed little else. But now these detachments have grown into the mighty Army of National Liberation which is not only equal but superior to the enemy, despite his vastly greater technical resources, in morale and endurance. Our needs, too, have grown since those days when every village or parish could find enough food for its own soldiers. We now need to organize government machinery, political machinery which will mobilize and turn to account all our people's latent resources toward one end—the fight against the evil Fascist invader, against his henchmen, against the traitors, against the Ustaše and the Cetniks." After a grateful reference to the moral support which they derived from their "profound faith in the might of the Soviet Union and of the Red Army," which, he said, had carried them through all the difficulties and dangers of the past eighteen months, Tito spoke of the indissoluble bonds which the war was forging between the peoples of Jugoslavia. "This historic assembly," he concluded, "is itself evidence of the unity of our peoples: Serbs, Croats, Slovenes, Montenegrins, Moslems and others regardless of race or religion."[8]

There followed a succession of enthusiastic but not particularly constructive speeches from various delegates including some members of the Croat Peasant party, some Montenegrin Agrarians, a schoolmaster from Nikšić who was also the editor of the local paper, and a couple of Orthodox priests. Later on a president, two vice-presidents and an executive committee were elected. The new president was Dr. Ivan Ribar, the elderly Belgrade politician, whose two sons, Jurica and Ivo were both leading Communists and among Tito's closest associates, and who himself had after some narrow escapes left Belgrade and joined the Partisans two months before. Strangely enough, Dr. Ribar, long a prominent member of the Serbian Democratic party, had been president of that very Constituent Assembly which twenty years before had outlawed the Jugoslav Communist party. With his long white hair, his fine features and his dignified manner, he looked the very model of an old-fashioned liberal statesman.

The final resolution adopted by the Bihac assembly and broadcast all over the country was no less reassuring than the person of its president. "In view," it read,

of the calumnies and slander which the invaders, the Ustaše and the Cetniks of Draža Mihajlović have been spreading about the National Liberation Movement and its aims, it is deemed necessary to issue the following statements:

The Jugoslav National Liberation Movement is composed of all true patriots irrespective of political or religious convictions or of national origin. Its aims are as follows:

1. The liberation of the country from the invaders and the achievement of independence and true democratic rights for all the peoples of Jugoslavia.

2. The inviolability of private property and the provid-

ing of every possibility for individual initiative in industry, trade and agriculture.

3. No radical changes whatsoever in the social life and activites of the people except for the replacement of reactionary village authorities and gendarmes who may have gone over to the service of the invaders by popularly elected representatives, truly democratic and popular in character. All the most important questions of social life and State organization will be settled by the people themselves through representatives who will be properly elected by the people after the war.

4. The National Liberation Movement, which is fighting for the freedom of the people and for their social and democratic rights, renounces any kind of coercion or lawlessness.

5. Officers who join the National Liberation Army are assured of their rank and of a position commensurate with their abilities.

6. The National Liberation Movement fully recognizes the national rights of Croatia, Slovenia, Serbia, Macedonia and all other regions. It is a movement which is as much Croatian as it is Slovene and Serbian. It guarantees that the national rights of all the peoples of Jugoslavia will be preserved.[9]

Such, at any rate for the time being, was the line. One of the delegates noticed that Tito was much moved by the proceedings. After it was all over, some of them went back to the Hotel Bosna for supper and at supper they drank Tito's health. In replying to the toast, Tito came perhaps nearer than usual to revealing what was in his mind, in his heart even. "Whatever I have been able to do," he said, "has been the work of the party. I was young and ignorant, and the party took me under its wing, and brought me up and trained me. I owe everything to it."[10]

VIII 〰〰 FEARFUL ODDS

By the end of 1942 Pavelić had become thoroughly alarmed at the progress which the Partisans were making in the Independent State of Croatia. Already a great part of its territory was under Partisan control; the communication system was in confusion and the economic life of the country had become hopelessly disrupted. In the towns food was getting shorter and discontent increasing. More and more Croats were joining Tito, whose followers had up to now been predominantly Serb. "The Partisans," wrote Dr. Goebbels in his diary, "have made a football of the Croat Government."[1]

There was yet another disturbing aspect of the situation: the attitude of the higher Catholic clergy still left much to be desired. Archbishop Stepinac remained, it is true, scrupulosuly correct in his attitude toward the regime. He continued to attend official functions and ceremonies; he had become Chaplain General of the Croat Armed Forces; he accepted and wore the high decoration which Pavelić had bestowed on him.[2] But at the same time he continued to intervene on behalf of the victims of the regime, while his letters and speeches and sermons became ever more critical of the Ustaše, of their methods and of their racial theories and laws. So critical, that extracts from them were used by the B.B.C. for purposes of propaganda. So critical, in fact, as to be almost defiant. "The Church," the Archbishop wrote to Pavelić in March, 1943, on learning that there were to be fresh persecutions of the Jews, "does not fear any power in this world, when it is a question of defending the elementary rights of men."[3]

There were, it is true, still no renegades among the Ustaše, whose fanaticism equaled that of the Communists, but the conscript Croat militia or Domobran were much less reliable and deserted to the Partisans whenever they got the chance. Throughout the Independent State there was everywhere talk of the Partisans, of their victories, of their growing numbers, of the daring raids which they had carried out or were about to carry out. Even in his own capital of Zagreb, the *Poglavnik* did not feel entirely secure. At the street corners, pillboxes were being built in case disturbances should break out.

Nor was Pavelić the only person to feel disturbed by what was happening in Croatia. When he had visited Hitler at his headquarters at Vinnitsa on the Eastern front in November, he had found the *Führer* in a thoroughly fractious frame of mind. This, the *Führer* had explained to him, was not at all what he had intended when he had allowed him to set up his Independent Croat State. He had expected him at least to be able to manage his own affairs. He had even counted on his being able to make substantial contributions to Germany's war effort, in foodstuffs, in minerals and in troops for the Eastern front. Instead of which, he had let half his so-called country be overrun by a bunch of Bolshevik bandits who had tied up all his own troops and necessitated the presence of a lot of German troops as well. It was high time the Partisans were dealt with once and for all, especially in view of the manifest danger of Allied landings in the Balkans. In the end, Colonel General Alexander von Löhr, the German Commander-in-Chief for southeastern Europe, had been called in and preliminary plans made for an all-out drive against the Partisans early in the New Year. It would be on a larger scale than any operations undertaken in Jugoslavia since the original Axis invasion in April, 1941.

The final arrangements for this campaign, which was to be known by the Germans as Operation *Weiss* and to the Partisans as the Fourth Enemy Offensive, were made at a conference which was held in Rome on January 3, 1943, and was attended by General von Löhr, General Ugo Cavallero, the Chief of the Italian General Staff, General Roatta, the general commanding the Italian forces in Jugoslavia and one of Pavelić's generals.*

* According to some accounts the Cetnik *Vojvoda* or Leader, Dobrosav Jevdjevic, representing the Cetnik forces in Dalmatia and Herzegovina, was also summoned to Rome for consultation on this occasion. However this may be, the Cetniks certainly took an active part in the Fourth Offensive. It appears that the Germans and Pavelic at first objected to the employment of Cetnik units on Croat territory, but finally agreed to their being used on the understanding that they would be regarded as an integral part of the Italian forces and would be withdrawn as soon as the operations in question were completed. Hitler himself seems at this stage to have been in favor of disarming the Cetniks altogether on the grounds that they were not to be trusted, but the Italians,

The German plan was to encircle and annihilate Tito's forces in Bosnia. With this object, they launched on January 20, with the help of their various allies, a concerted attack on his positions from several quarters at once. The main weight of the attack was directed against the Partiasn positions round Bihac in the wooded, mountainous region of western Bosnia and the Lika. The Germans attacked from the north and east: 7 S.S. Division "Prinz Eugen" advanced from the direction of Karlovac; 369 Infantry Division, supported by a Croat brigade, from Petrinje; 714 Infantry Division from Prijedor; and 717 Infantry Division, with Croat support, from Sanski Most. At the same time the Italians attacked from the west and south: the "Lombardia" Division from the direction of Ogulin; the "Re" Division from Gospić; and the "Sassari" Division, with Cetnik support, from Knin. Meanwhile the Montenegrin Cetniks, with the support of the Italian "Murge" Division and of Italian artillery units, were preparing to cut off the Partisan retreat to the south and southeast. Air support for these operations was given by units of the German and Italian Air Forces operating from airfields at Zagreb, Sarajevo, Mostar, Banjaluka and Karlovac. The troops engaged were under the immediate command of General Lütters, commanding the German forces in Croatia, and General Roatta, commanding the Italian Second Army, and under the supreme command of General Alexander von Löhr, Commander-in-Chief, Southeast, who, shortly after the offensive had started, himself flew up from Salonika to see them in action.

Tito, for his part, was not taken unawares. His forces at this time were deployed over a considerable area. The First and Third Partisan Divisions were in central Bosnia near Banjaluka and Jajce; the Second Division was near Knin in Dalmatia; and the Seventh Division was in Croatia near Petrinje. The remainder of his forces, including the recently formed First Bosnian and First Croatian Corps, were deployed round Bihać. He himself and his headquarters staff were in-

---

who attached considerable importance to their assistance, got their way in the end.[4] It is possible that General Mihajlovic di dnot entirely approve of the particularly close collaboration which existed between the Italians and the Cetnik commanders in Dalmatia and Herzegovina, Jevdjevic, Trifunovic and Djuic. This did not, however, prevent him from recommending Jevdjevic for the highest Jugoslav decoration, the Karadjordje Star, which was duly awarded to him by the Royal Jugoslav Government in London.

stalled in a fine old castle belonging to Count von Berks at Ostrožać near Bihać.

Forewarned of the Axis plan to encircle him, Tito now decided to break through with his main striking force where the enemy was weakest, namely, in the southeastern sector, which was held by the Italians and the Montenegrin Cetniks. With this aim in view, he left his Seventh Division as a rear guard to bear the main weight of the German attack from the northeast and hold up the enemy's advance for as long as possible, before withdrawing in its turn. He dispatched the First and Third Divisions from central Bosnia on a forced march to the River Neretva in order to forestall the Cetnik and Italian forces who were beginning to assemble along the Neretva Valley and in the key town of Prozor which commanded its approaches. And finally he ordered his Second Division to push southward through Dalmatia to the Ustaša stronghold of Imotski, halfway between Split and the Neretva, capture it, and then push on to the Neretva Valley. His calculation was that if these objectives could be attained and if, in particular, the towns of Prozor and Konjic could be taken and held, it should be possible for him successfully to withdraw his main force across the Neretva into the wild highlands of eastern Bosnia and Montenegro which lay to the east of it, and there once again to take the offensive. Meanwhile, with the object of disrupting the enemy's communications and tying down as many of his troops as possible, he gave orders for all other Partisan units throughout the rest of Jugoslavia to launch immediate attacks on enemy garrisons and lines of communication everywhere.

Once again, Tito's answer to an all-out attack by enemy forces superior to his own in both numbers and equipment was to shift the bulk of his forces as rapidly as possible to another part of the country and there to resume the initiative. "We must," he wrote,

> avoid fixed fronts. We must not let the enemy force us by clever tactics onto the defensive. On the contrary, the spirit of our troops must be offensive, not only in attack, but in defense as well. During an enemy offensive the offensive spirit must find expression in vigorous and audacious guerrilla tactics, in operations behind the enemy's lines, in the destruction of his communications, in attacks on his supply centers, and on bases which are temporarily weakened. We must be no more afraid

of being surrounded now than when we had fewer troops. We must make up for the loss of one area by the conquest of a larger and more important area.[5]

This time his task was complicated by having to take with him some three thousand Partisan sick and wounded who, if abandoned, would have met with an unpleasant death at the hands of the enemy. These were divided into those who could walk, those who could ride and those who had to be carried. They were then organized as a military formation. Each group had its officers and noncommissioned officers, and all who were strong enough carried arms. Besides the wounded, the Partisans were accompanied by many thousands of civilian refugees flying in terror before the advancing enemy.

For the sick, the wounded and the refugees the withdrawal was a severe ordeal. Food was short and there were very few horses. Typhus was raging. The weather was bitterly cold and the country lay under thick snow. Clear, bright weather was even less welcome than blizzards for it brought swarms of German and Italian aircraft, bombing and machine-gunning. The enemy's ground forces, too, harassed them continually from all sides and had constantly to be fought off.

Ten days after the opening of the Fourth Offensive, on January 31, 1943, Tito, perhaps more moved by what he saw around him than, as an orthodox Communist, he should have been, and resentful at the lack of recognition he had received, dispatched yet another telegram to Moscow. "I must once again ask you," he wrote,

if it is really quite impossible to send us some sort of help. Hundreds of thousands of refugees are threatened with death from starvation. Is it really impossible, after twenty months of heroic, almost superhuman fighting, to find some way of helping us? For twenty months we have been fighting without the least material assistance from any quarter. I assure you that these splendid, heroic people from Bosnia, the Lika, the Kordun and Dalmatia fully deserve all the help you can give them. Typhus has now begun to rage here, yet we are without drugs; people are dying like flies from starvation, yet they do not complain. These starving people give our men their last crust, while they themselves die like flies. They give their last sock, shirt, or boot, and themselves, in midwinter, go barefoot. Do your utmost to help us.

There was no answer for ten days. Then on February 11 came the following reply:

> You must not for an instant doubt that, if there were the least possibility of giving you any material help in your wonderful, heroic struggle, we should long ago have done so. The Soviet people, together with its leaders, is in its entirety on your side, full of enthusiasm and profound fraternal sympathy for the National Liberation Army. Josif Vissarionovich [Stalin] and myself have [many times?] discussed ways and means of helping you. Unfortunately, hitherto we have not been able to find a satisfactory solution to the problems on account of insurmountable technical difficulties [groups undecipherable] possibility of affording you assistance. The moment it is possible, we shall do all we can. Can you doubt this? Try to understand the present situation and explain it all to your comrades at arms. Do not lose heart, but gather all your forces to bear the present exceptionally hard trials. You are doing a great thing, which our Soviet land and all freedom-loving peoples will never forget. With fraternal greetings to yourself and best wishes to all the comrades in their heroic fight against the accursed enemy.
>
> GRANDPAPA[6]

As far as the tone went, it left nothing to be desired. But what was needed was material help.

Moscow's apparent failure to grasp this simple fact was at times more than Tito could bear. Particularly provoking was a message which arrived at the height of the Fourth Offensive, complaining because the Partisans had agreed to a limited exchange of prisoners with the Germans. To this he reacted sharply. "If you cannot understand what a hard time we are having," he signaled, "and if you cannot help us, then at least do not hinder us."*[7]

---

* One of the prisoners exchanged on this occasion was Tito's wife, Herta. The negotiations with the Germans were conducted by Vladko Velebit, who paid a visit to Zagreb for the purpose. While he was there, the Germans seem to have mentioned to him the possibility of some kind of "truce" and of "parallel action" by their respective forces in the event of a British landing in Jugoslavia. Clissold, *Whirlwind*, p. 151, Hagen, *Die Geheime Front*, p. 264, and Leverkuehn, *German Military Intelligence*, p. 152, give rather different accounts of this episode, but all are agreed that no truce was arranged.

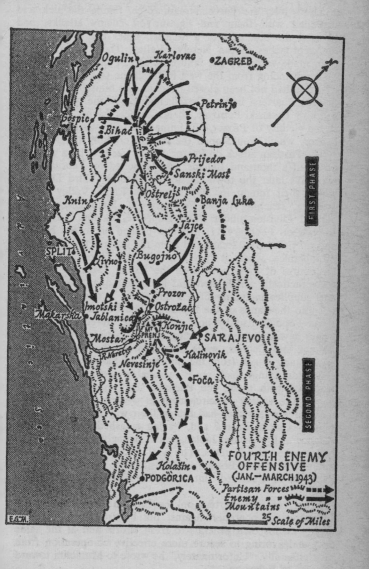

FOURTH ENEMY
OFFENSIVE
(JAN.—MARCH 1943)

Partisan Forces
Enemy "   "
Mountains

0   25 Scale of Miles

Meanwhile, the Partisan main force, taking the sick and wounded with them and fighting off enemy attacks, had covered the best part of a hundred miles and had reached the approaches to the Neretva Valley. Their breakout had been made easier by the failure of one of the Italian formations advancing from the west to fulfill the task allotted to it. The ring had not been closed in time. Tito himself had moved his headquarters, first to Ostrelj, high up in the wooded hills south of Bosanski Petrovac, thence to near Livno, and finally to the vicinity of Prozor. His immediate task was now to take Prozor, which would open the way to crossing the Neretva.

The Partisan attack on Prozor, which was held by a garrison of about a thousand Italians, was launched on February 15; two days later the town fell to the Partisan Third Division, which then fought its way along the Rama Valley to the Neretva, reaching it on February 20. Simultaneously the Second Division under Peko Dapčević, having duly taken Imotski on February 11, had also pushed on to the Neretva and on February 22 captured from the Italians the little town of Jablanica, where it linked up with the Third Division. In the course of these operations the Italian "Murge" Division was practically annihilated and important quantities of arms and supplies including fifteen tanks and a number of guns fell into the hands of the Partisans. The First Division under Koča Popović had by now reached the Neretva at Konjic, where it was besieging a strong, mixed garrison of Germans, Italians and Cetniks, while also securing the Partisan flank against any attack from the direction of Sarajevo.

So far things had gone reasonably well. Taking their wounded with them, the Partisans had managed to break out of the enemy's encirclement in western Bosnia. In less than three weeks they had fought their way across the snowy hills of central Bosnia and, having smashed the Italian resistance at Prozor and Jablanica and strongly invested Konjic, had reached the Neretva. The way across the river into the mountains of east Bosnia and Montenegro now lay open to them. Or so it seemed. But in fact their troubles had scarcely begun.

From his headquarters on the Eastern front, Hitler was following the operation against the Partisans step by step, urging on his own generals to fresh efforts and at the same time endeavoring to secure more effective co-operation from his Italian ally. "Unfortunately," he wrote to Mussolini toward the end of February,

Italian 5 Corps failed to advance rapidly enough to close the ring round the Grmec Mountains and so prevent strong Communist formations from escaping to the south and southwest. We have nevertheless succeeded in destroying a large number of Tito's troops and in inflicting on his forces considerable losses in men and material. It is both impressive and alarming to observe what progress the insurgents have made with their organization. We are only just in time to suppress the rebellion if we are not to run the risk of being stabbed in the back in case of an Anglo-Saxon landing in the Balkans. I consider it equally desirable that Italian troops should take part in the second phase of the operation. . . . I must ask you, *Duce,* to issue the necessary instructions to ensure prompt and friendly co-operation between our commanders on the spot and the full employment of all available resources. I have instructed General Löhr to maintain close liaison with the Italian commanders concerned in planning and carrying out operations.[8]

Meanwhile, alarmed by the fate which had overtaken the "Murge" Division and fearful for the future, General Robotti, who had succeeded General Roatta in command of the Italian Second Army, was now appealing urgently to General von Löhr to "undertake immediate measures to relieve the pressure on our forces."[9] To this appeal General von Löhr responded without delay: 717 German Division was at once sent southward to attack the Partisans at Prozor, while 718 Division, hitherto held in reserve at Sarajevo, was rushed to the relief of the beleaguered garrison still holding out at Konjic. Soon the Partisans, whose movements were grievously hampered by their thousands of wounded, found themselves seriously threatened from the north and east, while the Italians in Dalmatia kept up the pressure on them from the west. Finally, to the south and southeast, across the Neretva, they were confronted by their former allies, the Cetniks.

From Montenegro and Bosnia, from Serbia and the Sandzak the most prominent Cetnik leaders were massing their forces to administer what they hoped would be the *coup de grâce* to the Partisans. Colonel Stanišić was in command of three thousand Montenegrin Cetniks who had been sent by Italian transport. Colonel Djurišić commanded 2,500 men and Major Bačević landed with a force of three thousand men on the

coast at Makarska and fell upon the Partisan flank. Mihajlović
himself had moved to Foča, whence he was personally directing operations, with Major Ostojič as his Chief of Staff.*
From Foča he urged on his followers in Montenegro to renewed efforts against the Partisans. "Now that they have
been driven out of their Soviet Republic in western Bosnia,"
he wrote to Colonel Stanišić on February 17, "they have
come to rally the proletariat of Hercegovina, Montenegro and
Serbia and to set up another one here. . . . Now is our chance
to beat the Communists to their knees. If we do not take it,
it may be the worse for us."[10]

The Cetnik forces beyond the Neretva, totaling about twelve
thousand men, were arrayed in three main columns, the right
wing under Major Keserović, the left under Colonel Stanišić,
and the center under Major Pantic. Strongly supported by
Italian mortars and mountain artillery, their task was to make
a sudden attack on Jablanica with the object of cutting off
the Partisans in Prozor.

They did not, however, succeed in this assignment, much
to the fury of Major Ostojić. "Your columns," he wrote to
Colonel Stanišić on February 28, "did practically nothing. It
is perfectly disgraceful that all your senior officers with all
their staff college training should have to be taught what to do.
I have reported all this to the Minister and, if your columns
do not today reach the objectives allotted to them, I shall be
obliged to remove all your commanders from their posts and
have them court-martialled for incompetence and disobedience,
on instructions from the Minister."†[11]

But if the Montenegrin Cetniks were a disappointment to
Major Ostojić, they had nonetheless succeeded in firmly establishing themselves on the rocky slopes of Mount Prenj
beyond the Neretva, thereby further aggravating the position

* Major Ostojic was one of the officers who had landed from a
British submarine with Captain Hudson in 1941. He has been described as "an impressive man with a black mustache." On Mihajlovic's recommendation Major Djurišic was fortunate enough to
be awarded the Karadjordje Star by the Royal Jugoslav Government in London. According to some accounts he later received
the Iron Cross from the Germans. He was certainly warmly com-
mended by Radio Belgrade for his services to the Axis cause
(broadcast of July 13, 1944).

† General Mihajlovic held the post of Minister of War in the
Royal Jugoslav Government in London.

of the Partisans who were now confronted with the hazardous task of transporting themselves and their wounded across the Neretva in the face of fierce opposition from a strongly entrenched enemy on the other side. Their intervention had moreover given the Germans time to bring up the strong reinforcements who were now advancing from the north on Prozor and pressing forward to the relief of Konjic, where, despite all Partisan attempts to capture it, the mixed garrison of Germans, Italians and Cetniks was still holding out, threatening their flank and blocking what seemed their only practicable line of advance.

A few miles north of the little town of Jablanica the valley of the Neretva turns sharply eastward, skirting round the craggy heights of Mount Prenj in the direction of Konjic. At this same point its stream is joined from the west by a tributary, the Rama, a clear mountain river flowing rapidly along a narrow valley between high wooded hills. At the far end of this valley, some fifteen miles from the point where it joins the Neretva, lies Prozor. Shortly after the capture of Prozor by the Partisans Tito had established his headquarters in a rough gray stone shack by a little water mill in the Rama Valley midway between Prozor and the Neretva. In front there was a patch of Indian corn. A vine trailed untidily over the rough wooden porch. All round, the dark, scrub-covered hills sloped steeply down.

It was here that on the last day of February Tito held a council of war, attended by Djilas, Marko Ranković, Black Žujović and a few others. He first explained to his companions just how serious the situation was: the Germans advancing in strength from the north were now very close indeed and the Partisans were hemmed in from all sides. Then he unfolded his plan. First the Partisans must destroy all the bridges across the Neretva and withdraw such units as had already crossed from the left bank, in order to make the enemy think they had changed their plan and were going to try to break out somewhere else. Next they must attack the Germans to the north of Prozor in order to relieve pressure on the wounded assembled there. And then, rapidly changing direction, they must swing back into the Neretva Valley and, improvising a rough bridge, force the river and break through the Cetnik forces on the far side, taking the wounded with them.[12]

As a first step, the bridges were demolished and the First and Second Partisan Divisions withdrawn from the Neretva and dispatched to counterattack German 717 Division advancing on Prozor from the north. After some heavy fighting, in which the Partisans employed with good effect the tanks and guns they had captured from the Italians a few days before, the advancing Germans were first checked and then forced to fall back on Bugojno. Meanwhile with his Third Division Tito held the advance of German 718 Division from Sarajevo, and so secured his flank.

Having thus gained a brief respite and temporarily thrown the enemy off their guard by giving them the impression that he was seeking to break out to the north, Tito directed his attention to forcing the Neretva. It was a formidable undertaking. The Partisan main force and the wounded, assembled in the narrow Rama Valley, were now completely surrounded by overwhelmingly strong forces of the enemy. The Germans attacking from the north had been further reinforced and it could only be a question of time before they broke through. To the west were the Italians. To the south, beyond the Neretva, rose the mountain barrier of Mount Prenj six thousand feet high and strongly held by the Cetniks, now regrouping for an attack. To the east the Partisan line of advance along the Neretva Valley was effectively blocked by the enemy garrison at Konjic, now further reinforced by German 718 Division from Sarajevo.

In such a situation delay would have been fatal. Leaving the First Division as a rear guard to hold up the German advance on Prozor for as long as they could, Tito ordered the Second Division to force the Neretva at Jablanica, storm the Cetnik positions on Mount Prenj and advance across the mountains in the direction of Kalinovik. They were to be followed by the main force and the wounded. Meanwhile the Third Division was to cross the river at Ostrožac and secure the Partisan left flank against attacks from the enemy forces in Konjic, while the Seventh Division secured the right flank against the Italians attacking from Dalmatia.

These decisions were taken on March 5. By the night of March 6 the Second Division had reached Jablanica. At Jablanica the Neretva is a deep turbulent mountain river about seventy yards wide, flowing strongly between high, steeply sloping banks. In early spring the melting snows make of it the wildest torrent in Jugoslavia. Immediately beyond it, to the south, rise a range of medium-sized, scrub-covered hills. Beyond them again the jagged limestone crags of Mount Prenj stand massive and forbidding against the skyline.

The point chosen for the crossing was the site of the former railway bridge, now a tangled mass of girders half in and half out of the swirling waters of the Neretva. On the far bank, immediately opposite and commanding the crossing, was a medium-sized concrete blockhouse. This was now in Cetnik hands. So were the scrub-covered hills beyond. And so was Mount Prenj.

The first step was to establish a bridgehead on the far bank. Under cover of darkness a small detachment of Partisans, armed with hand grenades and submachine guns accordingly picked their way across the wreckage of the old railway bridge, and, creeping up to the blockhouse, managed to throw two hand grenades into it before the occupants had realized what was happening. They were followed by stronger forces and a bridgehead established. A rough plank bridge, threaded in and out of what remained of the old railway bridge, was now thrown across the Neretva and the crossing began.

It was to last for a week. On the first day—March 7—the sun shone brightly and the sky was soon full of aircraft, bombing and machine-gunning. The weather remained fine. From now onward the Partisans were under constant air attack. Flight after flight of Stukas would come swarming in over the surrounding hills and, peeling off in turn, swoop down one after the other on their target. Soon Jablanica was a heap of ruins, its streets littered with dead horses and wreckage and human corpses. It took a good Communist to be able to say cheerfully, as one of them did: "Every bomb that falls on us is one less on Russia"—a Russia, incidentally, that up to now had not stirred a finger to help them.[13]

Somehow, twenty thousand men and, by now, four thousand wounded, many of whom could not walk, had to be got across the one narrow ramshackle bridge and up the mountainside beyond. All the Partisans' heavy equipment, the trucks, the artillery and the light tanks they had captured from the Italians, were jettisoned and sent crashing down onto the rocks below. Every now and then a pony would lose its footing on the slippery planks and go hurling after them with its load. Some of the wounded crawled across on all fours; others were carried over by terrified Italian prisoners, all shouting and calling out together. From the hills round about came the thud of enemy artillery and mortars and the rattle of machine-gun fire.

At first the evacuation of the wounded, now concentrated in a disused tunnel near the bridge, was only attempted at night, but as the danger increased, it became necessary to work by daylight as well. Tito and his staff crossed on March 10 and took up their position on the mountainside opposite. On both sides of the river the Partisans were fighting desperately to keep back the enemy. Finally, at dawn on March 14, the last of the wounded were taken across and on the fifteenth they were followed by the last remaining Partisan troops. After more than a month of bitter fighting, the crossing of the Neretva had been accomplished, though with heavy losses.

A few days later the Partisans, having successfully fought off the Cetniks and, despite continued enemy shelling and bombing, somehow transported the wounded over the rocky heights of Mount Prenj, passed once again to the offensive. The Neretva had been crossed and the way to Montenegro lay open. "And now," in Tito's own words, "began the hunting down of the Cetniks."[14] Breaking through the Cetnik lines, Tito advanced eastward, driving what was left of Mihajlović's force of twelve thousand men in confusion before him into Montenegro and the Sandžak. One Partisan column struck southward to Nevesinje, while another, having by-passed Konjic, pushed on and cocupied Kalinovik, until recently the advanced headquarters of Mihajlović's elegant Chief of Staff, Major Ostojić.

The latter, from a safe distance, was once again bombarding Colonel Stanšić with peremptory appeals to stop the rot. "Investigate all cases of desertion," he wrote in his brisk military style, "and send the men back to their positions. Set up a court-martial and execute the ringleaders and all suspects on the spot. Tell the deserters that a hundred have already been caught and executed and that the same fate awaits the others. Their morale must be restored at all costs."[15]

All in all, things were in a bad way in the Cetnik camp. Mihajlović had little or no control over his commanders and these were mostly at loggerheads with each other. Discipline was weak. Drunkenness was rife. "He was going downstream on a tide of drink," a British liaison officer wrote of one Cetnik commander, "and there was an undercurrent of violence and treachery in his entourage that I did not like."[16] As for the rank and file, their heart was not in it. Many of them had joined with the idea that they were going to fight against the Germans and Italians. They had little liking for collaboration with the enemy or for this bloodthirsty war against the Partisans in which they usually came off worse. "For a soldier like me," one Cetnik said to the same British officer, "fighting should be something you enjoy. I enjoy fighting

against the Germans. I have also fought against the Partisans.
But it has always made me sad, because they are my
brothers."[17] As time went on, more and more Cetniks sought
a suitable opportunity to change sides.

Nor was it even certain that the equivocal but advantageous
relationship which had gradually grown up between the
Cetniks on the one hand and the Germans and Italians on the
other would continue indefinitely. The Italians, for their part,
liked the idea of playing off one resistance movement against
another and the German commanders in the field had also
found the arrangement a convenient one.[18] But Hitler, taking
a longer view, thought otherwise. If there were to be an Allied
landing in the Balkans, might not the Cetniks appear in a
different role? Might they not bite the hand that fed them?
Might they not use the arms and equipment which they had
been given to stab their benefactors in the back? Might they
not even make common cause with the Partisans?

The *Führer* had never liked Slavs. In a succession of letters
and telegrams he now endeavored to impress on the *Duce*
the dangers of trying to be too clever and warned him against
the "innate cunning and deceitfulness of these races" and
their "unbounded hatred not only for Germany but, perhaps
to an even greater extent, for Italy." "Mihajlović's aim," he
wrote,

> is to get arms and supplies for his own purposes by pre-
> tending to help your troops to pacify the country. In this
> way his formations are getting everything they need so
> as to be able to start fighting us when the time comes:
> arms, ammunition, supplies and strategical positions.
> *Duce*, I am bound in all conscience to warn you seriously
> against continuing such a policy. I can assure you that
> at the highest level in Mihajlovic's movement large-scale
> preparations are being made to destroy or disarm your
> forces in Herzegovina and Montenegro. I consider it
> desirable, in the interest of our common aims that your
> Second Army should regard Mihajlovic and his move-
> ment as bitter enemies of the Axis powers and I request
> you, *Duce*, to issue orders in this sense to your military
> commanders. . . . In my view, *Duce*, these are problems
> which cannot be solved by political astuteness but only
> by the ruthless employment of force.[19]

But Mussolini, while declaring his agreement in principle

and denying that he entertained any illusions in regard to General Mihajlović, was determined to go on using the Cetniks for as long as possible. They were, he explained to the *Führer*, of particular value for guerrilla operations and, after being "armed by the local Italian commanders," had "fought against the Partisans with great energy."[20] Cavallero and Roatta agreed with him. Politically, too, the Italians were glad of the Cetniks to counterbalance the Ustase, who bitterly resented Italian encroachments in Dalmatia and with whom their relations had steadily deteriorated from the very beginning. In the words of General Roatta the Cetniks were "their only asset in that sector."[21] In the end it was decided during a visit of Ribbentrop's to Rome that use should be made of the Cetniks for the time being, but that they should be disarmed "once the Partisan danger has been eliminated." Their disarmament, wrote Mussolini, would present no difficulty.[22]

Meanwhile the performance put up by the Cetniks during the Fourth Offensive had convinced Hitler that they were not only unreliable but useless. In the spring, despite Italian protests, Colonel Djurišić and some of his men were actually disarmed at Kolašin and sent to internment in Germany.[23] But they were not to stay there long. The events of the next few months in Jugoslavia and elsewhere were to make the Germans only too glad of such help as they could get from the Cetniks, while the Cetniks, for their part, were by now too heavily committed to their struggle with the Partisans and had advanced too far along the path of collaboration with the enemy for it to be possible for them to turn back.

During the past few weeks the Partisans had not only extricated themselves from a very dangerous military situation; they had also dealt a serious blow to their principal political rivals. But they still had a long way to go. As Tito and his staff sat talking at a house in the little village of Drača near Kalinovik one day toward the end of the Fourth Enemy Offensive, Djilas summed up the position by saying: "This is merely the end of Act II. Act V will bring the climax and dénouement," and Tito agreed. Meanwhile, the curtain was already going up on Act III.[24]

While Tito was following up his advantage against the Cetniks in Montenegro, the Germans were preparing to wipe him out. The war in Africa was almost over. It could now only be a matter of months before the Allies invaded Southern Europe. On the Eastern front, too, the tide had turned and was already rolling westward. For Hitler, it was of the utmost importance that at this critical stage of the war there should be no weak spots in the defenses of *Festung Europa*, no centers from which trouble could spread, no ready-made bridgeheads for the enemy. Last time Tito had barely escaped destruction. This time he must be annihilated. And this time the German High Command were determined to leave nothing to chance.

In one way Tito himself had inadvertently simplified their task. Having successfully crossed the Drina, his intention was now to push on southeastward through Montenegro into the Kosovo area on the borders of Serbia and Macedonia, spreading the revolt and at the same time linking up with the Albanian Partisans under Enver Hodja with whom he had recently established contact through Tempo Vukmanović. Meanwhile, his main striking force, consisting of his First, Second, Third, and Seventh Divisions, was temporarily concentrated in the same wild mountainous region from which, just a year before, he had begun his great march to the northwest. Situated partly in Montenegro and partly in eastern Bosnia, this area lies within a rough quadrilateral bounded by the main roads linking Kalinovik, Foča and Plevlja on the north, Plevlja, Savnik and Nikšić on the east, Nikšić and Bileća on the south and Bileća, Gacko and Kalinovik on the west. It is traversed by a series of high mountain ranges, divided one from the other by deep-cut valleys along which flow the four or five mountain torrents which together form the headwaters of the River Drina. Farthest to the east, between the Piva and Tara valleys, towers Durmitor, the highest range of all. South of Durmitor, across the River Kormarnica, rises the Njegoš Range. Northwest of Durmitor, between the valleys of the Piva and the Sutjeska lies the Maglić Massif, made up of Mounts Vućevo, Volujak and Maglić itself. Beyond the Sutjeska is Zelengora—"the Green Mountain." And beyond Zelengora lies the valley of the Bistrica along which runs the main road from Foča to Kalinovik.

There can be few wilder or more inhospitable regions upon earth than this great tangle of mountains, forests and rock-strewn uplands, broken at random by sheer precipices of limestone falling sharply away to the beds of swirling torrents three or four thousand feet below. There are no roads. Picking his way along narrow goat tracks, up and down mountainsides, across great wastes of crag and rock, along the stony beds of rivers and through vast forests where the trunks of huge trees lie rotting where they have fallen, the traveler may walk all day without coming on a single human habitation or indeed on any sign of life. There is little in this barren land to feed man or beast. On the high ground even water is hard to find: wells and springs are few and far between and for the most part there is nothing to quench the thirst save melted snow. Here and there a rare patch of more fertile soil supports a thin crop of maize or corn or provides meager pasture for a few goats or sheep. Living all the year round on bread, cheese and sour milk, the peasants in their hamlets and scattered homesteads grow barely enough to keep themselves alive. They weave their own homespuns and make their own rough shoes. Once their own needs are supplied, nothing is left over. Nor are there any markets in which they could sell their goods. For most of them it is a long day's march on foot across the mountains to the nearest small town where such luxuries as matches or salt can be found. In winter and far into the spring the snows cut them off entirely from the outside world. In the summer the sun beats down mercilessly on the arid limestone rocks.

In past centuries their native mountains had enabled the Montenegrins to hold out indefinitely against the Turkish invaders. In 1942 the Partisans themselves had been glad enough to fall back into them when hard pressed by the enemy. Now they were to see them in a different and less favorable light. Their main force was concentrated in an area which, they were to find to their cost, was relatively easy for the enemy to encircle and from which it was very much less easy for them to scrape—an area, too, in which food was very hard to come by. Even the wild and mountainous nature of the country was of less help to them than might have been assumed. "It might be thought," Tito wrote later,

that difficulties of terrain and natural obstacles are always of great importance for our army in defensive battles. But this is not so. In Montenegro, difficulties of terrain and natural obstacles proved a disadvantage to us, and an advantage to the enemy. They restricteed our maneuvering power and very nearly prevent our main striking force in Montenegro from breaking out of the enemy's encirclement. Great technical superiority, long-range guns, numerous aircraft and special units trained in mountain warfare gave the enemy, for his part, a definite advantage over us by helping him to surmount these difficulties. . . .

There are [he continued, pursuing the same idea] other factors to be borne in mind, which for ordinary armies, who possess all that is needed for waging war, are of second- or even third-rate importance, but for our army are vital. For example, the economic position of the population in the area of operations is of first-rate importance to our troops. Unlike the enemy we have no stores of food or food-producing factories in our rear. That is a factor we are often obliged to take into account in making our strategic plans. Secondly, we have no factories for producing arms or ammunition. That is another factor we have to take into account. Thus our decision whether or not to defend any given area or position may depend on how much ammunition we have there; or we may be forced to attack a town or village not because of its strategic importance, but simply in order to capture arms and ammunition. Thirdly, the political factor is of the first importance to us. We are a people's army and we cannot afford to ignore the attitude toward us of the people in the area in which we are fighting. We do not depend simply on our armed strength. We depend first on the people and only secondly on our armed strength.[25]

By the middle of May the Germans had completed their preparations. Their Fourth Offensive had been called "Weiss" —"Operation White"; they called their Fifth "Schwarz"— "Operation Black." To the German forces engaged in the Fourth Offensive they had now added the First Alpine Division, the specially trained "Brandenburg" S.S. Regiment and other individual units bringing their numbers up to over fifty thousand. Three Italian Divisions and the elements of others amounted to forty thousand more, while a number of Croat quisling formations and a regiment of Bulgarians made the total number of enemy troops engaged more than one hundred thousand, against less than twenty thousand Partisans. These enemy forces were based on half a dozen of the larger towns surrounding the area in which Tito's main striking force was concentrated. The Germans had rightly deduced from the disposition of his troops that it was Tito's intention to strike southeastward. Accordingly the three bases to the east and south of the Partisan positions—Plevlja, Kolašin and Nikšić—were held in great strength, while those to the north and west—Foča, Kalinovik and Gacko—were held more lightly.

During the first half of the month the enemy had made a number of moves which struck the Partisans as suspicious. News had reached them of the steps which the Germans were taking to strengthen their garrisons, particularly those at Foča and Kolašin. An attack which they themselves launched southeastward in the direction of Kolašin was thrown back and at the same time other enemy forces started closing in on them from the north and west. By May 20 it was apparent to them that a Fifth Offensive had begun and that their own position was rapidly becoming extremely dangerous.

This time the enemy employed new methods. His aim, as before, was to encircle and pin down the Partisans; to deny them the freedom of movement and the advantage of surprise which are a guerrilla's most valuable assets; to force them to present a target against which he could strike repeated and deadly blows. But this time the encirclement of the Partisan positions was better prepared and carried out with much greater thoroughness and ingenuity than in their earlier offensives. Nor was this all. The Germans now turned some of the Partisans' own weapons against them, in particular, mobility and surprise. They no longer advanced solely along the main lines of communication, but, while making the best possible use of these to shift their mechanized and armored forces rapidly from point to point, they at the same time sent specially trained mobile shock units ahead of their main force by devious ways in order to take their opponents unawares—a method that proved particularly effective against concentrations of Partisan wounded and sick. They were also quicker to seize any point of vantage and dig themselves in than hitherto; better, too, at preparing ambushes. Forward units were supplied by air and regularly reinforced with fresh troops so that constant pressure could be exerted on the Partisans. The latter were also kept under constant attack from the air, a weapon against which they were, practically speaking, defenseless. Finally, realizing the dependence of the Partisans on the civil population, the Germans forcibly mobilized every civilian they could lay hands on in the whole area. Their instructions were clear enough: "Every Partisan

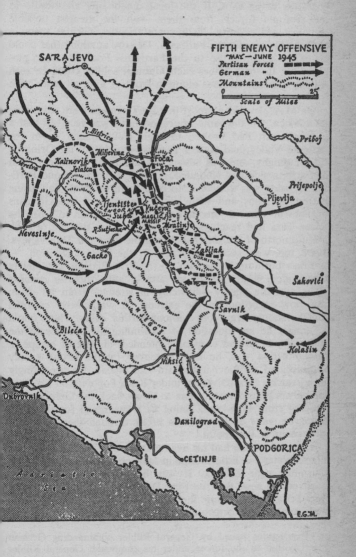

FIFTH ENEMY OFFENSIVE
MAY—JUNE 1943
Partisan Forces
German
Mountains
0   25
Scale of Miles

SARAJEVO

Priboj

R. Bistrica

Mrtvica
Kalinovik
Jelašca
Miljevina
Foča
R. Drina

Prijepolje
Pljevlja

Ljentište
ZAGOR'A
Suha
Vučevo
MAGLIČ
MASSIF
Mratinje

Nevesinje
R. Sutjeska

R. Tara
Žabljak
DURMITOR
Sakovići

Gacko

N J E G O Š

Savnik

Kolašin

Bileća

Nikšić

Dubrovnik

Danilograd

PODGORICA

CETINJE
B

Adriatic
Sea

E.G.M.

found is to be shot. If the local inhabitants are hostile to the German forces, treat them with the greatest possible brutality and severity. If they are friendly, harness them in the struggle against the Partisans. Destroy anything that could be of the slightest use to the Partisans. Foul all water supplies."*[26] In some places each German soldier could be seen driving a dozen civilians along in front of him, all laden with food or munitions.

On May 21 came a report that the Germans were advancing from Foča. On the same afternoon news was received that a German unit had broken through from Gacko down the Sutjeska Valley, had made a surprise crossing of the Drina by rubber dinghy, and was advancing rapidly on a concentration of Partisan sick and wounded. A brigade of the Second Partisan Division was thrown in to hold them up. Next day, using mountains guns and with heavy air support, the Germans brought up more troops in a determined attempt to cross the River Tara and reach the Piva Plateau, the triangle of high ground north of Durmitor, between the Piva and Tara valleys. They, too, were successfully held by the Second Division.

Tito's position, bottled up on the Piva Plateau, completely surrounded, under heavy air attack, with supplies running short and the enemy advancing in strength from all sides, was now hazardous in the extreme. It was clearly essential that he should break out without further delay. There could no longer be any question of continuing his advance to the southeast, as he had originally intended; his line of escape in that direction was, he knew, blocked by the strong enemy forces based on Plevlja, Kolašin and Nikšić. He accordingly now sent his First Division, under Koča Popović, on a forced march northward with orders to throw back the Germans advancing from Foča and, acting as a spearhead for the main force, to make every effort to break through the enemy encirclement at that point.

Tito at this time had his headquarters by Crno Jezero—"the Black Water," a little mountain lake on the slopes of Mount Durmitor near Zabljak. It was here that on May 26 he received the news that the First Division had fought their way into Foča, but, finding themselves hopelessly outnumbered, had been forced to withdraw. An intercepted enemy message

* Instructions issued by General Rübler commanding German 118 Division to the forces under his command. General Rübler was himself captured by the Partisans two years later in May, 1945.

showed that the Germans were now holding Foča in great
strength. That line of escape was also blocked.

There was, however, another possibility. A week earlier
Tito had sent a small force westward across the Piva to Mount
Vučevo with the object of holding a bridgehead there in case
of need. He now decided to reinforce the Partisans holding
this position and to follow them up with stronger forces. At
the same time he dispatched a brigade across the Maglić
Massif to the valley of the Sutjeska to seize and hold a point
commanding the river crossing at Suha. If he could secure
these two points, he might, with luck, be able to withdraw
his main force across the Maglić Massif, fight his way across
the Sutjeska, and then continue northward over Zelengora
toward the Foča-Kalinovik highway.

Accordingly, while the Third Partisan Division held the
enemy forces advancing from the south in a series of fierce
battles on the River Kormarnica, Tito's main force, with the
First and Second Divisions leading, began their advance westward and northward. At the same time an urgent message
was sent to Arso Jovanović, now with the Fifth Bosnian Division in central Bosnia, asking him to create a diversion by
attacking the Germans in the rear. Similar instructions were
sent to all other Partisan commanders outside the immediate
area of operations.

But by now the enemy had guessed Tito's intentions. Already German mountain troops, moving in from the west,
had managed to establish themselves on the Maglić Massif
beyond the Piva, while from the northeast another enemy
force was attacking the existing Partisan positions on Vučevo.
In these circumstances the crossing of the Piva and of the
Maglić Massif must needs be a hazardous undertaking. It
could only succeed so long as the Partisans held the village
of Mratinje. On May 30, however, two Partisan battalions
managed to reach the ridge above Mratinje a bare fifteen
minutes in advance of the Germans attacking from the other
side and to throw them back as they climbed up to it. At
the same time the Partisans on Vučevo not only beat off the
German attacks on their position but succeeded in capturing
a large quantity of food and ammunition, of which by now
they were extremely short. In this manner Tito's line of advance was secured, and the main force, picking their way
three thousand feet down the almost vertical eastern side of
the valley, crossed the Piva by a frail rope bridge which
despite repeated enemy air attacks had somehow remained

intact and, passing through the little hamlet of Mratinje, started on their climb another three thousand feet up the sheer rock face of the equally precipitous western side.

Tito himself, meanwhile, had assembled his staff in a little cave in the mountainside near Mratinje for the purpose of considering his next moves in detail. Vučevo, he knew, was still in Partisan hands. Farther west his troops had successfully established a bridgehead at Suha in the Sutjeska Valley and had also seized the heights commanding the crossing on the far side of the river. He now decided that the First and Second Divisions should advance in strength across the Maglić and make an all-out attempt to break through the enemy's encirclement on the Sutjeska. He himself would go with them. Meanwhile, the Third and Seventh Divisions under the command of Djilas would act as rear guard and escort the wounded.

These decisions were taken on June 3. Sensing what was afoot, the Germans were already strongly reinforcing their positions on the Sutjeska and fierce fighting was soon in progress in the valley itself. From the southwestern end of the valley the Seventh S.S. Division was closing in on the Partisans defending Suha, while German 369 Division, advancing along the Drina from Foča, forced their way up the valley from the northeast. Meanwhile German 118 Division, based on Kalinovik, were advancing southward from the Kalinovik-Foča highway across Zelengora for the purpose of meeting and throwing back any Partisan units that succeeded in crossing the river.

It had been Tito's original intention to cross the Sutjeska on a wide front. But by June 5 the whole of the far bank of the river was in German hands except three miles between Tjentište and Suha. At this point the Sutjeska runs through a narrow canyon between Zelengora to the north and the Maglić Massif to the south. On both sides almost perpendicular limestone cliffs rise to a height of three or four thousand feet. For part of their height, these are covered by a thick forest of beech and oak. Above, bare crags and pinnacles of rock thrust up toward the sky. Far below, the swirling waters of the Sutjeska surge tumultuously along the narrow, boulder-strewn riverbed. At either end, at Tjentište to the east and Suha to the west, the canyon opens out into a green smiling valley, where at the foot of the mountains a few farmsteads cluster among the meadows and orchards beside the river. The Germans had already reached Tjentište, and a battle was raging at the mouth of the defile. But three miles upstream at Suha, at the far end of the canyon, the bridge and an old Austrian guardhouse, though already under heavy fire from the enemy's guns, were still held by the Partisans. On the far side of the river, a narrow path, cut out of the sheer rock, led three thousand feet up the mountain side to a small plateau, also in Partisan hands. This was now the only remaining place where the crossing could be made.

On June 6 Tito, having reached Suha, gave orders for all heavy weapons, including all artillery and even heavy machine guns, to be buried and for the crossing to begin. It was a wrench to leave behind weapons which had been so hardly won, but mobility was all-important. All surplus pack horses were now killed and eaten. On the night of June 7, while the forward troops held the Suha bridgehead against overwhelming odds, part of the wounded were successfully transported across the river. Then Tito and his headquarters staff crossed, leaving the Third and Seventh Divisions to bring up the rear with the remainder of the wounded. They did not march far that night after crossing the river, but camped on the other side in a thick wood some way up the mountain, waking a few hours later to the sound of the German guns putting down a barrage along the whole length of the valley.

Having crossed the river, Tito and his staff, with the First and Second Divisions, the First Divison leading, now set out across the heights of Zelengora. Even though another obstacle had been surmounted, their strategical position was as desperate as ever. They were still completely surrounded by the enemy, and the Germans, taking full advantage of their own control of the roads, were now rapidly regrouping ahead of them so as at all costs to prevent them from breaking out across the Foča-Kalinovik road. The forces defending this little winding hill road were strongly reinforced and a number of strategical points along the Partisan line of advance were seized and hurriedly fortified. Meanwhile, from the rear and from both flanks enemy units were fast closing in for the kill. With their long-range guns they kept the Partisans constantly under fire. "Now that the ring is completely closed," ran a captured German operation order, "the Communists will try to break through. You will ensure that no able-bodied man leaves the ring alive."[27]

"Never," said Marko Ranković, during one of their rare halts, with shells bursting all around them, "have we been in a worse situation. We are bound to suffer heavy losses. For us the most important thing has always been to preserve the cadres which we have built up at such cost during the last two and a half years. And now those cadres are in danger of annihilation." [28]

Nor was it their own fate alone which was causing them concern. The Third and Seventh Divisions and the wounded were in even greater danger. They had not yet caught up. Wireless communications with them had broken down. And now the whole of the Sutjeska Valley was in German hands. A courier had, it is true, managed to reach the Seventh Division and there was some hope that they might join up with the advance guard, but the position of the Third Divison seemed hopeless. "It is a question of two thousand five hundred lives," said Tito, pacing slowly up and down, as he always did when he was worried. "How can we leave them behind? And yet we cannot stay where we are without running the risk of having our whole force wiped out." His companions waited for a word of encouragement, but none came. He felt it was no good raising their hopes. The next day, he said, would be a difficult one and they had better get ready for it. That was all. He, for his part, knew full well the dangers of their present position and how unlikely it was that any of them would come out of it alive.[29]

At six in the evening Tito gave the order to move. Pushing on they came at dusk to the Majevica Brigade. It had lost three-quarters of its men in the recent fighting. Most of those who were left were boys of sixteen or seventeen, worn-out and starving. The bones of every pack pony that was killed were picked clean, and still there was not enough to go round. Meanwhile, the Germans, weary, but well fed and well equipped, were pressing in from every side. High above them on the mountainside they could see the flash of the enemy's guns. Then, with a screech and a roar, shells began landing in the ravine, plowing into their little column, as they picked their way along the stony track above the stream. They were glad when night fell and the shelling stopped.

Next day the weather, which had been wet and cloudy, cleared. The sun came out and at once the sky was full of Stukas and Dorniers, methodically bombing and machine-gunning, day after day, from dawn till dusk. With true German thoroughness the pilots worked backward and forward over every square yard of the hillside. Then, when they had run out of ammunition, they came in low and, scorning Partisan rifle fire, flew past once more, leaning over the side and giving the Hitler salute as they roared overhead.

The Partisans plodded doggedly on, marching all night and some of the day, over rough, precipitous country, keeping alive by eating their skinny pack ponies and the leaves off the beech trees, and fighting as they went. All round them the mountain echoed with the rattle of machine guns and the thud of mortars and every now and then there would come the whistle and crash of a salvo of howitzer shells. Tito marched with his men, his face drawn by the stresses and strains of the last fortnight and his arm in a sling. He had had a narrow escape during the recent air attacks. A bomb had landed a few feet away from him, killing several of his companions and blowing him into the air. His own life was only saved because, as the bomb fell, his dog Lux had thrown himself across his master's head and received the fragments of the bomb and the full force of the blast in his body. "I thought," Tito said afterward, "that I was done for." During one of their brief halts he sent a signal to Moscow describing their position. "We request your help," it ended, "in this supreme trial."[30] But as he wrote it, he knew in his own mind that it was useless to expect help.

Meanwhile, on ahead, the First Proletarian Division, fighting desperately, were seeking to force their way through the German ring. Each time they attacked, the enemy counter-attacked. Each time they broke through, the enemy rushed fresh reinforcements in to the breach. Then, on June 12, just as they were giving up hope, came the news that the First Proletarian Brigade, the oldest Partisan formation of all and the one with the best fighting record, had broken right through to the Kalinovik-Foča road. Other units followed and more bitter fighting ensued, but all enemy attacks were beaten off and within twenty-four hours the whole force was over the road and in the deep forest on the far side.

"The fighting," said General von Löhr afterward, "was exceptionally heavy. All the commanders agreed that their troops were engaged in the most bitter struggle of the war. A ferocious Partisan attack directed against the Second Battalion of 369th Divison effected a breakthrough on this front near Jelašća and Miljevina. All the enemy forces managed to retreat through the resulting gap and disappeared in the mountains to the north. The Germans were too exhausted to stop them and there were no reserves."[31]

With the Kalinovik-Foča road, one of the enemy's main

lines of communication, at last behind them, the Partisans were safer than they had been for a longe time—safe, above all, from the sudden arrival of enemy reinforcements, mechanized or armored. For the first time for weeks they could afford to spend a day resting by a stream in the depths of the forest and idly watch the enemy's reconnaissance planes trying in vain to seek them out. The peasants from the nearby farms stared wide-eyed at these weary, battle-stained men and crossed themselves as though they were looking at ghosts come back from the dead. "Why, you're still *alive!*" they cried in astonishment. "There were so many guns and tanks and airplanes against you that we thought that, even if there had been a million of you, not one would have come out alive."[32]

Djilas and the Third Division, it will be recalled, had been left to fight their way through as best they could. On reaching the Sutjeska near Tjentište they could at first see no sign of the enemy. But when they had crossed the river and were advancing toward the hills on the other side, they suddenly found themselves under heavy fire from a whole series of concealed German strong points on the high ground. It was too late to withdraw. There was nothing for it but to try to storm the strong points. Under withering fire they started to climb the hill. In the ensuing battle the Partisans suffered heavy losses. Almost all the wounded and sick whom they were escorting fell into the hands of the enemy and were slaughtered. Sava Kovačević, the Divisional Commander, was shot through the head; and it was only after fierce hand-to-hand fighting that Djilas and a few other survivors succeeded in breaking through the German positions. A week later they, too, joined up with the main body under Tito.

Tito, meanwhile, had decided that the whole force should push on together into eastern Bosnia, and there divide up, each division going to a different part of the country to spread the revolt. From now onward, he decreed, the Partisans were to fight their war "on a wide front." The lessons of the last month had not been wasted. On June 21 they crossed the Sarajevo-Višegrad railway. By the end of the month they were in the heart of eastern Bosnia and had once again resumed the offensive.

More than once during the Fourth and Fifth Offensives, the main force of Partisans had only narrowly escaped annihilation. But they had escaped it nonetheless and, despite their terrible losses—eight thousand killed in the Fifth Offensive alone—had emerged from their ordeal more resilient and more confident than ever. Ever larger numbers of new recruits were now flocking to their standards. Tito's fame had grown and spread throughout Jugoslavia. It had spread at long last to the outer world as well. After all they had been through and all they had suffered, the Partisans and their leader could, in that eventful summer of 1943, look forward with new hope to better times ahead.

ON the evening of July 25, 1943, Mr. Winston Churchill, who
was spending the week-end at Chequers, received the news of
the fall of Signor Mussolini. "This," he said, turning to the
present author, who had recently been appointed to command
the British Military Mission to the Jugoslav Partisans, "makes
your job more important than ever. You must be got into
Jugoslavia at once."

The British Government's decision to recognize the existence of the Partisans by dropping liaison officers to them
had not been easily reached. Since the summer of 1941 King
Peter and the Royal Jugoslav Government had been established in London in company with various other Allied governments whose countries had been overrun by the enemy. It
was only natural that in deciding what resistance movement
to support in Jugoslavia the British Government should take
their views into account. It was no less natural that the Royal
Jugoslav Government in exile should be strongly in favor of
the Royalist Cetniks (with whom they were in direct wireless
contact) and bitterly hostile to the Communist-led Partisans.
Nor was it long before their likes and dislikes had communicated themselves to their British opposite numbers. The result
was a widely shared enthusiasm for Mihajlović and something
very like a conspiracy of silence in regard to Tito.

It was not until the spring of 1943 that the first doubts seem
to have crept into the minds of those responsible for British
policy—doubts as to the reliability of their information about
Jugoslavia, doubts as to Mihajlović's value as an ally, doubts
as to the validity of his claim to be regarded as the only true
resistance leader.

One of the first minds in which these doubts arose was that
of Captain F. W. Deakin, a young Oxford don who was working at the time in Cairo in the branch of GHQ Middle East
which was responsible for the conduct of Jugoslav affairs. On
the strength of the information which was coming in from
Jugoslavia, including signals received from Captain Hudson

and the other British liaison officers with the Cetniks, he arrived at the conclusion that the achievement of the Cetniks had probably been greatly exaggerated and that the military value of the Partisans was at any rate worth investigating. His ideas were not well received either in London or in Cairo. However, Deakin persisted, and on May 19, 1943, a first British liaison officer, Major Jones of the Black Watch of Canada, was dropped to the Partisans in Slovenia. A few days later Deakin himself and Captain Stewart of the Royal Engineers were dropped to Partisan Headquarters, at that time in Montenegro.

Deakin arrived to find the enemy's Fifth Offensive at its height. He spent the next month or two marching through the mountains of Montenegro with the hard-pressed Partisans, sharing with them the hazards and hardships of those strenuous days. Within a few days of his arrival his companion Stewart was killed and he and Tito were wounded by fragments of the same bomb. During this time he had abundant opportunities of judging for himself the fighting qualities of the Partisans. He also received first-hand evidence of the part played by the Cetniks. When the situation permitted, he reported his conclusions by wireless to Cairo. There, for one reason or another, his messages do not seem to have received the attention they deserved. An occasional aircraft load of supplies, it is true, was from time to time dropped to the Partisans. But larger quantities were still going to the Cetniks and in Great Britain the press and wireless, while continuing their panegyrics of Mihajlović, scarcely mentioned the Partisans.

However, the Allied invasion of Italy made it necessary for the High Command to exploit to the full every opportunity of making trouble for the enemy on the other side of the Adriatic. And so things did not stay where they were. In the course of the summer the decision was taken to increase the scope of the British missions, both to the Partisans and to the Cetniks, and to place each under the command of an officer holding the rank of brigadier. In September Brigadier Armstrong was dropped into Serbia to join Mihajlovic, while the present author was dispatched to Tito, still a shadowy figure as far as the outside world was concerned. Each had instructions to report on the military situation and to make recommendations as to how resistance could best be increased and intensified.

Tito, who outside Jugoslavia was still variously described as
a committee, a secret terrorist organization, and a young woman of great beauty, was now in his fifty-second year. He
was sturdily built, with iron-gray hair. His rather wide, smooth-
skinned face with its high cheekbones showed clearly enough
the stresses and strains which he had endured. It also gave
some indication of his character. His regular, clearly defined
features were haggard and drawn and deeply burned by the
sun. His mouth was ruthlessly determined. His alert, light-blue
eyes missed nothing. He gave an impression of great strength
held in reserve, the impression of a tiger ready to spring. As
he spoke, his expression changed frequently and rapidly, in
turn illumined by a sudden smile, transfigured with anger or
enlivened by a quick look of understanding. He had an agreeable voice, capable of sudden harshness. His dress was neat
and workmanlike: a plain dark tunic and breeches without
the badges of rank now worn by his subordinates; at his belt
a pistol in a leather holster; in his cap a small red five-pointed
star with hammer and sickle. Almost the only contrast was
furnished by the fine diamond ring which he had bought
himself in 1937 and which he still wore as a reminder of those
bygone days.

He made no secret of being a Communist. On the contrary,
he gloried in it. But, for a Communist, he was unusually ready
to discuss any question on its merits and to take a decision
there and then, without reference to higher authority. He
seemed perfectly sure of himself: a principal, not a subordinate. There were other unexpected things about him: his surprising breadth of outlook; his apparent independence of
mind; his never-failing sense of humor; his unashamed delight
in the minor pleasures of life; a natural diffidence in human
relationships, giving way to a natural friendliness and conviviality; a violent temper, flaring up in sudden rages; an
occasional tendency to ostentation and display; a considerate-
ness and a generosity which constantly manifested themselves
in a dozen small ways; a surprising readiness to see both
sides of a question; and, finally, a strong instinctive national
pride.

This he shared with every one of his followers, from the
highest to the lowest. To the Partisans, the outside world did
not seem of immediate interest or importance. What mattered
to them was *their* Revolution, *their* War of National Liberation, *their struggle* against the invader, *their* victories, *their*
sacrifices. Of this they were proudest of all: that they owed

nothing to anyone; that they had got so far without help from outside.

That they had achieved much was undeniable. Tito had now built up an effective guerrilla force numbering, he claimed, some 150,000 Partisans. These were divided into eight corps and twenty-six divisions distributed over a great part of Jugoslavia. Each Partisan formation had its own headquarters, and these subordinate headquarters were linked by wireless or courier to Tito's General Headquarters. In the areas temporarily held by them the Partisans invariably set up an efficient provisional administration in which the key posts were everywhere held by party members. Already it seemed clear enough that Tito and his followers must in the long run become masters of Jugoslavia.

Of the Partisan leaders Tito himself stood head and shoulders above his fellows. He brought to the war of resistance against the Germans the same qualities which had stood him in such good stead in the past: leadership, courage, realism, ruthless determination and singleness of purpose, resourcefulness, adaptability and plain common sense. He imposed on the National Resistance Movement the same merciless discipline that he had imposed on the party; he endowed it with the same oracle: the party line. Where there were important decisions to be taken, whether political or military, he took them; took them calmly and collectedly, however precarious the situation. He possessed and could inspire in others an absolute devotion to their common cause, an utter disregard for the dangers and difficulties which beset them. And, most important of all, by throwing together Serbs, Croats, Slovenes and the rest of them in the fight against the common enemy, he had caused them to forget their old internecine feuds and thus achieved within his own ranks an entirely new sense of national unity.

Amid the varying fortunes of war Tito shared the hazards and hardships of his troops under his command. When his Partisans were on the move, he moved with them, covering immense distances on horseback or on foot, through forests or across mountains, in fair weather or foul, with a resilience and a capacity for endurance which would have been remarkable in a much younger man. When there was a lull in the fighting, he would establish his headquarters in whatever accommodation was available: in a hut or a cave or a castle or in a shelter made of branches in the forest. His rule was to make himself and those with him as comfortable as the cir-

cumstances allowed. An efficient system of communications
kept him continuously in touch with his subordinate commanders throughout Jugoslavia. From wherever he was he exercised effective military and political control. The greater
part of his day and night was spent in perusing the signals
and reports which came in from all over the country, discussing them with his colleagues, planning future moves and
sending out fresh instructions and directives. He would also
regularly inspect neighboring Partisan units and formations
and personally investigate the problems of the civilian population. He believed in seeing all he could for himself at first
hand. Having dealt with the immediate problems requiring
his attention, he would join the members of his headquarters
staff in a convivial meal or a game of chess, or simply lie
down on the ground and go to sleep. He had the gift, when
he chose, of putting his cares aside and relaxing completely.
Then he would laugh and joke as if he had not a worry in
the world. But at all times of the day and night, whether
working or sleeping or eating, he would be ready, on the
receipt of an urgent signal, at the sound of nearby fighting or
at the warning cry of a sentry, to spring into immediate and
effective action. Alertness and quick reactions had long been
part of his stock-in-trade. He was a man who was at his
best in a crisis. An emergency served to sharpen and heighten
his powers.

He was later briefly to sum up the principles which underlay
his conduct of the war. "Our fundamental purpose," he said,
"was to make our revolt into a movement of national liberation, to enlist for it the armed support of the greatest number of people from all classes of the population. We sought to
instill in our units the strictest possible discipline, not by ex-
tra drills, but by ceaseless political instruction with the object
of improving both individual and collective morale and of
securing a proper attitude toward the population. Our aim
was to build up from our Partisan detachments an army which
would win the devotion of the civil population. Hence the
severe sanctions inflicted on those who did anything calculated
to alienate the population. From every point of view we attached the highest importance to morale. Militarily and tactically our principles were: to prevent what had started as a
partisan war from turning into a war for the defense of
towns and villages; to overcome the tendency of villagers to
stay in or near their villages and gradually to accustom them
to the idea of fighting wherever they were needed; to avoid,

above all, pitched battles, which were particularly dangerous on account of our shortage of ammunition. In view of our inferiority in numbers and in armament it was necessary for us to fight as far as possible at night. It was also necessary for us to avoid heavy losses ourselves, to inflict as heavy losses as possible on the enemy, and to plan our attacks so that they brought in the biggest possible return in arms and ammunition. Every defeat had at once to be made up for by a victory—anywhere—so that morale did not suffer. For this reason even our worst defeats, even the big enemy offensives had no effect on the morale of our men, for we ourselves at once went over to the offensive, choosing the place where the enemy least expected it. There were a lot of factors to be taken into account in our kind of war. It was particularly important for us to look after our wounded and never to relax our care for them whatever the difficulties. That had a very great effect on the morale of our troops, though very often to save one wounded man cost us the lives of three or four soldiers. It was vital also to impress upon our men that they must never allow the fact of being surrounded to demoralize them, but must regard it as the normal situation in our kind of war. By concentrating our efforts against one point, we could always break out of any encirclement. We were always encircled and always came through. Of great importance, too, was offensive action in the enemy's rear. Whenever the enemy launched an offensive, we sent out Partisan detachments to destroy communications behind his lines. That had a demoralizing effect on our opponents and prevented them from bringing up the supplies which they needed. Finally—and this, too, is important—we were always in dangerous and difficult situations; but our men never cursed us because we were always exposed to the same dangers as they were. There was no difference in that respect between our troops and their leaders—and that, too, was good for morale."[1]

Tito's immediate associates had the same background as himself. They were the little group of revolutionaries whom he himself had brought together, who had shared his exiles and his imprisonments, who had helped him organize workers' cells and promote strikes, who had run with him the gauntlet of police persecution, who together with him had formed the new leadership of the party after the purge of 1937 and who under his leadership now formed the High Command of the Movement of National Liberation. Edo Kardelj, the schoolmaster from Slovenia, now the party's leading Marxist dialectician; stocky, pale-skinned, sensible and immensely reliable, with steel-rimmed spectacles and a neat little black mustache. Marko Ranković, the peasant's son from Serbia with his air of conspiracy who, under Tito's supervision, now operated with subtlety and ruthlessness the party machine and its widespread intelligence organization. Djilas, the Montenegrin intellectual, handsome, intolerant and impetuous, with a look of inspired fanaticism. Black Žujović, all and saturnine, Tito's Deputy Commander-in-Chief, thown in again and again where there were dangers to be overcome or difficulties to be straightened out. Koča Popović, small, brilliant and vital, the millionaire's son from Belgrade, once a poet and philosopher and now the most dashing of Partisan commanders. Ivo Ribar, young, energetic and dedicated, with the wide brow and high cheekbones of the typical Slav, a brilliant speaker. Vlado Dedijer, an enormous Serb with the physique of a prize fighter, who before the war had been a journalist and also one of the best all-around athletes in the country and who in his spare time now noted down day to day in his diary his personal impressions of all that happened round him. Vladko Velebit, the general's son, tall and good-looking, the perfect liaison officer, with an easy friendly manner which in the past had served as an admirable cover to his clandestine revolutionary activities. Nearly all were in their twenties or thirties, an exception being old Moša Pijade, the little Jewish intellectual who had been Tito's companion in jail and now shared with Kardelj the distinction of being the party's leading theoretician. Then there were the girls, Olga and Ždenka, who took turns at working for Tito, keeping his maps and bundles of signals. Zdenka was small, pale and fanatical. Olga, tall and well built, was the daughter, strangely enough, of King Peter's Minister for Foreign Affairs, but neither a London season before the war nor a spell in prison as a dangerous agitator had weakened her devotion to the Communist cause. Finally, there were Tito's personal bodyguards, Boško and Prlja, a formidable pair, heavily armed, who never left his side, and his dog, Tigar, a large German wolfhound captured from the enemy during the Fifth Offensive and now his constant companion.

There were two striking things about this oddly assorted group over whom Tito presided with an air of amused benevolence; first, their devotion to the Old Man, as they still called him; and, secondly, the fact that all of them, young and old, men and women, intellectuals and artisans, Serbs and Croats, had been with him "in the woods" since the early days of the resistance, and had worked underground with him before that, sharing with him hardships and dangers, setbacks and successes. This common experience had overcome all differences of race or class or temperament and had forged between them lasting bonds of loyalty and affection. They had, in short, become comrades in the deeper, nonpolitical, sense of the word.

At the beginning of September, further events had taken place in Italy which were to have the most far-reaching consequences on both sides of the Adriatic and to demonstrate still further the interconnection of the two theaters of war. The Italian Government, formed by Marshal Badoglio after the fall of Mussolini, having first secretly come to terms with the Allies, had on September 8 proclaimed the surrender to them of the Italian Armed Forces.

The arrangements for the Italian surrender had been a closely guarded secret, with the result that it was as much of a surprise to the Partisans and Cetniks as to the Germans. The failure of the Allies to inform him in advance of what was afoot incensed Tito and he expressed himself forcefully on the subject to the newly arrived Head of the British Mission. But in the three-cornered scramble for the spoils which now ensued he nevertheless managed to secure for himself a far larger share than either of the other two competitors. The chief aim of the Italians was to get back to Italy while they could. The Partisans acted promptly and decisively. Within a few days of the surrender, they had occupied most of Dalmatia including the islands and, for a short time, the town of Split and large areas in Slovenia and Istria. What is more, they had seized the supplies, arms and equipment of ten Italian divisions. Not only were they able to rearm and reequip their existing forces; they could also put arms into the hands of the large numbers of new recruits who now flocked to their banners.

And so, in the autumn of 1943, Tito had two major causes for satisfaction. First, his forces had received a sudden accession of military strength, which not only greatly increased their capacity for resistance to the Germans, but seemed likely in the long run to have a decisive effect on the outcome of the internal struggle for power in Jugoslavia. And secondly, he had been recognized as an ally—belatedly perhaps, but nevertheless recognized, by one of the Great Powers; indeed by two, for an officer of the United States Army, Major Lynn

Farish, had now joined the British Mission at his headquarters.

Had he, perhaps, a third reason for satisfaction? It seems probable that, secretly, he had. For the past two years, while he had been fighting for his life, and for the Communist cause, he had tried, and tried in vain, to obtain help from the quarter from which he had most reason to expect it—from Russia. All that he had got in return was advice—most of it not very good—and criticism. He had not even been able to persuade the Russians to send him a military mission, so that they might see his needs for themselves and at the same time show the world that they had not abandoned those who were fighting so bravely for them. Now, thanks to no one but himself he had been able to arm and equip his troops on a scale which no amount of airborne supplies from Russia could ever have achieved. He had also, thanks purely to his own achievements, succeeded in wresting from a basically hostile capitalist government a degree of recognition which his own patrons in Moscow, which Grandpapa, had still not seen fit to accord him.

There had been times during the past two years when Tito had resented the tone of some of the messages he had received from Moscow. It was a tone which did not show proper understanding of the special problems which confronted him; which did not indicate due appreciation of the sacrifices which he and the people of Jugoslavia were making in the common cause, of their revolutionary spirit, or of the successes which they had achieved; which, finally, was not the tone to use in addressing the future ruler of Jugoslavia. Now, perhaps, there might be an improvement. Perhaps Grandpapa might at long last learn to appreciate his loyal friends at their true value. And if he did not . . . if the long-requested help were not forthcoming . . . why, there were now other sources from which help might be obtained. If Moscow could have directed dealings with the capitalist West, so could he. To sup with the Devil, you needed a long spoon. But Tito's spoon, he reckoned, was as long as anybody else's—longer in fact. Self-confidence was a quality which he had never lacked.

The directive issued to the British Mission to Tito laid particular emphasis on the purely military aspect of the situation. The policy of the British Government was to do as much damage to the enemy as possible. With this object in view, they would help anybody who was fighting the Germans.

Politics were a secondary consideration. Jugoslavia's future form of government, it was constantly said, must be settled by the Jugoslavs themselves after the war.

This greatly simplified the issue—oversimplified it, some might say. There could be no doubt that Tito was a Communist and that the Partisan Movement was Communist controlled. There could be very little doubt that, once the war was over, they would play a decisive part in Jugoslav affairs. On the other hand, they were an extremely effective military force and their operations were undoubtedly causing grave embarrassment to the enemy. Such was the gist of the reports sent home by the British Military Mission, in the light of which it was now decided to give the Partisans all the help that was available. Before long airborne supplies began to reach them on a much increased scale, while, wherever possible, the Allied Air Forces based in Italy supported their operations from the air. In order to facilitate the co-ordination of his own operations with those of the Allied Forces in Italy, Tito agreed that British officers should be attached to the principal Partisan formations throughout Jugoslavia. These were under the command of the central mission at his headquarters and linked to it by wireless.

Captain Deakin's cheerful and courageous conduct during the Fifth Offensive had won the admiration of the Partisans. His friendly nature endeared him to all who came in contact with him and did much to overcome the deep-seated prejudice and suspicion which these fanatical Communists naturally felt toward the representatives of a capitalist power. Ever since his arrival in May excellent personal relations had existed between the Partisans and the British. As supplies increased and military collaboration became closer and was extended to a wider field, these were still further consolidated. There remained, however, one substantial stumbling block to any further improvement. The Partisans bitterly resented the support which the Allies were continuing to give to the Cetniks.

So far no British officer who had served in occupied Jugoslavia either with the Partisans or with the Cetniks had returned to the outside world to report. In November the present author, having reached the Island of Vis off the Dalmatian coast was picked up by motor launch and subsequently flown to Cairo, where he saw both the Foreign Secretary, Mr. Eden, who was on his way back from Moscow, and the Commander-in-Chief, Middle East, General Wilson, and also delivered a full written report.

Meanwhile, Tito had expressed the wish to send a military mission of his own, under Ivo Ribar, to General Headquarters, Middle East, and this was now agreed to by General Wilson. A first attempt to send the mission out was prevented by a German bombing attack which destroyed the captured enemy aircraft in which they were about to take off and killed Ivo Ribar, a sad loss to his comrades and to his old father whose other son had been killed in action a few weeks before. After this a British aircraft—the first—was successfully landed on some flat ground near Glamoć in Bosnia at the beginning of December. In it, Vladko Velebit, who had been given the rank of colonel and appointed to take Ribar's place, Captain Deakin, and the present author flew to Cairo. Their arrival there coincided with that of Mr. Churchill, recently come from Teheran.

The Jugoslav situation had been touched on at both Moscow and Teheran. At Moscow, Mr. Eden had been surprised to be told by Molotov that the Soviet Government were thinking of sending a military mission to Mihajlović. But, whatever lay behind it, this idea was dropped and at Teheran the Big Three formally recorded their decision to give all possible help to the Partisans. "The Conference," ran the minutes, "agreed that the Partisans in Jugoslavia should be supported by supplies and equipment to the greatest possible extent, and also by commando operations."

Mr. Churchill had from the first taken a personal interest in the growth of resistance in Jugoslavia. It was the sort of question which by its very nature was calculated to appeal to him. He now took advantage of the presence in Cairo of two members of the British Mission to the Partisans to discuss the whole problem with them. He did not himself receive Colonel Velebit, but conferences were arranged for the latter with General Wilson and with the Naval and Air Commanders-in-Chief, at which it was agreed that the scale of British support for the Partisans should be considerably increased and that as soon as it was possible, a number of Partisans should be sent to Egypt to be trained under British auspices as pilots and tank crews. By the end of 1943 the British Government and High Command were considerably better informed regarding the situation in Jugoslavia, and, on the strength of what they knew, they now formally accepted the Partisans as allies on a strictly military basis.

From the political point of view, things were not so simple. There was no escaping the fact that the British Government still had very definite obligations toward King Peter, who had brought his country into the war on their side in 1941, and toward the Royal Jugoslav Government in exile, whom they continued to recognize as the legal government of Jugoslavia. What is more, there was still a British Mission with Mihajlović, nominally Minister of Defense in the Royal Jugoslav Government, and the Cetniks were still receiving supplies on approximately the same scale as the Partisans.

In all this, one thing was clear enough. There was no hope of a reconciliation between Tito and Mihajlović. The time for that, if indeed the opportunity had ever existed, was long past. The civil war was raging with renewed vigor. On both sides there were British officers; both sides were using British arms and ammunition. It was a situation which could only benefit the Germans.

Mr. Churchill now decided to give the Cetniks a last chance. For some time past the British officers attached to General Mihajlović's Headquarters had found it increasingly difficult to induce him to take even token action against the enemy. Morover his attitude, when pressed to do so, was anything but friendly. "The British," he had been reported as saying in a speech to his men in February, 1943, "are now fighting to the last Serb in Jugoslavia . . . trying to purchase Serbian blood at the cost of an insignificant supply of arms." He had, it seemed, gone on to say that he would "never be a party to this shameful commerce, typical of English traditional perfidy," and had concluded by proclaiming that his enemies were the Partisans, the Ustaše, the Moslems and the Croats; when he had dealt with them, he would turn his attention to the Italians and the Germans; he needed no further contact with the Western democracies, whose aim was to win the war at the expense of others; as long as the Italians remained his sole inadequate source of benefit and assistance, nothing the Allies could do would make him change his attitude toward them.[2] Meanwhile, the evidence that most of Mihajlović's subordinate commanders had reached accommodations with the enemy was becoming ever harder to ignore. Many of those who had hitherto mainly collaborated with the Italians, notably the Cetnik leaders in Dalmatia and Herzegovina, had since the Italian collapse transferred their allegiance to the Germans, who were now ready enough to accept them as allies. In these circumstances, Mihajlović was invited, through Brigadier Armstrong, to destroy a specific bridge on the Belgrade-Salonika railway. It was decided that

if, in three months' time, he had not carried out this operation, the British Mission to the Cetniks would be withdrawn
and all supplies would cease.

But this was only half the problem. Politically, the situation was thornier than ever. The British decision to support
Tito as well as—perhaps instead of—Mihajlović had been
bitterly opposed by the Royal Jugoslav Government, who regarded it, not without reason, as a step toward the establishment of a Communist regime in Jugoslavia and a serious blow
to any hopes they might have of ever returning to their own
country. It was useless to expect a co-operative attitude on
their part. Tito, meanwhile, on his side, had taken a step
which was calculated to deepen the rift still further.

Early in October, hearing that a meeting was to take place
in Moscow between the British, American and Soviet Foreign
Ministers, Tito had sent to Moscow the following signal, a
signal rather less deferential in tone than some of his earlier
messages, a signal which resembled not so much an agent's
request for instructions as a communication addressed by one
independent government to another:

> In connection with the preparations for a conference
> between the representatives of the U.S.S.R., Great Britain
> and America, it is probable that the question of Jugo-
> slovia will be raised. In this connection I beg you to in-
> form the Soviet Government as follows: The Anti-Fascist
> Council of Jugoslavia and Supreme Headquarters of the
> National Liberation Army and Partisan Detachments of
> Jugoslavia have empowered me to declare:
>
> First, we acknowledge neither the Jugoslav Govern-
> ment nor the King abroad because for two and a half
> years they have supported the enemy collaborator, the
> traitor Draža Mihajlović, and thus bear full responsibility
> for this treason to the peoples of Jugoslavia.
>
> Secondly, we will not allow them to return to Jugo-
> slavia, because that would mean civil war.
>
> Thirdly, we speak in the name of the overwhelming
> majority of the people who want a democratic republic
> based on National Liberation Committees.
>
> Fourthly, the only legal government of the people at
> the present time is the National Liberation Committee
> led by the Anti-Fascist Council.
>
> We shall give a statement to this effect to the British

Mission attached to our Headquarters. The British general has already informed us that the British Government will not insist on supporting the King and the Jugoslav Government in Exile.*³

But in Moscow, where they met during the second half of October, the representatives of the powers had had other things to think about, and Tito's telegram, with its defiant message, had not been placed on the agenda. Jugoslavia, it is true, had been mentioned in Moscow. Mr. Eden had informed Mr. Molotov that the British Government now had a mission with the Partisans; and Mr. Molotov, somewhat to Mr. Eden's surprise, had, as recorded, informed him in return that the Soviet Government were thinking of sending a mission to General Mihajlović. But beyond this there was no formal discussion of Jugoslav affairs. And the Soviet Government, being no doubt a little tired of Tito's continual outbursts on the subject of Mihajlović and the government in exile, and thinking perhaps that they had explained their attitude on these questions often enough already, had left this telegram unanswered.

Accordingly, having made his position, as he hoped, clear and received no reply, Tito, taking advantage of the comparative lull which followed the end of the Fifth Offensive, had called a second plenary meeting of the Anti-Fascist Council, to take place at the end of November in the little Bosnian hill town of Jajce, where he had established his headquarters amid the crumbling walls of the old Turkish castle on a hill above the river.

A few days before the council actually assembled, Tito had gathered together his Politburo to decide what else, if anything, should be said to Moscow. Following this meeting a short signal was sent to Moscow on November 26, briefly announcing that the council was to meet forty-eight hours later and that the occasion would be used to reorganize it as a provisional legislature and at the same time to form a National Committee, responsible to it, which would act as a provisional executive. The signal did not mention that the occasion

* In accordance with his instructions, the Head of the British Military Mission had informed Tito that the British Government had no intention of trying to impose any government on the Jugoslav people against their will. The future form of government was a matter which they would have to decide for themselves after the war.

would also be used to declare the Royal Government in exile illegal and to forbid King Peter's return to Jugoslavia. The view of the Politburo had been that it would be as well to say nothing about this.[4]

Just a year had elapsed since the Bihać assembly. Once again the delegates assembled from all over Jugoslavia, traveling long distances and slipping through the enemy lines by night in order to reach their destination, amongst them Edo Kardelj, who after eighteen months in Slovenia had now rejoined the High Command. On November 29 Tito addressed them. The time had come, he said, to turn their council into a proper constitutional body and to form a National Committee of Liberation with all the powers of a provisional government. The monarchy and the exiled government were completely discredited. Only a republican, democratic government could save the Jugoslav people from the misfortunes which had overtaken them in the past.

Tito's speech, needless to say, was greeted by the delegates with a display of tumultuous enthusiasm, after which a number of resolutions were unanimously passed. These provided, *inter alia*, for the transfer of power from the Royal Jugoslav Government in exile to the newly formed National Committee of Liberation, in which Tito himself held the posts of Prime Minister and Minister of Defense; for King Peter's exclusion from Jugoslavia until such time as the Jugoslav people were able freely to decide for themselves what form of government they wanted; and for the eventual introduction of a federal constitution. At the same time the council, at the proposal of the delegates from Slovenia, unanimously conferred on Tito the title of Marshal of Jugoslavia. On this occasion he was officially described as Josip Broz, or rather as Josip Broz-Tito. It was the first time that his real name had been publicly revealed. Indeed it was the first time that he had used it at all since he had come out of prison nearly ten years before. And now that he used it, it was in order that he might be proclaimed a marshal, that he might, in effect, be proclaimed the future ruler of Jugoslavia.

It was some days before the Russians woke up to what had happened: they had been presented with a *fait accompli*. Having once grasped this, they were furious, Stalin in particular. At his meeting with Mr. Churchill and President Roosevelt at Teheran, the Jugoslav question had been treated as a purely military problem. The British and Americans had shown themselves surprisingly ready to recognize the military value of the Partisans and had even agreed to support them. The much thornier political question had been conveniently shelved. And now Tito, like a dog with a stinking bone, had dug it up and proudly deposited it in the middle of the carpet. "The Boss," said Manuilski to Vlahović, the official representative of the Jugoslav Communist party in Moscow, "is quite unusually angry. He says that this is a stab in the back for the Soviet Union and for the Teheran decisions."[5]

It was not until in due course it became clear to him that the Western powers had not been unduly disturbed by the Jajce Resolutions, in fact, had hardly noticed them, that Stalin grudgingly revised his attitude. But even then, deep down in his vindictive mind, there lingered and rankled a grain, perhaps more than a grain, of resentment at the effrontery of Josip B. Tito, self-styled Marshal of Jugoslavia.

The Germans, meanwhile, had launched a fresh offensive— their Sixth, to which they gave the code name of *"Kugelblitz"* or "Thunderbolt." With the end of the Fifth Offensive the war in Jugoslavia had entered a new phase. Having broken out of the enemy's encirclement in Montenegro, Tito had deliberately dispersed to different parts of the country the group of Partisan formations which during the past year had constituted his main striking force. In this manner, he would no longer present to the enemy a target against which the latter could strike a single decisive blow. Nor would he again run the risk, at one moment very real, of seeing the pick of his troops pinned down and wiped out by an overwhelmingly strong enemy force. For the time being, it was true, he would no longer have at his disposal a force capable of striking such powerful or concentrated blows or of undertaking such large-scale operations. But, against this, by dispersing these seasoned shock formations to different parts of the country, he would, in accordance with his constant aim, be still further "spreading the revolt" or, as he had once put it, "waging the war on a wider front." With the large quantities of arms and equipment seized from the Italians he had armed many thousands of new recruits. There was now no part of the country where the Partisans did not possess substantial resources of manpower and it now became his object to build up in each area a strong, self-contained, self-reliant force capable of conducting large-scale operations on its own initiative.

To the Germans, hard pressed on the Eastern front and in Italy and still afraid of an Allied landing in the Balkans, the

Partisans were becoming an ever more serious source of concern. It was like grappling with a many-headed monster. Temporarily driven out of one area, they at once assumed the offensive in several others simultaneously. In most parts of the country it was becoming as much as the Germans could do to maintain their garrisons in the larger towns and secure their main lines of communications, now under constant attack. After the failure of their Fifth Offensive the German High Command had set about regrouping, reorganizing, and above all reinforcing their troops in Jugoslavia which, by force of circumstances, had ceased to be an army of occupation and had become willy-nilly an operational fighting force. A new command, to be known as Army Group "F," was set up in Belgrade under Field Marshal von Weichs with operational control of all forces in the "southeastern" or Balkan theater of war, which now included strong armored and mechanized forces recently transferred from the Russian front and regrouped to form the Second German Panzer Army.

There were now stronger German forces in Jugoslavia than ever before. According to an official German appreciation, these comprised at the end of 1943 fourteen German divisions, two German S.S. regiments and five divisions of non-Germans under German command, amounting in all to well over 200,000 men. In addition to these, Field Marshal von Weichs had under his command at this time another 160,000 Bulgarian and Serb or Croat quisling troops, making a grand total of over 360,000. According to the same German appreciation, the Partisan forces amounted at this time to some 111,000 fighting troops.

Even with these powerful reinforcements, the Germans could no longer hope to wipe out the Partisans altogther in the course of a single offensive. But a strong German force supported by armor, artillery and aircraft, could in the end always dislodge the Partisans from any given position. Henceforth it became the policy of the Germans to deal with the Partisans piecemeal, to pin down and eliminate one group of them at a time.

It was against this background that the Germans, during the second half of September, 1943, launched their Sixth Offensive. Taking advantage of the Italian collapse, the Partisans had succeeded in occupying large areas of Dalmatia and of the Italian zone of Slovenia. In Dalmatia, Split, the islands and a considerable stretch of the coast were in their hands. In Slovenia, they were threatening Ljubljana and the Ljubljana-

Trieste railway. With the danger of a possible Allied landing hanging over them, the Germans could clearly not afford to leave things as they were. Using fast-moving armored and mechanized columns, with plentiful air support, they attacked these newly liberated areas in strength. Most of Slovenia was reoccupied and in a few weeks they had succeeded in occupying the Dalmatian coast and in cutting the Partisans' communications with the sea. Using the Pelješac Peninsula as a jumping-off place, they then rapidly recaptured the islands of Korčula, Brač, Hvar and Mljet.

By the beginning of January only Vis, the outermost of all the islands, was in Partisan hands. In view of its obvious strategic importance this was by mutual agreement now jointly occupied by a British Commando Brigade and a corresponding force of Partisans and used as a temporary base for Allied air and naval operations in the Adriatic. It also served as a base for the armed fishing boats and schooners of the growing Partisan Navy.

Having consolidated their gains in Dalmatia and firmly reoccupied the coastal areas, the Germans next turned their attention to eastern Bosnia, where a powerful Partisan force was on the one hand threatening Serbia and on the other the vital Brod-Sarajevo-Mostar railway. In December strong German forces based on Mostar, Sarajevo, Tuzla and Prijepolje converged on the Partisans in the hills east of Sarajevo. In the words of a German staff officer, "a certain degree of encirclement was achieved on paper, but the enemy, who knew the country, managed to slip through and disperse in the hills." This time, however, the Germans were better prepared and, using special mobile columns including ski troops, followed up each individual Partisan unit in a determined attempt to bring it to battle. Here they achieved some success. Despite the desire of the Partisans in Bosnia to avoid pitched battles, there was much heavy fighting. The winter was unusually cold and, in addition to heavy casualties in the fighting, the Partisans suffered severely from lack of food and clothing. "They were," to quote the same German staff officer, "obliged to abandon further operations and spend some months reorganizing their forces."[6]

Toward the end of December the main theater of operations again shifted, this time to central Bosnia, where Tito, in order to relieve the pressure on his forces in eastern Bosnia, had ordered an all-out attack on the town of Banjaluka, at that time the headquarters of the Second German Panzer Army.

After some fierce fighting the Partisans succeeded in forcing their way into the town, only to be driven out again by the Germans, who retaliated by pushing along the Vrbas Valley and attacking Tito's own headquarters at Jajce, with the result that toward the middle of January he and his staff were forced to withdraw hurriedly westward to the comparative security of the wooded hills above Bosanski Petrovac.

It was among these hills, in a hastily improvised wooden hut in the forest with deep snow all round, that the Head of the British Military Mission, who had been dropped back into Jugoslavia by parachute some hours earlier, handed him a personal letter from Mr. Winston Churchill together with a signed photograph. When they had last met, Tito had been wearing a plain dark tunic without badges of rank. Now, roughly embroidered on his sleeve in gold thread were the laurel wreath and five-pointed star which had been chosen to denote the rank of Marshal of Jugoslavia. Tito made no attempt to hide his pleasure at receiving the letter and the photograph. Like the wreath and star on his sleeve, they were outward and visible signs of the recognition which his achievements had won for him. And outward and visible signs were something to which he had never been indifferent.

Mr. Churchill's letter was couched in the friendliest terms and its contents were from Tito's point of view no less satisfactory. After a flattering reference to the "valiant efforts" of the Partisans, the Prime Minister gave a categorical assurance that "we British have no desire to dictate the future government of Jugoslavia." He was, he continued, "resolved that the British Government shall give no further military support to Mihajlović and will only give help to you, and we should be glad if the Royal Jugoslavian Government would dismiss him from their councils." "Please correspond with me through Brigadier Maclean," he concluded, "and let me know of anything you think I can do to help, for I will certainly try my best."

This was the beginning of a friendly personal correspondence between Mr. Churchill and Tito on a variety of topics which was maintained for the most part over the British Mission's wireless link. Jugoslavia had become one of Mr. Churchill's favorite subjects. "I wish I could come myself," he telegraphed to Tito some weeks later, "but I am too old and heavy to jump out on a parachute."

Meanwhile it seemed as though long-awaited recognition

were finally coming to the Partisans from another quarter, from the quarter which mattered to them most of all, from Moscow. The Russians had, as we have seen, been displeased by the proceedings at Jajce. Tito was going ahead too fast for their taste. They had no wish to alarm their British and American allies unduly at this stage; the time for that would come later. Nor was it for Tito to take the initiative in such matters. The Kremlin would decide in good time when and how a Communist regime was to be established in Jugoslavia and when, if ever, the rank of marshal should be assumed by Josip Broz. The Jajce Resolutions did not, however, seem to have shocked the British and American Governments as much as might have been expected; in fact, they seemed hardly to have noticed them. In the meantime British help to Tito was increasing in scale and the number of British officers with the Partisans growing steadily larger. Perhaps, after all, a Russian Mission should have gone to Jugoslavia before now, if only to find out what was going on there.

Having at long last decided to send a mission to Tito, the Russians set out to do the thing in style. Lieutenant General Korneyev, a distinguished officer who until recently had been Chief of Staff of an Army Group, was appointed to command it, with Major General Gorshkov, a noted expert on Partisan warfare, as his second-in-command. A quantity of colonels and majors, including at least one obvious representative of the NKVD, completed its strength.*

Even now, it was some time before the mission actually arrived in Jugoslavia. For geographical reasons, the task of conveying it there was entrusted to the Royal Air Force. The normal way of entering Jugoslavia at this time was by parachute. But the Russians, for some reason declined to jump. The aircraft, they said, must land. It was pointed out to them that the only available landing place was deep in snow. At once, a number of Partisans, battle-weary and weakened by lack of food, but proud to clear the snow from the ground on which the Soviet Mission would land, set to work. Scarcely had the snow been cleared from the chosen strip than there was a new, far heavier fall of snow. When the strip had again been cleared, the Germans, intrigued by so much activity, made a determined attack and captured it. This happened more than once. Something else would have to be thought of. Resourceful as ever, the R.A.F. suggested gliders. Their sug-

* NKVD: Peoples' Commissariat for Internal Affairs: Secret Police.

gestion was accepted and in the end it was in two Horsa gliders, with an impressive fighter escort, that General Korneyev and his staff made their appearance on a fine frosty afternoon toward the end of February.

It was a big moment for the Partisans. For Tito and the little group of dedicated Communists at the head of the party it was as though, after all they had been through, their reward had come at last. Now there would be no more misunderstandings. Stalin would be informed directly of all they had suffered, of all they had achieved, of all their special problems, and any difficulties there had been before would vanish.

For the rank and file, the thrill was, if possible, even greater. Most of them had never seen a Russian before. But for the past three years they had heard of little else. It was for Russia, after all, that they were fighting. Tito himself had told them so. It was thanks to Russia that they had survived. It was through Stalin and Russia and the glorious Red Army that they would ultimately triumph over the powers of evil—over the Germans, over the Cetniks, over the King, over the Ustaše, and possibly someday over Great Britain and America too. To them, the Russians were superhuman, larger than life, bigger and stronger and wiser and kinder and far more democratic than anybody else in the world. And now at last a mission of real Soviet Russians, officers of the Red Army, generals, even, had descended on them out of the sky, bringing, no doubt, in their train arms and food and boots and all the other things they needed so badly. Eagerly they clustered round to gaze at the new arrivals.

There was nothing particularly the matter with the Russians. They wore the new Red Army uniforms, chocolate-colored breeches and tunics with large stiff gold epaulettes and shiny boots. They were neither larger nor smaller than anybody else, and looked as if some fresh air and exercise would not do them any harm. General Korneyev was a plump, amiable-looking elderly gentleman with a slight limp. He had been an officer in the Imperial Army before the Revolution, but looked more like a bank manager than a soldier. His second-in-command had a more military appearance, but a less amiable expression. The more junior officers carried attaché cases. On being shown their quarters, the Russians asked where the lavatory was. It was explained to them that there was no lavatory. In that case, they said, a lavatory must be constructed. At once some Partisans were set to work building a lavatory according to their somewhat elaborate specifications.

Meanwhile, as the weeks and months went by, it became clear that the hero worship which the Partisans lavished on the Russians was far from being reciprocated by the latter. The Russians felt but little enthusiasm for the task which had been entrusted to them. The Partisans, it seemed to them, were *"nekulturni"*—they lacked culture. General Korneyev, for his part, made no secret of the fact that he would have far preferred the post of Military Attaché in Washington, while General Gorshkov left no one in any doubt that he considered his own Russian partisans greatly superior to the local product. When it became apparent to them that there was no question of their taking over command of the Partisan forces, as they had evidently expected to do, they became even less enthusiastic.

Before very long there were signs that the disenchantment was mutual. Tito had soon grasped that these were not the men to comprehend his point of view, still less to convey it successfully to Stalin. As to interpreting the party line, Tito did not, or thought he did not, require their help. Still less did he want their advice on military matters. There was one thing he could hope for from them—that they would provide him with an additional channel of supply. When he realized that there was at present no question of this, and that their total resources amounted to a dozen or so shiny new sub-machine guns and the abundant supplies of vodka and caviar which they had brought with them by glider, he began to lose interest.

The British officers at Partisan Headquarters had, for their part, expected to be left out in the cold as soon as the Russians arrived. They were pleasantly surprised when this did not happen. Whatever his motives, Tito went out of his way to treat both missions on a basis of rigorous equality. Indeed there were times when he seemed to take pleasure in putting the Russians at a disadvantage in relation to their British colleagues.

One such occasion was the weekly conference to which he would summon the two heads of mission in order to discuss the supply situation. First he would ask the Head of the British Mission what supplies he could expect from British sources. The scale of British assistance was now steadily increasing and the reply was usually not unsatisfactory. He would then turn to General Korneyev. "And what, Mr. General, can *you* do to help us?" he would ask amiably. Once more the unhappy General would be obliged to explain that, as there were no Russian airfields in reach of Jugoslavia, his country was unfortunately not able to take part in supplying the Partisans. "In fact," Tito would say dryly, "you can do nothing." And the following week the performance would be repeated. Each time, as General Korneyev, limping slightly, made his way down the steep, rough path leading to the cave, Tito's wolf-hound Tigar would growl and snap threateningly at his heels. "An anti-Russian dog," Tito would say, and laugh.

There were now British liaison officers all over Jugoslavia, and supplies of food, arms, clothing and ammunition were dropped to Partisan formations throughout the country in accordance with a system of priorities agreed by Tito and the Head of the British Mission. The Royal Air Force and U.S. Army Air Force in Italy also gave the Partisans both tactical and strategical air support whenever possible. The British Mission included demolition experts and artillery instructors whose services were placed at the disposal of Tito's forces and medical officers who were able to give valuable help to the Partisan wounded. The care and disposal of the wounded had from the first presented a formidable problem and whenever the possibility of landing an aircraft presented itself, every effort was made to evacuate as many Partisan wounded as possible to Allied hospitals in Italy. In this way, many lives were saved and Tito's forces relieved of a serious burden.

By the end of February the impetus of the enemy's Sixth Offensive had spent itself and Tito with his usual resilience had gone over once more to the attack. Close operational liaison now existed with Allied Force Headquarters at Caserta and, in addition to containing twenty or so enemy divisions which might otherwise have been transferred to other fronts, the Partisans were able to give valuable help to the Allied commanders in Italy by specific operations undertaken at their request and timed to coincide with their own operations on the other side of the Adriatic. A notable instance was the destruction by the Slovene Partisans at the request of General Alexander of the Stampetov Viaduct on the railway linking Trieste to Ljubljana.

Tito himself, meanwhile, had moved down from the hills and established his headquarters amid the ruins of the once busy little Bosnian town of Drvar. There he lived in a large cave in the rock face sixty feet above the ground, overlooking the valley in which the town was situated. At the back of the cave a waterfall made an agreeable rushing noise and provided water for drinking and washing; ferns and moss grew in the interstices of the rock. Farther up the little green valley, at Mokri Nogi, were the headquarters of First Partisan Corps, commanded by Koča Popović, which was the formation entrusted with the defense of Partisan Headquarters. To the north, Fifth Corps under Slavko Rodić was based on Bosanski Petrovac.

From his new capital Tito dispatched missions of his own to the outside world. One night at the beginning of April Vladko Velebit, now promoted to major general, was picked up from Bosanski Petrovac by a British aircraft and flown first to Algiers and thence to London, where he was received by Mr. Churchill. After a brief visit to England he established a permanent headquarters at Bari in Italy.

At the same time Djilas was sent to the Soviet Union, where he spent the best part of two months and was received by Stalin in person. He took this opportunity of raising the question of supplies and extracted from the *Vozhd* the promise that Soviet aircraft, operating from bases in the Ukraine, would drop supplies to the Partisans in eastern Jugoslavia. And indeed toward the end of April a few such drops were actually made. At the same time ten American-made lease-lend Dakotas, bearing Soviet markings, were dispatched to Bari whence they brought to the Partisans arms and ammunition provided by the Western Allies. It was thus that two years after Tito's first request for help and a year after the arrival of the first British supplies, the first driblet of aid reached the Partisans from the Country of the Revolution.

Altogether Djilas found Stalin most affable. The unpleasantness over the Jajce Resolutions seemed to have been forgotten. The *Vozhd* showed a most flattering interest in the achievements of the Partisans. "The eyes of the whole world," he remarked benignly, "are fixed upon you." And, on being asked whether the line they were taking was correct, "You yourselves know best," he replied, "and you yourselves should judge." There was only one thing that seemed to worry him, the red stars the Partisans wore in their hats. "What do you need red stars for?" he asked. "You are only frightening the British. The form is not important."[7]

When he left Moscow, Djilas took with him a gold sword which the Presidium of the Supreme Soviet had presented to Tito and a pair of binoculars sent him by Marshal Konyev.

But he did not bring back what Tito had sent him to get: recognition of the National Committee as the legal Government of Jugoslavia.

With the rapid growth of the Partisan Movement problems of operational and administrative control had multiplied and there had been a resulting increase in the size of Tito's Headquarters at Drvar. In addition to the British and Soviet Missions an independent American Mission had now arrived and some meteorological experts from the American Army Air Force who from time to time would send a large scarlet balloon floating up into the sky above the village. There was also the new "Provisional Government" to be accommodated. There were even some dancers from the Zagreb ballet. None of this made for secrecy or for mobility. The Partisans, after being constantly on the move for three years, were beginning to feel more and more the need for a fixed base, for an island of permanently liberated territory, which from this point of view would also possess considerable political advantages. And now the failure of the German Sixth Offensive, the apparent stability of the situation in central Bosnia, the increased help they were receiving, the progress which the Allies were making on other fronts, all encouraged them to think that such a thing might at last be possible.

They were to be sharply disillusioned. One day toward the end of May a single German aircraft made its appearance over Drvar, flying at a height of about two thousand feet. There was nothing unusual about this, as the enemy was in the habit of making frequent air attacks on Partisan Headquarters. But this time, instead of bombing or machine-gunning, the pilot spent half an hour flying up and down over the valley, comfortably out of range of small-arms fire, and then flew off again in the direction from which he had come. It seemed clear enough that he had been making a detailed reconnaissance of Drvar and those who noticed him surmised that his visit would shortly be followed by an unusually heavy bombing raid.

For three days nothing happened. On the night of May 24 Tito and Kardelj ate their evening meal as usual in his cave and then lay down to rest with forty or fifty feet of reassuringly solid rock between them and the sky above. It was the eve of Tito's fifty-second birthday. He awoke not many hours later, just as it was getting light, and, going to the mouth of his cave, saw two Focke-Wulf aircraft flying up the valley. They were followed by others and soon a number of medium-sized enemy aircraft were bombing the village and its surroundings. Then, as he listened, a deeper note fell on his ear, and out of the sun came six big JU-52's flying in formation down the valley. They reached the village and circled overhead. Those watching waited for the ominous whistle of descending bombs.

It did not come. Instead, something that was not a bomb fell from the leading aircraft, something that billowed out into a great canopy with a man suspended from it. More followed. In a few seconds the air was full of them. Already the first German parachute troops had gone into action and were shooting their way into the village. Next came gliders with arms and more men. One glider seemed about to land immediately opposite the entrance to the cave, a few yards from where Tito and Kardelj were standing, when at the last moment, instead of coming down smoothly like the others, it suddenly nose dived and crashed. The crew, it seemed, were killed, for no one emerged from the wreckage. This was a lucky escape for those in the cave, but already some other Germans, despite fierce resistance from the handful of Partisan Headquarters troops stationed in the village itself, had managed to establish themselves on the flat ground beyond the river and were firing into the cave with a heavy machine gun, while yet another party moved up toward it. It was with difficulty that his companions restrained Tito from engaging them with a rifle. But there could be no question of making a stand against such odds. It was imperative that they should get out at once. The trouble was that the path leading down from the entrance of the cave, indeed the whole face of the cliff, was under heavy fire. A Partisan who started out to make a reconnaissance was shot through the head and fell in his death agony at Tito's feet. There was no escape that way.

Only one hope remained: the waterfall at the back of the cave. It was dry now, and its channel led up through a tunnel in the rock to the top of the cliff. Up this, with the help of a rope, Tito and the others climbed and pulled themselves to safety. The dog Tigar was dragged up after them. From the top of the cliff, which Marko Ranković and a few Partisans had managed to keep clear of Germans, they made their way across country to the nearest Partisan unit.

By now, the Partisans, though heavily outnumbered, had counter-attacked and had even succeeded in driving the enemy out of the village. But the latter were still firmly established

on the surrounding slopes and now came the news that strong
enemy motorized and armored forces were closing in on Drvar
from all sides. The neighboring Partisan formations were holding them as best they could, but they had already suffered
heavy losses and could not hope to hold out indefinitely
against such odds. Tito accordingly gave the order for a
general withdrawal into the hills. That evening, after some
narrow escapes, he and his staff reached the little group of
huts deep in the woods at Potoci which they had left just four
months earlier. They were joined there by the British and
Soviet Missions, who had also succeeded in extricating themselves from Drvar. Soon the British wireless operator had
established contact with R.A.F. Headquarters at Bari and
was asking urgently for air support.

The strong German armored and motorized forces based on
Bihać, Banjaluka, Jajce, Livno and Knin, whose arrival had
been intended to coincide with the airborne attack, did not
in fact reach Drvar until the next day. By then the birds had
flown. All they found of interest was one of Tito's new
uniforms and a pair of his boots, which they flew to Vienna
and exhibited in a museum. Operation *Rösselsprung*—
"Knight's Move," as the Germans called their Seventh Offensive, had failed. Having missed Tito, the Germans revenged
themselves on the defenseless civilian population of Drvar,
well known for their loyalty to the Partisans. Men, women and
little children were ruthlessly slaughtered. Very few of the
inhabitants lived to tell the tale.

No sooner had Tito reached the comparative safety of
Potoci than the Germans began to close in on him in the
woods. He decided to break out. This he did, surprisingly
enough, by train. An engine and some trucks had been laid
up at Potoci, out of harm's way. With fierce fighting in progress all round, Tito and his party climbed on board and
steamed off majestically down the five miles of track through
the woods, while bullets whined through the trees around and
Very lights illuminated the night sky. After that they walked.

For the next few days Tito and his staff, accompanied by the
Allied Missions and a force of a few hundred Partisans,
dodged through the woods, moving mostly at night and lying
up during the day. They had many narrow escapes. German
patrols, aircraft and light tanks were everywhere. Food and
ammunition were short. Once they were able to stop long
enough in the same place to receive a supply drop. British

aircraft also gave the Partisans all possible air support, flying more than a thousand sorties during these critical days.

Ever since they had left Drvar, Tito had personally directed the operations of the little force which accompanied him as well as those of the larger Partisan formations in the neighborhood. All who were with him were struck by his calmness and the resoluteness of his demeanor. This was not the first time he had found himself in such a situation. Soon he had regained the initiative and, with the four Partisan divisions which he now had under his command in the immediate neighborhood, he felt that he had every hope of holding his own.

His own inclination was to remain in Bosnia at the head of his troops. For some time, however, General Korneyev, the Head of the Soviet Military Mission, who was himself beginning to show signs of strain, had been urging him to leave by air at the first opportunity. He even told him that it was the wish of the Soviet Government that he should leave and that he had received a signal from Moscow in this sense. In the end Tito decided to accept this advice, or, perhaps it would be more correct to say, to do as he was told, for the old relationship with Moscow still remained and the message he had received was a reminder of its existence. Besides, there was something in what the Russians said. It was impossible for him to direct the operations of his forces all over Jugoslavia, while being kept constantly on the move by the enemy. The increased complexity of his task made a relatively firm base essential and for the moment there seemed no chance of establishing such a base on the mainland. He would not, moreover, need to leave Jugoslav territory and establish a second "Jugoslav Government in Exile" in a foreign country. He could establish his headquarters on the island of Vis, which was strongly held by Partisan and British forces, and offered all the advantages of a firm base while being at the same time part of Jugoslavia.

Having arrived, though reluctantly, at this conclusion, Tito informed the British Mission of his decision and asked for their help in arranging for the evacuation of himself and his staff by air to Italy. In reply to a signal, the R.A.F. promised to try to land the necessary aircraft that night on some flat ground near by which for the time being was held by the Partisans. When Tito and his companions reached the appointed place, it was raining and there was low cloud. It seemed improbable that an aircraft would be able to land.

But, just as they were giving up hope, there came the hum of airplane engines; bonfires were lighted and the first plane landed. Tito, his dog Tigar, half a dozen members of his staff, the Russian Mission and Colonel Street of the British Mission climbed on board. As he did so, Colonel Street was surprised to notice that the aircrew were Russians. The aircraft was a Dakota, supplied under lease-lend, which the Russians were operating from Bari under British operational control. Somehow the pilot had managed to obtain this particular assignment for his plane, thereby enabling his government to claim that they had rescued Tito. An hour or two later they were landing in Bari.

Disliking the status of refugee, Tito remained in Italy no longer than was necessary. After spending a few days in a villa on the outskirts of Bari which had been placed at his disposal by the British authorities, he crossed by night to Vis in H.M.S. *Blackmore,* a Hunt Class destroyer. On the way over he was entertained at dinner in the wardroom in the best naval style. The atmosphere was hilarious, there was plenty to drink, and Tito's natural shyness soon wore off. By the end of the evening he was reciting "The Owl and the Pussy Cat" in fluent English to an admiring audience of young naval officers. The *Blackmore* reached Vis just before dawn. From her deck as she approached the little harbor of Komiša, Tito could see the massive shape of Mount Hum looming above him in the half-light, while farther away, across another twelve miles of sea, the jagged mountains of the mainland stood outlined against the eastern sky.

The rocky little island of Vis, the Issa of classical times, possesses by virtue of its geographical position considerable strategical importance. The most outlying of the Dalmatian Islands, it offers a convenient base from which to raid the other islands and the mainland or to attack shipping in the Adriatic. During the Napoleonic Wars it was held by the British for several years and to this day Fort Wellington and Fort George still bear the Royal Cipher of King George III, while an elegant marble obelisk commemorates a naval victory won against the French by Captain William Hoste, R.N., in 1811.

Following the decision to hold it against all comers, taken jointly in the previous January by the Allies and the Partisans, Vis had become, by the time Tito arrived there in June, a miniature military, naval and air base, and, incidentally, a kind of Anglo-Jugoslav condominium. A British Commando

Brigade, together with an equivalent force of Partisans, not only furnished the garrison, but had already carried out a number of successful raids against the enemy forces on the neighboring islands and mainland. A "Balkan School of Artillery" under British command instructed the Partisans in the use of the 75 mm. pack-howitzer. A British Naval Headquarters at Komiša was responsible for a force of motor torpedo boats operating against enemy shipping in the Adriatic, a task in which they were joined by a number of armed schooners and fishing boats which formed the nucleus of a Partisan navy. Finally, the central plain had been cleared of vines and olives and converted into a full-sized airfield from which a squadron of rocket-carrying Hurricanes was operating against shipping and targets inland, while other aircraft, based in Italy, used it for refueling, thereby considerably increasing their range. The roads of the island were congested with British military vehicles, and on every side brightly painted signboards advertised the presence of REME, NAAFI, DADOS and the Corps of Military Police.

Thus Tito, on arriving at Vis, found himself at very close quarters with the British Armed Forces. From the cave, high up on the slopes of Mount Hum, where he had installed himself, he could see the fighters and bombers of the R.A.F. landing and taking off and could hear the skirl of the pipes and the bugle calls of the Commandos, while a British guard shared with his own Partisans the responsibility for his personal safety.

Already the news from the mainland was better. The Seventh Enemy Offensive had had a limited objective: the destruction of Tito and his headquarters. Having failed in this objective, it was, like the six other offensives which had preceded it, petering out. Once again the initiative was passing to the Partisans, who were now receiving help on a considerable scale from the Western Allies. In the place of the somewhat haphazard arrangements which had existed hitherto, a new R.A.F. formation, known as Balkan Air Force, had been created in Italy under the command of Air Vice-Marshal Elliot with the special task of supplying the Partisans and affording them air support. The headquarters of this force were in direct wireless communication with the British Military Mission at Tito's Headquarters, which coordinated and transmitted to them the Partisan requests for assistance.

Not long after his arrival on Vis, Tito was joined there by his son Zarko, newly arrived from the Soviet Union. Zarko, a tall, lightly built, good-looking youth with defiant blue eyes and a mop of fair curly hair, had served until now in the Red Army, in which he had attained the rank of sergeant. He had only one arm, having lost the other in the fighting before Moscow, where he had also won a medal for bravery. He could speak little or no Serbo-Croat. During the fifteen years which had elapsed since he had been smuggled out of Jugo-slavia with his mother in 1929 he had learnt to look upon the Soviet Union as his country and on Russian as his mother tongue. But no sooner had he arrived on Vis than he dis-carded his Russian uniform for that of a Partisan lieutenant and set to work to relearn his native tongue. Soon his natural high spirits and wild charm had won him a firm place in the affections of his father's personal entourage, already strongly predisposed in his favor by the fact of his Soviet upbringing and of his service in the Red Army.

By this time the British Government had at last settled a question which had long complicated and disturbed their relations with the Partisans: the problem of their parallel commitments to the Cetniks. During the past two years the Cetniks had slid farther and farther down the slippery slope of collaboration. Though Mihajlović himself kept as far as possible aloof from such arrangements, since the collapse of Italy more and more of his subordinate commanders in Serbia, Bosnia, Dalmatia and Montenegro had come to terms with the Germ ns Occasionally Mihajlović appears to have sought to discourage too blatant collaboration, but without much success. This is evident from a confidential report sent to him early in 1943 by his representative for western Bosnia, Major Vranješević.

The orders of the High Command not to tolerate any further relations with the Germans could not [wrote Major Vranješević] be carried out, on account of the necessity of obtaining munitions and supplies from the Germans. Should relations be broken off, the supply position would become critical. . . . I can say quite frankly that, had we not relied on the support of the local Croat garrisons in the course of our operations, we should have been destroyed by the Partisans, whose forces were always superior to ours, particularly during the winter months. The morale and fighting spirit of the Cetniks were at their height in 1941 and they were whole-hearted in their struggle both against the Germans and the Ustaše and against the Partisans. Later, however, morale fell considerably, particularly since the Bosnian Cetnik detachments concluded their agreement with the Germans and Croats for joint military action against the Partisans.

Major Vranješević also reported that "senior officers make it a rule to be otherwise occupied when fighting is going on" and added that some "have even simply handed over their units to German Command. I opposed this, for collaboration is not the same thing as subordination."[8]

Discipline, never good among the Cetnik commanders, was becoming worse. This emerged clearly at a conference held between representatives of Mihajlović and representatives of the Cetnik command for Bosnia at the village of Kokovi in February, 1943. "We must recognize," said one Cetnik, "that our organization has been bad and that our troops are not sufficiently disciplined, since they are led by people for whom they have not sufficient respect. . . . Looting has made an ugly appearance in our ranks and compromises us and serves to discredit our army." "Individual commanders," according to another delegate, "have shown themselves to be useless. They are given to corruption and drunkenness and ride about on bicycles and have become like great lords."[9]

The Cetnik rank and file, for their part, found it all extremely puzzling, as is shown by a letter from Captain Wuriamek of the German Headquarters at Banjaluka to Radoslav Radić, Milhajlović's commander for west Bosnia, complaining that Cetniks under his command had been heard to shout: "Long live King Peter II, Queen Marie and London." "It is forbidden," continued Captain Wuriamek, "to shout 'long live' with reference to the enemies of the German Reich. I must draw your attention to this and ask you to explain it to your troops. Incidents of this kind may disturb the excellent relations which have existed up to now between you and the German armed forces."[10]

Meanwhile, Mihajlović himself continued strongly to discourage anything approaching active resistance to the Germans. "In the actions against Tito's bands on the Drina," he wrote to Major Djurić, his commander for southeast and central Serbia, on May 8, 1944,

the Germans did not touch us. On the contrary many of our commanders were helped and enabled to avoid attacks made by the Communists from Bosnia and Serbia. As we have not sufficient munitions and forces, we cannot carry on fighting on two fronts. At present our most dangerous enemies are the Communists. Therefore, I order that every kind of armed action against the occupier's forces cease but the occupier will be attacked in propaganda. Every commander will be personally responsible to me for the above being carried out.[11]

Although every effort was made by Mihajlović to disguise from the British officers attached to his forces the existence of actual collaboration between his subordinates and the enemy, his own continued failure, indeed refusal, to undertake any active operations against the Germans could hardly pass unnoticed. "From the operational point of view," the Head of the British Mission at his headquarters wrote in April, 1944,

Mihajlović's orders for inactivity are known and followed almost without exception. Numerous ambushes and acts of sabotage could have been carried out during the last six to eight months virtually without loss; whether there would have been reprisals or not is a question which will never be answered. We were constantly assured that there is a plan which will swing into operation when "the Day" is ordered by Mihajlović, and that, when that happens, all communications will be interrupted if not blocked entirely. We were never able to find out what the plan is, and we don't believe that it exists except in vague words, though one or two commanders such as Ljuba Mihajlović and Osokolić might have scheduled definite personnel for definite operations. . . .

The main preoccupation [the report continued] ever since the end of October, has been propaganda. This has never wavered from the line that Serbia is hitched, for worse, to the Anglo-American star and that no compromise is possible with the occupying powers. Equally strong is the propaganda against the Partisans who have, in the minds of the people, taken the place of the Germans as Enemy No. I.

The report added that the British Mission had no actual evidence of collaboration but that "it seemed fairly clear from the desperate attempts of the local commanders to avoid any action in that region that a sort of non-aggression pact existed which conduced to the comfort of all concerned." The conclusions drawn by the writer were:

> 1. As a military organization the Mihajlović set-up could never do more, now that it has reached its present stage of military ill-preparedness and moral defeatism, than accelerate by a few days the already inevitable German withdrawal or collapse.
>
> 2. The organization will continue to fight the Partisans with such weapons as it has, either until it is finally beaten or until there is a Partisan representation in the Jugoslav Government.[12]

The period of three months set by General Headquarters, Middle East had by now elapsed without Mihajlović having even attempted the operation which he had been asked to carry out. The Head of the British Military Mission at his headquarters was accordingly instructed to inform him that he would receive no further supplies and that the Briitsh officers with his forces would be withdrawn at the first opportunity. In fact, no opportunity of extricating them presented itself until May when Brigadier Armstrong and his officers finally took leave of a reproachful, resentful, but still courteous Mihajlović.

In the House of Commons Mr. Churchill explained this decision. "The reason," he said, "why we have ceased to supply Mihajlović with arms and support is a simple one. He has not been fighting the enemy and, moreover, some of his subordinates have been making accommodations with the enemy." British support of the Cetniks had from the first been based on a misapprehension. With the help of their own propaganda, the British had in their imagination built up Mihajlović into something he had never seriously claimed to be. They were now dropping him because he had failed to live up to their expectations. Henceforward all Allied help went to the Partisans. The B.B.C., whose broadcasts were widely listened to by the population and carried great weight, supported them wholeheartedly.*

Hitherto, the British, reluctant to do anything which might exacerbate civil strife, had given little or no help to Tito's forces in Serbia, which they were inclined to regard as a Cetnik preserve. Now all such scruples vanished. Serbia was an area of considerable strategic importance. The Belgrade-Salonika railway was the enemy's chief line of communication in the Balkans and his principal line of withdrawal from Greece. For years the Cetniks, though ideally situated for such operations, had taken no effective action against it. Now, having finally abandoned Mihajlović, the Allies did everything they could to build up the Serbian Partisans.

This suited Tito. Both politically and militarily Serbia was vital to him. The Partisans had begun their resistance in Serbia. It had been the scene of their early triumphs. It had also witnessed their first major setback. Unless they re-established themselves there, their chance of ultimately dominating the whole country would be seriously diminished. When Tito had trudged wearily out of Uzice under the fire of the advancing Germans in November, 1941, it had been with the firm intention of returning. Hitherto this had not been possible. The scattered Partisan detachments he had left behind him in that fateful hour to carry on the resistance in Serbia as best they could while he and the main body of his forces withdrew into Montenegro had not prospered. The fertile rolling country was less suited to guerrilla warfare than the mountains and forests of Montenegro and Bosnia. The population, by nature conservative and loyal to the monarchy, were inclined to prefer the passive attitude of the Cetniks or even the open collaboration of General Nedić to the all-out resistance and revolutionary policies of the Partsians. As a result, the enemy forces of occupation had for some time past enjoyed greater security in Serbia than anywhere else in the country. The Serbian Partisans, hunted by the Germans, by Nedić, by the Cetniks, by the Albanians, and by the Bulgars, out of sympathy with the local populations and out of touch with their comrades in the rest of the country, short of arms

---

* In August, 1944 the United States Government resumed contact with Mihajlovic by sending him an independent "Intelligence Mission" under Colonel R. H. McDowell. Colonel McDowell's principal duty seems to have been to arrange for the evacuation of American aircrews who had been shot down over Jugoslavia and had managed to reach the Cetniks. He also served as a channel for peace proposals put forward by the Germans in September through a certain Herr Staerker. His presence in Jugoslavia, after the Allies had announced that they would have no further dealings with the Cetniks, gave Tito a grievance which he not unnaturally exploited to the full.

and equipment, had again and again come near to annihilation. Under their leader, Peter Stambolić, they had continued to carry out guerrilla raids and ambushes, but their forces still consisted only of scattered bands instead of the larger Partisan units and formations which existed in other parts of the country. Nor did they possess in Serbia the same powerful political and administrative organization as elsewhere.

But now at long last things were changing. Partisan successes elsewhere had their echo in Serbia. New brigades and divisions were raised and in the spring of 1944 Tito sent Koča Popović, one of his most successful and popular commanders, to Serbia to take command.

The Allied decision to withdraw support from the Cetniks and at the same time to give all possible assistance to the Partisans also had its effect. Supplies to the Cetniks ceased altogether, while arms and ammunition were dropped to the Partisans in substantial quantities. The local Partisan commanders were thus enabled not only to re-equip their existing forces, but also to arm large numbers of volunteers whom they had hitherto been obliged to turn away through lack of equipment.

Nor was the change in Allied policy without its effect psychologically. The prestige with which British and American support had hitherto endowed the Cetniks was now transferred to the Partisans. The civil population began to realize that the more strenuous policy of the Partisans, which had once seemed so foolhardy, had in the long run won for them the Allied support which Mihajlović had forfeited by his caution and inactivity. They realized, too, that the Germans, who had for so long seemed invincible, were at last beginning to weaken and, that when in the end they withdrew or were driven out, power would almost certainly pass to the Partisans. There ensued a marked increase in popular support for the Partisans and a corresponding decrease in the popularity of the Cetniks. In May, 1944 the defection to the Partisans of Major Radoslav Djurić, Mihajlović's commander for central and southeast Serbia, and his subsequent appeal to all Cetniks to follow his example, helped still further to hasten the disintegration of the Cetniks forces throughout the area.

With the collapse of his movement in Serbia, where it had had its origin and where it was most firmly rooted, Mihajlović's last chance of success finally vanished. The Cetniks had never possessed the qualities to which the Partisans owed their triumph: strong leadership, iron discipline, unity, a relentless determination to attain at all costs certain clearly defined aims. "In war," Napoleon once said, "it is not men, but the man that counts." Though a brave man and a well-trained, experienced soldier, Mihajlović lacked the ruthless determination, the unwavering singleness of purpose of his rival. Though personally popular, he was unable to control his subordinates or to preserve order in his forces. In guerrilla warfare ideas are of paramount importance. The Cetniks were inspired by no idea which could equal Communism in its strength, its persistence, in its power over the mass as over the individual. In character, their movement was static rather than dynamic, passive rather than active, negative rather than positive. In their anxiety to avoid casualties, to prevent the Partisans from gaining power, to prevent the disruption and destruction of the old, established way of life, they lost sight of what they had originally set out to do. By waiting eternally for the ideal opportunity which never presented itself, they missed countless lesser opportunities. Though in reality hostile to the Germans and Italians, they drifted inevitably into a policy of collaboration with them. Having started as patriots, they had from the best of motives become something very like traitors.

In Serbia, these various developments had a cumulative effect. Allied support and supplies brought more volunteers; more numerous and better equipped, the Partisans were able to increase the scope of their operations; their resulting successes led to the capture of more arms and equipment from the enemy and at the same time still further increased their prestige. In the space of a few months the situation underwent a revolutionary change.

Toward the middle of the summer Tito decided that the moment had come to start shifting his main striking force to Serbia. The time seemed ripe for an all-out effort there. During August a strong force of nine divisions, grouped in two corps under the over-all command of Peko Dapčević was accordingly dispatched from east Bosnia and Montenegro into western Serbia, whence, after a series of sharp and on the whole victorious encounters with Germans, Bulgarians and Cetniks, they pressed northward in the direction of Belgrade. At the same time the forces already in Serbia under the command of Koča Popović were brought up to seven divisions, likewise grouped in two corps, and made responsible for the future conduct of operations in southern and eastern Serbia. Everything was now ready for the reconquest of Serbia. And, with Serbia in his grasp, Tito would have little more to worry about.

X 🔲🔲🔲 HOW MANY MILES TO BABYLON?

On other fronts and in other theaters of war, things were moving equally fast. Rome had fallen and the Eighth Army stood before Florence. The Allies had landed in France. The Russians were advancing rapidly on nearly every sector of their immense front; already their victorious armies were pushing down toward the Balkans. The end of the war in Europe was at last in sight. With its approach, the need for a settlement of a number of outstanding problems became daily more urgent both from Tito's point of view and from that of the Allies.

First of all, it seemed possible that, as things began to go worse for them, the Germans would decide to cut their losses and withdraw their forces of occupation from the Balkans. If so, it was important that effective steps should be taken to cut off their retreat. In any case, it seemed likely that before long the Partisans and the Allies would join hands in northern Italy. This made it desirable that their respective operations should be more closely co-ordinated than ever.

There were also a number of no less urgent political problems to be faced. Tito had already announced his intention of laying claim to Istria, Trieste, Venezia Giulia and part of Carinthia. It was the hope of the British and American Governments that all such questions would be settled by the peace treaties and not before. But there was clearly a distinct possibility that if Tito got there first he might take the law into his own hands. Nor did Tito feel any more certain about the intentions of the Western Allies. Supposing they got there first, might they not somehow contrive to cheat Jugoslavia of her due? Both parties felt the need to reassure themselves as to the other's intentions.

Finally there was the political future of Jugoslavia to be considered. For the Western Allies the problem was how to reconcile their *de jure* obligations to the Royal Jugoslav Government in exile with the *de facto* situation which existed in the country and with the military alliance which they had contracted with the Partisans. Tito, for his part, knew exactly what he wanted. He was determined to seize power at all costs.

226

While he assumed that he could count on Soviet support for this project, he could not be certain what the attitude of the British would be. They would hardly welcome a Communist regime in Jugoslavia; it might even be their intention to restore the monarchy by force, though in view of their present attitude this now seemed less likely than formerly. But, for the time being, it was clearly desirable to avoid a showdown. Allied recognition, if it could be obtained, would be definite asset. It might even be necessary to make certain concessions, to compromise temporarily on certain issues, in order to make certain of getting what he wanted in the long run.

As it happened, the way to a compromise was already being prepared in London. In May King Peter had on British advice dismissed the government of M. Purić, which was bitterly hostile to the Partisans, and invited Dr. Ivan Subašić to form one in its place for the avowed purpose of reaching agreement with Tito. Dr. Subašić was a Croat. In 1941 he had held the position of *Ban* or Governor of Croatia and had escaped abroad at the time of the German invasion. Before the war he had been known as a moderate whose aim was somehow to bridge the gap between Serbs and Croats. Now he saw himself once again in the role of mediator, this time between King Peter and Tito. He was by nature an optimist.

Having collected a group of fellow exiles who like himself were anxious to come to terms with Tito, Dr. Subašić next suggested to the latter through the intermediary of the British Government that he should come to Vis in order to talk things over with the Partisans. After a suitable show of reluctance Tito agreed, and early in June Dr. Subasic and several of his colleagues landed from a British destroyer at Komiša where they were received with some formality by representatives of the National Committee and by a Partisan guard of honor. The visiting statesmen, with their pale faces and town clothes, provided a strange contrast with the hard-bitten, sunburnt Partisans.

The negotiations which now began in Tito's cave were from the first almost completely one-sided. Tito held all the cards except one. In order to obtain Allied recognition for his regime, and in order not to risk forfeiting the help he was getting from the Allies, it might conceivably be worth his while to make certain temporary, limited and largely formal concessions to these halfhearted, rather pathetic representatives of an exiled monarch. In the long run he was bound to come out on top, but for the time being an understanding with King Peter and his government might even bring him certain political benefits in Serbia and elsewhere. Besides, the Russians kept urging him, through General Korneyev, to come to terms with Subašić, in order, as they put it, "not to complicate" their relations with the British.[1]

It did not take long to reach a provisional understanding. An agreement was concluded on June 16. This provided that Dr. Subašić's Government should include no elements hostile to the Movement of the National Liberation and that its "main task" should be to organize aid for the Army of National Liberation. Dr. Subašić also expressly recognized the decisions of the Jajce Congress of November, 1943 and the institutions which had then been set up and undertook to appeal publicly to the people of Jugoslavia to support the Partisans. It was further agreed that the question of the monarchy should be left for the Jugoslav people to decide after the war and that, in the meantime, neither side should do anything to "emphasize it or render it acute." Finally the agreement envisaged the early formation of a united Jugoslav Government composed jointly of elements of the government in exile and of the Partisan National Committee. Having thus, on paper at any rate, bridged the gap between himself and Tito, Dr. Subašić returned to London to lay the results of his labors before King Peter. With him went Vladko Velebit to keep an eye on him and to act as a link between the London Government and the National Committee.

The agreement which had been concluded had one immediate result. General Mihajlović was deprived of his post as Minister of War and excluded from the government which Dr. Subašić now formed on his return to London. Henceforward the Royal Jugoslav Government had no further official dealings with him. Not long afterward King Peter himself made a broadcast to Jugoslavia denouncing him and calling on all loyal Jugoslavs to support Tito. For Mihajlović, to whom the monarchy meant so much, this final repudiation must indeed have been a bitter blow.

The presence of Tito on Vis clearly offered a convenient opportunity for the Allied High Command to discuss with him personally a number of questions of mutual interest, and, toward the end of July, he received an invitation from General Wilson, the Supreme Allied Commander, Mediterranean, to visit him at Caserta for the purpose of military conversations at the highest level. Some weeks earlier Tito had at the last

minute refused such an invitation on learning that King Peter
was to be in Italy at the same time. Now he accepted. It was
arranged that the visit should take place at the beginning of
August.

Tito's entourage completely filled the airplane which the
Supreme Commander had sent over to Vis to fetch him. There
was Arso Jovanović, his Chief of Staff. There was Black
Žujović, his Deputy Commander-in-Chief. There were several
other Partisan staff officers. There were Tito's two bodyguards,
Boško and Prlja. There was his private secretary, Olga Nincić.
There was his son, Žarko. There was his personal physician.
There was his security officer. There was his dog, Tigar.

Before leaving Vis, the whole party had been fitted out with
brand-new uniforms, cut by Tito's personal tailor from the
heavy gray serge worn by the former Jugoslav Army, but
adorned with Partisan insignia and badges of rank. Tito, for
his part, was dressed as a Marshal of Jugoslavia. On his head
he wore a handsome new hat, with a patent-leather peak and
a scarlet band heavily decorated with gold oak leaves. It was
not, perhaps, an ideal costume for the sweltering heat of a
Mediterranean August. But then it was not designed for comfort. It was designed to show conclusively to all concerned
that Tito and his staff were not just Communist guerrillas in
borrowed battle dress, but members of the high command of a
properly constituted national army, come to negotiate on equal
terms with an Allied high command.

And indeed they were received as such. General Wilson had
sent his Chief of Staff, General Gammell, to Capodicchino airfield to meet them. There was a guard of honor for Tito to
inspect. There was a fleet of high-powered cars, waiting to
carry them up to the hunting lodge above Caserta, where
special accommodations had been prepared for them and
where the Supreme Allied Commander in person was waiting
to entertain them at luncheon. Allied Force Headquarters had
done everything they could to celebrate this, Tito's first public
appearance outside his own country, in a manner worthy of the
occasion, and he, for his part, soon shook off any uneasiness
or apprehension he might have felt at this first contact with
the outside world and encountered his Western hosts with the
same good-humored friendliness which they showed toward
him.

The discussions that followed gave Tito an opportunity of
explaining personally to the Allied High Command the needs
and requirements of the National Army of Liberation. They

also provided General Wilson and his staff with an opportunity of explaining to Tito the practical difficulties which stood in the way of meeting many of his requests. For example, Tito had of late been pressing more and more insistently for tanks and heavy artillery. A visit to the Eighth Army's colossal tank maintenance workshops at Naples, employing twelve thousand workmen, now served to give him a useful insight into the logistics of modern warfare, even if it still did not altogether convince him that the operation of an armored force was as yet beyond the means of the Partisans.

More important still, Tito's talks at Allied Force Headquarters, helped reassure him as to the Allies' intentions toward him. He found on the part both of the British and of the Americans a genuine admiration for the fight the Partisans had put up and a genuine desire to help them. He himself was also able to form a more correct appreciation than hitherto of the scale and intensity of the British and American war effort in this and other theaters and of the spirit in which the Western Allies were facing the sacrifices which it demanded of them severally and collectively. He was also impressed by something else, by the easygoing friendly comradeship, by the lack of formality which he found everywhere. "The thing in Italy which struck me most," he said afterward, "was the integration of the British and American staffs. I could not have believed that such close co-operation was possible between independent sovereign states."[2]

After four or five days most of Tito's business with Allied Force Headquarters had been more or less satisfactorily concluded. The supply problem had been discussed. So had the question of air support. A number of minor problems had also been disposed of. With General Wilson he had reviewed the wider strategical picture. He now began to notice that, on one prextext or another, his departure from Italy was being delayed by the British authorities. There was someone else, it appeared, who wanted to talk to him, but not just yet. In the meantime, would he not like to visit Fifteenth Army Group? Or Rome? Or the Island of Capri? A little impatiently he agreed to postpone his return to Vis.

It was on Capri, on August 11, while having tea in the garden of an agreeable villa, with his dog Tigar lying at his feet, that, hearing the roar of aircraft engines overhead and glancing up at the sky, Tito caught sight of a great four-engined York transport aircraft, with an escort of fighters all round it, coming in to land at Capodicchino airfield. By now he had guessed for whom it was he was waiting. "Here," he said with a smile, "comes Mr. Churchill."

The two met next day on the wide balustraded terrace of General Wilson's villa, once a favorite residence of Queen Victoria. Tito, resplendent in gold braid, red tabs and tight-fitting gray serge, had arrived first and was looking out across the glittering waters of the bay to where a plume of smoke rose lazily from the summit of Vesuvius, when suddenly he became aware of the Prime Minister of Great Britain advancing on him with outstretched hand. Mr. Churchill was wearing loose white ducks and an open-necked shirt. His face was round and pink and at the same time awe-inspiring, his expression welcoming and friendly. He had long wanted to see Tito for himself.

The conversations which now opened in the sweltering mid-August heat, amid the faded Victorian splendors of the Villa Rivalta, ranged over a wide field. The two protagonists got on well enough. Mr. Churchill told Tito of his admiration for the military achievements of the Partisans and assured him of the Allies' intention to afford them all possible help. He then turned to more general topics. Taking Tito into General Wilson's war room, he told him of his plans for the future and showed him how he thought the military situation would develop. He spoke of the pressure that was being brought to bear on the Germans on the various fronts and of their obstinate refusal to yield an inch of territory if they could avoid it. Hitler's correct strategy, he said, would be to withdraw his troops from the Balkans and concentrate them on the main battle fronts. But it could not be assumed that he would necessarily do this. Pointing on the map to Istria, he mentioned the possibility of an Allied landing there and obtained from Tito in return a prompt assurance that the Partisans would welcome such a landing and do everything in their power to assist it.

The political issues were a good deal thornier. On the subject of the British Government's obligations toward King Peter, Mr. Churchill was quite frank; he made it clear that they could not grant the Partisans any kind of political recognition unless they came to terms with the King, or rather with his government. That must be the first step. What happened after that was for the Jugoslavs themselves to decide, but in his view there was a lot to be said for a constitutional monarchy. Might it not be a good idea for him to meet King Peter and talk things over?

By questioning him as to his plans for the future and urging on him the need for moderation, Mr. Churchill showed clearly enough that he recognized the preponderant part which Tito and his followers were likely to play in the new Jugoslavia. Was it, he asked, his intention to establish a Communist regime on Soviet lines in Jugoslavia? And, if so, what were the reactions of the Jugoslav people likely to be? Stalin had once told him that his battle with the Russian peasants over collectivization in the early thirties had been a more perilous and formidable undertaking even than the battle for Stalingrad. The Partisan movement, he suggested, enjoyed less support in Serbia than in other parts of the country. "I hope, Marshal," he concluded, "that you will think twice before you join such a battle with your sturdy Serbian peasantry." He asked, too, about the Cetniks. Must the civil war go on? Was no compromise possible? Could not national unity somehow be achieved? The Allies, he must remember, were not providing him with arms and equipment in order that he should fight a civil war. If they gained the impression that this struggle against the Germans was becoming a side issue, they would naturally lose interest.

Tito replied to these questions with studied moderation and restraint. The Jugoslavs, he said, had much to learn from the example of Russia, but what they learned would need to be adapted to their own special circumstances. In regard to Serbia, Mr. Churchill must have been misinformed. He could assure him that, save for a minority of quislings, the population there was wholeheartedly behind the Partisans. Only when he spoke of Mihajlović and the Cetniks did his voice take on for a moment a petulant and angry tone. It was a subject about which, for all his powers of self-control, he could not bring himself to speak with equanimity. "I told him," he wrote long afterward, "what I thought of Mihajlović."

There were altogether three meetings and also a dinner and a luncheon, at which speeches were exchanged. At times the conversation would leave the subject immediately under discussion and drift to more personal themes. His son Randolph, Mr. Churchill said, had told him about his life with the Partisans.* It made him want to go to Jugoslavia himself, but perhaps it was rather late in life for him to start parachuting. The

* Major Randolph Churchill was dropped into Jugoslavia by parachute in January, 1944 and remained there until the spring of 1945.

task of translating what was said fell in the main to Tito's secretary, Olga, whose gentle charm did not escape the Prime Minister. At the last meeting, as he was taking leave of Tito, he gave her a little gold locket, bearing the inscription: "To Olga from Winston S. Churchill."

On the conclusion of his talks with Mr. Churchill, Tito flew back to Vis, taking with him Dr. Subašić, who had also been present at some of the meetings and with whom it had been agreed that he should pursue the discussions which they had begun two months earlier.

All in all, Tito had reason to be well satisfied with his visit. Quite apart from the assurances he had been given concerning the continuance of Allied assistance, the manner of his reception was in itself a mark of the recognition which he and his followers had won for themselves from the Western Allies. A year ago, the Partisans had scarcely been heard of outside their country. Now, he, their leader, the one-time jailbird, had been received as an honored guest by one of the Big Three. It was true that, in order to obtain formal recognition for his regime from the Western powers, he would first have to go through the motions of reaching agreement with Dr. Subašić. But that was a small concession in comparison with the advantages which would accrue from it. And, once he and his friends were in power, Dr. Subašić could soon be disposed of.

Was it not possible to discern yet another cause for satisfaction in this initial contact with the outside world? All Tito's past training and experience made it natural that he should turn his back on the West and look eastward to Moscow for guidance and help. But the fact remained that geographically Jugoslavia lay between East and West. The art of playing off one great power against another was a long-established tradition in the Balkans. There could of course be no question of a good Communist like Tito making use of such methods in his dealings with the Soviet Union. But, to look at it in another way, might not the fact that he had secured such generous recognition from the West perhaps make the Kremlin rather more inclined than hitherto to appreciate him at his true value?

By the end of August the Red Army, having entered Rumania, was rapidly advancing toward the Danube and the frontiers of Jugoslavia. If the Germans were to prevent their flank from being turned and the retreat of their forces in the Balkans from being cut off, their only hope was to withdraw their troops from Greece and Jugoslavia, where their position was in any case daily becoming more difficult, to a defense line farther north. They now adopted this course. On September 1 General von Löhr, commanding Army Group E, was entrusted by Hitler in person with the task of carrying out the withdrawal. The necessary orders were issued immediately and the retreat began during the first week in September. Simultaneously, the Partisans, in concert with the R.A.F. and United States Air Force, launched a series of vigorous and extremely successful combined attacks against German lines of communication all over the country in accordance with a plan which had been previously agreed with Allied Force Headquarters in anticipation of an enemy withdrawal and which bore the name of "Operation Ratweek." Everywhere along the enemy's line of retreat convoys were ambushed, bridges blown up and trains dynamited. Simultaneously, the German situation in the Balkans was still further aggravated by the sudden defection of the Bulgarians, who, after signing an armistice, immediately re-entered the war on the side of the Allies, handing over to the Partisans the areas which they had been occupying in Serbia and Macedonia. By the end of September Koča Popović's forces were in possession of most of southern and eastern Serbia, while the nine Partisan divisions under Peko Dapčević, advancing northward through western Siberia, had reached a line some twenty miles south of Belgrade stretching from Obrenovac across the Kosmaj to Smederevska Palanka.

How, it may be asked, did the Germans regard the man who could claim, with some justification, that, after three years of bitter fighting, he was now driving them out of his country? The notes of a lecture delivered on September 21, 1944, to an audience of senior military officers by Heinrich Himmler in person, provide the answer. "I should like," said Himmler, "to give another example of steadfastness, that of Marshal Tito. I must say that this old Communist, Herr Josip Broz, is a consistent man. Unfortunately he is our opponent. He has really earned his title of Marshal. When we catch him we shall kill him at once. You can be sure of that. He is our enemy. But I wish we had a dozen Titos in Germany, men who were leaders and had such resolution and good nerves that, even though they were forever encircled, they would never give in. The man had nothing, nothing at all. He was always encircled, and he always found a way out. He has never capitulated. We know better than anyone how he gets under our skin in the Serbo-Croat district, and that is only because he fights consistently. He has the cheek to call a battalion a brigade, and we fall for it straight away. A brigade? In Heaven's name. The military mind at once imagines a group of six or eight thousand men. A thousand vagabonds who have been herded together suddenly become a brigade. Divisions and corps are knocked to pieces by us, and the man forms them up again every time. Be sure he only succeeded in doing that because he is an uncompromising and steadfast soldier, a steadfast commander."[3]

Meanwhile the first Soviet troops had crossed the Jugoslav border from Rumania and were now advancing in the direction of Belgrade. The need for comprehensive high-level discussions with the Russians had become urgent. Early in September Tito put forward through General Korneyev the suggestion that he should visit Moscow for the purpose of co-ordinating the operations of his own forces with those of the Red Army during the next phase of the campaign. The answer was favorable, and added, according to Jugoslav sources, that Tito should keep his departure from Vis strictly secret.*

The airfield on Vis was under British command. It was, however, occasionally used by the Soviet-piloted Dakotas based on Bari. It was in one of these that Tito, accompanied by two members of his personal staff and by General Korneyev, took off just before midnight on September 21, having successfully avoided detection by the R.A.F. security guards. At the last moment his dog Tigar, realizing that his master was going away, made such a fuss that Tito decided to take him too. A sack was put over his head to keep him quiet while the party was getting into the aircraft. It was thus that Tito and his entourage, reverting easily to the clandestine habits of their earlier existence, left Vis by stealth.

From Vis Tito flew first to Marshal Tolbukhin's Headquar-

---

* If this version is correct, it seems possible that the object of the Russians in insisting on secrecy was to make trouble between Tito and the British. If so, they were entirely successful. Mr. Churchill was particularly annoyed by this clandestine departure and in an indignant telegram spoke of Tito as having "levanted" from Vis.

Molotov, on the other hand, assured Mr. Eden, when they met in Moscow in October, that it was at Tito's wish that his journey had been kept secret. Such behavior, he added, was all that you could expect of a Balkan peasant.

ters at Craiova in Rumania. There he received a delegation of
Bulgarians with whom he signed an agreement providing for
an armistice between their respective forces, to be followed by
joint action against the Germans. Then he flew on to Moscow.
On his tunic he proudly displayed the ribbon of the Order of
Suvorov, First Class, which the Soviet Government had a-
warded him a fortnight earlier.

Tito had not visited the Soviet Union since 1940. Then, he
had gone there as a Comintern agent, the representative of a
small and not particularly successful illegal Communist party.
He had even been shunned by his fellow lodgers at the Hotel
Lux. Now, he came as the leader of a Communist party which
would shortly assume power, as the commander of a victorious
army, a marshal in his own right, accustomed to dealing with
foreign governments on equal terms.

On his previous visits to the Land of Socialism, Tito, or
Walter, as he was still known in Moscow, had not been important enough to be received by Stalin. He had only seen him
from a distance, at the Seventh Comintern Conference and
at parades on the Red Square. Now he was on quite a different footing. A special, lavishly equipped *dacha* was placed at
his disposal, the same, he noted with satisfaction, that Mr.
Churchill had occupied on his visit to Moscow. No sooner
had he arrived than he was swept off to the Kremlin to see
Stalin, who at this, their first meeting, embraced him with
such vigor that he lifted him clean off his feet, while Molotov, Zhdanov, Malenkov and Beria, looked on appreciatively.
What greater reward could there be than this for the faithful
Communist who had deserved well of the party and emerged
triumphant from all his ordeals?

And yet, once the initial greetings were over and they had
begun their discussions, was it Tito's imagination, or did he
notice a certain reserve, a certain coolness, in Stalin's attitude
toward him? It was true that the *Vozhd* had spoken in appre-
ciative terms of what the Partisans had done. He had even
observed, somewhat cryptically, that it was a good thing that,
whereas he, Stalin, was getting old, Tito was in his prime and
had acquired much valuable experience during the war. But
from his general attitude and from certain remarks that he
dropped, it soon became clear that all was not well.

Seen from close to, Stalin was smaller and rather less per-
sonable than he appeared in his photographs. His skin was
sallow. His mustache was sparse and straggling and his teeth,
when he smiled, were discolored and crooked. He also had

narrow, sloping shoulders and held his arms a little away from his body. But he moved with the muffled ease of a polar bear and, however unprepossessing his appearance, there could be no doubt as to the force of his personality. At this and every other meeting, he completely dominated the proceedings, while his subordinates, Molotov, Zhdanov, Malenkov and Beria, cringed before him.

Confronted with this formidable phenomenon, it was a little difficult for Tito to know just how to behave. Five years ago it would have been quite simple: he would have behaved as a not very important junior officer in the presence of his Supreme Commander. But a lot of water had flowed under the bridges since then. Now he represented much more than two or three thousand party members, hunted and harried by the police. He represented a nation in arms, an army of a quarter of a million men, a *de facto* government that had already started to build Socialism along lines of its own. And so he treated Stalin with respect, with the respect due to a great revolutionary, to a great statesman, to the Leader of the International Proletariat, to the Supreme Ruler of the Land of Socialism. But he did not treat him as someone from whom he was ready to take orders at any time, on any subject. He allowed at times the slightest suggestion of independence to creep into his manner.

Stalin noticed this and did not like it. It was not the only thing he did not like about Tito. He had not been pleased by the tone of some of the telegrams Tito had sent him, especially the one beginning "If you cannot help us, at least do not hamper us. . . ." Indeed that particular message had caused him literally to stamp with rage. He did not like all the publicity Tito and his Partisans had been receiving. He did not like Tito's good looks and spectacular uniforms. He had, in short, a feeling that Tito might be getting too big for his boots. For, after all, in Stalin's eyes, there was precious little difference between Comrade Walter of the Lux Hotel and Marshal Josip B. Tito of Jugoslavia, between one Moscow-trained Communist and another. They were all simply puppets to be used as long as they served any useful purpose and then discarded or liquidated. But there would be time for such minor adjustments later. For the moment expediency required that he should put up with him, even treat him with a certain degree of consideration. Nevertheless, in the Kremlin (and outside it), it became known that the impression made on the *Vozhd* by this colorful Communist from the Balkans had been far from favorable.

Tito, it must be admitted, was not being altogether easy. Stalin had quite naturally assumed that, when the Red Army entered Jugoslavia, the Partisans and anyone else who might be there would automatically come under the orders of his Commander-in-Chief, Marshal Tolbukhin, who commanded the Third Ukrainian Front. Nor had it occurred to him that he might have to ask anyone's permission before allowing his troops to cross the Jugoslav frontier in pursuit of the enemy. But he did not know Tito. The latter, it appeared, had come in the name of his National Committee (formed, as we know, against Stalin's express instructions) to negotiate an agreement which, on certain specified conditions, would permit Soviet troops to enter Jugoslavia for a limited period for the specific purpose of conducting operations against the German forces in Hungary, on the clear understanding that they withdrew again as soon as their task was completed. He was also prepared to discuss joint operations by Partisan and Soviet forces and would be glad to accept the support of one Soviet armored division in the forthcoming assault on Belgrade. There could, he made it clear, be no question of the Partisans being placed under anyone's command except his own, or of the Russians exercising any civil or administrative powers while on Jugoslav territory.

Stalin accepted these terms. It did not matter anyway and this was not the moment for a showdown. There would be time for that, if necessary, later. Meanwhile, instead of the armored division for which Tito had asked, Stalin announced that he would send a corps, as a reminder, perhaps, that armed force on a sufficient scale did count for something.

Once the purely military problems had been settled their conversation ranged over wider fields. Tito himself has given a vivid account of it. Stalin, it appears, like Mr. Churchill before him, tried to give Tito a little advice as to the way in which he should tackle some of the political problems which confronted him. "Be careful, Walter," he said, "the bourgeoisie in Serbia is very strong." "I disagree with you, Comrade Stalin," Tito replied with bland assurance, "the bourgeoisie in Serbia is very weak." At this there was an awkward silence. Stalin, unused to being contradicted, frowned, while Molotov and the others sat aghast. Then the *Vozhd*, having recovered his composure, went on to ask Tito about various non-Communist Jugoslav politicians. "Oh," said Tito at the first name he mentioned, "he's a scoundrel and a traitor; he collaborated with the Germans." Stalin did not look very pleased and mentioned another name. The result was the same. This was too much for Stalin. "Walter," he said angrily, "to you they are all scoundrels." But Tito was unabashed. "Exactly, Comrade Stalin," he replied sententiously, "anyone who betrays his country is a scoundrel."

"From now onward," Tito tells us, "the talk proceeded in a very painful atmosphere." The next subject to be discussed was the restoration of the Jugoslav monarchy. Stalin, it appears, was all for it. But on this issue Tito was more uncompromising than ever. He said that it was impossible, that the people would not stand for it. He was carried away. He used the words "treason," "terror," "hatred" and "corruption." Another awkward silence ensued. Then patiently Stalin said: "You need not restore him forever. Take him back temporarily. Then you can slip a knife into his back at a suitable moment."

But at this interesting stage in the conversation they were suddenly interrupted by Molotov, who had been called out and now returned bringing with him an agency report that the British had landed in Jugoslavia.

"Impossible!" said Tito when it was shown to him.

"What do you mean—impossible?" said Stalin. "It's a fact." And he listened irritably while Tito explained that the agency must have got it wrong; that he had asked Generel Alexander to land three batteries of artillery to help the Partisans with their operations in the neighborhood of Mostar and Sarajevo and that this had probably been confused with a full-scale invasion.

"Tell me, Walter," he said, when Tito had finished, "what would you do if the British really tried to land against your will in Jugoslavia?"

"We should offer determined resistance," Tito answered at once. After which there was yet another awkward silence.

Then, after dressing down one of his marshals by long-distance telephone, Stalin slammed back the receiver and took Tito off to supper at his house in the country. At supper the *Vozhd* plied his guest with wine and vodka. After a time, Tito, who was not used to such heavy drinking, felt sick and had to go out of the room.. As he was cursing himself for having drunk so much, he heard Beria, who had followed him out, saying: "It doesn't matter. These things will happen!" Which made him feel sillier than ever. There was no doubt about it, the visit had not been an unqualified success.[4]

From Moscow Tito flew to Vršac in the Banat, arriving in time to join up with the Russians as they came streaming over the Rumanian border. The battle for Belgrade was now about to begin. While one strong Soviet armored force closed in on Belgrade from the northeast, another, having crossed the Danube lower down, converged on the city from the southeast, linking up with Peko Dapčević's First Army as they advanced to the attack from the south. From Vršac Tito personally co-ordinated the movements of his own troops with those of the Red Army.

The Germans, anxious to hold Belgrade for as long as possible and thus secure their communications with the south until they had withdrawn the remainder of their forces from Serbia and Macedonia, had reinforced the garrison with all the troops they could lay hands on and the ensuing battle was a singularly fierce one. Farther south, more heavy fighting was in progress round Kraljevo, the key to the Ibar and Morava valleys. For the first time in Jugoslavia, the Germans found themselves up against an enemy plentifully supplied with heavy armor and artillery. They, for their part, were fighting for their lives and their antitank gunners performed prodigies of valor, leaving the surrounding country and the approaches to the city littered with shattered Soviet tanks.

But by October 14 Peko Dapčević's Partisans had, with Russian support, broken through the enemy's front to the south of Belgrade and reached his second line of defenses on the outskirts of the city. The prize for which they had waited so long and suffered so much was now within their grasp. Led by the First Proletarian Division, they began their final assault on the center of the city. In spite of strong Soviet armor, artillery and air support, this was to last for nearly a week, the enemy fiercely defending every street and every house. But in the end the German resistance began to fail. A strong German force which tried to fight its way through to the city from the south was cut off and almost entirely destroyed. Early on October 20 the First Proletarian Division, fighting its way along one of the main avenues, stormed and took the old Turkish citadel, the Kalimegdan, and a few hours later what was left of the German garrison was falling back across the Sava to Zemun. In the battle for Belgrade the Germans had lost sixteen thousand killed and eight thousand captured.

The Partisans, too, had suffered severely. But Belgrade was theirs at last.

All through the war, through all the setbacks, through all the hazards and hardships which he had endured, Tito, with characteristic steadfastness and singleness of purpose, had constantly looked forward to this moment. The Partisans had begun their uprising in Belgrade; it was fitting that Belgrade should witness their triumph. And now, at last, this had come to pass, though at a heavy cost in lives and in human suffering.

A few days after the fall of Belgrade, Tito held a review of the troops who had taken part in the battle for the city, led by the First Proletarian Brigade. The Partisans who now marched past their leader were a ragged, battle-stained throng. They were of all sizes and ages. They looked underfed and weary. Their arms and equipment had only this in common: that it had been captured from the enemy in battle. Their uniforms, also stripped from the corpses of their foes, were discolored and torn. But they marched well and held themselves proudly. They had spent the last three years fighting up and down the length and breadth of the country. They had endured innumerable hazards and privations. And now at long last they had gained their reward. They had routed the enemy and were entering the capital of their country as conquerors.

After they had marched past, Tito spoke to them. He was clearly much moved. "In the most difficult hours of the war," he said, "during the most terrible offensives, I always thought to myself, 'In Belgrade we began the uprising; in Belgrade we shall end it in victory!' That great day has now come. Among us there are very few of those who set out in 1941. They built their lives into the foundations of this country that it might be free and what the people wish it to be. Their example was followed by thousands of others. Every rifle that fell to the ground was seized by ten other hands. Glory to the fighters who fell for the liberation of Jugoslavia, for the liberation of her capital, Belgrade!"

The fall of Belgrade marked the end of the guerrilla phase of the war in Jugoslavia. Henceforward, from being a war of movement, it became to a great extent a war of position, something entirely new to the Partisans. By now the Germans were in full retreat, and within a few weeks Serbia, Macedonia, Montenegro, Herzegovina and Dalmatia, as well as

large parts of Bosnia were clear of them. In order to safeguard their line of withdrawal, the Germans concentrated on
holding the main Sarajevo-Brod-Zagreb line of communication together with the bare minimum of territory necessary
for its defense. They also clung to the lateral communications
connecting it with Bihać, Banjaluka and Mostar, thus protect-
ing their southwestern flank against the attacks of the Partisans and against the risk of an Allied landing in Dalmatia.
Their northeastern flank, seriously threatened by the Russians
in Hungary, they protected by holding as strongly as possible
the wedge of territory bounded on three sides by the Sava, the
Drava and the Danube and known as the Srem. Here a fixed
front was formed, the Germans desperately resisting the efforts of a combined Russian, Bulgar and Jugoslav force to
break through toward Brod, while in the north, in Croatia
and Slovenia, they hurriedly prepared in those bitter winter
months the defense line to which they eventually hoped to
fall back.

The capture of Belgrade also marked the beginning of a
new phase politically. Partisan statesmen no longer needed to
creep through the enemy lines at night in order to perform
their duties. The members of the National Committee were
now installed in such of the official buildings of the capital
as were still standing. Their business, instead of stirring up
trouble, was now to govern and administer the country and
restore order, to quell resistance instead of organizing it. It
was a task before which less resolute or less self-confident
men might have flinched. The Partisans, though possessing but
little experience of such matters, threw themselves into their
new work with characteristic assurance, enthusiasm and ruthlessness.

Tito, for so long an outlaw, now took up his residence in
Prince Paul's charmingly furnished White Palace at Dedinje
on the outskirts of the city. From now onward his suits and
uniforms were made by the best tailor in Belgrade; the horses
he rode were the finest in the country; he ate the best food
and drank the best wine; his official receptions were on the
most lavish scale. But amid all this magnificence it is only
fair to say that, to his former companions, he remained as
simple and as friendly in his approach as ever. Indeed there
was nothing he liked better than to collect half a dozen old
friends in a corner of one of the great gilded salons and
there, over a glass of *rakija*, talk of the old heroic days "u

šume"—"in the woods," and sing the old familiar Partisan
songs.

During the weeks which followed its liberation, Belgrade
itself presented a forlorn aspect. It had suffered severely in

the recent fighting. It also bore the marks of the Luftwaffe's
bombardment in April, 1941 and of subsequent Allied air
attacks. Every fourth or fifth house along the tree-lined avenues bore signs of damage. The Royal Palace had received a
direct hit and lay in ruins. Derelict tanks, destroyed in the

fight for the city, still littered the streets. In the squares and public gardens, rough wooden crosses marked the graves of Partisans or Russians who had been killed in the battle. On the walls of the houses there still hung ominous notices signed by the German Commandant, proclaiming mass executions of civilians as a reprisal for Partisan activities. Outside the town the derelict hutments of a former German concentration camp furnished a grim reminder of the occupation. At night shooting could be heard in the streets, as stray Germans, who had been hiding in cellars or attics, emerged and ran the gauntlet of the sentries, or drunken Russians brawled and fought among themselves. In the Kalimegdan, the old fortress where the Turks had once held sway, a detachment of Russian women troops with rifles and bayonets and pasty, moonlike faces mounted guard.

Gradually, as time passed, things became more normal. The bulk of the Russian contingent was withdrawn. The streets were cleared of debris. Shops, schools, churches and theaters reopened. Food supplies, at first disorganized by lack of transport, resumed on a more normal scale. Slowly, a number of citizens who had thought it at first wiser to lie low, began to emerge. For, though many had cheered the Partisans and the Russians when they entered the city, some still went in terror of their lives, while others, after living through three and a half years of German occupation, had consciences that were far from clear.

Tito was now in undisputed control of the greater part of the country. His troops were in occupation of all the areas from which the Germans had withdrawn, while his civil authorities had taken over their administration. Members of the Communist party occupied all the key positions. War conditions favored centralization. A policy of state control and large-scale requisitioning was easily justified. Soon the greater part of industry and commerce was more or less directly controlled by the National Committee. The press and wireless automatically followed the party line. Conscription gave the central authority a hold over every able-bodied individual in the country and at the same time provided it with a considerable armed force with which to back its decisions. Nor should it be supposed that by the end of the war the Partisans did not enjoy a considerable measure of genuine popular support. By their relentless struggle against the invaders they had won widespread admiration and approval, which increased when they finally emerged victorious. To many peo-

ple they seemed to present the only prospect of stable government, and this was an important consideration in a country
which for the past four years had been tortured by every
kind of strife and dissension. They were also known to enjoy
the support of the great Allies, and in particular of the Soviet
Union, whose Red Army, even after its withdrawal, continued
to dominate the situation militarily from across the frontier.

Moreover there were now no serious rivals for power. The
puppet administrations set up by the Germans were doomed
to collapse as soon as German support was withdrawn. Nedić,
having formally handed over the command of his remaining
forces to Mihajlović, had fled from Belgrade in September.*
Pavelic, it is true, was still in Zagreb, but his supporters by
now were divided among themselves and already most of the
territory of this Independent State was in Partisan hands. As
to the Cetniks, many had taken advantage of the amnesty
which Tito had offered them and joined the Partisans. Others
fled northward with the Germans. Some said that in the
spring, when the leaves were on the trees, there would be a
Cetnik rising throughout Serbia, but for the present there was
no sign of any such thing. Meanwhile, the position of the
Partisans was daily becoming stronger.

It was against this background that Tito resumed his negotiations with Dr. Subašić, who had returned to Jugoslavia
shortly before the fall of Belgrade. Tito's position was now
stronger than ever and by November 2 a draft agreement had
been drawn up. This provided that Tito's Anti-Fascist Council
should remain the supreme legislative body, while a united
government was formed from members of both the National
Committee and of Dr. Subašić's Government. The united
government would in due course hold elections to decide the
future form of government of the country. In the meantime
this would in theory continue to be a monarchy, the King
remaining abroad and being represented in Jugoslavia by a
regency.

Tito had made it quite clear that his only object in accepting such a compromise was to secure immediate recognition
from the Allies. The next step was to submit the proposed
arrangements to the latter for their approval. Accordingly the
Head of the British Mission now flew to London, taking with

* General Nedic was later handed over to the Partisans by the
Allies and fell, jumped or was pushed out of a window with fatal
consequences.

him the draft agreement, while Kardelj and Dr. Subašić flew to Moscow. A week or two later they returned from their respective destinations, having received the assent of the British and Soviet Governments to the draft as a possible basis for an understanding.

Stalin, it appeared, had taken the opportunity to lecture Subašić and Kardelj on the blessings of true democracy. "None of your rigged elections!" he had warned them with sardonic jocularity. And he had gone on to tease Kardelj about the unreliability of Partisan military claims. "I know those Partisan figures," he said, "they're always exaggerated."[5]

Mr. Churchill, for his part, while accepting the draft agreement, showed but little enthusiasm for it, or indeed for Tito, who had earned his displeasure by "levanting" so unceremoniously from Vis in September. On his return to Belgrade, the Head of the British Mission endeavored to convey to Tito the irritation which his behavior had caused in London and the harm it had done to Anglo-Jugloslav relations. But Tito could not, or would not, understand. "Only recently," he observed, "Mr. Churchill went to Quebec to see President Roosevelt, and I only heard of this visit after he had returned. And I was not angry." He was clearly taking to his new position like a duck to water. Visitors noticed that a small bronze bust of Napoleon now occupied a prominent position on his writing desk.

It remained to obtain the assent of King Peter to the proposed agreement and with this object Dr. Subašić now left Belgrade for London. He was to stay there for some time. As was only to be expected, it did not prove easy to convince the King that the proposed agreement was really in his best interests. Nor had the fruits of victory made Tito any more amenable. It began to look as if the negotiations, which were conducted in a desultory manner by wireless, might drag on indefinitely.

This did not suit Tito, who had other fish to fry. After waiting for a couple of months, he decided that the time had come to exert a little pressure. Up to now, in accordance with the terms of the preliminary agreement reached on Vis, *Borba* and *Politika* and the rest of the Communist-controlled newspapers now appearing in Belgrade had scarcely made mention of the King or of the negotiations. Now, all of a sudden, they came out with violent attacks on King Peter, while simultaneously, despite the bitter winter weather, the streets of Belgrade filled with well-disciplined crowds of demonstrators chanting in dreary unison the endlessly repeated refrain, *"Hoćemo Tito; necemo Kralja"*—"We want Tito; we don't want the King."* Outside the Headquarters of the British Mission the demonstrators halted and sang with redoubled energy, as though the better to drive home their point. Above their heads, as they sang, flapped the flags of the Allies: Union Jack, Stars and Stripes, Hammer and Sickle—Hammer and Sickle now predominating, larger and more prominent even than the Jugoslav Tricolor. The pretense that for Jugoslavia the problem of her future form of government still admitted of more than one possible solution was daily wearing thinner. Even in Bulgaria, Hungary and Rumania, now firmly occupied by the Red Army, the process of Sovietization was proceeding more gradually.

Meanwhile, a few hundred miles to the south, in Greece, a similar situation was developing in a dissimilar way. There, British troops had landed close on the heels of the retreating Germans. With them had come the Greek Government in Exile. The Greek Communists, whose contribution to their country's wartime resistance had not been comparable to that of their Jugoslav comrades, but who nevertheless possessed a considerable political and military organization, now found themselves at a disadvantage. Instead of passing into their hands, as it might otherwise have done, power had passed automatically into the hands of the non-Communists, who could now count on the support of the British Forces of Occupation. The Communists' answer was armed revolt. Early in December they rose and attempted to seize power by force of arms. The British, determined to prevent any attempt on the part of the Communists to prejudge the ultimate issue, reacted promptly and decisively. After a month's fighing in and around Athens, the insurgents were defeated and on January 11, 1945, a truce was signed. For the time being the Greek Communist rebellion had been stifled.

Tito watched events in Greece closely. From his point of view, they were not very reassuring. If the British were prepared to back their fancy so vigorously in Greece, might they not try the same thing in Jugoslavia? Might this not be the

---

* Here and there a few bold spirits varied this with *"Hocemo Kralja iako ne valja"*—"We want the King, even if he is no good," thus displaying a frame of mind characteristic of many who, while preferring the monarchy to a Communist dictatorship, felt no particular enthusiasm for the person of the monarch.

real reason for the delay in reaching a settlement and for King Peter's intransigence? The old fears of a British attempt to restore the monarchy by force revived.

But on January 18, 1945, Mr. Churchill made a speech in the House of Commons which did much to set Tito's mind at rest. "It is," he said, referring to the Jugoslav negotiations, "a matter of days within which an agreement must be reached on this matter and, if we are so unfortunate as not to obtain the consent of King Peter, the matter will have to go ahead, his assent being presumed." "We have," he continued, "no special interest in the political regime which prevails in Jugoslavia. Few people in Britain, I imagine, are going to be more cheerful or more downcast because of the future constitution of Jugoslavia."

After that Tito knew that he had nothing more to worry about. His manner, when discussing the negotiations, became increasingly jocular. Even the news that King Peter had dismissed Dr. Subašić and that everything was once more in the air, left him completely unmoved. The whole thing, he said, was "as good as a play."

And, sure enough, within a day or two relations between the King and his Prime Minister had been resumed and negotiations reopened. By now the points at issue had been narrowed down to the choice of the three regents. This was a purely academic question, for it had long been clear that the regents would never be more than figure-heads. But there was still plenty of scope for argument. The rival claims of a number of elderly Serb, Croat and Slovene politicians were discussed from every angle, while charges of treason and corruption flew back and forth in true Balkan style. An agreement seemed as far off as ever.

Then, in early February, the news reached Belgrade that the Big Three, Churchill, Stalin and Roosevelt, were meeting at Yalta in the Crimea. It was known that the Jugoslav problem would be on the agenda and that a pronouncement might be expected. In due course it came. It was short and to the point. After the traditional reference to "democratic principles," Tito and Dr. Subašić were urged to conclude an agreement without further loss of time. There was no mention of King Peter. It was impossible for either side to ignore the Crimean oracle. The proceedings in London were hastily wound up and a few days later Dr. Subašić and his government arrived in Belgrade with instructions to come to terms with Tito as quickly as possible.

But there was still some fight left in King Peter, enough, at any rate, to find fault with Tito's latest choice of candidates for the regency. Abandoned by his government and by the British and faced with what had long been a foregone conclusion, he and his little circle of personal advisers managed to hold out for a few more weeks against the pressure which was being brought to bear on them to come to terms with Tito. Then, quite suddenly, at the beginning of March, resistance ceased. It was announced that the King's objections to Tito's proposals had been withdrawn and agreement reached.

The remaining formalities did not take long. The three regents were sworn in with due ceremony; Dr. Subašić's Government resigned; and on March 7 Tito, who had previously resigned his post as Chairman of the National Committee, announced that he had been successful in forming a new united government, with Dr. Subašić as Minister of Foreign Affairs and six other members of the former Royal Government holding office in it. It is scarcely necessary to add that the key positions in the new administration remained in Communist hands. Even at the Foreign Ministry Vladko Velebit, who held the post of Assistant Minister, had far more real power than Dr. Subašić. Now as always, the real business of the state was conducted, not by the government as such, but by the Politburo of the party, by that little band of able and devoted companions which Tito had gathered round him during the past ten years, by Kardelj, Randović, Djilas, Žujović, Hebrang, Kidrić and Moša Pijade.

It remained for the Allies to perform their part of the bargain by granting formal recognition to the new government. They did so with alacrity. Five days after the formation of the new government Mr. Ralph Stevenson, hitherto Ambassador to King Peter, arrived in Belgrade and took up residence at the British Embassy. Within a few weeks he was joined by United States and Soviet colleagues.

The war in Europe was nearly over. At the beginning of April the Partisans launched a final offensive which was to continue until May and in which all their available forces were engaged: the First Army under Peko Dapčević; the Second Army under Koča Popović; the Third Army under Kosta Nadj; the Fourth Army under Petar Drapšin. Harassed and attacked from every side, but still clinging stubbornly

to its vital communications and fighting back every inch of
the way, what remained of the German Army of Occupation
dragged itself through Bosnia and Croatia like a wounded
snake. An attempt by General von Löhr to arrange through
his contacts with Mihajlović for the orderly capitulation of his
forces to the Allies had failed. There was nothing for it but
to try and fight their way out. Only a few succeeded. During
the last two months of the war in Jugoslavia the Germans
were to lose close on 100,000 killed and over 200,000 captured. On Hitler's instructions, the evacuation of Bosnia had
been too long delayed. When the defense line south of
Zagreb was reached, it was no longer possible to hold it.
Falling back across it, General von Löhr's troops continued
their agonizing retreat toward their own country, now itself
in mortal peril. But, before the main force could reach the
frontier, there came on the night of May 7 the order for
unconditional surrender. Those who could, gave themselves
up to the British; others to the Russians; for the great majority
there was no choice but to surrender to the Partisans. General
von Löhr, for his part, chose to remain in Jugoslavia with the
main body of his troops. As they were setting out for Jugoslav Headquarters to arrange the surrender, his Chief of
Staff asked him what treatment he personally expected to
receive from the Partisans, *"Mit Sicherheit,"* he replied, *"den
Tod"*—"Death for a certainty." He was, as it turned out,
right.

With the retreating Germans went a number of Tito's internal
opponents, Ustaše, Cetniks, Serb Volunteer Corps, Slovene
White Guards, Montenegrin Nationalists, a pitiful rabble, part
traitors, part heroes, part bewildered peasantry, all finally
united in this last act of collaboration with an already defeated
enemy. On May 14 the *Poglavnik* of Croatia, Dr. Ante
Pavelić, made his last public appearance in Zagreb at a rally
of the Ustaša Women's Organization. "Never forget, my
sisters," he told them, his large, ugly face convulsed with
emotion, "that there is no life without freedom. It is better to
live one day as a lion than a hundred years as a sheep. If we
must die, let us fall as true heroes, not as cowards crying
for mercy." After which, outdistancing his own panic-stricken
forces, he left hurriedly for the Austrian frontier. When
Moskov, the commander of his personal bodyguard, urged
him to rally his remaining companions in a last heroic stand,
he made it clear that the idea did not appeal to him, and con-

tinued his headlong flight toward Austria. Four days later, on May 8, Zagreb fell to the Partisans.*[6]

Not far away, in Bosnia, another of Tito's enemies had decided differently. Draža Mihajlović, having declined a British offer of asylum, was making his way back through the Bosnian highlands to Serbia at the head of a few hundred faithful followers, determined to carry on the fight against his Communist adversary to the bitter end. But the Cetniks, regarded as an organized military and political force, had already ceased to exist.

The Germans were smashed. The Ustaše were smashed. The Cetniks were smashed. In a matter of days now the Partisans' "three and a half years of bitter fighting" would have come to an end, leaving them alone in the field, masters of the situation, and of their destiny.

* The *Poglavnik's* subsequent movements are somewhat obscure. From Austria, he seems to have made his way to Italy, remaining there under various disguises until 1947 or 1948, when he left for South America. At the time of writing he is living in the Argentine where he has formed a new Ustaša organization and is patiently waiting for the day when he will be able once again to assume supreme power in Croatia.

part three

★ ⌐⌐⌐⌐⌐⌐⌐⌐⌐⌐⌐⌐⌐⌐⌐⌐⌐⌐⌐⌐⌐⌐⌐⌐⌐⌐⌐⌐⌐⌐ ★

WHO, WHOM?

Who, whom? We or they?
                                    LENIN
*Une action populaire comme celle-ci—ou une
révolution—ou même une insurrection—ne main-
tient sa victoire que par une technique opposée
aux moyens qui la lui ont donnée. Et parfois
même aux sentiments.*
                        ANDRÉ MALRAUX, *L'Espoir*

XI ꜱꜱꜱ "PEOPLE'S DEMOCRACY"

At the Moscow Conference of October, 1944 it had been agreed by Mr. Churchill and Generalissimo Stalin that after the war British and Soviet influence in Jugoslavia should be on a fifty-fifty basis. Mr. Churchill had jotted down these and other figures on a half-sheet of paper and pushed them across the table to Stalin, who without a moment's hesitation had ticked them with his big blue pencil. But in practice there now seemed little doubt that the Soviet share would be very much larger.*

The Russians were by now beginning to make their presence felt in Jugoslavia to an ever-increasing extent. During the latter months of the war the task of supplying the Partisans had passed very largely into their hands. The Soviet armored corps which had taken part in the battle for Belgrade had not, it is true, remained on Jugoslav territory longer than was strictly necessary. But a horde of Russian military advisers and technicians had soon made their appearance and settled busily down to the task of converting the Partisans into a satellite army on Soviet lines, wearing Soviet-type uniform and using Soviet equipment and training methods. Simultaneously, other Soviet advisers had appeared in most of the main departments of state. Finally on April 11, 1945, a Soviet-Jugoslav Treaty of Friendship and Mutual Assistance formally set the seal on the intimate relationship which already existed between the two governments. Tito, taking Djilas with him, and wearing an even more resplendent uniform than on his previous visit, had himself gone to Moscow to sign it. This time, as an Allied

* Under the terms of this remarkable arrangement it had been further agreed that in Rumania and Bulgaria Soviet influence should predominate on a basis of 90 to 10 and 75 to 25 respectively. Hungary, like Jugoslavia, was to be on a 50-50 basis. In return Great Britain was given a controlling influence (90-10) in Greece.[1]

The Jugoslavs do not seem to have heard about the agreement until a good deal later. When they did, they were considerably enraged.

Prime Minister, he had been treated with even greater respect than before. Molotov and Vishinsky, both in diplomatic uniform, had been at the airport to meet him. And once again he had been received by Stalin. "I," he told a reporter, "had a talk with Marshal Stalin. Calmly and simply the great soldier and statesman displayed the exceptional interest which he takes in our country's requirements. It is indeed fortunate not only for the people of the Soviet Union but for all liberty-loving peoples that the Soviet Union has so great a leader."[2] And was not the new ruler of Jugoslavia in any case Moscow's man? Could not the Russians count on him to carry out their instructions as faithfully as he had done in the past? Was that not perhaps the reason why Stalin had shown himself so ready to agree to the British proposal to go halves?

Even before the hostilities in which they were jointly engaged had been brought to a victorious conclusion, the period of limited collaboration which since 1941 had existed between Russia and the Western powers had already come to an end. For a time the West was to cling to the illusion that what in the Soviet eyes had never been more than a temporary expedient could somehow be converted into a permanency. But the Russians were already busily preparing for the next phase in their advance toward world domination, a phase in which their erstwhile allies would occupy the role of Public Enemy Number One. As time went on, they no longer bothered to keep up even an appearance of friendliness; bitter hostility for the West marked their every utterance and their every action. The Cold War had begun.

Moderation has never been a national characteristic of the Jugoslavs. Taking the new line from Moscow, they applied it with a vigor and a virulence all their own. Soon they were in the forefront of the political and ideological battle between East and West. The reasons for this were partly temperamental and partly geographical.

One of Tito's war aims had always been to incorporate in Jugoslavia Trieste and certain of the surrounding areas which Italy had taken from Austria after the First World War and which were largely Slovene in population. He had informed the Western Allies of these and other claims and had been told in reply that they were matters which would be settled at the peace conference and not before.* In particular he had

---

* Tito also claimed Zara, Fiume and the Istrian Peninsula from Italy, and Klagenfurt from Austria.

discussed the question of Trieste with Field Marshal Alexander on the occasion of his visit to Italy in the summer of 1944 and during a visit which the Field Marshal had paid to Belgrade in February, 1945. On both occasions the Field Marshal had made it clear to him that on purely military grounds it was essential that, when the time came, the Allied Armies should have the use of the port of Trieste and of the adjacent roads and railways in order to continue their advance northward. These exchanges, however, in no way lessened the desire of either party to reach Trieste in advance of the other. As Alexander's Fifteenth Army Group advanced northward up the Italian pennisula and Tito's Army of National Liberation closed in on Trieste from the other side, each watched the other's progress with growing attention. "The great thing," Mr. Churchill telegraphed to President Truman on April 27, "is to be there before Tito's guerrillas are in occupation."[3]

The first contact between the two armies was made at Monfalcone, a dozen miles west of Trieste, on April 30. By then Tito's troops were already fighting in Trieste itself and were also across the River Isonzo in a number of places. The Germans, however, were for obvious reasons anxious to surrender to the British rather than to the Partisans, and it was not until General Freyberg's Second New Zealand Division entered the city on May 3 that they finally capitulated. There were now both British and Jugoslav troops in Trieste, but the Jugoslavs predominated and had taken over the civil administration as a matter of course. The ensuing Forty Days, as they were to be known, were used by them for, among other things, the ruthless settlement of a number of old scores.

Feeling that it was imperative that these questions should be regulated in a more orderly manner, Field Marshal Alexander, having failed to secure the withdrawal of the Jugoslav forces to a line farther east, now dispatched his Chief of Staff, General Morgan, to Belgrade to see Tito. General Morgan arrived in Belgrade on May 9, the day on which hostilities ended in Europe. He found Tito, who was wearing a magnificent new white summer uniform, in a truculent mood and not at all disposed to withdraw his troops from the positions they occupied. In the end General Morgan was obliged to come away empty-handed.

This enraged Field Marshal Alexander, who considered that Tito had gone back on what had been agreed between them. On May 19 he issued a strongly worded communiqué comparing Tito's behavior to that of Hitler and Mussolini and concluding with the following words: "We are now waiting to hear whether Marshal Tito is prepared to co-operate in accepting a peaceful settlement of his territorial claims or whether he will attempt to establish them by force."

This in turn provoked a no less violent reaction from Tito, who expressed bitter resentment at the comparison which the Field Marshal had drawn between his actions and those of Hitler and Mussolini. His troops, he claimed, had gallantly advanced to the Isonzo and beyond in pursuit of the enemy. They were prepared to co-operate with the Allies but they would not allow themselves to be humiliated or cheated of their rights.

The two armies were now facing each other at very close quarters indeed, and the strong reinforcements which the Allies had brought up left no doubt as to their intentions. Unless he was prepared to risk hostilities with a greatly superior adversary, Tito was bound to give way. Having first ascertained from the Russians that they were not prepared to back him, he let it be known that he was ready to negotiate. On June 9 agreement was reached in principle and on June 11 the Jugoslavs withdrew from the city of Trieste. Under the terms of the detailed agreement which was now negotiated between General Morgan and Tito's Chief of Staff, General Arso Jovanović, they remained in occupation of Istria and of the Slovene littoral as far as Trieste (Zone B), while the Allies occupied the city itself and the country to the west of it (Zone A). For the time being, Zone A was placed in trust under Allied administration, while Zone B was placed in trust under Jugoslav administration, on the understanding that the whole question would be finally settled at the peace conference.

In the end a peaceful solution had been arrived at, but it left the Jugoslavs seething with resentment, while the British, for their part, no longer felt very well disposed toward their former allies.

Meanwhile another cloud, the size, it is true, of a man's hand, but a cloud nonetheless, had appeared on Tito's horizon —on his eastern horizon. And once again the occasion was Trieste.

The Russians were in two minds about Trieste. They wanted, of course, to make sure of it for themselves. But they wanted more than just Trieste; they wanted, if possible, to bring the whole of Italy under Communist and thus under Soviet control. If Trieste were given to Tito, it would, they reasoned, become in effect a Russian port. But there was also strong feeling about Trieste in Italy, and by actively supporting Tito's claim to it they would be weakening the position of the Italian Communist party and thus lessening their chances of success. Quite apart from this, if they gave Tito the slightest encouragement, he might attempt to seize Trieste by main force and thus involve them in an open conflict with the West, for which they were not as yet prepared. And so, instead of encouraging Tito, the Russians used their influence with him in a moderating sense—with the result that, as has already been recorded, a peaceful settlement was eventually arrived at.

This inconclusive solution suited everyone except Tito, whom it left with a lively sense of grievance. This he ventilated in a speech which he made on May 28 at Ljubljana, the newly liberated capital of Slovenia, barely a month after his return from Moscow. "It is claimed," he said, "that this is just a war, and up to now we have considered it as such. But we also want a just end to it. We demand that everyone shall be master in his own house. We do not want to pay other people's bills. We do not want to be used as a bribe in international bargaining. We do not want to get involved in any policy of spheres of influence. Why should it be counted against our peoples because they want to be completely independent and why should their independence be limited or contested? Never again will we be dependent on anyone."[4]

Stalin may have been in two minds about Trieste. On one point he had no doubts at all, namely the attitude which he expected from his subordinates. This attitude was not, in his view, reflected in Tito's Ljubljana speech. Not reflected either in certain other actions and utterances which had been reported to him from Belgrade. Nor indeed in the bearing and manner of this overdressed upstart on the occasions when he himself had received him in Moscow. It was time, he decided, to call him to heel.

After an earlier verbal exchange with Kardelj during which the latter, on instructions from Tito, had expressed surprise that the Soviet Government should assume that the speech necessarily applied to them, Sadchikov, the Soviet Ambassador in Belgrade, on June 5 addressed to the Jugoslav Government a formal communication in the following terms:

We regard Comrade Tito's speech as an unfriendly attack on the Soviet Union and Comrade Kardelj's explanation as unsatisfactory. The public here understood Comrade Tito's speech in the manner stated; nor can it be understood in any other. Tell Comrade Tito that, if he should once again permit such an attack on the Soviet Union, we shall be obliged to reply with open criticism in the press and disavow him.[5]

In Tito's temporary absence from Belgrade, Sadchikov, a disagreeable-looking functionary with narrow eyes and a hard sardonic mouth set in a pudgy Soviet face, delivered this startling message to Edo Kardelj. It placed the latter in an awkward position. On the one hand, there was his duty to his leader; on the other, his duty to Moscow. It was something very like a conflict of loyalties, a predicament which no true Communist should ever have to face. Kardelj, calm, resolute and not easily ruffled, did his best under trying circumstances.

"The communication," Sadchikov reported to his government afterward, "made a serious impression on him. After some thought, he said he regarded our opinion of Tito's speech as correct. He agreed that the Soviet Union could not tolerate such statements. . . . Kardelj asked me to convey to you his gratitude for this well-timed criticism. He said it would improve their work."[6]

But this was not all. Communist ritual, the ritual of self-abasement, demanded that he should go further still. "In an attempt," the Ambassador's report continued,

to analyse (very carefully) the cause of their mistakes, Kardelj said that Tito had done great work in liquidating fractionalism in the Communist Party, but was inclined to regard Jugoslavia as a self-sufficient unit outside the general development of the proletarian revolution and of Socialism. Secondly such a situation had arisen in the Party that the Central Committee had ceased to exist as an organizational and political centre. They met by chance and made decisions by chance. In practice every one of them was left to himself. Their style of work was bad and lacked co-ordination. Kardelj said that he would like the Soviet Union to regard them, not as representatives of another country, capable of solving questions independently, but as representatives of one of the future Soviet Republics and the Communist Party of Jugoslavia as part of the All-Union Communist Party, that is, that their relations should be based on the prospect of

Jugoslavia becoming in the future a constituent part of
the U.S.S.R.

A soft answer to turn away wrath? Or had the Russians succeeded in inserting a wedge between Tito and his right-hand
man? Or was the Ambassador just painting the lily? Time no
doubt would show. Meanwhile, there could be no doubt of one
thing: Tito had aroused the Kremlin's ire in no uncertain
fashion.*

Nor was this all. There had been trouble with Moscow
even before this—trouble over the behavior of the Red Army
in Jugoslavia during the war. In the moment of victory most
armies behave with a certain amount of abandon. Marshal
Tolbukhin's forces had been no exception. During their brief
stay in Jugoslavia they had, according to Jugoslav official
sources, committed 1,219 rapes, 329 attempted rapes, 111
rapes with murder, 248 rapes with attempted murder, and
1,204 robberies with violence. One Russian officer had actually raped a Partisan girl orderly while she was in the act of
delivering an important message during the battle of Belgrade.
Another Jugoslav girl, it was reported, had been so unsettled
by her experiences at the hands of a group of Russian soldiers
that, although formerly a keen Communist, she had lost all interest in politics and announced her decision to give up her work
for the party. A drunken Russian officer had shot at and
wounded Tito's son Žarko in a night club in Belgrade. The wife
of a member of the National Committee had been assaulted.
Even if the Partisans had not possessed a preconceived and altogether exaggerated idea of the military, political and moral
virtues of the Red Army, they could scarcely have failed to be
unfavorably impressed by such an outstanding display of
brutality and license. As it was, they were profoundly shocked
and disillusioned.*

Nor was it only the civilian population or the rank and file
of the party who were thus affected. Concern was felt at the
highest level. In the end, after a more than usually deplorable
episode, the Politburo decided to draw the attention of Gen-

* In *Tito Speaks*, Vladimir Dedijer has denied the accuracy of
Sadchikov's report of this conversation. It is of course quite likely
that the Russians rewrote the Ambassador's report before publishing it in the hope of making trouble between Tito and Kardelj (see p. 330 below).

* To an eyewitness of the liberation of Belgrade there seems
nothing inherently improbable about these statistics.

eral Korneyev, the head of the Soviet Military Mission, to the
harm which such incidents were doing to the prestige of the
Red Army. But General Korneyev did not take these represen-
tations in the spirit in which they were intended. He had never
thought much of the Partisans. That they should now try to
teach the Red Army how to behave was really the last straw.
It brought out all the imperial instincts which he had absorbed
years before as a young officer in a crack Czarist regiment.
"I protest," he shouted, before they had even finished speaking, "in the name of the High Command of the Red Army, I
protest against these untruths."[7] After which he went off and
dispatched an indignant and seemingly somewhat inaccurate
account of the meeting to Moscow. The result was that a few
days later Tito received an angry telegram from Stalin himself
complaining in particular that Milovan Djilas, who had been
present at the meeting with Korneyev, had declared at a meeting of the Central Committee of the Communist party of
Jugoslavia that "Soviet officers were morally inferior to British
officers." "If the soldiers of the Red Army," Stalin concluded,
"were to find out that Comrade Djilas and those who did not
challenge him consider English officers superior from a moral
standpoint to Soviet officers, they would cry out in pain at
this undeserved insult."[8] In reply to this outburst it was at once
explained that Djilas had not expressed these views on his
own behalf but had merely attributed them to the bourgeoisie
of Belgrade, an explanation which was proffered once again
verbally when Tito and Djilas visited Moscow in the following
April. But the harm was done. Although at the time Stalin
seemed more or less satisfied by their explanation and even
expressed mild interest in the further accounts of Red Army
misdemeanors with which Tito and Djilas proceeded, perhaps
a little tactlessly, to regale him, the incident, along with various
others, continued to rankle in his resentful mind and was
duly stored up for future use.

But the disorderly behavior of the rank and file of the Red
Army was by no means the only difficulty to be contended
with. The presence in Jugoslavia of numerous Soviet military
and technical advisers also presented a variety of awkward
problems. For one thing, they were far too inclined to give
advice. The experience so painfully gained by the Partisans
during their "three and a half years of bitter strife" in the
forests and mountains did not impress them at all. The Jugoslavs, they said, must completely remodel their army on Soviet
lines, until it became in effect a subsidiary part of the Red

Army, to be employed in whatever role the Russians saw fit to use it. Moreover, in return for these highly unpalatable counsels, they demanded financial remuneration on an unheard-of scale, insisting that quite junior Red Army officers be paid three or four times the salary accorded to Jugoslav Army Commanders or cabinet ministers. They also insisted on having Jugoslav soldier-servants to black their boots and carry their wives' shopping baskets, menial tasks which the Partisan warriors concerned deeply resented. Before long, they had made themselves thoroughly unpopular, and it was being freely said at all levels of the Jugoslav Army that they were more trouble than they were worth.

Nor did the Russian advisers confine themselves to tendering advice. It soon came to the notice of the Jugoslavs that, in addition to their legitimate functions, both military and civilian experts were making it their business to recruit Jugoslav citizens for the Soviet intelligence service, and that the arguments they used on these occasions bordered on the subversive. Thus, in the autumn of 1945, Dušanka Perović, a girl cipher clerk employed by the State Security Organization, came to Marko Ranković with a story of how a certain Colonel Ivan Stepanov of the Soviet Military Mission had tried to enlist her services for his government. Colonel Stepanov, she said, had explained to her that the enemy might be anywhere—even among the leaders themselves. At the moment, he had said, Tito himself was not under suspicion; for the time being "he was working as he should." But this, Colonel Stepanov had added, could not be said of some of his colleagues. You never could be sure. If you were a good Communist it was better to take the broader view, better to enter the service of "the bigger and better tried organization"; better, in short, to enter the service of the Soviet Union. And similar approaches had been made by other Russians to other Jugoslavs occupying responsible positions.[9]

Earlier in the war Tito had hoped that, once direct contact had been established with the Russians, once the latter could really see the situation in Jugoslavia for themselves, all misunderstandings and difficulties would vanish. Now the closest contact had been established between the two countries, and yet the difficulties still persisted, in fact, they grew from day to day in size and complexity. It was discouraging, disturbing even, but not as yet sufficiently disturbing to distract Tito's mind from the main issue: the successful prosecution of the conflict in which he was fast becoming involved with the West and the rapid elimination of all remaining anti-Communist elements in his own country.

Now that they had accorded him formal recognition, the usefulness of the Western powers from Tito's point of view was very largely exhausted: it seemed improbable that he would have any more favors to ask of them or they of him. This was even truer of the non-Communist elements whom he had been obliged to include in his provisional government in order to secure for it the blessing of the British and United States Governments. Having served their purpose, they could be discarded.

From the very first, Subašić, Grol, Šutej and the three other "imported" ministers were given no say whatever in the conduct of affairs. Nor was there any pretense at what, in the West, is understood by "democracy." As Tito himself put it, with brutal frankness, at a later date:

> Having created the main pre-conditions during the war and having in our minds already established a new type of state to take the place of the old, we could not during the the period of joint government make any concessions to those elements in the Government who actually represented the interests of the overthrown monarchy, the bourgeoisie and their patron abroad, international reaction. This was only a transitional period in the internal development of the new Jugoslavia. Even at this time our adversaries at home and abroad still cherished illusions as to "who would beat whom." But we had no such illusions. We knew how it would all end.

Tito in fact, had never had any intention of implementing the Tito-Subašić Agreement. As he went on to say:

> We had to accept this agreement because the Western Powers stubbornly insisted on it. . . . We decided to make it because we were aware of our strength. . . . We therefore had nothing to be afraid of and consented to this agreement which could do no harm, but only good— provided we pursued the right course of action. And that, in the event, is just what we did.[10]

Finding themselves powerless to secure the implementation either of the Tito-Subašić Agreement or of the Declaration on Liberated Europe which had been signed by the Big Three at

Yalta, Subašić and Grol invoked the help of the British and American Governments. But from that quarter no help was forthcoming. Unless they were prepared to stand by and see a mockery made of the arrangement to which they had expressly subscribed, the only course open to them was to resign. Grol, having first publicly expressed his disapproval of what was being done, resigned on August 20. He was followed two months later by Subašić and Sutej. Not long after, all three were placed under house arrest. Their places in the government were taken by more pliable and, from Tito's point of view, more reliable men.

It had long been agreed by all concerned that Jugoslavia's future form of government should be decided, once the war was over, by "the Jugoslav people." By the autumn of 1945 Tito felt that the time was ripe to hold elections for a constituent assembly. The elections were conducted on approved totalitarian lines. There was a single list, for which only the candidates of the People's Front were eligible. Though nominally a coalition, the People's Front was in fact completely controlled by the Communists. Of the candidates nominated, 470 were actual members of the Communist party; the remaining 40, though nominally not party members, were all Communist-sponsored. The remnants of the old political parties were shadowy in the extreme. "I am not," Tito had said some months earlier, "against parties in principle. . . . But, to create parties just for the sake of parties—that is something for which at present we have no time."[11]

At the ensuing elections, which were held in November and which, it was claimed, were "the most democratic elections ever held in Jugoslavia," all the candidates were elected by an overwhelming percentage of the votes cast, which was scarcely surprising as there was no one else to vote for and it required considerable courage to abstain. The press and wireless were government-controlled, the courts and the firing squads dispensed Communist justice. Meanwhile, in the background, and sometimes (for their methods were inclined to be crude) in the foreground, an efficient and ruthless Security Police, known first of all as OZNA and subsequently as UDBA, did their best to ensure that no "hostile elements" were allowed to contravene the wishes of "the Jugoslav people." "It has been suggested," said Tito speaking in Serbia that summer, "that the time has come to liquidate OZNA. Of course it has! There was a time when I myself wished that someone would liquidate the gendarmerie! But let no one have any illusions about that

. . . . If OZNA puts fear in the hearts of those who do not like our kind of Jugoslavia, all the better for the Jugoslav people. We shall never listen to such advice."[12] Meanwhile, in prisons and concentration camps all over Jugoslavia many thousands of those who "did not like our kind of Jugoslavia" were expiating their lack of enthusiasm for the regime behind iron bars and barbed wire, while others found themselves being gradually squeezed out of existence by social, political and economic pressure.

The opening session of the new Constituent Assembly was held on November 29, 1945, the second anniversary of the Jajce Declaration. Its first act was formally to abolish the monarchy and proclaim in its place a federal republic on Soviet lines, closely corresponding to the provisional constitution drawn up at Jajce two years before. The new Federative People's Republic of Jugoslavia, to give it its official title, was composed of six federal republics, Serbia, Croatia, Slovenia, Bosnia, Macedonia and Montenegro, each possessing its own Government and each, in theory at any rate, enjoying a certain measure of autonomy, while at the same time united to the others by the firm hand of the central government and the even firmer hand of the Central Committee of the party. It was the proud and constantly repeated boast of the rulers of the new Jugoslavia that, with their formula of "Brotherhood and Unity," they had solved the problem of the nationalities once and for all. For this claim there was in one sense a measure of justification. Under what was in effect a thoroughgoing Communist dictatorship, no one nationality, neither Serbs nor Croats, Slovenes, Montenegrins nor Macedonians, any longer enjoyed any particular advantage over the others. It could thus fairly be claimed that the days of the old Serb hegemony were over and that with it at any rate one grievance had vanished. Moreover, among the government's own supporters and particularly among those who had fought as Partisans during the war, a new sense of comradeship and common purpose was beginning to replace the old national hatreds and rivalries which still flourished in less "progressive" circles. For the other claims made on behalf of the new constitution by its sponsors it is hard to find even the flimsiest foundation of fact. In practice, if not in theory, it placed power fairly and squarely in the hands of a single party or rather of the little group of men who controlled that party; placed it there and left it there for good and all.

The federal Constitution, after being formally passed by the

Constituent Assembly, was finally promulgated on January 31, 1946. The "new type of state" to which Tito and his comrades had for so long looked forward was in being. The Dictatorship of the Proletariat, or at any rate of the Communist party, was an accomplished fact. But even now there was still a lot of cleaning up to be done, a lot of "adversaries" to be liquidated.

Mihajlović, for one, was still at large, somewhere in those wild Bosnian highlands on which Tito himself had so often fallen back when hard-pressed by his enemies. It remained to hunt him down and bring him to book.

By June, 1945 the dwindling force of several hundred Cetniks, with which Mihajlović had set out to fight his way back to Serbia, had been reduced to a mere handful of men. He had lost his papers, his baggage and his wireless equipment. He was cut off from contact with the outside world. The population of the Sandžak in which he now found himself was far from friendly. He was worn out and short of food. In the autumn of 1945 he fell seriously ill and his remaining companions were obliged to carry him on a litter from village to village, picking up food where they could get it and hiding as best they could from the pursuing Partisans. But still he refused to leave Jugoslavia and still he clung to his belief in the possibility of a national uprising—an *ustanak*—against Tito and his regime, an uprising which, like that other much talked-of uprising against the Germans, would take place not now, not immediately, but at some future date, when conditions were more favorable. "Under no conceivable circumstances," he wrote in a letter smuggled out to friends abroad and dated February 2, 1946,

> will I leave my country and my people. "You cannot carry your country with you on the soles of your shoes," said Danton when he was urged to leave France. I can do no more than repeat those words today. . . . I know what an uprising would mean at the present time. A national uprising will be militarily justifiable only when there are no longer foreign troops in our country to bolster up the terrorist regime which holds power today. . . . My forces consist of practically the entire nation, both those inside and those outside the country. In our free mountains there are today over 100,000 fighting men. . . . You know my strategic purpose: to maintain myself at all costs for the great task which lies ahead.

It may be that I shall fall in our sacred cause. But you all know well that this would not mean that the righteous cause for which our nation is fighting would fall with me.[13]

By March, 1946 Mihajlović was left with only four companions. All the others had been killed or captured or had deserted him. The pursuit was closing in. He had now reached the wooded, mountainous country round Višegrad on the borders of Bosnia and Serbia; he was once again in sight of his Serbian homeland. He decided that for the time being he would stay where he was. His men dug a trench for him in a little wood above a village, a kind of foxhole, half open with some straw in it. There he remained during the day, alone, starving and frozen with cold. At night, if it was safe for him to do so, he went to a house in the village.

One evening, early in March, he crept out of his hole and went, as usual, to this house. But this time he found waiting for him, not his friends, but Tito's police. Before he had grasped what was happening, there were handcuffs on his wrists and he was being led off, filthy and in rags, his steel-rimmed spectacles awry, his hair and beard tangled and matted, to the car which was waiting to take him to Belgrade. An hour or two later a telegram was dispatched to Tito, then on his way to Warsaw, to inform him that his old rival was finally at his mercy. It was from Marko Ranković and consisted of two words: *"Plan ostvaren"*—"The plan is fulfilled."*[14]

Toward the end of May, 1946, while those responsible were putting the final touches to the case against Mihajlović, shortly to be tried for his life on a charge of high treason, Tito, accompanied this time by Ranković, Kidrić and Koća Popović, set out on a state visit to Moscow.[15] From the moment of his arrival there, Tito was treated with every mark of consideration and respect. Molotov was at the station to meet him and the same evening he received a message to say that Stalin was anxious to see him and his party at the Kremlin immediately.

On reaching the Kremlin the Jugoslavs were ushered along a succession of well-lit, thickly carpeted corridors, bright with

---

* It appears that, on reaching Warsaw, Tito informed Stalin by telephone of Mihajlovic's capture. The *Vozhd* expressed satisfaction at the news and then, having rung off, proceeded to issue a sharp personal reprimand to Timofeyev, the head of the NKVD in Jugoslavia, for not having known what was afoot.

new paint and shining brass, and then through a series of equally spick-and-span antechambers until finally they were shown into a room containing a conference table and ten chairs. Awaiting them there stood Stalin in person with Molotov on his right and on his left Lavrentiev, the new Soviet Ambassador in Belgrade. As Tito entered the room, Stalin, with an affable smile, walked jauntily forward to meet him.

As Tito introduced his companions, Stalin shook hands with each of the Jugoslavs in turn, staring them up and down as he did so. "Look what fine strong men, Vyacheslav Mikhailovich!" he said to Molotov. "What a sturdy race!" Then he sat down at the head of the table and the others arranged themselves round him.

After inquiring politely whether Tito had had a good journey, Stalin asked what had happened to "Comrades" Subašić and Grol since they had left the government, and some witty exchanges followed at which everyone laughed. Next he asked after Djilas and Kardelj and, on being told that Djilas was ill: "Tell him I'll cure him," he said, "he must spend his holidays at Sochi on the Black Sea, that'll soon put him right." They noticed that all the time he was talking, he kept drawing intricate designs on his writing pad and then crossing them out and starting again. "The English and Americans don't want to give you Trieste, do they?" he asked suddenly. And then, before Tito had had time to answer, he had started talking about agriculture.

It was some time before Tito succeeded in bringing the conversation round to what he really wanted to talk about, namely Jugoslavia's prospects of economic development. Stalin asked him whether he liked the idea of Soviet-Jugoslav joint-stock companies. A little naïvely Tito explained that the advantage of these companies to the Jugoslavs was that they would help with the industrialization of Jugoslavia. Stalin did not bother to dissent from this point of view, but, continuing to doodle on his scribbling pad, went on to ask some pertinent questions about Jugoslav deposits of oil, bauxite, copper and lead—a subject which seemed to interest him a good deal more than Tito's plans for the industrialization of his country. "You have good bauxite," he said, still doodling.

After discussing various military problems, they next turned to foreign policy. Stalin seemed particularly interested in Albania, especially in what was going on inside the Albanian Communist party. "Do you know Enver Hodja?" he asked.

"What kind of man is he? Have they any internal problems? What is your information? . . . Should we receive them here in Moscow? . . . It seems to us that there is no need for us to do so. It would be embarrassing for them and for us. It would be better if we helped them through you. There is trouble in the Albanian Politburo." ·

"Leave it to us," said Tito reassuringly. "We can settle it with them direct."

"Excellent," replied Stalin, with the air of someone handing over a difficult problem to a completely dependable colleague. After that they talked about Bulgaria and Hungary.

It was long after midnight when they finished their business. As the meeting was breaking up, Stalin asked Tito what their plans were for that evening. "We have none," replied Tito.

"Aha!" said Stalin. "A Government with no State Plan!"

"We have arranged our plans to fit in with yours," said one of the Jugoslavs ingratiatingly.

"Then you had better come and have something to eat with me," said Stalin and, summoning his secretary, a short, fat, bald man wearing a colonel's uniform, he told him to get the cars.

For the next two or three minutes Stalin continued to play the genial host, laughing and joking with his guests. Then he sent for his secretary again and asked where the cars were. The secretary shuffled uneasily. At this Stalin flew into a fury and started to curse and swear, roaring and grimacing and waving his arms, while the wretched secretary stood white and trembling before him. His guests were relieved when the cars finally arrived and they were swept off in them through the darkness down the special *Pravitelstvennoye Chaussee* or "Government Highway" to Stalin's *dacha*.

The *dacha* was comfortably furnished in a quiet, unobtrusive style. One of the guests was struck by the feeling of silence and isolation it gave him, of remoteness from the outside world. A silent middle-aged woman in a clean white apron brought in silver covered dishes, containing a variety of Georgian specialties and left them to help themselves. The drinks stood on a side table. They began by drinking toasts, starting on *pertsovka,* a particularly potent variety of vodka with red pepper in it.

At supper Tito sat on Stalin's right. In addition to Molotov they had now been joined by Zhdanov, who, they noticed, looked ill, by Bulganin, quiet and rather deaf, with a little beard, and by Beria, spectacled and sinister. Over supper, the *Vozhd,* speaking Russian with a harsh Georgian accent, treated them to a series of thumbnail sketches of foreign Communist leaders. They were not very flattering. Togliatti, he said, was a professor, a theorist, but no leader. Thorez, Pieck and La Pasionaria also lacked the qualities which made good leaders. José Diaz had been a "good and wise comrade," but he, unfortunately, was dead.

Eventually, tiring of conversation, Stalin turned on the gramophone, humming the tunes—mostly Russian folk songs and dances—to himself. Then he started to dance all by himself in the middle of the room. "How vigorous you are, Comrade Josif Vissarionovich!" chorused Molotov and the others admiringly. But Stalin's mood had already changed. "No," he said, "I shall not live much longer. The laws of nature are taking their course." At this his companions protested loudly. "No, no, Comrade Josif Vissarionovich," they cried, "we need you. You still have a long life ahead of you." "No," Stalin repeated, "the laws of nature are taking their course." Then, looking at Tito, "Tito," he said, "should take care of himself and see nothing happens to him. Because I have not much longer to live and he will remain for Europe." "Churchill," he went on, "said Tito was a good man. He said so three times. In the end I replied 'I really don't know, but if you say so, I suppose he must be good. I will also do my best to get to know Tito.'" And once again his guests laughed politely.

Then he started drinking toasts again. He linked arms with Tito and embraced him and they drank *bratstvo*—"brotherhood"—together. Then suddenly he caught hold of him under the arms and lifted him off his feet three times in time to the music. His fit of depression had passed. He was cheerful once more. "There's strength in me yet!" he said. After that he drank *bratsvo* with the rest of them. *"Serb, pridi siuda!"* —"Come here, you Serb!" he cried, catching hold of whichever Jugoslav was nearest. Then, suddenly turning on Beria and Ranković, the two police ministers, "Now, you two," he asked, with grim jocularity, "which of you is going to catch the other?"

By now it was very late, but Stalin had not done with them yet. He lectured them on the virtues of the eucalyptus tree and urged them to try growing it in Jugoslavia. Then he told them about the great migrations of the fourth and fifth centuries, about the Avars and the Chechens and the arrival of the Slavs in Europe. It was five in the morning when they finally left. It had been a gratifying though exhausting evening.

The visit continued in the same style. Nothing was too good for Tito. The Pan-Slav Committee gave a special reception for him. Stalin gave an official luncheon in his honor at the Kremlin and there was another all-night supper party at the *dacha*. This time a Bulgarian delegation was there, led by Dimitrov, and Stalin amused himself by being deliberately rude to the Bulgars and in particular to Dimitrov, in front of the Jugoslavs. So wounding were his remarks on the subject of the Comintern that Dimitrov, for many years its Secretary General, turned first white and then crimson, while his fellow guests were overcome with embarrassment. He also made a point of selecting the Jugoslavs for special distinctions of one kind or another in public, while ignoring the Bulgars. President Kalinin had just died. At the lying-in-state, it was the Jugoslavs who stood on guard at the catafalque. At the funeral, Tito was chosen from all the foreign visitors to stand on Lenin's tomb with Stalin and the Politburo. On every possible occasion Stalin was courteous, agreeable, affable. It was too good to be true.

Tito, feeling pleasantly elated, returned to Belgrade from Moscow on June 10, just in time for the trial of Draža Mihajlović, which opened on the same day. The trial was held before the Supreme Military Tribunal in the barracks of the former Royal Guard at Topčider outside Belgrade, which were heavily guarded for the occasion. Indicted with Mihajlović were twenty-three other accused, including several members of the former Royal Jugoslav Government who were tried *in absentia*, and also various members of the Nedić administration, including Dragi Jovanović who had been Chief of Police under the German Occupation. The latter was by any standards a notorious war criminal, and his inclusion in the trial was clearly intended by implication to blacken his codefendants.

Under a new law the accused were considered guilty until proved innocent. When Mihajlović, slight and bespectacled, wearing an old uniform tunic stripped of military insignia, entered the court, he was greeted with jeers, hisses and cries of "Hang him!" While the deputy military prosecutor, grim-faced in his Soviet-type uniform, started, amid manifestations of approval from the crowd, to read the indictment, he sat listening quietly, peering through his spectacles and occasionally stroking his thick, graying beard. Behind him and behind each of the other accused stood a soldier armed with a submachine gun. The indictment took eight hours to read. The main charges against Mihajlović were: raising his "Jugoslav Army in the Fatherland"; using it to stifle resistance; and, finally, the commission of countless war crimes. The Cetniks, it was claimed, had committed every conceivable atrocity and act of terror; they burned villages, skinned Roman Catholic priests alive and murdered Moslems. Mihajlović, it was alleged, had personally commanded the Cetniks in their operations against the Partisans and had collaborated with the Germans, the Italians and Nedić. The British liaison officers at his headquarters, beginning with Captain Hudson in 1941, had, it was suggested, persistently encouraged him to exterminate the Partisans.

Next day the president of the court, also wearing the Soviet-type uniform of the new Jugoslav Army, began a cross-examination of the accused. In this he was assisted by the deputy military prosecutor. Mihajlović opened his remarks with the proud claim that he was the first insurgent against Germany in Europe, but under cross-examination agreed that the Partisans had struck the first actual blow against the enemy, while he was waiting for the right moment. He added that the Jugoslav Government in exile had given him no orders to fight the Germans at that juncture, nor had they forbidden him to fight the Partisans. He admitted Cetnik collaboration with Nedić as early as 1941 and said that when he reached Montenegro in 1942 he had found the Cetnik commanders there collaborating with the Italians. He did not like this, he said, but he did not want to interfere and in any case could not control his subordinates. With regard to the role of his British liaison officers, Mihajlović said that at the end of 1942 Colonel Bailey, who had recently taken over command of the mission at his headquarters, had urged him to "wipe out the Partisans," explaining that the British intended to land in Dalmatia in the spring of 1943 and wanted the coast clear. Under cross-examination, Mihajlović, while emphasizing the dissensions which existed between individual Cetnik commanders, admitted that there had been a certain degree of collaboration with the Germans and Italians, but added that Captain Hudson had known of this and had not condemned it. In conclusion, he denied that he himself had been guilty of collaboration, though he admitted that some of his commanders had entered into agreements with the enemy. He also denied most emphatically that he had been responsible for any massacres of the civilian population.

Mihajlović's cross-examination ended on June 18, by when he had been in the witness box for six days. It was followed by the cross-examination of the other accused. After this the court proceeded to the examination of witnesses and documents. One of the chief witnesses for the prosecution was Mihajlović's former commander for central and southeast Serbia, Major Radoslav Djurić, now a colonel in Tito's Army. Djurić testified enthusiastically against his former leader, accusing him of consistently fighting the Partisans and collaborating with the Germans. Subsequently, other witnesses were called by the prosecution to give evidence concerning the activities of the Royal Jugoslav Government in London and their links with the Cetniks. The prosecution also produced a stream of peasants in leggings and sandals who, one after the other, told in picturesque terms of atrocities committed by the Cetniks. When the oral evidence was finished, the court passed to the written evidence. For two successive days hundreds of documents of one kind or another were produced and read out in court in support of the charges brought against the accused. Finally, the wives of two Cetnik commanders were called by the counsel for the defense. Their evidence did not amount to much, but they showed, under trying circumstances, that they had the courage of their convictions. One of them consistently referred to Mihajlović as "the General" and, when told by the president of the court to call him "the Accused," retorted "accused by the Communist party, not by me" and, amid the pandemonium that ensued, defiantly left the court with a nod and a smile to Mihajlović.

On July 8 the deputy military prosecutor began his final speech. It lasted for five hours. During it he dwelt at length on the sinister role played by the British and American liaison officers who, he claimed, had egged on Mihajlović to fight against the Partisans. His remarks were greeted with frantic applause. He concluded by calling, amid louder applause than ever, for the supreme penalty "in the name of the Jugoslav People."

He was followed by Mihajlović's counsel, Dr. Dragi Joksimović. Small and resilient, Dr. Joksimović resembled a bull terrier in both appearance and behavior. Soon he was engaged in vigorous controversy both with the prosecutor and the president of the court. The more excited he became the faster he spoke, and soon the words were pouring from his mouth in a veritable torrent. Mihajlović collaboration, he said, was absolutely unproven. He was, he went on, amid a storm of protests, "the Master and Mountain King of Serbia." He had done what the Allies told him to do. Captain Hudson in particular had told him "not to turn the fight into one to the advantage of the Soviet Union." The indictment, he said, was based on the principle that Mihajlović must bear responsibility for all the acts of his subordinates; this contention he rejected absolutely. "I demand," he concluded, "acquittal on all charges."

Mihajlović began his final speech late on the night of July 10. He showed himself throughout respectful to the court and oblivious of the crowd, who for once forgot to hiss and listened in complete silence. Hitherto he had appeared incoherent and indeterminate. Now his character stood out clearly and for the next four hours he dominated the proceedings. He spoke without oratory, without rancor toward the political opponents or private enemies, lucidly and in detail. He was a professional soldier presenting a military report, compelling because of its simplicity. His care for details was astonishing. These were the notes he had been writing daily in court for weeks. He described what had happened, action by action and place by place.

He began by telling of his early life. "In the First World War," he said, "I was wounded and received medals for valor. I stayed at the front all the time when I could have left it." He went on to tell of his lasting hatred for the Germans and how between the wars he had tried to raise and train the youth of Jugoslavia for the fight he knew must come. He had sought, too, to modernize the Jugoslav Army, but for this and for the attempts which he had made to keep in touch with the British he had been severely punished by his military superiors. "When war came and our front broke," he continued, "I was left with a broken-spirited people and with the legacy of rottenness reaching back for twenty years. I went into the forest and told the people to hide their weapons. I wanted to continue resistance and so became a rebel against Hitler's Germany. At that time only England and I were in the war. The Partisans appeared as soon as Soviet Russia entered the war. I had three meetings with Marshal Tito to which I went sincerely. I told him I believed we could come to an understanding and that both sides had made mistakes, but unfortunately we spent our time in mutual

accusations and, even before I met him, the battle had begun.
The Germans began to withdraw and I decided to attack. It
is not true that I gave orders not to attack. I had little material
and I had to tell some officers who wanted to join me to stay
in Belgrade. My first contact with the outside world was
through the Soviet Embassy in Sofia; my second by means
of a home-made wireless set. After this Captain Hudson arrived from Great Britain with a message that I was not to
transform the struggle into a fight for the Soviet Union and
announced that all troops in Jugoslavia were to come under
my command."

He had, he said, wanted to co-operate with the Partisans,
but Tito had wanted to make a frontal attack on the Germans. This had struck him as military foolishness in view of
their lack of resources. Against his advice the Partisans had
attacked, lost territory and been forced to leave Serbia. This
he had known would happen, as they were led by inexperi-
enced men. He denied that he had at this time handed over
Partisan prisoners to the Germans. If that was done, it had
been the work of his lieutenant, Djurić, now the principal
witness for the prosecution, who, he said, was nothing but a
collaborator. The German reprisals, Mihajlović continued,
were terrible. He himself had seen villages burned. "My five
thousand men," he went on, "were nothing against five German divisions. I told the London Government of my predicament, but got no instructions and so went to the Germans
myself with two others. We took hand grenades in case of
treachery from the Germans. All we got from them was a
demand for unconditional surrender and I was called a rebel.
I was astonished and said I was fighting for my country and
they, as soldiers, must understand this. I was afraid one of
my two commanders would throw his grenade in anger. I
refused to drink wine with the Germans and there was no
agreement. Soon after the Germans attacked my headquarters
on Ravna Gora and killed many of us. I escaped through
their lines. Once they passed within a few yards of me, but
I was covered with leaves."

When Mihajlović came to speak of his commanders, he had
a sad tale to tell of disorganization, disloyalty and petty ambition. Some, despite his orders to the contrary, had collaborated with the enemy; some had fought each other; others
had plotted against him and sought to supplant him. He said
that he had been aware of some cases of collaboration, but
not of others. "The Partisans," he said, "had twenty years'

experience of underground work and I had to take things as they were and improve on what I had. I had many adherents and little time to do as I intended and put my organization in order." He specifically denied that he had ever had a representative at Italian Headquarters, but admitted that there might have been some kind of parallel action with the Italians which appeared to him then in quite a different light from now. He only showed signs of emotion when denying his responsibility for war crimes. He had, he said, never ordered any such measures against civilians. His ultimate aim had been a rising against the Axis forces of occupation. The court would remember Hitler's message to Mussolini in which he said that he, Mihajlović, was a bitter enemy of the Axis and only waiting for the moment to attack.

Speaking of his meeting with German representatives in September, 1944 Mihajlović said that Colonel McDowell, the Head of the United States Intelligence Mission at his head-quarters, had told him that his fight against the Germans was no longer of interest; what mattered was that he should stay among his people. By then 70 per cent of his men were ill with typhus. The Red Army were approaching. Nothing came of his attempt to send them a mission. His object in meeting the Germans with Colonel McDowell had not been to arrange for collaboration, but rather to negotiate for a German sur-render.

Toward midnight Mihajlović came to the end of his speech. Quietly folding his paper, he said: "I wanted nothing for my-self. The French Revolution gave the world the Rights of Man, the Russian Revolution also gave us something new, but I did not wish to start today where they started in 1917. I never wanted the old Jugoslavia, but I had a difficult legacy. I am a soldier who sought to organize resistance to the Axis for our own country and for the whole Balkan Peninsula. I am sorry that anyone should think I have been disloyal to the government, but documents exist concerning that. I was caught in the whirlpool of events and in the movement for a new Slav unity which I have long favored. Believing that the world would follow the course of the Russian Revolution, I was caught among the changes in the Western democracies. They are for our peoples' good and so are the Russians. I had against me a rival organization, the Communist party, which seeks its aims without compromise. I was faced with changes in my own government. I was surrounded by every imaginable intelligence service, British, American, Russian and German

—all the intelligence services in the world. I believed I was on the right road and invited any foreign journalist or Red Army Mission to visit me and see everything. But a merciless fate threw me into this maelstrom. I wanted much, I began much, but the gale of the world carried away me and my work. I ask the court to judge what I have said according to its true value."

The verdict on General Mihajlović and his codefendants was given on July 15. All twenty-four were found guilty of war crimes and collaboration with the enemy. Mihajlović himself and ten others were sentenced to be shot and the remainder to various terms of imprisonment. The verdict was received with applause by the crowd and impassively by Mihajlović, who, still dressed in his old uniform tunic, stood to attention while it was being read out.

That night Tito, speaking at Cetinje during a tour of Montenegro, said that the sentence passed on Mihajlović had been "a sentence on international reaction." Next day the court rejected Mihajlović's appeal against its sentence. On the same afternoon, the British Foreign Secretary, Mr. Ernest Bevin, announced in the House of Commons that the Jugoslav Tribunal had refused to admit evidence from British liaison officers who had wished to testify in favor of Mihajlović. At the same time he rejected the suggestion that the British officers attached to the Cetniks had encouraged Mihajlović to fight the Partisans. No such instructions, he said, had ever been sent to these officers by His Majesty's Government. On the contrary their whole endeavor was to unify Cetniks and Partisans and to persuade both factions to combine against the enemy.

After sentence had been passed, Mihajlović's wife was allowed to visit her husband in prison and spend some hours with him. He did not see his son and daughter, who already during the war had denounced their father as a traitor and gone over to the Partisans. The sentence of the court was carried out in the early morning of July 17, Mihajlović and his companions being shot, it was said, on the former golf course at Topčider, once a favorite resort of the Diplomatic Corps.

The execution of Mihajlović symbolized the removal of a potential danger to Tito's regime in Serbia. In Croatia, solidly Catholic, opposition centered from the first round the Catholic Church.

Tito himself was an atheist. His creed was a strictly materialist one. In his new state he was determined to tolerate no division of loyalties and, with one apparent exception, no interference from outside. These were the considerations which dictated his attitude toward the churches in general and in particular toward the Church of Rome.*

Trouble began as soon as he assumed power. The victorious Partisans, needless to say, lost no time in settling their old scores with the Ustaše. Owing to the sympathy which many of the Catholic clergy had shown for the Ustaša movement, there were a number of priests among those imprisoned or executed as collaborators or war criminals. Although the charges brought against individual priests were frequently unfounded or exaggerated, there was often an element of truth in them which provided a ready-made pretext for repressive measures. These not unnaturally provoked a hostile reaction from the Church, which led in turn to fresh repression. On top of this came a series of land reform measures involving the nationalization without compensation of over 160,000 acres of Church lands in Croatia and Slovenia. In a strongly worded pastoral letter issued in September, 1945 the Catholic hierarchy protested vigorously against this confiscation of Church property and against the continuing persecution of the clergy. Tito replied to this personally in a no less strongly worded article published in *Borba* of October 25, recalling the atrocities committed by the Ustaše during the war and asking why the bishops had made no protests then. Thenceforward the conflict became increasingly violent.

Religious services, it is true, were freely held in crowded churces, but other church activities were discouraged, if not by direct, then by indirect means. Religious education was to a great extent abolished. Discrimination of one kind or another was practiced against church-goers. The Catholic newspapers were squeezed out of existence. Crippling taxes were levied on church organizations and institutions. The

* Despite its national character and despite the patriotic behavior of many of its clergy during the war, the Serb Orthodox Church also came in for a good deal of persecution. Among the Orthodox clergy a resolute opponent of the regime was Metropolitan Josip, Acting Head of the Serb Orthodox Church. It is related that when a Communist crowd gathered beneath his windows shouting "Death to Josip," he at once appeared on the balcony and invited them to desist. "It is a sin," he said, "to wish the death of your leaders. And anyhow, which of them are you shouting against, Josip Broz or Josip Stalin?"

government-controlled press and wireless kept up a constant campaign of villification and abuse. Public demonstrations against the clergy by groups of hooligans became increasingly frequent and often culminated in acts of violence which the police did little or nothing to prevent.

At the head of the Catholic hierarchy during these difficult times stood Archbishop Aloysius Stepinac. Some of the other clergy and bishops, notably Archbishop Sarić of Sarajevo, who had been one of Pavelić's most enthusiastic supporters, had found it advisable to leave Croatia with the Germans. Stepinac, who had shown considerably less enthusiasm for the Ustaše and had even sought to restrain Pavelić from some of his worst excesses, remained to face the *Poglavnik's* no less formidable successor. His duty, as he saw it, was to his flock.

From Tito's point of view, Archbishop Stepinac presented an awkward problem. In June, 1945, shortly after Stepinac's release from a fortnight's imprisonment, the two men had met in Zagreb for the purpose of finding a *modus vivendi* between church and state. Their meeting had not been unfriendly. Each had expressed his understanding for the other's point of view and his desire for an agreement. "Render unto Caesar the things that are Caesar's," the Archbishop had said, "and to God the things that are God's." And they had parted with mutual expressions of good will.[16] But Caesar in the event had claimed a larger share than the Church had seen fit to accord him and soon relations were more strained than ever. In upholding what he regarded as his Church's rights, Stepinac showed himself adamant. Nor did he hesitate to make his views as widely known as possible by means of his sermons and pastoral letters.

In Tito's eyes such an attitude was openly subversive of the government's authority. And subversion was something that he was not prepared to tolerate. He was thus confronted with a dilemma. Clearly, it would be difficult to liquidate the Archbishop, as Mihajlović had been liquidated. On the other hand, there could be no question of allowing him to continue his activities unhindered. In the end he decided to ask the Vatican, through the papal nuncio in Belgrade, to replace Stepinac. But here he met with an abrupt refusal. The Holy See, he was told, did not allow temporal authorities any say in Church appointments. He had encountered an organization as uncompromising as that to which he himself owed allegiance.

It had not been Tito's intention to force, at this stage, a showdown with the Vatican, which still commanded the unswerving loyalty of several million devout Catholics in Croatia and Slovenia. A further period of cold war would have suited him better. But if the Vatican wanted a showdown, he was ready for one. Without further delay he gave instructions for the public prosecutor to prepare a case against Stepinac as a collaborator with the enemy during the war and as an active opponent of the present regime. Material, of a sort, was not lacking.

The Archbishop was arrested on September 18, 1946. His attitude remained unyielding. During the preliminary investigation of his case he roundly attacked the government for their persecution of the Church and claimed that "his only crime was that he had refused to yield to the demands of Communism." He would not, he said, offer any personal defense nor would he appeal against whatever sentence was passed on him. If the government wanted better relations with the Church, their right course was to open negotiations with the Vatican. If they persisted in their present attitude, it would do them no more good than it had done Hitler. Let them remember that behind the Church stood Christ, who had said: "Whoever falls on this stone will be broken and he on whom it falls will be dashed to pieces."

The trial opened in Zagreb on Monday, September 30. In the dock with the Archbishop were his own secretary, a number of other priests and a high Ustaša functionary, Colonel Erik Lisak. Just as Nedić's Chief of Police had, for tactical reasons, been tried at the same time as Mihajlović, so care had been taken to include a prominent Ustaša in the present trial. The recital of his notorious and abundantly proved crimes could not fail to confuse the issue and create from the first an atmosphere prejudicial to the Archbishop.

For some days past the government-controlled press and wireless had been conducting a violent campaign against the Archbishop and public demonstrations had been organized all over the country to demand a particularly heavy sentence against him. The arrival in court of the judges and public prosecutor was now the signal for a frenzied show of enthusiasm by the carefully selected throng of spectators, who throughout the trial lost no opportunity of displaying their sympathy for the prosecution and their detestation of the prisoners.

As soon as he could make himself heard, the public prosecutor started to read the indictment. Three main charges were brought against the Archbishop. He was accused of collaboration with the enemy during the war; of collaboration with the Ustaše and complicity in their crimes; and of resistance to and conspiracy against the present government of Jugoslavia. In support of these charges the public prosecutor adduced the Archbishop's numerous public appearances in company with prominent Ustaše and Germans; his messages glorifying the Independent State of Croatia; his prayers for that state and for its rulers; and his acceptance of a high Ustaša decoration and of the post of Chaplain General to the Croat Armed Forces. At the same time, he dwelt at length on Ustaša atrocities in general and in particular on the forced conversions, for which he sought to fasten responsibility on Monsignor Stepinac, who, he pointed out, had presided over the Committee of Bishops set up to handle this whole question. He also sought to show that since the end of the war the Archbishop had, through Colonel Lisak among others, maintained contact with Ustaše refugees abroad while at home he had given active encouragement to the terrorist *Križari* or *"Crusaders,"* whose special standard had been secretly blessed in his own private chapel.

But, despite prolonged cross-questioning and badgering both by the public prosecutor and by the president of the court, who gave him no real chance to answer the questions they put to him, the Archbishop continued steadfastly to deny that he had committed anything that could be called a crime. "When there is peace," he said, answering the charge of collaboration, "when it is possible to publish documents, when everyone can say what he has to say without fear, then there will be no one who can say a word against me." He would, he said, give an account of his activities "when conditions in this country are settled," a reflection on the permanency of the Communist regime, to which the public prosecutor indignantly retorted, "I consider conditions here *are* settled." A rather clearer indication of the prosecution's real intentions was given when the public prosecutor produced in court a copy of a pastoral letter issued by the Archbishop in March, 1945, while the Germans were still in Zagreb, attacking the Partisans for the persecution of the Church and clergy. But here again the Archbishop stood his ground and took the opportunity of saying that he considered that numbers of priests were still being "improperly punished."

As counsel for the Archbishop, his friends had retained

a certain Dr. Ivo Politeo. Just eighteen years before Dr. Politeo had in this same court conducted the defense of another rebel against established authority. On that occasion his client had been Josip Broz, then Secretary of the Zagreb branch of the Communist party and now Prime Minister of Jugoslavia. Once again, at an interval of eighteen years, Dr. Politeo assumed the task of defending a prisoner who had earned the hatred of a powerful authoritarian government. Under changed circumstances he showed himself no less courageous in his defense of Archbishop Stepinac than he had done eighteen years earlier in his defense of Josip Broz. He strongly criticized the generalizations contained in the indictment and vigorously attacked the whole basis of the prosecution's argument. To the charge that the Archbishop had consorted with the enemy occupation authorities, he replied that these contacts had been purely official in character. Monsignor Stepinac had met representatives of the German Army and Government at official functions and he had communicated with them on official subjects, often in an attempt to secure better treatment for one section or another of the community. The same applied to his contacts with the Ustaše. There was at the time no other established authority to deal with, and so he had dealt with the Ustaše. But that did not mean that his dealings with them had been particularly cordial. On the contrary, he had, by standing up to them, earned the dislike both of the Germans and of the Ustaše. The Archbishop could not, said Dr. Politeo, be held responsible for crimes said to have been committed by individual Catholic priests, most of whom were not under his jurisdiction, less still for those committed by the Ustaše. Nor could he be held responsible for the attitude of the Catholic press, which was largely controlled by the Ustaša Government. As regards the forced conversions, the Archbishop had never given these his approval. His client, he maintained, had invariably acted in accordance with international law and canon law and had even gone out of his way to protest against the persecution of Serbs, Jews and gypsies.

On the afternoon of October 3, after the interrogation of the accused had been concluded, the Archbishop was at last afforded an opportunity of stating his case without other interruption than the derisive laughter with which most of his remarks were greeted by the crowd. Having first declared, amid hoots of merriment, that he had a completely clear conscience, he went on to say that, although there had been a lot of talk in court about "the accused Stepinac," this was

not so much Stepinac's trial as the trial of the Archbishop of
Zagreb and of the representative of the Church in Jugoslavia.
He had been charged with responsibility for the forced conversions. Once again his conscience was clear. The verdict of
history would put the whole business in its perspective. He
would only say that during the war the Church had been
obliged to contend with innumerable difficulties. He himself
had been obliged to move a priest to another parish because
the local Orthodox population were threatening to kill him
for not admitting them quickly enough to the Catholic faith.
As to his decision to accept the chaplaincy of the Croat Forces,
it had been dictated by the same motive which had led him
to accept a similar post in the old Jugoslav Army, namely,
his duty to afford spiritual comfort to Catholic soldiers. He
had, he continued, never been popular with the Germans or
with the Ustaše, but he would have been a poor creature if
he had not at that time shared the patriotic enthusiasm of the
Croat people, who in the old Jugoslavia had been no better
than slaves. It was this feeling of Croat patriotism that inspired his speeches and his pastoral letters. Everything that
he had said about the right of the Croat people to liberty and
independence was based on sound principles of morality and
no one could deny them that right. "If you think," he continued, "that the people of Croatia are satisfied with their
present lot, then give them a chance to declare themselves
freely. I, for my part, will gladly abide by their decision. I
have done so in the past and will do so again." Turning to
the charge that he had shown himself an enemy of the state
and of the people, who, he asked, were the civil authorities
in 1941? The Jugoslav Government in exile or the Partisans
hiding in the forests? He had no choice but to accept the
authority of Pavelić's established government in Zagreb, just
as, since May, 1945, he had accepted the authority of the
present government of the country. As to the charge of subversive activities, it was true that since the war Lisak and
other secret Ustaša emissaries had come to him under false
names and that letters had been sent to him, which he had
not even read. If that was all they could prove and if that
was a crime, he was ready to be condemned for it, ready
even to suffer death. He could face his Maker with a clear
conscience. "But let us," he continued, "examine the real
point of difference between us, the real reason why it has
been impossible to pacify our country. The public prosecutor
has said again and again that nowhere is there such complete

freedom of conscience as here. I will now quote some facts which will prove exactly the opposite." And for the next twenty minutes, the Archbishop, thin, stubborn and ascetic-looking, proceeded to give the Church's side of the case: over 260 Catholic priests put to death; the Catholic schools closed; the work of Catholic seminaries and of Catholic charitable and cultural organizations made impossible; Church property confiscated; the Catholic press squeezed out of existence; civil marriages; antireligious teaching in the state schools; and the constant persecution of the Catholic clergy, now exposed to every sort of injury and insult. The Church did not want war. Although it would not accept a *Diktat*, it would welcome a fair settlement, negotiated with the Vatican. He would say this to the Communist party, who was his real accuser. The attitude of the Church was not dictated by material considerations; it was not opposed to social or economic reforms. But if others were to be allowed to preach materialism, Catholics should be allowed freely to profess and defend their principles. They had died for this right in the past and were still ready to die for it.

There followed next the examination of witnesses. Those for the prosecution, seventy-one in number, were called on October 5. Their evidence concerned in the main the forced conversions and the other misdeeds of the Ustaše and most of it had but little direct bearing on the part played by the Archbishop. Of the thirty-five witnesses called by the defense, only seven were admitted, the remainder being for one reason or another disqualified. After they had been examined, on October 7, the public prosecutor made his final speech, denouncing Stepinac in the strongest terms as "the emissary in our country of a foreign power," as an agent of papal and Italian imperialism, who had "wanted to win Bosnia for Catholicism with the sword." He was followed on October 8 by the counsel for the defense, and on the same evening Archbishop Stepinac made a concluding statement.

Reverting to the question of the forced conversions, the Archbishop emphasized that he could not be held responsible for what had happened outside his own diocese of Zagreb. Within that diocese any conversions which had taken place without his written authority were not valid. "When applications for admission to the Church came in," he said, "we had to ask ourselves whether they should be accepted or rejected. To say that the Church used force to obtain conversions is ridiculous. We were not so blind as not to see the difficulties which existed on both sides. Force was undoubtedly used by the civil authorities. The Church therefore had to bear in mind that if it rejected such applications it would make the position of the Orthodox applicants even more difficult. And so, taking all things into consideration, we gave, not orders, but permission that they should be received into the Catholic Church (except for persons living in sin and so on). And now we are being tried for these acts of kindness. . . . And so, if one thinks this whole matter over calmly, it takes on quite a different aspect and I can be said to have no personal responsibility." "You can," he concluded, "pass whatever sentence you like on me . . . You will be condemning an innocent man; my conscience is clear, as the future will show."

The verdict was announced on Friday, October 11. Under the prevailing system of justice the outcome of the trial, like that of Mihajlović, was a foregone conclusion. Archbishop Stepinac was found guilty of "crimes against the state," of political collaboration with Pavelić, of sanctioning compulsory conversions to Catholicism, of accepting in 1942 nomination by the Vatican to the post of Chaplain General to the Ustaše and Domobran, and finally of associating indirectly with Mihajlović and negotiating with foreign imperialist powers with the object of securing their intervention in Jugoslavia. He was sentenced to sixteen years' imprisonment with hard labor and deprived of his civic rights for a further five years. The prison to which he was sent to serve his sentence was Lepoglava, the same prison to which Josip Broz had been committed eighteen years before. The other priests tried with him were sentenced to various terms of imprisonment, while Colonel Lisak, whose active participation in the misdeeds of the Pavelić regime had been proved beyond doubt, was condemned to death. Shortly afterward the Vatican retaliated by formally excommunicating all those directly or indirectly concerned with the trial. In the West, feeling against Tito and his regime became stronger than ever.

By dethroning King Peter, shutting up Subašić, shooting Mihajlović and imprisoning Stepinac, Tito had eliminated four potential adversaries. There remained to be dealt with, however, perhaps the most formidable adversary of all—that "sturdy peasantry" of which Mr. Churchill had spoken to him when they met at Naples during the war.

By the time Tito formally assumed power in 1945, the economic revolution, which formed an essential part of his program, was in practice already far advanced. As a Communist, it was naturally his aim to bring under state control the means of production and distribution. As far as commerce and industry were concerned, this presented a relatively simple problem. For the past four years all the main centers of industry and population had been under German occupation. The owners of most large industrial or commercial enterprises had, therefore, either collaborated with the enemy, or had been liquidated, or had fled abroad. Thus, when it came to nationalization there were relatively few capitalists left to expropriate. Most of the former owners had either been deprived of their civic rights and property as collaborators; or they were simply not there. It only remained for the government to take over. This they did with alacrity, allotting managerial appointments as often as not on a basis of military and ideological merit rather than of technical skill and experience. A decree of November 21, 1944, had provided for the transfer to state ownership of all enemy property and for government control of the property seized by the enemy during the war. This was followed in December, 1946 by laws nationalizing all industry, commerce, trade, insurance, banking, transport and communications.* Soon the only exponents of private enterprise left were a few cobblers, tailors, watchmakers and pastry cooks. Planning and administration for all state concerns were centralized in Belgrade. Investment, production, prices, wages and profits for every enterprise throughout the country were controlled by the appropriate department of the central authority.

In the case of the land, which Tito was equally determined to nationalize or collectivize, things were not quite so simple. There were relatively few large properties in Jugoslavia and in any case the Land Reform Act, passed in August, 1945, had already limited to sixty acres the amount of land which could be held by any single owner. The problem centered rather round the peasant farmers whose small holdings came well below the prescribed minimum and comprised most of the agricultural land in the country. The vast majority of these had stubbornly continued to till their land throughout the war regardless of the fighting which from time to time swept over it, and were equally determined to cling to it now,

---

* Matters were slightly more complicated in the case of foreign-owned enterprises. But this did not deter Tito, who nationalized them first and negotiated afterward.

come what might. Moreover, as Jugoslavia was primarily an agricultural country, depending on their produce for the needs of the population as well as for exports, the attitude of these small holders was bound to be of considerable importance.

The nationalization of the few large properties and their conversion into state or collective farms caused relatively little difficulty. It was when the government tried to force the individual small holders to form collective farms on the Soviet pattern, or at any rate to pool their resources and join together in agricultural co-operatives, that they ran into serious trouble. They were, it is true, in a position to exercise considerable pressure on the peasants. Large parts of Jugoslavia had been completely devastated during the war and left devoid alike of agricultural machinery and livestock. UNRRA and other relief was in practice administered through the government. On a national scale the government controlled the collection, distribution, and sale of foodstuffs, and now set up a system of compulsory government purchase of foodstuffs, known as the *Otkup,* under which the peasants were compelled to sell 80 per cent of their produce to the state at controlled—and extremely low—prices. Finally, the government had at their disposal, and were at all times ready to use for the purpose of enforcing their will, a large and well-disciplined army and police force. But the fact remained that, once the peasants had made up their minds not to cultivate their land or to cultivate only enough to supply their own needs, no amount of pressure was of any use. The government could threaten them, could impose quotas and fix prices, could withhold supplies, could seize their property, could turn them off their land, could arrest them. None of this would produce food. And without food the life of the country could not go on. Tito was stubborn. But the peasants, who came of the same stock from which he himself had sprung, were no less stubborn. Soon a battle was engaged which was marked by retreats and advances on both sides and which Tito, like Stalin before him, was to find as exacting as any of the campaigns he had fought against the enemy during the war.

One engagement in this battle was that fought against Dr. Dragoljub Jovanović, the leader of the Serb Peasant party. Dr. Jovanović, who during the war had done what he could to organize resistance among the Serbian peasantry, had been welcomed by the Partisans as a useful ally and in 1944 had joined Tito's National Front. In 1945 he had stood for election and had been made a member of the Presidium of the National

Assembly. He seems at this stage to have believed that he could exert a moderating influence on the regime and in 1946 he emerged as a bold critic of the government's attitude toward the freedom of the individual. The government retaliated by arranging for his expulsion from what was left of his own party. Undeterred, he continued openly to attack the government's policy of nationalization and industrialization, which he described in a speech before the Assembly as "rash, tricky and tyrannous." Even physical violence at the hands of a gang of Communist roughs did not deter him and, after a violent campaign against him in the government press, he was finally arrested on May 14, 1947. His trial, which took place in October, found him still undaunted. Like that of General Mihajlović, it was made the occasion of violent attacks on Great Britain. He was accused of having, at the instigation of the British Secret Service, tried to organize "a Peasant bloc," hostile to the government. But he strongly refuted this charge and defended himself so vigorously that the prosecution made but a feeble showing. He was nevertheless sentenced to eight years' imprisonment.

Such were Tito's internal preoccupations. "For us," he had said to a friend in 1945, "the most dangerous thing of all would be to stop halfway. What we achieved during the war was only a beginning."[17] And indeed within two years of taking power he and his comrades had, with characteristic ruthlessness and singleness of purpose, advanced farther toward their ideal of a Communist state than any of the other satellite governments—farther, perhaps, than the Kremlin had intended them to advance. At the same time, Jugoslavia had under their guidance vigorously maintained her position in the forefront of the rapidly developing conflict between East and West.

Nothing that Tito had done since coming to power had endeared him to public opinion in the West. The memory of his brave fight against the common enemy during the war was soon obliterated by the ruthlessly totalitarian tendencies which he was displaying and by the seemingly ever clearer signs that he had always been, and still remained, first and foremost a Soviet agent.

It was from this angle in particular that the governments of the Western powers approached the problem of Trieste when it came up for discussion before the Paris Peace Conference in 1946. In their discussions with the Royal Jugoslav

Government during the war the British Government had shown themselves frankly favorable to Jugoslavia's claim to Trieste and the surrounding areas. Nor had they given any indication that they intended to oppose it during the various exchanges which they had had on the subject with Tito in 1944. Ethnographically, after all, the Jugoslavs could make out at least as good a case as the Italians. And the Jugoslavs had been Great Britain's allies during the war, while the Italians had been her enemies.

It was what had happened since that had caused the British and American Governments to modify their attitude. In the first place, Tito's attempt to anticipate the decisions of the Peace Conference by seizing Trieste without further ado, though possibly understandable from a Jugoslav point of view, had been scarcely reassuring. Secondly, the fast-accumulating evidence of the aggressive tendencies of the Soviet Union and of Tito's subservience to the Soviet Government soon convinced the Western powers that to let Tito have Trieste would be to make a present of it to a potential enemy. The Soviet Government's support of the Jugoslav claim, though not vigorous enough to satisfy Tito, helped to confirm this impression. Trieste became a danger point where the armed forces of East and West faced each other across a few strands of barbed wire and where from one moment to another a spark might be struck which would set the whole world in flames.

It was against this explosive background that there occurred in August, 1946 a series of events which for a few days seemed likely to precipitate a conflict. From time to time since the end of the war the Jugoslav Government had complained to the United States Government that American aircraft based in Austria and Italy were flying over Jugoslavia without permission. Between July 18 and August 8, they claimed, no less than 172 American aircraft had "violated Jugoslav territory." On several occasions Tito himself had publicly protested against what he described as violations of Jugoslav sovereignty. But amid the welter of hostile exchanges between East and West, the Americans seem to have paid little or no attention to these protests and, according to the Jugoslavs at any rate, the flights continued.

Then, on August 9, an American transport aircraft was reported missing on its way from Vienna to the Italian town of Udine. On inquiry it transpired that, having lost its way in a storm, it had been fired on and forced to land by Jugoslav fighters near Kranj in Slovenia. Scarcely had the American Ambassador in Belgrade delivered a strongly worded note, protesting against this "wicked, inexcusable and deliberate attack on a friendly nation's airplane" and demanding the release of the crew, when, on August 19, came the news that another American transport aircraft was missing on the same route. In his last message the pilot had reported "tracer bullets streaking past" his aircraft.

Tito himself had the best of reasons for knowing exactly what had happened to the second aircraft. It had been shot down by Jugoslav fighters in broad daylight before his very eyes while flying over his own country house at Brdo in Slovenia. All five of the crew had been killed.

The crisis sharpened. On August 20 the Jugoslavs had replied to the first American note with a strong protest against the deliberate violation of their frontiers. To this the State Department now replied on August 21 with a peremptory note, describing the Jugoslav action as "outrageous," demanding the release of the crew of the first aircraft and a full investigation into the loss of the second, and adding that if these demands were not met within forty-eight hours they would summon a special meeting of the Security Council.

At first it seemed as though Tito might reject this ultimatum. His immediate reaction was to reinforce his troops on the frontier. Then more prudent counsels prevailed. The crew of the first aircraft were set free. Tito expressed his regret for what had happened, announced that he had instructed his pilots not to attack foreign aircraft over Jugoslav territory and undertook to pay compensation. The incident was closed. But the compensation and apologies grudgingly tendered by Tito could not bring the dead American airmen back to life. American public opinion, already far from friendly, had been deeply stirred by what had happened, and the existing tension between Jugoslavia and the West sharply aggravated.

Simultaneously another international danger area was coming into being, this time on Jugoslavia's southern frontier. After the abortive Communist coup of December, 1944, Greece had remained under British occupation. In March, 1946 elections had been held which resulted in an overwhelming victory for the right and in September, following a plebiscite on the question of the monarchy, King George II had returned to Greece and resumed the throne. This was the signal for revival of the civil war. Hardly had the King returned when an armed Communist rising took place in Greek Macedonia. Moreover it soon became clear that, in addition to what they already possessed, the Greek Communist guerrillas were receiving fresh supplies of arms and equipment from Jugoslavia, Bulgaria and Albania and that, when it suited them, they were withdrawing into the territory of these countries to rest and re-form before continuing their operations. As the months went by, these increased in scope until, despite the strenuous efforts of the government forces, a large part of Greek Macedonia was in Communist hands. Toward the end of 1947 the Communists announced that a "Democratic Greek Government" had been formed in the "free mountains of Greece" under Markos Vafiades, who during the war had been Chief Political Commissar of the Communist resistance forces in Greek Macedonia. All attempts by Greece or the Western powers to secure effective action by UNO were blocked by the systematic use of the Soviet veto.

In their political support of the Soviet Government at UNO and in the military support which they afforded the Communist guerrillas in Greece, none of the satellite governments showed themselves more zealous than the Jugoslavs. In Greece the cold war had turned into a shooting war and, once again, Tito's Jugoslavia was well to the fore.* When, in the autumn of 1947, it was announced that Belgrade had been chosen as the seat of the newly created Cominform or Communist Information Bureau, Jugoslavia's position as the leading Soviet satellite seemed to the world at large to be more firmly established than ever. In reality, however, things were not quite as they seemed.

* There are indications that in their support of the Greek Communist insurgents the Jugoslavs went farther than Stalin considered advisable. "We do not agree with the Jugoslav comrades," he is reported as saying to Kardelj in February, 1948, "that they should go on helping the Greek Partisans. . . . That struggle has no prospects whatsoever." In his attitude over Greece, as over Spain and China, it seems probable that Stalin was influenced partly by fear of unwelcome international complications and partly by a characteristic distrust of revolutionary movements not under his own immediate control.[18]

XII 😂😂😂 GATHERING STORM

TITO, as we have seen, had lost no time in pushing ahead with the nationalization of industry and commerce and the collectivization of agriculture. His next care, as befitted a good Communist, was to launch a Five Year Plan.

For many years a recurrent theme in the propaganda put out by the Jugoslav Communist party had been the dependence of the old Jugoslavia on foreign capital and the exploitation of her rich natural resources by grasping foreign capitalists, who had succeeded in reducing her to the status of a "colonial territory." The declared aim of Tito's Five Year Plan was to "industrialize and electrify" the new Jugoslavia and render her as far as possible economically self-sufficient. At last his dreams of *industrializacija* and *elektrifikacija* were to be fulfilled. At last vast state-owned mills and factories and power stations were to bring happiness and prosperity to the wretched struggling peasants in their miserable villages. The Five Year Plan, he proclaimed, would mean a better life for everyone.

It was a bold project. The sudden industrialization of a backward agricultural country would at the best of times have been a formidable undertaking. The devastation wrought in Jugoslavia during the war made it more formidable still. The national economy had to be rebuilt from its foundations. The war had taken a terrible toll. More than a tenth of the population, 1,685,000 out of a total of 16 millions, had lost their lives. Half a million more had been wounded or disabled. Countless men, women and children had contracted tuberculosis. The country's labor force had been dangerously reduced and it had lost tens of thousands of technicians and skilled workers. Agriculture, Jugoslavia's basic industry, had suffered heavily. Two-thirds of her livestock and horses had been lost; a quarter of her vineyards and orchards devastated. Most of the farm carts and agricultural implements had been broken or lost. The reserves of timber had been exhausted. Such industry as there was had been largely destroyed. Trade and commerce were paralyzed. The mines were no longer in working order. Finally, the communications system had been

wrecked: thousands of railway wagons, coaches and locomotives had been destroyed or removed; the permanent way
had been ripped up all over the country, and practically every
road and railway bridge had been dynamited. Indeed, during
the period which immediately followed the war it was only
thanks to the very considerable material assistance afforded by
UNRRA that the new Jugoslavia had managed to keep going
at all. And even so there had been widespread starvation and
economic distress.

Such was the background against which, on November 29,
1946, on the first anniversary of the proclamation of the Republic, Tito announced his Five Year Plan, due to come into
force in 1947. It aimed at the rapid industrialization of the
country, with special emphasis on heavy industry. UNRRA
supplies, mostly provided by the United States, would, it was
hoped, continue for a time to furnish immediate needs. But
the ultimate intention was that the imports of additional raw
materials and industrial equipment required by Jugoslavia for
the implementation of the plan should be obtained as far as
possible from the East, from Soviet Russia and from the other
People's Democracies with whom appropriate trade agreements would duly be concluded.

The new plan was extremely ambitious. It took little account of realities, least of all of Jugoslavia's almost complete
lack of trained industrial specialists and technicians. Inadequate investment in agriculture meant that there would not
be enough agricultural exports to pay for the capital equipment
which would be needed before industrial exports could begin.
But criticism, even informed criticism, was regarded as tanta-
mount to treason. The national income was to increase by 93
per cent, the value of industrial production by 223 per cent
and of agricultural production by 52 per cent in comparison
with 1939. The new industries were to include the production
of heavy and medium machine tools, of heavy constructional
machinery, of steam boilers, water turbines and electrical
equipment. Iron ore output was to be doubled, the output of
steel trebled. Electric current was to increase fourfold, the
production of pig iron fivefold. The output of the metal industry was to be seven times that of 1939, of building materials
eight times, of chemicals nine times. Tens of milliards of
dinars were to be spent on hydroelectric plants, on boring and
drilling machinery, on refineries and cracking plants. Lakes
and marshes to be drained, the road, railway and canal system
extended and entirely new industries set up in the most back-

ward areas. In commerce and industry, the Five Year Plan would mark the end of private enterprise and the complete nationalization of the means of production and distribution.

Only in agriculture, which, despite its vital importance to the national economy, was allotted a secondary role, would the process be slower. Peasants were to be "encouraged" to join co-operatives rather than forced into collective farms, and as yet there was to be no wholesale nationalization of small holdings. The decision to adopt such a relatively mild attitude toward the peasants had not been reached without considerable discussion and even opposition in the Central Committee. The chief opponent of this policy was Andrija Hebrang, the President of the State Planning Commission, who claimed that it was both economically and ideologically unsound. Tito had called the peasants the cornerstone of the new Jugoslavia and the party was full of peasants. But, Hebrang pointed out, the vanguard of any true revolution should be the industrial proletariat. The peasants were notoriously reactionary. They must be steam-rollered into submission.

Hebrang, a short, stocky man with a swarthy complexion and only one eye, was one of the ablest of the Croat Communists. Before the war he had spent many years in jail and had emerged to find that in his absence Tito had been entrusted with the leadership of the party. The rivalry between the two was no secret. Hebrang had spent the first months of the war working underground in Zagreb. Early in 1942 he had been caught by the Ustaše. While in prison he had been savagely tortured and Pavelić himself had come to look at him as he lay in his cell. Then, somewhat unexpectedly, the Ustaše had agreed to exchange him for several of their own high officials who had fallen into the hands of the Partisans. Soon after reaching Partisan Headquarters he had been made Secretary of the Croat Communist party. But Tito had not felt entirely happy about his conduct of affairs and had later sent Kardelj to Croatia to investigate matters. The confidential report submitted by Kardelj on his return confirmed Tito's doubts. "Things will never go well in Croatia," wrote Kardelj, "so long as Andrija Hebrang continues to be Secretary of the Croat Communist party, in fact so long as he continues to be there at all. His whole attitude and mentality tend to undermine the attachment of the Croats to the idea of Jugoslavia. I have concrete evidence of this. We are always having trouble with the same negative elements. Hebrang's nationalist network is evident at every step." Accordingly in 1944 Hebrang had been removed from his post as Secretary of the Croat party. But he was too able for his services to be entirely dispensed with and shortly after he had been made Minister for Industry and President of the Economic Council and Planning Commission. Unofficially, he had another important function: on a number of subjects he kept up a private correspondence direct with Moscow.

In his opposition to Tito, Hebrang had an unexpected ally in Black Žujović, Tito's wartime Deputy Commander-in-Chief. Just as during the war Tito had entrusted *Crni* with a succession of difficult and responsible tasks, now in peacetime he had given him one formidable assignment after another. First, as Minister of Finance he had had to wrestle with Jugoslavia's shattered financial system. Now, as Minister of Transport, he was trying to restore her disrupted communications. But despite his close wartime association and long-standing friendship with Tito he had found that there were many aspects of the latter's postwar policy with which he could not agree, and he had accordingly joined Hebrang in his criticism of the government's economic and agricultural plans.

In the spring of 1946, during Tito's absence in Prague and Warsaw, Hebrang brought matters to a head by sending a letter to the Central Committee of the party in which he declared that his position as Minister for Industry and President of the Economic Council and Planning Commission was made impossible by the personal animosity with which he was being treated by Tito and calling for a thorough investigation into his personal position. The Politburo was summoned to consider the letter and after a heated debate, during which Žujović supported Hebrang, it was decided to refer the whole matter to a special commission which would in due course make recommendations to the Central Committee.

In due course the Commission reported as follows:

> 1. Comrade Hebrang's letter, both in its tone and contents, represents something unprecedented in the history of the Central Committee since it was set up in 1937. In this letter Comrade Hebrang maliciously and, according to party standards, quite impermissibly alleges that Comrade Tito bears him a private grudge for receiving cables addressed personally to him from Moscow, and that this is the real reason why Comrade Tito distrusts Comrade Hebrang's economic policy. Comrade Hebrang's attitude during the session of the Central

Committee held on April 19 was anything but self-critical and shows that his letter was not really concerned with some personal difference with Comrade Tito, but with an attempt to shift the political differences between himself and Comrade Tito, as representing the policy of the Central Committee, on to a personal plane and introduce unhealthy relationships and impossible methods of work into the Central Committee. The very fact that a free interchange of opinions, criticism and self-criticism does exist within the Central Committee gives the lie to Hebrang's unfounded and uncomradely assertions.

2. The attitude adopted by Comrade Žujović in the Central Committee's session of April 19 over Comrade Hebrang's letter had the effect not only of condoning Comrade Hebrang's offense, but also of strengthening his hand and confirming him in his incorrect attitude toward the Central Committee and Comrade Tito, both as regards the internal relations inside the Central Committee and also regarding his mistaken economic and financial policy.

In the light of the above, the Commission recommends to the Central Committee that Comrade Hebrang be removed from the Politburo, thereby enabling the party to carry through a correct economic policy; the Commission furthermore recommends that a severe reprimand be administered to him as punishment. The Commission recommends that Comrade Hebrang relinquish his post of Minister for Industry in the Central Government and that of the President of the Economic Council. The Commission considers that Comrade Hebrang should continue to hold that of the President of the Planning Commission.[1]

The Commission's report was endorsed by the Politburo. Hebrang was expelled from that body and dismissed from all his offices, except, strangely enough, that of President of the Planning Commission. Žujović was severely reprimanded. The revolt had come to nothing. The Five Year Plan was launched notwithstanding.

But Hebrang's revolt had been a straw in the wind. Although, in launching his Five Year Plan, Tito was doing no more than follow the example which Stalin himself had set in Russia some twenty years earlier, it was not long before it became all too apparent that his new project—indeed his economic policy as a whole—did not enjoy Soviet approval.

This was first brought home to the Jugoslavs in the course of their negotiations with the Russians for the establishment of Soviet-Jugoslav joint-stock companies. The decision to establish such companies had been taken in principle during Tito's visit to Moscow in May, 1946, when he had discussed the matter with Stalin personally. On that occasion, it will be recalled he had somewhat naïvely explained to Stalin that the advantage of these companies to the Jugoslavs was that they would contribute to the industrialization of Jugoslavia. Stalin, for his part, had not bothered to dissent from this view, but, continuing to draw intricate designs on his scribbling pad, had gone on to ask some pertinent questions about Jugoslav deposits of non-ferrous metals—a subject in which he seemed rather more interested than in Tito's plans for industrialization. It was only after the Jugoslavs had returned home and the negotiations had actually begun that it became clear to them that the Russians had quite different ideas from their own about Jugoslavia's economic future.

From the outset, Yatrov, the chief Soviet negotiator, left no doubt as to his government's requirements and intentions. The joint-stock companies which he had in mind would not help the Jugoslavs to industrialize their own country. On the contrary, they would give the Russians virtual control over large sections of the national economy, including most of the existing industrial and economic enterprises, and would enable them to exploit Jugoslav raw materials and other natural resources to their hearts' content. When the Jugoslavs, ideologically correct as ever, protested that, with no industry, there would be no foundation on which to build Socialism, he retorted with brutal directness: "What do you want with a heavy industry? We have everything you need in the Urals."[2]

The ensuing negotiations were equally unfruitful. The Jugoslavs, it is true, continued to assure the Russians of their desire for the closest economic co-operation with the Soviet Union, provided their national resources were developed and provided their national interests were safeguarded. But in the Russian scheme of things there was no room for such provisos. What the Russians wanted was a free hand, a free hand to exploit Jugoslav resources, a free hand to decide the lines on which the Jugoslav national economy should develop. It was the same thing every time. In every section of the national economy that came under discussion, oil, steel, iron, non-ferrous metals, they demanded a monopoly—a monopoly for their joint-stock companies. These in practice would be Russian-dominated. Exempt from Jugoslav taxation and jurisdiction, they would be so constituted as to impose a maximum burden on the Jugoslav partner, while bestowing every possible financial and other benefit on the Russian. They would even make it impossible for the Jugoslav Government to draw up any general economic plans without first obtaining Soviet approval.

It was beginning to look very much as though the Russians did not want to see Jugoslavia industrialized and self-sufficient, but preferred her to remain simply a source of raw materials, an integral part of their economic empire, in short, a "colonial territory." Worse still, it looked as though the Russians had the whip hand. The Jugoslavs depended almost entirely on Russia and her satellites for the machine tools and technical assistance without which their Five Year Plan would be an impossibility. Delivery of the necessary heavy equipment had, it is true, been promised but, when it came to the point, the promised equipment had a way of not materializing, and even when it did materialize, the quality was often poor and the prices far too high. Meanwhile Russia was buying up at ruinously low prices the greater part of Jugoslavia's output of raw materials.

Russian intentions had been made clearer still by the Soviet Government's proposal for the setting up of a Soviet-Jugoslav Bank, under a Soviet director general, which would have given them a veritable stranglehold on the financial and economic life of Jugoslavia. When the Jugoslav Government refused to agree to this, the Soviet negotiators made no attempt to disguise their resentment and spoke openly of Jugoslav "megalomania."

By the end of February, 1947, after nine months of negotiating, only two joint-stock companies, neither of them, properly speaking, industrial in character, had been set up: the "Justa" Air Transport Company and the "Juspad" River Shipping Company. Of these, the former gave the Russians virtual control over all Jugoslav airlines, both inside and outside Jugoslavia, while the latter made them a present of all the Jugoslav shipping on the Danube. The directors of both companies were Soviet citizens and the financial conditions were in both cases overwhelmingly favorable to the Soviet Union.

From a Soviet point of view this was satisfactory so far

as it went. But it did not go nearly far enough. Nor was this all. If the negotiations had awakened some doubts in Jugoslav minds as to the purity and disinterestedness of Soviet intentions, they had provided Stalin with renewed and overwhelming proof of Jugoslav stubbornness and independence. And stubbornness and independence were qualities which he was not prepared to tolerate in his subordinates. Before very long a showdown would be necessary. Meanwhile, like a cat playing with a mouse, he decided to give his intended victim a little more quite illusory encouragement, before gathering himself for the final pounce.

Kardelj, who visited Moscow in March, 1947 in connection with the Four Power Talks on the Austrian Peace Treaty, found the *Vozhd* in exceptionally jovial mood.[3] "And how," he inquired, "is Comrade Tito?" while Molotov, echoing his master, chipped in with "Is he well after his operation?" for Tito had recently been operated upon by Dr. Smotrov, a Soviet surgeon especially sent by Stalin. "He is," Kardelj replied politely, "feeling very well. The operation was a complete success. We are only sorry that Dr. Smotrov has since died."

This amused Stalin. A dead doctor was the sort of joke that appealed to him; he had had some of the Kremlin doctors tried and shot just before the war. "What did he die of?" he asked, having been told that he had died of a heart attack: "Perhaps he drank too much," he went on in the same jocular tone. "Surgeons like drinking." Then, to Molotov: "Did you send Tito a note about it?" "No," said Molotov, "it didn't come to that. There wasn't time. Tito got his story in first."

It was not until he had been treated to a lot more of this heavy-handed Kremlin banter that Kardelj finally managed to edge the conversation round to the subject he wanted to raise: the joint-stock companies. When he did, the result was most surprising. "Do you consider," Stalin asked, before he had finished speaking, "that, as joint-stock companies are of no especial use to you, it would be better not to set any up?" and then, without waiting for an answer: "How would it be if we did not set up joint-stock companies, but helped you; how about our giving you an aluminum factory and a steel plant, and helping you extract and refine oil? Of course it is not a good basis for co-operation to found joint-stock companies in an allied and friendly country like Jugoslavia. There would always be misunderstandings and differences; in a way the very independence of the country would suffer and friendly relations would be spoiled. Such companies are only suitable for satellite countries. Have you a plan?" he went on. "What capacity of steel and aluminum do you require?" And then: "We shall let you have this on credit," he concluded, "we shall also help you with men, with specialists, and you shall pay nothing in money, or however you can—though you should," he added with a disarming grin, "give us *something* in return."

Kardelj accepted this generous offer with alacrity. "We agree fully to your proposal," he said, as soon as he could get a word in edgeways. "We thank you very much." A few months later an agreement was concluded by which the Soviet Union undertook to grant Jugoslavia a credit of $135 million for capital goods, especially heavy industrial equipment.*

Meanwhile Tito had not lost all personal contact with the West. During the summer of 1947 he received several visits from his war-time associate, the former Head of the British Military Mission, now an opposition back bencher. The latter, who had been charged by Mr. Ernest Bevin with the task of clearing up a number of points outstanding between the two governments, found him affable and, considering the tension between their two countries, unexpectedly co-operative. They spent long hours riding together through the forests of Slovenia. Tito had put on weight since the war, but showed himself both physically and mentally as alert and as energetic as ever. At Brdo, Tito lived in a charmingly furnished country house, once Prince Paul's summer residence, where he and his closest associates spent the summer months. Kardelj and Marko Ranković were there with their families. Prlja, Tito's wartime bodyguard, now drove the Marshal's immense open touring car. Tigar, beginning to get a little gray round the muzzle, was more sedate than in the days when he used to snap at General Korneyev's ankles in the cave at Drvar.

At times, it is true, the cares of state appeared to weigh heavily on Tito and his friends; they seemed tense and abstracted. No doubt the strain of the war years, the stresses of their administrative responsibilities were beginning to tell— perhaps other stresses, too, whose existence they hardly liked to admit even to themselves. But one thing seemed unimpaired, the comradeship which for so long had united this particular

* It was never honored. Of the $135 million promised the Soviet Government only furnished equipment to the value of $800,000. They finally denounced the agreement in 1949.

little group, which had carried them through the conspiratorial period in the thirties, through the hazards and hardships of the war and which now enabled them to confront together the difficulties and dangers of the peace.

In September these preliminary contacts culminated in a more formal gathering at which the British Ambassador, Sir Charles Peake, and General Steel, the British Commander-in-Chief in Austria, were also present and at which an agreement was signed regulating the difficult question of the Jugoslav Displaced Persons in Germany, Austria and Italy, and conversations initiated concerning various frontier problems. None of these were matters of the first importance, but it showed that, despite ideological differences, it was, in practice, not impossible to reach agreement with the West over day-to-day questions.

To the inmates of the Kremlin, however, this resumption by Tito of his wartime contacts with the West was anything but agreeable. They signified their displeasure in a curious way. On October 22 there appeared in the Moscow *Literary Gazette,* an article, entitled "The British Mission in the Drvar Cave," purporting, with a wealth of heavy Soviet innuendo and sarcasm, to prove that the present author, aided and abetted by Major Randolph Churchill and under instructions from the Prime Minister himself, had in May, 1944 deliberately engineered the German parachute attack on Drvar with the object of eliminating Tito, whose continued existence was a source of displeasure to the British Government. "Our reader," the article observed, "is a clever reader and will, I am sure, be able to put two and two together."

The hint, it might have been thought, was clear enough. But Tito did not take it—he did not "put two and two together." On reading the article he showed signs of marked irritation and instructed his Ambassador in Moscow to inform those responsible that the article was both untrue and unhelpful.[4] What is more, he remained indirectly in touch with the former Head of the British Mission.

By the latter half of 1947 the stage was set for the final phase of Stalin's plan for the subjugation of Eastern Europe. Most of the spadework had already been done. It now remained, as in Czechoslovakia, for example, to sweep away the few surviving bourgeois politicians who by their co-operation had, wittingly or unwittingly, helped to prepare the way for a Communist dictatorship and who, here and there, had

managed to linger on in public life after their usefulness had
been exhausted. It also remained to remove from the Com-
munist-dominated satellite governments any remaining vestiges
of independence and to fit them and their countries militarily, politically and economically into the rapidly expanding framework of the Soviet Empire.

There was no reason to expect that either process would
give rise to any serious difficulties. Everywhere in Eastern
Europe the key positions were held by Moscow-trained men
who knew what was expected of them. Nor was any trouble
to be anticipated from the Western powers who, unlike the
Soviet Union, had disarmed after the war and whose policy
of bewildered appeasement made it in any case most unlikely
that they would offer any serious resistance to anything.

In short, at first sight, a relatively simple operation. But
Stalin had never believed in leaving anything to chance. Nor
had he ever placed implicit confidence in anyone, whether
Moscow-trained or not. His practice in approaching any
enterprise had always been thoroughly to prepare the ground
in advance, to build up elaborate systems of checks and
counterchecks, to eliminate at once any figures who, now or
later, might conceivably give rise to trouble and to play off
one protagonist against another and, each against all, until
finally he succeeded in gathering all the reins of power firmly
in his own hands. It was to this congenial and familiar task
that, in that sunlit autumn of 1947, he addressed himself with
all his old ruthlessness and skill.

To anyone subjecting the Eastern European scene to the
careful and informed scrutiny which it was now receiving
from the Kremlin, it might, it is true, have seemed to possess
one or two mildly disquieting features. First of all there was
an occasional tendency on the part of individual satellite
governments to behave in matters of secondary importance
as though they were not satellite governments at all, but the
governments of sovereign independent states, a tendency to
argue and answer back, instead of obeying implicitly the
orders they were given. Secondly, there were times when,
instead of co-ordinating their own policies with the Kremlin's
master policy, they were inclined to co-ordinate them mutually
among themselves. To say that they showed signs of "ganging
up," of forming anything that could be described as a *bloc*,
would be grossly to exaggerate what was never more than a
scarcely discernible tendency. But Stalin was a man who,
after long experience of the political jungle, believed in acting

on very slender indications indeed. What is more, it had not escaped him that these tendencies had a way, on further investigation, of leading the investigator back with disturbing regularity to the same quarter, namely Belgrade.

Since the end of the war Tito had paid a number of visits to the rulers of the other People's Democracies and had concluded with them a variety of agreements. In March, 1946 he had gone to Warsaw where he had signed a Treaty of Friendship and Mutual Assistance with Poland. From Warsaw he had gone to Prague and in May, 1946 a similar treaty had been concluded between Jugoslavia and Czechoslovakia. Tito had not bothered to go to Albania, which was now, practically speaking, an appendage of Jugoslavia, the satellite of a satellite; but Enver Hodja had come to Belgrade in June, 1946 and a treaty had been signed between the two countries in July. Later on Tito had gone to Bulgaria and Hungary. In the summer of 1947 he had received Georgi Dimitrov at his summer residence at Bled. And now, in the autumn of the same year, he was preparing to go to Rumania. Most of these visits had been returned and there had been more treaties and more conversations with more Eastern European statesmen. On some of these contacts the Kremlin had full reports, but on some they had not. Nor were the reports they received always entirely reassuring; here and there there were indications that their satellites might be comparing notes behind their back. There was another thing. Wherever Tito went, he received an enthusiastic reception. In Prague, Warsaw and Sofia, in Budapest and Bucharest, enormous crowds turned out to see this legendary figure, each of whose uniforms was more magnificent than the last. Tito's fame had spread far beyond the frontiers of his own country. He was in a different class from any of the other rather drab satellite rulers. He was well on the way to becoming, in his own right, an international figure of the first magnitude. None of which caused any great satisfaction in Moscow, where the impression prevailed that in some respects the situation had got a little out of hand.

From Stalin's point of view, the first necessity was to set up machinery which would enable him to exercise an increased measure of direct control over the individual Communist parties of the various satellite countries and, through them, over the governments of these countries. Such, though this does not seem to have been apparent to all the participants at the time, was the idea which lay behind the foundation of the Communist Information Bureau, or Cominform.

Since the liquidation of the Communist International in 1943, contact between foreign Communist parties and the Kremlin had been maintained through a variety of channels. Changed circumstances now called for a chance in organization. Though the ultimate aim of the new body might be to establish over its members an ascendancy no less absolute than that possessed by the Comintern, it was nevertheless considered advisable to pay lip service to their nominal independence. From the first it was emphasized that the purpose of the Cominform was, as its name indicated, to provide for the "exchange of information" between individual Communist parties. It was also, it was announced, intended to facilitate mutual consultation and the co-ordination of policy "on a basis of mutual agreement."

These aims were proclaimed in a resolution passed at the first meeting of the Cominform which was held in September, 1947 at a convalescent home for sick secret policemen near a small spa in western Poland. The meeting, which lasted for seven days, was attended by representatives of the Soviet, Jugoslav, Bulgarian, Czech, Rumanian, Polish and Hungarian Communist parties and of the Communist parties of France and Italy. No other parties were invited to send delegates. The Soviet party was represented by Zhdanov, and Malenkov; the Jugoslav party by Kardelj and Djilas. Gomulka and Minc represented Poland; Anna Pauker and Gheorghiu Dei, Rumania; Chervenkov and Poptomov, Bulgaria; Slansky and Bastovansky, Czechoslovakia. The French representatives were Duclos and Fageon, while Longo and Reale represented the Italians. Both the building in which their deliberations took place and the surrounding park were heavily guarded.

The meeting was dominated from the start by Zhdanov, with his little black mustache and puffy red face, who opened the proceedings with a harangue on the conflict between the Communist and non-Communist worlds. Later he loudly interrupted any speaker whose remarks did not appeal to him. He even instructed some of the delegates as to the line they were to take. For example, Kardelj and Djilas were told to criticize the conduct of the French and Italian Communist parties. This they did with alacrity and assurance, much to the fury of Jacques Duclos, who went off into the park and sat on a bench by himself, a small, angry figure with his long nose, his clipped mustache and his big horn-rimmed spectacles, refusing to talk to anyone and irritably swinging his plump little legs which were too short to reach the ground. His pride was hurt. A wedge had been successfully inserted between the Communist parties of France and Jugoslavia.[5]

Altogether the Jugoslavs came in for a good deal of seemingly rather flattering attention. Their party was always mentioned first in the various resolutions, and when it came to choosing a home for the new organization Zhdanov put through a long-distance call to Stalin, who replied in person that he wished it to be situated in Belgrade.

Yudin, the permanent Soviet representative on the Cominform, arrived in Belgrade in October. He was a philosopher by profession, but was also known to be connected with the NKVD. He also made it his business to keep in with the great. An eyewitness has described how, on taking leave of Zhdanov he walked backward all the way to the door, bowing as he went, and finally misjudged his position and collided violently with the door in an agony of servility.

Yudin's first action on arrival was to take over a large building in the middle of the city as Cominform Headquarters. There he at once established a private wireless link with Moscow and the editorial offices of the official Cominform newspaper, which appeared simultaneously in Russian, French, English and Serbo-Croat and bore the somewhat cumbrous name of *For a Lasting Peace, for a People's Democracy*. Much of Yudin's time was spent in editing and producing this periodical—an arduous and worrying task, involving numerous sudden journeys to Moscow and the last-minute destruction of whole issues which had belatedly been discovered to contain some ideological error. But the Jugoslavs, who, in view of what they knew about his past, had thought it worth while to keep track of him, found that the pursuit of journalism and philosophy did not take up all his time. Some of it was spent in other, less admissible activities, concerning which long and illuminating reports were in due course laid before Marko Ranković in his office at the Ministry of Internal Affairs. The spy was being spied on.

The chief of these activities, and one for which, by virtue of his position, Yudin was exceptionally well placed, consisted in making trouble between Jugoslavia and her partners in the Cominform. Meanwhile, the same thing was being done at a higher level—a much higher level.

At the beginning of January, 1948, Lavrentiev, the Soviet Ambassador, a large man with an expressionless face and gray, fishlike eyes, called on Tito with a personal telegram from Stalin; it asked that a member of the Jugoslav Politburo, preferably Djilas, should come to Moscow immediately to discuss a number of current issues, especially Albania. There was nothing very surprising about this. Albania had been discussed at both the previous meetings of the Jugoslav leaders with Stalin: in 1946, when Stalin had so ostentatiously put Tito in charge of Albanian affairs, and in 1947, when he had asked Kardelj for his views on the same subject. As usual there were plenty of questions that needed settling, for example, the defense of southern Albania and Jugoslavia's own defense needs. Moreover, Djilas was well qualified to discuss them. It could surely be safely assumed that the feeling aroused back in 1944 by his alleged aspersions on the conduct of the Red Army had long since been dispelled. Had not Stalin, after all, sent him a special invitation through Tito in 1946 to come and spend a holiday on the Black Sea coast?

Accompanied by a military delegation with Koča Popović, now Chief of the General Staff, at its head, Djilas left Belgrade by train for Moscow early in January.[6] They traveled by way of Rumania, stopping in Bucharest to have dinner with Anna Pauker. At Jassy, where the wide gauge began, they changed into a saloon coach specially sent for them by the Soviet Government. In this, they crept on at a snail's pace across the bleak snow-covered expanse of the Ukraine, past a succession of towns and villages battered and blasted by the war. At mealtimes, waiters in white coats would bring them caviar and little glasses of vodka, and hot cabbage soup with sour cream in it, and black bread and white bread, and large dishes of fish and meat. The steam heating in the coach was slightly oppressive. From time to time the locomotive would emit the long-drawn melancholy wail peculiar to Soviet locomotives. It took them five days to reach their destination.

On reaching Moscow, they were driven to the Moskva Hotel, a portentous modern building near the Kremlin. Djilas, who had been given a room to himself, said that he would prefer to share Koča's room on the fourth floor. At this the management seemed distressed, but eventually produced a double room on the second floor. The reason for their concern became apparent when, shortly after, an electrician arrived to make some adjustments. Djilas and Koča, who had been to Moscow before and knew about microphones, had no difficulty in guessing what he had come to do.

Scarcely had the Jugoslavs settled in than Djilas was told that Stalin would like to see him at once. A large, shiny, closed car carried him across the Red Square and up to the main gate of the Kremlin, a city within a city, with palaces and towers and the golden cupolas of its churches rising from behind the high crenelated red brick walls. An electric bell above the gate rang persistently as the car approached and a red light flashed on and off. Beneath the arch an officer of the Kremlin Guard, wearing a long gray overcoat and a red and blue peaked cap, checked the identifications and saluted and the car drove on up an inclined slope to the yellow stucco-fronted building containing Stalin's private office. There Stalin and Molotov were waiting.

Stalin lost no time in coming to the point, namely Albania. "The Soviet Government," he said, "lay no claim to Albania. Jugoslavia is free to swallow Albania whenever she chooses." And at the word "swallow," with a crude but expressive gesture, he greedily licked the fingers of his right hand.

Djilas was surprised. "But, Comrade Stalin," he said, "there is no question of our swallowing Albania. All we want is friendly relations as between allies." "Which," said Molotov, interrupting, "comes to precisely the same thing!" Whereupon they pressed Djilas to embody these somewhat startling conclusions in a telegram which Stalin would send to Tito.*

From this rather bewildering · beginning the conversation turned to the question of the military supplies required by Jugoslavia. Djilas explained what was needed. Being a Jugoslav, he was careful not to understate his country's requirements. But Stalin was at his blandest. *"Chepukha!"* he exclaimed with an expansive gesture, "A mere trifle! We will give you everything you need." Djilas observed that the Jugoslavs did not expect the Rusians to provide them with any secret weapons. "We have no secrets," said Stalin, "from the army of a friendly and allied power like Jugoslavia," and, seizing the telephone, he instructed Marshal Bulganin, the Minister of Defense, to give the Jugoslavs everything they

* Djilas duly drafted a telegram and sent the draft to Stalin next day. But he was careful to tone down what had been said and the telegram was never sent. It was evidently not what was required. In *Tito Speaks* Dedijer suggests that the object of this elaborate gambit was to furnish proof of Jugoslavia's imperialist designs on Albania. This explanation seems as likely as any other. One thing is clear enough: Stalin did not mean what he said.

wanted. After which, with that bluff geniality, so encouraging to foreign visitors, so chilling to those who knew him better, Stalin swept his guest off to a cozy supper at his *dacha* with Molotov, Zhdanov, Vosnesenski and Beria. The last-named, spectacled and podgy, talked a lot, watching everyone with his cold, staring blue eyes. Vosnesenski, preoccupied with economic problems or perhaps with a sense of his own impending doom, hardly spoke at all.

At five the next afternoon Djilas, Koča Popović and the rest of the delegation were received by Marshal Bulganin. A strangely unmilitary figure with his little pointed beard wagging above his uniform collar, Bulganin listened politely while Djilas enumerated his country's requirements. "You shall have everything," he said reassuringly as soon as Djilas had finished, and at once appointed a committee of experts to work things out over the weekend and report on Monday. The Jugoslavs were delighted.

Monday came, but they heard nothing more; Tuesday, Wednesday and Thursday went by: still nothing. On Saturday they asked what was happening. They were told that "complications had arisen." There was nothing for it but to wait. They waited.

The days passed. They spent their time sight-seeing. They went to the Red Army Museum and were surprised to find how few of the exhibits illustrated the part played by Lenin in 1918; there was, they noticed, much more about Stalin. At the request of the NKVD officer escorting them, they recorded their impressions in the visitors' book. In the evenings they went to the Bolshoi Theater and saw *Swan Lake* and *The Sleeping Beauty*. When they got back to their hotel at night, they talked things over among themselves, not always perhaps very discreetly. Still nothing more was heard from the Kremlin.

When they had seen Moscow, they asked if they might go to Leningrad. A villa there was at once put at their disposal by the Leningrad Soviet. Dutifully, piously, they visited the historic scenes of the October Revolution: Kronstadt, the Winter Palace, the Finland Station, the Nevski Prospect, the Fortress of St. Peter and St. Paul. Wherever they went, they were accompanied by a major from the NKVD.

Then they came back to Moscow. Still there was no answer from the Kremlin. Djilas tried a new line of approach. He proposed to Mikoyan, the Minister of Foreign Trade, the revision of the agreement governing the sale of Soviet films to Jugoslavia, which, as it stood, was burdensome to the Jugoslavs. But Mikoyan, handsome, elegant, aloof and unfriendly, replied with Armenian inscrutability that he did not wish to revise the agreement; it might create a precedent. In regard to various other matters which Djilas sought to raise he was even less forthcoming. It was now the beginning of February. Nearly a month had gone by since the Jugoslavs had first arrived in Moscow. Meanwhile elsewhere there had been new and dramatic developments.

The question of a Balkan federation, and in particular of some kind of federative union between Jugoslavia and Bulgaria, had been under discussion on and off ever since the winter of 1944, when Kardelj and Dimitrov had first talked it over in Sofia. At that time, though both parties were agreed as to its desirability in principle, no progress had been possible, partly owing to the unfavorable attitude of the Western Allies and partly owing to the difficulty of deciding on what terms federation should take place, the Bulgars wishing for a union between the two countries on equal terms, while the Jugoslavs suggested that Bulgaria should simply become a seventh federal republic in the existing Jugoslav Federation. Subsequently the idea had been shelved, but it had again been raised on the occasion of Dimitrov's visit to Tito at Bled in the summer of 1947, when the two old comrades had reached the conclusion that federation between their countries must be arrived at gradually. Meanwhile a Jugoslav-Bulgarian Treaty of Friendship and Mutual Assistance had been drawn up, providing for the closest political and economic co-operation between the two countries. This was signed at Evxinograd in Bulgaria in the following November, after being duly approved in Moscow. "We shall establish co-operation so general and so close," Tito said in speech at Sofia on this occasion, "that the question of federation will be a mere formality." And the listening crowds had roared their applause.

Such was the background against which, two months later, toward the end of January, 1948, Dimitrov, while on a visit to Rumania, made a statement to the press on the subject of a Balkan federation. "The question," he said, "of a federation or confederation is premature for us. It is not on the agenda at present, and therefore it has not been a subject of discussion at our conferences. When the question matures, as it must inevitably mature, then our peoples, the nations of People's Democracy, Rumania, Bulgaria, Jugoslavia, Albania,

Czechoslovakia, Poland, Hungary and Greece—mind you, and Greece!—will settle it. It is they who will decide what it shall be—a federation or confederation—and when and how it will be formed. I can say that what our peoples are already doing greatly facilitates the solution of this question in the future. I can also emphasize that when it comes to creating such a federation or confederation, our peoples will not ask the imperialists, and will not heed opposition from them, but will solve the question themselves, guided by their own interests, which are bound up with the interests and international co-operation necessary to them and to other nations.'

To Stalin, Dimitrov's statement, coming on top of a speech in which Kardelj had set forth at length the happy results of Tito's round of visits to his neighbors in Eastern Europe, was the last straw. He reacted promptly and violently. On January 29 *Pravda* published a scathing counterstatement referring to Dimitrov's statement and declaring that "these countries require no questionable or fabricated federation or confederation or customs union; what they require is the consolidation and defense of their independence and sovereignty by mobilizing and organizing internally their people's democratic forces, as was correctly stated in the well-known declaration of the nine Communist parties." At the same time telegrams were sent to Sofia and Belgrade, calling on the two governments to dispatch delegations to Moscow immediately.[7]

Dimitrov, having first hastily retracted all he had said and publicly abased himself, at once left for Moscow accompanied by Vassili Kolarov and Traicho Kostov. At the same time, the Russians made it clear that they wished Tito himself to head the Jugoslav delegation. The Jugoslav Central Committee, however, decided that it would be enough if Kardelj and Bakarić* were to join Djilas, who was still in Moscow. The Russians continued to drop hints, but these Tito ignored. He did not, as it happened, feel like going to Moscow just then.

Meanwhile, before Kardelj and Bakarić left for Moscow, a fresh issue had arisen. The Albanians asked Belgrade to send them two Jugoslav divisions to help defend their southern borders against a possible attack by the Greeks. The Jugoslavs, who had already sent an air formation to Albania,

* Prime Minister of Croatia and Secretary of the Croat Communist party.

agreed in principle. But before the divisions could be moved, a sharply worded telegram arrived from Molotov expressing strong disapproval of what had been decided and declaring that the Soviet warning would be published in the press, unless the two governments at once canceled their agreement. It was the same threat of the ultimate sanction—public denunciation—which had been leveled against Tito three years earlier, after his speech at Ljubljana. Moreover, taken in conjunction with Stalin's recent invitation to "swallow up" Albania, it looked very much as though the Albanian Government's request for help had been an act of deliberate "provocation" undertaken at the instigation of Moscow. It looked, in fact, as if the Russians were determined at all costs to pick a quarrel with Jugoslavia. Things were hotting up.

Kardelj and Bakarić reached Moscow on Sunday, February 8. Nothing was said to them for two days except that "the top Bulgarians" had arrived, apparently an allusion to Tito's absence and to their own inferior status. Djilas, they found, had been told nothing by the Russians and had only learnt of their impending arrival from a telegram which Tito had sent him from Belgrade.

On Tuesday, February 10, the Jugoslavs received a message saying that they were to be in Stalin's office in the Kremlin at nine that evening. In the anteroom they were joined by Dimitrov and the two other Bulgars. The meeting started at a quarter past nine. Stalin sat at the head of the table with the Jugoslavs and Bulgars on his left and his own men, Molotov, Zhdanov, Malenkov, Suslov and Zorin, on his right. The proceedings were opened by Molotov. There were, he said, serious differences between the Soviet Union, on the one hand, and Jugoslavia and Bulgaria, on the other. These differences were "inadmissible both from the party and from the state point of view." While Molotov was speaking, Stalin sat in silence, scowling and doodling ceaselessly on his scribbling pad. Quite clearly there was serious trouble ahead.

Molotov went on to enumerate the points at issue: the Jugoslav-Bulgarian Alliance, which he said had been concluded against the wishes of the Soviet Government; Dimitrov's statement on federation; the recent Jugoslav exchanges with Albania. As Molotov mentioned Dimitrov's statement, Stalin interrupted him. "We observe," he said with his harsh Georgian accent, "that Comrade Dimitrov allows himself to be carried away at press conferences. He does not guard his tongue. Whatever he says, whatever Tito says, is thought abroad to have been said with our knowledge. For instance, the Poles were here. I asked them what they thought of Dimitrov's statement. 'A wise thing,' they said. I told them it was not a wise thing. Then they said that they also thought that it was not a wise thing. Comrade Dimitrov later tried to correct his statement by some sort of communiqué put out by the Bulgarian News Agency. Nothing was corrected by his correction." And more in the same surly, sardonic vein, while his visitors sat appalled.

When Dimitrov's turn came to answer, Stalin kept interrupting him. In vain he tried to explain that nothing had really been concluded at Bled; that Bulgaria had great difficulties to contend with. In vain he admitted that his statement to the press had been a mistake.

"You wanted to shine by saying something new," Stalin interrupted. "That's all wrong. Such a federation is an impossibility."

"There is no essential difference between the foreign policy of Bulgaria and that of the Soviet Union," said Dimitrov.

"There are enormous differences," Stalin retorted angrily. "It is no good trying to hide the facts. Leninist practice has always shown that it is necessary to realize an error and to repair it as quickly as possible."

"It's true," Dimitrov answered, "that we did make a mistake. But we are also learning by these mistakes in foreign policy."

"Mistakes!" said Stalin, "you are an old political worker and you have been in politics for more than forty years, and now you want to rectify mistakes. Mistakes are not the issue; the issue is a conception different from ours." That, Stalin kept repeating, was what he was concerned with, and that was what he was determined to stop. He then went on to say that he had nothing against a federation between Jugoslavia and Bulgaria. What he was not prepared to tolerate was a federation or customs union between Rumania and Bulgaria.

At this Kolarov, one of the Bulgars, pointed out that the Bulgars had duly submitted their draft agreement with Rumania to Moscow, and Molotov was obliged to admit that this was so. This made Stalin angrier than ever. "There you are," he shouted, "now we've made fools of ourselves too." And, turning on the wretched Dimitrov, who had clutched at Kolarov's intervention as a drowning man clutches at a straw, "You've acted like a Komsomol,"* he said, "you answer back like a woman of the streets. You try to astonish the world as if you were still Secretary of the Comintern. Bulgaria and Jugoslavia never tell us what they are doing. We have to find out for ourselves. We are simply confronted with the accomplished fact."

The Jugoslav's turn came next. Kardelj began by recalling that the Jugoslav-Bulgarian Treaty had also been submitted in draft to the Soviet Government. The only point the Russians had questioned concerned the duration of the treaty, which they suggested should be concluded for a period of twenty years and not for all eternity as its enthusiastic drafters had originally proposed. Apart from this, he knew of no differences in foreign policy between Jugoslavia and the Soviet Union.

"There are differences and big differences too," broke in Stalin, who had been scowling at Molotov all the time Kardelj was speaking. "What have you got to say about Albania?"

But again Kardelj's explanations about Albania and his protestations that Jugoslavia had consulted the Soviet Government on every major issue of foreign policy were interrupted. Even when, on a side issue, he endeavored to convince the *Vozhd* that the Netherlands formed part of Benelux, he was sharply put in his place. "When I say NO," Stalin roared, "it means NO." And that was that.

Having thus bludgeoned his visitors into silence, Stalin now proceeded to give his own views on East European federation. He wanted three federations formed: Bulgaria and Jugoslavia; Hungary and Rumania; Poland and Czechoslovakia. "The federation of Bulgaria and Jugoslavia," he added, "should be proclaimed immediately—the sooner the better. The time is ripe. First Bulgaria and Jugoslavia should unite and then they should annex Albania." And he went on to say that the new state should have a special name of its own.

Before the meeting broke up, Kardelj made a final attempt to convince Stalin that there were no serious divergences between Jugoslav and Soviet policy. But once again he was unsuccessful. "It is not true," Stalin said. "There are differences between us." And it was only after he had told the Jugoslav delegates that he wished them to sign on behalf of their government an agreement providing for mutual consultation with the Soviet Government on all questions of foreign policy that he finally let the matter drop.

Later the conversation turned to Russia's support of Italy's

* Member of the Young Communist League.

demand for the return of her former colonies. "Emperors," said Stalin, "when unable to agree on the division of their spoils, used to give the disputed territory to the weakest feudal lord, in order to be able to seize if from him the more easily at a suitable moment. The feudal lord was usually a foreigner, so the emperors overthrew him all the more easily when he became a nuisance." At which, for the first time that evening, he laughed. The meeting dispersed at midnight. This time Stalin asked neither the Jugoslavs nor the Bulgars to supper at his *dacha*.

Once back at their Embassy, Kardelj, Djilas and Bakarić sat down to talk things over among themselves. They decided that Stalin's primary object in insisting on immediate federation with Bulgaria was to destroy Jugoslav unity and gain control of Jugoslav. They also decided that they must resist immediate federation.

But before leaving Moscow they were to be subjected to a final humiliation. At midnight on February 11, Kardelj was suddenly summoned to Molotov's office. On arrival Molotov handed him two sheets of paper in a blue folder. It was the agreement on mutual consultation between the two governments, ready drawn up. "Sign it," said Molotov peremptorily. Kardelj hesitated. Should he sign it or not? He reflected that to refuse would only aggravate an already tense situation. He decided to sign. But, for all his native calmness and imperturbability, he was so disturbed, so angry and so upset that when it came to the point he wrote his name in the wrong place, and the whole agreement had to be copied out again. On the following night he signed the fresh copy, after which he and his companions left Moscow for Belgrade to report to Tito.

XIII 〰〰 ST. VITUS'S DANCE

ALREADY the signs of impending trouble were multiplying on all sides. From Bucharest came reports that the Rumanian Communist party, always in close touch with the Kremlin, had suddenly ordered Tito's portraits to be taken down. At an official reception in Tirana, when the Jugoslav Minister proposed the health of Stalin and Tito, the Soviet chargé d'affaires replied: "I drink to Tito, *provided* Tito is for unity in the democratic bloc." In Moscow the Soviet Ministry for Foreign Trade broke off negotiations for a new trade agreement with Jugoslavia, thus virtually putting an end to trade between the two countries. There could no longer be any doubt about it. Jugoslavia's relations with the Soviet Union were rapidly approaching a crisis. Such was the appalling, but nonetheless inescapable fact which now stared Tito in the face.

How had such a situation arisen? And what would be its outcome? To find the answer to these questions, it is necessary to go back some way. When Tito had been made Secretary General of the Jugoslav Communist party in 1937, it was because he was regarded in Moscow as an essentially reliable and trustworthy man. The appointment had been his reward for long years of devoted service to the Communist cause, long years of unquestioning obedience to the party line.

But a lot had happened to Tito since 1937. In company with many thousands of his fellow countrymen, South Slavs like himself, he had undergone the hazards and hardships of a savage, bitter war against a foreign invader. He had built up from nothing a formidable military and political machine of which he was the absolute master. He had tasted the triumph of ultimate victory. And, when all was said and done, he could claim that it was by his own efforts and those of his followers that the Germans had been driven from his country and he and his party established in power. Unlike the rulers of the neighboring satellite countries, he had not returned home in the baggage train of the Red Army. Human experience shapes human character. The impact of events on the individual cannot altogether be left out of account even when the individual in question is a Communist. It would indeed have been surprising if, after such experiences, Tito had still been as ready as ever to take his orders from a foreign master.

"Much," the present author wrote in 1943 in a secret report to Mr. Churchill, "will depend on Tito, and whether he sees himself in his former role of Comintern agent or as the potential ruler of an independent Jugoslav state." This, in fact, was the problem which arose in acute form as soon as the war was over and Tito duly established in power in Belgrade. To what extent was he going to take his orders from Moscow? What was going to be the relationship between the new Jugoslavia and the Country of the Revolution, between himself and Stalin?

In the old "illegal" days before the war Tito's relations with Moscow had presented no problem. He had simply done what he was told. With all its imperfections, the Soviet Union was, in his own words, "the only country where the Revolution had succeeded and where Socialism was being built." It was the "mighty country where all the dreams for which we were fighting had been fulfilled." It was "the Workers' Fatherland." Without Soviet help and guidance he and his comrades could hope to achieve nothing; with them, they might achieve anything.

But now the situation had changed. Now they, too, had had their Revolution. They, too, were building Socialism. They had seen their dreams fulfilled in their own country. Their workers had their own Fatherland. And all this with precious little help from anyone. In theory, a conflict between Communist states was an impossibility. In practice, things had turned out otherwise. As early as 1942, in Montenegro, after less than a year of war, Tito had found himself, for the first time in his life, disagreeing with Moscow—and saying so. As the war went on, the occasions for disagreement had multiplied.

Disagreement with Moscow . . . Before the war such a thing would have been unthinkable. From Moscow's point of view, it still was unthinkable. But, after what they had been through, the Jugoslav Communists had come to believe in working things out for themselves. For them Marxism-Leninism was not an unalterable dogma, but something to be adapted to their own needs. "The Jugoslav brand of Communism," Tito once said, "had its origin in the hills and forests and was not imported ready-made from Moscow."

There had been much speculation as to the precise cause of the trouble between Tito and Moscow. But it is not really necessary to go beyond this Jugoslav belief in the possibility of working things out for oneself, this refusal to accept the Kremlin's lightest word as gospel, this tendency to argue and to answer back. The subject or occasion of the dispute was of secondary importance. What mattered was that there should be a dispute at all. The Soviet system was based on the absolute infallibility of the Kremlin. And Tito, on a number of issues, was challenging that infallibility.

The orthodox Communist must be immune to ordinary human feelings: he must be without pride, without love or hatred, without pity or resentment, without patriotism or loyalty, save to Moscow. During the war, under the terrific stresses and strains to which they had been subjected, Tito and the men round him had to some extent lost this immunity. Fighting side by side, they had come to feel pride in their achievements and in those of their fellow countrymen. They had allowed feelings of comradeship, of loyalty and affection to grow up between them. They had at times even felt pity for the sufferings of the civilian population. They had felt anger and resentment at the lack of understanding they so often encountered. In short, they had acquired a point of view of their own, a national point of view, very nearly, for which in the ultimate resort they would have been prepared to die. They had experienced the stirrings of something, which, if not old-fashioned patriotism, was certainly very like it. And they had experienced it with the violence, the intensity of feeling, which is one of the characteristics of their race. "After this war," Djilas had said to a friend in 1943 at a moment of crisis, "I could not live in any country but ours."[1]

Consciously or unconsciously, it was in this new frame of mind that Tito and the little band of men round him had, in the closing months of the war, confronted the problem of their relations with Moscow. If they had been asked to explain their attitude, they would have replied that the change lay not in themselves but elsewhere. Now that the Communist party was in power in Jugoslavia, they would have explained, its relationship with Moscow had automatically changed. In a world where there were other Communist countries, the Soviet Union was no more than *primus inter pares*. The other

Communist countries would be linked to it by a common tradition, by common interests, by common aims and aspirations, but they would be the masters of their own destiny. At the same time, it is hard to see how, deep down in their revolutionary subconscious, they could have failed to sense that this could not be so; that the only relationship which Stalin would ever tolerate was the old one of master to man; that he would expect of them now the same unquestioning obedience as heretofore, obedience which on certain issues they, it seemed, were no longer prepared to give him.

But, whatever their feelings may have been on the subject, there was no doubt what Stalin felt about it. Whether or not they realized in what direction they were heading, Stalin was quite certain of it, had been quite certain of it for some time. Disagreement, disobedience, insubordination—whatever you chose to call it—was something which he would not tolerate, something which he was determined to root out. Up to now he had bided his time. Now he was preparing to strike. And now, at long last, Tito and the men round him seem fully to have grasped the extent of the danger which threatened them.

In this critical situation, Tito turned, as he was bound to turn, to the party, to his own party, to the Communist party of Jugoslavia, which he himself had built up and on which, in error, his power was founded. As a first step he called a meeting of the Central Committee for the morning of March 1 at his own house, Rumunska 15, an agreeable suburban villa in which he now lived, keeping the White Palace for official purposes. By a strange coincidence it was situated only a few yards from the house in which, as Engineer Slavko Babić, he had lived illegally during the spring and summer of 1941.

Tito opened the meeting with an account of the present state of Soviet-Jugoslav relations.[2] They had, he said, reached a deadlock. He spoke of the difficulties there had been over the joint-stock companies, of the trouble over Albania, of the Russian refusal to admit the need for a strong Jugoslav Army, of the economic pressure which the Russians were now exerting on them. This, he said, they must resist.

He was followed by Kardelj, Djilas and Tempo Vukmanović, who described their experiences in Moscow, and by Kidrić, the Minister for Heavy Industry, who spoke in greater detail of the economic pressure that was being brought to bear on them and of the effect it was likely to have. What it came to, Kardelj observed, was that they and the Russians had different ideas on the subject of Socialist development. They believed in co-operation on equal terms between different countries advancing toward Socialism. The Russians, on the other hand, were solely interested in the aggrandizement of the Soviet Union. Djilas, who followed, expressed the same view.

In regard to Bulgaria it was agreed that the Russian demand for immediate federation must be rejected. To accept union with Bulgaria at the present time, said Tito, would be to allow a Trojan Horse to enter the Jugoslav party. On some subjects they had different ideas from the Russians. "We are not," he said, "a mere pawn on a chessboard." In Bulgaria, Marko Ranković pointed out, the Russians had a finger in everything. The Ministry of the Interior was completely under their control. What was at stake, they concluded, was the independence of Jugoslavia, and all who spoke agreed that the Soviet demands must at all costs be resisted.

All who spoke . . . There was, however, one member of the Central Committee who did not speak, but sat silent, taking notes of everything that was said: Black Žujović, *Crni*. Some of the other members of the Central Committee, noticing it, recalled that of late they had seen very little of him. He had seemed to avoid them. He duly attended meetings of the government and of the National Assembly, but he no longer dropped in on Tito for a drink in the evening or went out shooting with his old friends, as he used to formerly.

It had naturally been decided to keep the proceedings of the Central Committee and the issue involved absolutely secret. The general public had no idea of what was happening, and outwardly everything seemed serene. Meanwhile Soviet pressure was daily being intensified. On March 18, General Barskov, the Head of the Soviet Military Mission, informed Koča Popović that the Soviet Government had decided to withdraw all their military advisers and instructors from Jugoslavia on the grounds that they were "surrounded by unfriendliness and treated with hostility." On the following day the Soviet chargé d'affaires read out to Tito a telegram from Moscow ordering all Soviet civilian specialists to leave Jugoslavia. Both military and civilian specialists started leaving forthwith, to the astonishment of the Jugoslavs with whom they had been in touch.

In these circumstances Tito decided to address himself directly to Molotov. In a note dated March 20 he declared that he and his colleagues of the Central Committee were "surprised and hurt" by the Soviet Government's decision to withdraw its experts and by its failure to state "the real reason" for doing so. They refused to accept the reasons given, which in their view were completely unfounded. It was not true to say that the Soviet experts had been "surrounded by hostility." Nor was it true that Soviet requests for information made through the proper channels had been refused. They accordingly asked to be "told straight out" what the trouble was.[3]

It was more than a week before Tito received the Russian reply. It was delivered to him by the Soviet Ambassador at his villa at Tuškanac outside Zagreb. With the Ambassador came the Counselor of Embassy. Tito got up from his desk when the Russians came in, and shook hands with them. He did not ask them to sit down. All three remained standing while Tito opened the letter. It was in Russian and consisted of eight closely typed pages. At the foot were the signatures of Stalin and Molotov and the date: March 27. At the top the word "Confidential" was written in purple ink. As Tito read the opening sentence he felt, in his own words, thunderstruck. "We consider your answer," the letter began, "untruthful and therefore wholly unsatisfactory." As he read on, he could see Lavrentiev watching him closely. "When," he inquired, before Tito had finished reading, "may we expect an answer?" With an effort Tito contained himself. "I did not," he said afterward, "wish him to see that it had made any impression on me." "We shall give the letter our attention," he replied coldly. They shook hands again and the Ambassador was shown out. The interview had not lasted five minutes.[4]

After Lavrentiev had gone, Tito read carefully through the whole letter. It more than fulfilled the promise contained in its first sentence. Its tone was consistently offensive. It raked up the aspersions allegedly cast on the Red Army by Djilas in 1944. It complained that Soviet representatives in Jugoslavia, including Yudin of the Cominform, were spied on and followed by Jugoslav Security Agents. It asserted that "anti-Soviet rumors are circulating among the leading comrades in Jugoslavia, for instance that the Communist party of 'the Soviet Union is degenerate,' that 'great power chauvinism is rampant in the U.S.S.R.'" It pointed out that it was "laughable to hear such statements about the Communist party of the Soviet Union from such questionable Marxists as Djilas,

Vukmanović, Kidrić, Ranković and others," and that "the great mass of the Jugoslav party would disown this anti-Soviet criticism as alien and hostile, if they knew of it." "Trotsky," it continued significantly, "also started by saying that the Communist party of the Soviet Union was degenerate and that it was suffering from the limitations inherent in great-power chauvinism. Naturally he camouflaged himself with leftist slogans about world revolution. But in fact it was Trotsty himself who was degenerate and who, on being found out, sided with the sworn enemies of the Soviet Communist party and of the Soviet Union. We think that the political career of Trotsky is not uninstructive." After which the authors launched into a violent ideological attack on the Jugoslav Communist party, accusing it of being "undemocratic," of not practicing "self-criticism," of being neither Marxist-Leninist nor Bolshevik in its organization, of failing to check the development of capitalism, of letting itself be submerged in the Popular Front, of being a mere tool of Marko Ranković and his secret police, of borrowing ideas from Bernstein and Bukharin on the one hand and the Mensheviks on the other. Then, returning from the general to the particular: "We cannot understand," they continued,

why the English spy, Velebit, still remains in the Ministry of Foreign Affairs of Jugoslavia as First Assistant Minister. The Jugoslav comrades know that Velebit is an English spy. They also know that the representatives of the Soviet Government consider Velebit a spy. Nevertheless Velebit remains in the position of First Assistant Foreign Minister of Jugoslavia. It is possible that the Jugoslavia Government intends to use Velebit precisely as an English spy. As is known, bourgeois governments think it permissible to have spies of great imperialist states on their staffs with a view to insuring their good will, and would even agree to placing their peoples under the tutelage of these states for this purpose. We consider this practice entirely inadmissible for Marxists. Be that as it may, the Soviet Government cannot place its correspondence with the Jugoslav Government under the censorship of an English spy. It is understandable that as long as Velebit remains in the Jugoslav Foreign Ministry, the Soviet Government considers itself placed in a difficult situation and deprived of the possibility of carrying on open correspondence with the Jugoslav Government through the Jugoslav Ministry of Foreign Affairs. . . .

These are the facts [the letter wound up] that are causing dissatisfaction to the Soviet Government and to the Central Committee of the Communist party of the Soviet Union and which are endangering relations between the U.S.S.R. and Jugoslavia.[5]

There could be no doubt about it: such a letter betokened the very worst kind of trouble. There was the reference to Trotsky; the mutually contradictory, but no less disturbing references to Bunkharin and the Mensheviks. There was the word "anti-Soviet" which occurred again and again. There was the term "questionable Marxist" applied to four leading members of the Jugoslav Politburo. There was the scarcely veiled threat that the rank and file of the Jugoslav party would be violently opposed to what was going on, *if they knew about it*. There was the flat announcement that Velebit was a British spy and the sinister implication that, in spite of this, perhaps even because of this, he was being protected by some high-placed person or persons. There was the sneering, menacing tone which prevaded each of those eight typed pages. Finally, there was at the bottom that signature which gave to every single word the weight and sanctity of holy writ, the signature of J. Stalin.

When Tito had finished reading the letter, he telephoned to Kardelj, Djilas, Ranković and Kidrić and asked them to come and see him. Then he read the letter through again and, after a few moments' thought, picked up his pen and sat down to draft a reply. It took him two hours. At the end of this time he had covered thirty-three sheets of foolscap with his bold, rather irregular handwriting.

Meanwhile, Kardelj, Djilas, Ranković and Kidrić had arrived. Tito showed them the letter from Stalin and Molotov and his own proposed reply. They agreed with him that it was essential to take a firm line. They rejected his suggestion that he should resign. He rejected their suggestion that they should resign. "What the devil," he asked, "should I do without you?" All five were much moved. Then they sat down to consider seriously what should be done. They decided that their right course was to lay the whole matter before the Central Committee of the party. A plenary meeting was accordingly called for April 12. Traveling back to Belgrade in the train, Kardelj and the others continued to discuss the question which was now uppermost in all their minds. "There can," said Kardelj, "be no turning back now. I know the Russians. I know the way their minds work. They will next proclaim that we are Fascists, so as to provide in the eyes of the world the necessary moral and political justification for their campaign against us. If they could, they would liquidate us by force, but I think that they will not go as far as that for reasons of external policy."[6]

On the morning of April 12 the twenty-six members of the Central Committee assembled in the library of King Alexander's former palace at Dedinje outside Belgrade, a distressing building in the early Serbian manner. At ten o'clock exactly Tito came in and sat down. The doors were closed and the proceedings began.[7]

Tito, who spoke first, began by explaining briefly what had happened and by reading out the text of the Soviet letter of March 27 and of his draft reply. He then put the issue quite frankly to the meeting. "Remember," he said, "that this is not a matter of theoretical discussion, of errors committed by the Jugoslav Communist party, or of any ideological deviation that we have committed. Nor must we allow ourselves to become involved in a discussion of such matters. The real issue at stake is the relationship between one state and another. In my view they are only using ideological questions as a pretext for putting pressure on us and on our state. That, Comrades, is the issue."

He then announced that each member of the Committee would be called upon to declare himself one way or the other. The minutes of the meeting would, he added, be sent to Moscow, if the Russians asked for them.

Tito was followed by Kardelj, who declared himself in agreement with what he had said and with the proposed draft reply. He recalled the party's achievements, especially during the war, and rejected the charges brought against it as ridiculous. "It would not," he concluded, "be the action of sincere men, but of traitors, if we were to admit things which were not true."

The members of the Central Committee spoke one after the other in the order in which they were sitting round the conference table. The next sixteen all spoke in the same general sense as Tito. Then came the turn of Black Žujović. The others had spoken sitting down. Žujović, tall, dark and cadaverous, now stood up and said in a loud voice: "Comrades, I appeal to your revolutionary conscience. I am against sending such a letter to the Soviet party. Do not forget that tremendous issues are involved. I am against adopting such an attitude toward the Soviet Union and the Soviet party."

At these words a hush fell on those assembled in the library. Tito rose to his feet and walked up and down muttering: "This is treason, to the people, the state and the party." But Zujović paid no heed to him. "Where," he asked, "do we go from here? What will be Jugoslavia's place in the struggle against imperialism? I have thought deeply about it all. Let us not make a fatal mistake. We did our duty during the war. The present situation has brought us to power, and thus into contact with the Soviet Union. Every word, every observation, even the slightest, from the Soviet party, should be a warning to us to re-examine everything before deciding on further action. We must seek the full sense of Stalin's very word. How can we convince ourselves and the people that we are on the right path, if the Soviet party and Stalin do not approve? I believe that we and not they are wrong in this matter." Next he turned to the deviations of which the Jugoslav party was accused. From now onward he was constantly interrupted. "Do you think I'm a Trotskyist?" cried Djilas in a state of great excitement, while others shouted "Out with it!" and "No beating about the bush!" but Zujović did not allow himself to be put off. It was a full ten minutes before he finally sat down.

When the meeting was resumed after luncheon, Tito spoke again. "It is painful to me," he began, "to hear Zujović speak as he does. What he is in effect saying is: 'How dare pygmies like us oppose the Soviet party?' But we, too, made sacrifices for our country. . . . I am sure that none of those who laid down their lives ever thought that after the war their country would be without a name. . . . The road and the incentive to Socialism are not incorporation in the Soviet Union but the development of each country individually. That is where we differ from the Soviet party. And suddenly we hear *Crni* say: 'You are wrong to defend yourselves'. . . . To accept the Soviet letter would be contemptible. It would be to admit what is untrue. We are entitled to speak on an equal footing with the Soviet Union. . . . You, *Crni*, have assumed the right to love the Soviet Union more than I do. Our party is as pure and honest as the day. You, *Crni*, want to wreck its unity, you want to disrupt the leadership that has been working as one man for eleven years, a leadership that is bound by blood to the people. We called upon our people to make the supreme sacrifice. They would refuse to stand by us for a single day if we proved unworthy of their sacrifices. Our revolution, Comrades, does not devour its children. The children of this revolution are honest."

The next to attack *Crni* was Marko Ranković, who, besides being a member of the Politburo, was, as no one in the room could forget, Minister of the Interior and Head of UDBA, the dreaded Security Police. "Does he consider," he asked, "that our party is not a Marxist-Leninist party?" And then, after a number of other ideological questions: "Remember, *Crni*," he said, "that, if anyone tried to help you and save you for the party, it was Comrade Tito, who proposed you for election to the Central Committee at the Fifth National Conference in 1940, in spite of what you had done abroad, in spite of your connections with Gorkić"—a sinister allusion to Žujović's past that was wasted on one.

Next was raised the question of Žujović's contacts with the Russians. Djilas, it seemed, had seen his car outside the Soviet Embassy. What, it was asked, was he doing there? Had he reported to Lavrentiev on the proceedings of the Central Committee? Had he, in particular, reported on the meeting which had been held at Tito's house on March 1? Žujović refused to admit that he had done anything of the kind, but his denials did not carry conviction and, afterward, when he had left to go to a meeting of the Finance Committee, Tito said: "Our Plenum must take a stand on the case of Žujović. Further co-operation with him is impossible. Personally, I am not sure he did not report to Lavrentiev. That would be treason. No one has the right to love his own country less than the Soviet Union." After that the meeting was adjourned until the following morning. Next morning the Central Committee's first action was to appoint a commission of three (including Marko Ranković) to examine the case of Sretan Žujović and of Andrija Hebrang, like him, once again under suspicion.[*]

Having thus disposed of its only dissident member, the Central Committee settled down to work on the reply to Moscow. By the time they had finished with it, the final version was somewhat shorter than Tito's original draft and various other amendments had been made, but its sense was the same and the general tone was as uncompromising as ever. Having

---

[*] Žujović later admitted that he had given the Soviet Ambassador a full account of the Central Committee's meeting of March 1 and of their subsequent meetings.

first blandly enunciated the entirely subversive principle that "no matter how much each of us loves the Land of Socialism, the U.S.S.R., he can, in no case, love his own country less," it went on categorically to deny the Soviet accusations. These, it said, were "surprising and insulting" and could only be explained by the fact that the Soviet authorities had been misled by such dubious informants as Hebrang and Žujović. It dwelt at great length on the remarkable achievements of the Jugoslav Communist party.

> The great reputation which our party has won for itself by its achievements, not only in our country, but in the whole world, speaks for itself. . . . We cannot believe that the Central Committee of the Communist party of the Soviet Union can dispute the services and results achieved by our party. . . . We are of the opinion that there are many specific aspects in the social transformation of Jugoslavia which can be of benefit to the revolutionary development in other countries, and are already being used. This does not mean that we place the role of the Communist party of the Soviet Union and the social system of the U.S.S.R. in the background. On the contrary, we study the Soviet system and take it as an example, but we are developing Socialism in our country in somewhat different forms.

It further emphasized that the Russians were wrong if they thought that they were naturally or traditionally popular in Jugoslavia. On the contrary, any feeling there might now be for them had been "stubbornly inculcated into the masses of the party and of the people in general by the present leaders of Jugoslavia." As regards the Soviet charge that Velebit was an English spy, the Jugoslav note stated quite briefly that the matter was being looked into.* It then went on to accuse

* In actual fact Tito seems to have paid little or no heed to this charge. On its first being brought to his notice, he sent for Velebit, who arrived thinking that he had been summoned to discuss some question concerning the work of his department. Without saying anything Tito handed him the Russian note in which the charge was made. He then told him that he did not believe the Russian accusation and that it would in no way affect his good opinion of him. For the time being, however, it would be as well for him to occupy a rather less prominent position than

the Russians of trying to organize a widespread espionage system in Jugoslavia. "We cannot," it observed, "allow the Soviet Intelligence Service to spread its net in our country." In conclusion the note expressed the desire of the Jugoslav Central Committee to see any misunderstandings cleared up and suggested that the best way of achieving this object would be for the Soviet Central Committee to send one or more of their members to Jugoslavia to see things for themselves. It was dated April 13 and signed, with "comradely greetings," by Tito and Kardelj.[8]

Tito's decision to place the matter fairly and squarely before the Central Committee had been a bold one. For years past he had done his best to instill into its members and into the party as a whole an unquestioning belief in the infallibility of the Kremlin. Had the meeting gone against him, he would have been lucky to escape alive. But, as he himself said later, life had taught him that the most dangerous thing in a crisis is to hesitate, not to take a stand; reactions, at such moments, must always be bold and determined. Certainly in the present instance his boldness had paid a rich dividend. The reactions of the Central Committee had been the same as his own; with one exception, their loyalty to their country had outweighed their royalty to Moscow. And now he could face Stalin with the knowledge that at any rate the leaders of the party were solidly behind him.

Žujović, it is true, had come out openly against him and Hebrang had also been found wanting. But they, it seemed, were the only two, and in any case it was far better that they should have shown their true colors at this stage and thus enabled him to take the necessary preventive action. From Tito's point of view, the great thing was that the Russians had not by their scarcely veiled threats and ideological bluster succeeded in dividing the leaders of the Jugoslav party among themselves, in driving a wedge between him and the little group of men who had been through so much with him.

Having failed in this first object Stalin now shifted his line of attack. He had already sent copies of his letter of March 27, not only to the Jugoslav Central Committee, but to the Central Committees of all the other Cominform countries,

---

that of Deputy Minister of Foreign Affairs. He was accordingly appointing him Chairman of the Federal Committee for Social Welfare.

with the request that they should define their attitude to the dispute. On April 16 Yudin delivered to Tito a letter from Zhdanov enclosing a resolution from the Hungarian Central Committee couched in terms even more wounding to Jugoslav pride than those of Stalin's letter. It was followed in due course by similar communications from the Polish, Czech, Rumanian and Bulgarian Central Committees. The intention, quite clearly, was to indicate to Tito that, internationally, he stood alone.

One incident, however, which took place at about this time gave a somewhat contrary impression. On April 19 a Bulgarian delegation, which included Dimitrov, passed through Belgrade on their way to Prague. For a few moments, Djilas, who had gone to meet the Bulgars at the station, was left alone in the railway carriage with Dimitrov and one other Bulgar. Taking advantage of this opportunity, Dimitrov, according to Djilas, at once seized his hand and whispered "Stand firm!"[9]

At the beginning of May the Russians followed up their ranging shots with a broadside. In an official note, dated May 4 and covering twenty-five typed pages of foolscap, Stalin and Molotov replied on behalf of the Soviet Central Committee to the Jugoslav note of April 13. This, they wrote, "showed no improvement on earlier Jugoslav communications; on the contrary, it further complicated matters and sharpened the conflict." "Our attention is drawn," the joint authors continued, "to the tone of these documents which can only be described as excessively ambitious. They show no desire to establish the truth, to admit errors or to correct them. The Jugoslav comrades do not accept criticism in a Marxist manner . . ." After which they settled down with renewed venom and vigor to the agreeable task of recapitulating all their old complaints: the hostile atmosphere surrounding the Soviet military advisers; the way in which Soviet civilians were spied on; Velebit's retention at the Ministry of Foreign Affairs; the treatment of the Soviet Ambassador in Belgrade; Tito's speech at Ljubljana in 1945;* Djilas's remarks about the Red Army in 1944; the horrifying ideological deviations of the Jugoslav party and the "unbounded arrogance" of its leaders.

* In this connection the note reproduced Sadchikov's report on his conversation with Kardelj quoted at page 267 above. Whether this document was genuine or not, it is quite clear that Stalin's object in reproducing it was to make trouble between Tito and Kardelj.

It was on these last two subjects that the Russians had most to say. The Jugoslav leaders, it seemed, were not taking proper steps to suppress capitalism and liquidate the *kulaks*. They had allowed the party to be merged in the nonparty People's Front. They had abandoned all attempts at democratic procedure within the party. And finally they had got an altogether exaggerated idea of their own importance. "The services," wrote Stalin and Molotov,

> of the Communist parties of Poland, Czechoslovakia, Hungary, Rumania, Bulgaria and Albania are not less than those of the Communist party of Jugoslavia. However, the leaders of these parties behave modestly and do not boast about their successes, as do the Jugoslav leaders, who have split everyone's ears with their unrestrained self-praise. It is also necessary to emphasize that the services of the French and Italian Communist parties to the revolution were not less but greater than those of Jugoslavia. Even though the French and Italian Communist parties have so far achieved less success than the Communist party in Jugoslavia, this is not due to any special qualities of the Communist party of Jugoslavia, but mainly because, after the destruction of the Jugoslav Partisan Headquarters by German paratroopers, at a moment when the Jugoslav Movement of National Liberation was passing through a serious crisis, the Soviet Army came to the aid of the Jugoslav people, crushed the German invader, liberated Belgrade and in this way created the conditions which were necessary for the Communist party of Jugoslavia to achieve power. Unfortunately the Soviet Army did not and could not render such assistance to the French and Italian Communist parties. If Comrade Tito and Comrade Kardelj bore this fact in mind they would be less boastful about their merits and successes and would behave with greater propriety and modesty.

Finally, after rejecting the suggestion that representatives of the Soviet Central Committee should visit Jugoslavia, Stalin and Molotov announced that they proposed that the whole question should be discussed at the next session of the Cominform.[10]

By seeking to belittle the wartime achievements of the Partisans, Stalin and Molotov had, in Jugoslav eyes, committed the ultimate, the unforgivable sin. Nothing could have been better calculated to produce an attitude of complete intractability on Tito's part and at the same time to ensure for him the unswerving support not only of the party, but of the country as a whole.

On May 9 the Jugoslav Central Committee met to consider the latest Soviet note and drew up a short reply rejecting the suggestion that the dispute should be settled by the Cominform. The balance, they pointed out, would be too heavily weighted against them.[11]

At the same time the Central Committee also considered the report submitted by the commission set up to investigate the case of Žujović and Hebrang. This traced the misdeeds of both men back to before the war when Hebrang, although in prison at the time, had been reprimanded for "fractionalism," while Žujović had been an adherent of Tito's predecessor and rival Gorkić. Hebrang, it recorded, had been further reprimanded in 1941 for his failure to carry out the directives of the party in regard to the organization of resistance. There had followed the misdemeanors which had led to his removal from the post of Party Secretary for Croatia in 1944 and to his expulsion from the Politburo in 1946. Since then, the report stated, he had used his position as President of the State Planning Commission to sabotage the economic development of the country and, in particular, to impede the fulfillment of the Five Year Plan. He had also given "a distorted picture of the situation in our country and slandered the Central Committee of the Jugoslav Communist party and some of its individual members to our friends in the Soviet Union. In this way he sought to cloak his antiparty, hostile and disruptive work and activities behind a mask of feigned friendship to the Soviet Union." "Finally," the report continued, "the Commission is in possession of recently acquired documents which show A. Hebrang to have been guilty of treacherous conduct when he was arrested in 1942 by the Ustaša Police in Zagreb and prove that he then undertook to work for the Ustaša regime and Ustaša Police." Žujović was likewise denounced by the Commission as a "confirmed fractionalist," who, both during and since the war, had criticized Tito and other members of the Central Committee and had opposed and obstructed their financial and economic policy. He had also "spread around his distrust in our own strength and in our ability to achieve the Five Year Plan and to build Socialism in our country." Finally, like Hebrang, he had "slandered the Politburo and our party to the Soviet Union." On all these counts the Commission recommended that both men should be expelled from the party and that their activities should be "investigated by the appropriate branches of the People's Authorities."[12] Having considered the report, the Central Committee adopted its recommendations in their entirety. Shortly afterward it was publicly announced that both Hebrang and Žujović had been expelled from the party and arrested on a charge of high treason. An angry protest from Moscow was ignored.*

Meanwhile the Russians had not yet abandoned all hope of inducing the Jugoslavs to attend the forthcoming meeting of the Cominform. On May 19 a young man called Mossetov arrived in Belgrade from Moscow with a letter from Suslov, the Secretary of the Soviet Central Committee, again pressing them to attend. Taking advantage of the division of opinion which still existed on this particular issue in Jugoslav party circles, he put it about in Belgrade that Stalin himself was to be present at the meeting, which would be held in the Ukraine, and that the least Tito could do was to come too. But the Jugoslavs, who remembered seeing Mossetov in the uniform of an NKVD colonel and hearing that he had taken a leading part in the liquidation of Gorkić and other Jugoslav Communists in Moscow in 1937, were not taken in by this somewhat transparent maneuver. On May 20 the Central Committee met and decided unanimously against taking part in the Cominform meeting.

A few days later yet another note, dated May 22, was received from Moscow, attributing this Jugoslav refusal to the arrogance of the Jugoslav leaders and to their sense of guilt. They had, it said, been ready enough to criticize the French and Italians at the first meeting of the Cominform. Why would they not in their turn submit to criticism? "The refusal of the Jugoslav Communist party to report to the Informburo," the note continued,

> means that it has taken the course of cutting itself off from the united socialist people's front of People's Democracies headed by the Soviet Union, and that it is now preparing the Jugoslav party and people for a betrayal of the united front of People's Democracies and the U.S.S.R. Since the Informburo is a party foundation of the united front, such a policy leads to the betrayal of the work done for the international solidarity of the

workers and to the adoption of an attitude of nationalism
which is hostile to the cause of the working class. Irrespective of whether the representatives of the Central
Committee of the Communist party of Jugoslavia attend the meeting of the Informburo, the Communist
party of the Soviet Union insists upon the discussion
of the situation in the Communist party of Jugoslavia at
the next meeting of the Informburo. In view of the request
of the Czechoslovak and Hungarian comrades that the
meeting of the Informburo take place in the second half
of June, the Communist party of the Soviet Union ex-
presses its agreement with this proposal.[14]

The implied threat was clear enough. For all this, when
the official invitation to attend the Cominform meeting reached
them some weeks later, the Jugoslavs politely but firmly turned
it down.

Spring was succeeded by summer, the breathless, blazing
summer of southeastern Europe. If, as seems possible, Stalin
had hoped to subdue Tito during the weeks which remained
before the meeting, he was doomed to disappointment. Not
only did the Jugoslavs show no signs of yielding to pressure.
They chose this moment to announce their intention of holding a full-scale Party Congress at the end of July, in other
words, of giving the rank and file of the party an opportunity
to express itself on the dispute. Once again Tito had chosen
the bold course.

The Cominform met in Bucharest toward the end of
June. All the member parties were represented except the
Jugoslavs. Again Zhdanov was in charge. Among the other
delegates were Rakosi, Kostov, Anna Pauker, Slansky, Duclos
and, finally, Togliatti, the Secretary General of the Italian
party, who, as "Ercoli," had helped discipline the Jugoslav
party ten or twelve years earlier on behalf of the Cominform.
For several days the assembled delegates remained closeted
together. Then the oracle spoke, and spoke, this time, not
only to the initiated, but to the world at large.

The twenty-eighth of June, the Feast Day of Viddo or St.
Vitus, a pagan deity later conveniently transformed into a
Christian saint, has been marked by many fateful events in
Serbian and Jugoslav history. It was on Vidovdan or St.

---

* It appears that the Russians had made plans to rescue Zujovic
by airplane, but these were frustrated by his arrest.[13]

Vitus's Day, 1389, that the Turks defeated the Serbs at Kosovo and brought Serbia under Turkish rule for the next five centuries. It was on St. Vitus's Day, 1914, that Gavrilo Princip shot the Archduke Franz Ferdinand at Sarajevo and thereby precipitated the First World War. It was on St. Vitus's Day, 1919, that the Treaty of Versailles was signed which ended that war. It was on St. Vitus's Day, 1921, that the new Jugoslav state, created at Versailles, was endowed with its first constitution. And now, in 1948, it was on St. Vitus's Day that *Rude Pravo,* the official organ of the Czech Communist party, published in full the astonishing resolution which had been unanimously passed by the assembled Cominform delegates at their meeting in Bucharest.

The resolution contained, first of all, a scathing denunciation of Tito and other Jugoslav leaders. "The Information Bureau," it began, "notes that recently the leadership of the Communist party of Jugoslavia has pursued an incorrect line on the main questions of home and foreign policy, a line which represents a departure from Marxism-Leninism. . . . The Information Bureau declares that the leadership of the Jugoslav Communist party is pursuing an unfriendly policy toward the Soviet Union. . . . The Information Bureau denounces this anti-Soviet attitude of the leaders of the Communist party of Jugoslavia as being incompatible with Marxism-Leninism and only appropriate to nationalists." The resolution next examined in some detail the deviations and shortcomings of the Jugoslav leaders: their failure to suppress capitalism; their failure to recognize the importance of the industrial proletariat; their tendency to let the party become merged in the National Front; their disregard for democratic principles; the intolerably "Turkish and terroristic" character of their regime, as demonstrated by the arrest of Hebrang and Žujović. "The criticism of the Central Committee of the Communist party of the Soviet Union and of the other Central Committees," it continued, "provides the Communist party of Jugoslavia with the means of correcting its mistakes. But, instead of accepting it in a Bolshevik manner and mending their ways, the leaders of the Communist party of Jugoslavia, suffering from boundless ambition, arrogance and conceit, have met this criticism with belligerence and hostility." After which, having first dismissed as "leftist demagogic measures" the recent attempts of the Jugoslavs to accelerate the liquidation of capitalism and the collectivization of agriculture and denounced as the most revolting hyprocisy their "loud declaration of love and devotion for the Soviet Union," the Information Bureau expressed complete agreement with the conclusions arrived at by the Soviet party. "The Information Bureau," it went on, "considers that, in view of all this, the Central Committee of the Communist party of Jugoslavia has placed itself and the Jugoslav party outside the family of the fraternal Communist parties, outside the united Communist front and consequently outside the ranks of the Information Bureau." Finally, after declaring that "such a nationalist line can only lead to Jugoslavia's degeneration into an ordinary bourgeois republic, to the loss of its independence and to its transformation into a colony of the imperialist countries," the resolution addressed to the rank and file of the Jugoslav party a direct appeal to take the law into their own hands. "The Information Bureau," it concluded,

> does not doubt that inside the Communist party of Jugoslavia there are sufficiently healthy elements, loyal to Marxism-Leninism, to the international traditions of the Jugoslav Communist party and to the united Socialist front. Their duty is to compel their present leaders to recognize their mistakes openly and honestly and to rectify them; to break with nationalism, return to internationalism; and in every way to consolidate the united Socialist front against imperialism. Should the present leaders of the Jugoslav Communist party prove incapable of doing this, it is their duty to replace them and to advance a new internationalist leadership of the party. The Information Bureau does not doubt that the Communist party of Jugoslavia will be able to fulfill this honorable task.

Hitherto no whisper of the gathering storm had reached the world at large. On June 28, like a thunderclap, the news of Jugoslavia's expulsion from the Cominform, of the open breach between Moscow and Belgrade, broke on an astonished world. The threat of public denunciation, twice before held over Tito, had at last been put into execution. The fight was on.

XIV ⌂⌂⌂ LOATHLY OPPOSITE

AFTER reading the text of the Cominform communiqué, Tito spent the next two or three hours pacing up and down his study. The situation in which he now found himself was one of extreme peril. It was also one of great moral stress. The unthinkable had happened. The break with Moscow, with the Country of the Revolution, with the habit of thirty years, had come at last. He faced ideological isolation.

One thing at least was quite certain: there could be no turning back; he was bound to go forward. The ban of excommunication, which for some time past he had courted by disputing the supreme authority of the Kremlin and, more recently, by openly defying it, had fallen. In no circumstances would it be withdrawn. The big decision of his life had been taken earlier, in March, after he had received Stalin's first note, or perhaps even before that, when, deep down in his own heart, he had first begun to question the infallibility of the Kremlin. The main problem now was one which he had faced often enough before, namely how to survive. It was to this problem, as he walked up and down, that he addressed his active and resilient mind.

His prospects, at first sight, were not very good. He was up against the overwhelming might of the Soviet Union. Inevitably now, it would become a primary aim of the Kremlin to crush him. And no one knew better than he did with what utter ruthlessness that aim would be pursued. What is more, he faced this formidable threat almost completely alone. Jugoslavia was at enmity with the West. She had now incurred the undying hostility of the East. Even in Jugoslavia, on what support could he count with any certainty? Of the little band whom he had summoned to his villa at Tuškanac on that fateful day in March and who were themselves as irretrievably committed to the struggle as he was, of Kardelj, Djilas, Ranković and Kidrič, he could, he felt, be sure. He could also count with reasonable certainty on the continued support of the Central Committee. They, too, when it came to the point, had declared themselves for him and against Moscow; they, too, were compromised. And yet . . . might it not be that among their number there were others who felt like Žujović, but had lacked the courage to come out openly in his support? Might it not be that yet others would weaken when they realized the full implications of what had happened? A number, after all, had been doubtful about the wisdom of refusing the summons to Bucharest. And then, was it not also possible that there were among the members of the Committee hidden agents of Moscow, biding their time and waiting for the right moment to strike? Might not such agents be anywhere, even in his own circle, among his own personal friends?

As yet, the country at large knew nothing of the dispute. How would the Jugoslav people react when they learned of what had happened? Ever since the end of the war Tito's own propaganda machine had, as he himself had put it, been "stubbornly inculcating" into them love for the Soviet Union, the belief that everything in Russia was perfect, that Stalin could do no wrong. What would their reaction be when they learned that the infallible oracle had pronounced so overwhelmingly against its own high priest? How would the rank and file of the party feel? Would they react in the same way as the Central Committee? Would their loyalty be to their wartime leader or to Moscow? And the non-Communists? Would they think better or worse of him for having defied the Kremlin? Would they feel impelled to rally to the government of their country in time of national stress? Or would they just see in the recent crisis an opportunity for making trouble? Tito could not be sure. But he was determined to put the matter to the test without delay.

On the following day, June 29, he held a further meeting of the Central Committee. They, he found, showed no sign of weakening. A reply to the Cominform's resolution was drafted and agreed, vigorously refuting the charges which it contained and calling upon the members of the Jugoslav Communist party to "close their ranks in the struggle for the implementation of the party line." At the same time the decision was taken to publish both the Cominform communiqué and the Jugoslav reply in full in the Jugoslav press. Next day, in cities, towns and villages all over the country, seething crowds of ordinary citizens were to be seen round the newspaper sellers, jostling each other to buy copies of *Borba* and get news of the breach, the unbelievable breach, between Moscow and Belgrade.

There were just three weeks to go before the Party Congress, long enough to give Tito some idea of what to expect from the party and the country in general. On the whole the omens were favorable. All remained quiet and there was, practically speaking, no indication of any popular support for the Cominform point of view. In party circles there was pained indignation at the attitude of the Cominform. As for the non-Communists, many of them felt that it was perhaps time to revise their hitherto unfavorable opinion of Tito. He had, they were bound to admit, fought the Germans, and now he was standing up to the Russians, not to mention the Poles, the Bulgars, the Hungarians, the Rumanians and the Czechs. There might, after all, be hope for him yet. The reaction of one old Serbian lady to these events is perhaps as typical as any. "We are strange people," she said when she heard what had happened. "When Hitler was at the height of his power, when the whole of continental Europe was at his feet, we tore up the pact we had made with him. When the Americans were at the height of their power in 1946 and the whole world was afraid of the atomic bomb which they had dropped on Japan the year before, we shot down their aircraft because they had violated our national territory. And now, when Stalin is bursting with strength, we reject his ultimatum. It reminds me of little Serbia rejecting the Austro-Hungarian ultimatum of 1914. We are strange people, but we know how to defend our country."[1]

There was also encouraging news from abroad. Almost without exception, the considerable number of Jugoslavs, who at the time of the breach were for one reason or another in Russia or in the satellite countries, had resisted all pressure to make them defect and, despite their exposed position, had declared in favor of Tito. In the West, though there was still widespread doubt as to the true nature of the dispute, public opinion, until a few days before solidly hostile to Tito, was now beginning to show itself slightly more favorable to him.

Tito, wisely, did not allow any of this to go to his head. So far, it was true, things had gone well. But the biggest dangers and difficulties still lay ahead and it was vital that he should play such cards as he held with the greatest of care. The first necessity, if he was to survive, was to carry the party with him. Without the support of its five hundred thousand members, he would be lost. He must on no account do anything which might shock or antagonize party opinion or lend substance to charges brought against him by the Cominform, to the charges that he was a deviationist, that he was hostile to the Soviet Union, that he was making Jugoslavia into "an ordinary bourgeois republic." It was important to remember that the minds of all party members did not necessarily work as fast or as logically as his own. It was advisable to tread very warily indeed.

Certainly a high degree of wariness marked his conduct of the Party Congress which opened on July 21. This was the fifth congress held by the Jugoslav Communist party since its foundation and the first since it had assumed power. It was held in the great hall of the barracks of the former Royal Guard at Topčider, outside Belgrade, the same hall in which, just two years before, Draža Mihajlović had stood his trial and been condemned to death. Now it was decorated with busts of Marx, Engels, Lenin and, neither any larger nor any smaller than the rest, of Stalin. The place of honor was occupied by a big picture of Tito himself. The Congress was attended by over two thousand delegates from all over the country, representing a total of some half a million party members. Almost every man and woman present had fought under Tito's command as a Partisan during the war.

Tito opened the proceedings with a speech lasting no less than eight hours. The first seven and a half of these were taken up with a detailed historical survey of Jugoslav Communism from its earliest beginnings down to the present time. He told his audience of the ineffective struggle of the workers in Serbia and Austria-Hungary; of the internal dissensions and deviations which had hampered the work of the Jugoslav Communist party in the twenties and early thirties. Then he told them, amid bursts of obediently frenzied applause, how an entirely different spirit had possessed it once the "new leadership" took over in 1937, how in the space of three years the "new leaders" had strengthened, reorganized and united the party, and how "constantly and tirelessly, through the printed and the spoken word," they had "educated both its members and the peoples of Jugoslavia in a spirit of deep trust, love and devotion toward the Soviet Union, as being the most progressive country, the Country of Socialism and the selfless protector of small peoples." He told them how, on June 22, 1941, the day of Hitler's attack on the Soviet Union, the Jugoslav Politburo had issued a proclamation calling for a general armed uprising to "help the righteous struggle of the great, peace-loving Country of Socialism, the Soviet Union, our dear Socialist Country, our hope and beacon." He recalled the years that had followed, those "three and a half years of bitter strife" in which almost every man and woman there had taken an active part. He recalled their defeats and their victories, the hardships they had endured and the sacrifices they had made. He reminded them of those comrades of theirs who with their last breath had cried: "Long live the Soviet Union and Comrade Stalin." He also told them how, when the war was nearly over and the Western Allies had been helping them for some considerable time, the Russians had eventually given them some help in taking Belgrade and had sent them a certain amount of war material, for which, he was careful to say, they were duly grateful. Finally he spoke of the party's achievements since the war, of the good progress it had made with the liquidation of capitalism and the building of Socialism, of the success it had achieved with its Five Year Plan, of the benefits it had derived from the People's Front, of its fundamental ideological soundness, of its strength and unity and of its determination to continue in the same path in future.

It was only in the last twenty minutes that he "turned briefly" to the Cominform communiqué; with its "monstrous accusations against our party and its leaders"; with its "call to civil war" and its "call to destroy our country." "Those who attack us," he said, "the leaders of the Communist parties in the countries we have helped most, should at least have decency not to resort to such lies, to such shocking slander." And he recalled the generosity Jugoslavia had shown to Bulgaria despite "all the evil" she had suffered at the hands of the Bulgars during the war; and the thousands of tons of grain she had sent to Rumania, to Poland and to Czechoslovakia. "The leaders of the Jugoslav Communist party," he said, "showed themselves brotherly and forgiving; and now, in return, they are being shamelessly slandered and smeared." "Our critics," he continued, "now dispute the fact that we are Marxist-Leninists. But on what ideological basis did we achieve so much? Was it because we were Trotskyists that we entered the war on the side of the Soviet Union in 1941? Or out of loyalty to Marxism-Leninism, as practiced by Comrade Stalin himself in the U.S.S.R.? We entered it because we were Marxist-Leninists not only in words but in deeds." " 'Our teaching,' " said Tito, quoting Lenin quoting Marx and Engels, " 'is not dogma, but leadership for action' . . . that is what Lenin said and taught. And now *they* want us to confine ourselves to certain narrow formulas in building

Socialism." After which, he went on to declare his firm intention of doing everything in his power to restore good relations with the Soviet party and once again extended to them, this time publicly, a cordial invitation to come and see things for themselves on the spot.

When at the end of eight hours Tito concluded his speech amid enthusiastic shouts of "Stalin! Tito!" he had achieved a number of important objects. First, he had stated his own case. Without once using the first person singular, he had reminded his hearers of everything that he and the little group of men round him had done for the party and for the country. He had also reminded them again and again that he and they were comrades in arms. At the same time he had vigorously refuted the charges made against him and successfully roused the indignation of his audience against those who made them. And he had done all this without ever once directly attacking Stalin or the Soviet Union. His venom had been concentrated on the satellites and the Cominform. He had scarcely given an indication that the Russians were even concerned in the dispute. Less still had he given any justification to the charge that he was "anti-Soviet." On the contrary he had gone out of his way to demonstrate his longstanding and unswerving loyalty to the Soviet Union and its ruler. Never had a speech, on the surface at any rate, been less provocative. Deep in their own minds Tito and the little group round him had known for months past that between them and Moscow, between them and Stalin, there was war to the death. But, for tactical reasons, and above all in order to make quite certain of carrying with them the rank and file of the party, it was vital not to let this appear; vital, too, for the time being, to take no step which might be represented as provocation. "I had," said Tito afterward, "to give Stalin time to behave in such a way that people in Jugoslavia would say 'Down with Stalin' of their own accord without my having to suggest it to them."[2]

For all its totalitarian trappings, the Fifth Congress of the Jugoslav Communist party had been profoundly significant. It had shown that Tito was master in his own house and not afraid of his own party. The Cominform's summons to the rank and file of the party to get rid of him had been ignored, had, indeed, been flung back at them. The Kremlin would have to think again.

Certainly, from the Soviet point of view things could

scarcely have gone worse. There can be little doubt that when Stalin finally decided to bring his quarrel with Tito into the open he did so because the information at his disposal led him to believe that, when it came to the point, Tito could easily be got rid of. "I will shake my little finger," he had said to Khrushchev, "and there will be no more Tito." Now it had come to the point, and his information had proved incorrect. He had completely misjudged the situation. Tito, it turned out, was not at all easy to get rid of. He had neither eclipsed himself before the wrath of the Kremlin, nor had he been swept away by his own party. He was still most embarrassingly there.

In another important respect the Kremlin had so far failed badly. It had failed to establish in Jugoslavia any effective nucleus of opposition to Tito inside the party. Neither Hebrang nor Žujović had been quick enough. Tito, an old hand at such matters, had liquidated them before they could liquidate him. Nor had the Russians succeeded in their various attempts to drive a wedge between Tito, Djilas, Ranković, Kidrić and Kardelj, or to play them off against each other. The little group, despite all pressure, had stayed entirely loyal to each other.

There remained another possibility. After the war, in 1946, Tito had appointed Koča Popović as Chief of the General Staff in place of Arso Jovanović, whom he had sent to Moscow on a staff course. While in Moscow, it appears, Arso had taken up with a Russian girl, the daughter of a general in the Red Army. His demotion had already shaken his loyalty to Tito and it seems probable that, with the help of the general's daughter, the NKVD had little difficulty in winning him over to their point of view. It is even possible that in the recesses of his literal, rather narrow mind this relatively recent convert to Communism still clung to the belief in the absolute supremacy and infallibility of the Kremlin, which formed after all an essential tenet of the Communist creed. In any event, when given the opportunity, he sided with the Russians and against Tito. Exactly what use the Russians proposed to make of General Arso is not clear. No doubt they hoped either to carry out with his aid a military *coup d'etat* in Jugoslavia or else to smuggle him out of the country with the object of building round him a "Free Jugoslav Government" in exile. But once again their plans misfired.

On July 30, a month after the publication of the Cominform communiqué, the Danube Conference opened in Belgrade.

Great Britain, France and the United States were represented at it by their ambassadors. Vishinsky was the Soviet representative. Rumania was represented by Anna Pauker. Stanoje Simić, Tito's Minister of Foreign Affairs, and his Deputy, Aleš Bebler, represented Jugoslavia. Tito himself chose to spend August out of Belgrade.

The purpose of the Conference was to revise the Statutes of the Danube Convention. Before the war the Danube had been an international waterway. Now, to all intents and purposes, it had passed under Russian control. And the Russians, who possessed the necessary majority of votes at the Conference, had no intention of surrendering their monopoly. Vishinsky made this clear from the outset. His draft for the revision of the Danubian Statutes would, he announced with brutal frankness, be carried whether the Western delegates liked it or not. The door by which they had entered the conference room was, he reminded them, still there for them to leave by, if they so desired. The representatives of the Western powers watched with interest to see whether recent events would produce any change in the attitude of Jugoslavia. But here again Tito showed the same caution which had characterized his attitude hitherto. When it came to a vote, the Jugoslav delegates voted, as usual, with the Soviet bloc, and Vishinsky's draft was carried with an undiminished majority.

Despite this, the atmosphere at the various official receptions held in honor of the delegates was, as can be imagined, somewhat strained. But one delegate, at least, showed no signs of embarrassment. Anna Pauker had never been in better form. From time to time she let drop hints that "the trouble in Jugoslavia would very soon be cleared up once and for all." What exactly passed between her and Arso Jovanović is obscure. That there was a connection seems probable. All that is known for certain is that on the night of August 11-12. Tito's former Chief of Staff, who ostensibly had gone shooting wild boar, was himself shot dead by a Jugoslav frontier patrol as he was trying to cross the frontier into Rumania under cover of darkness. His two companions, Colonel Vlado Dapčević, a brother of the more famous Peko, and Colonel Branko Petričević, got away, but were subsequently captured and sentenced to twenty years' imprisonment.[3] Shortly after this incident the delegates to the Danube Conference, having signed the new Danube Convention, left Belgrade. Another Soviet gambit had failed. "If we had known how things were going to turn out," said Madame Pauker to a foreign diplomat, "we should have used other methods."

As a first step, the Russians now let loose against Tito the full fury of their propaganda machine. Henceforward the whole of the Soviet and satellite press and wireless kept up a campaign of unparalleled violence against their former favorite, who was freely denounced as a Fascist, a murderer and an agent of the imperialist powers. At the same time the Russians used every conceivable device to spread alarm and despondency in Jugoslavia itself. In August they flooded Belgrade with a pamphlet, printed in Moscow in Serbo-Croat, giving the text of the Soviet letters to Tito of March 27, May 4 and May 22. But the Jugoslav Government, nothing daunted, replied to this by publishing the whole corespondence. As they had rightly supposed, the Soviet letters, with their unflattering references to Jugoslav achievements during the war, did nothing to enhance Soviet popularity in Jugoslavia.* Nor were Soviet attempts to make trouble for Tito by encouraging separatist tendencies in the component states of the federation—in Croatia, in Montenegro and, most of all, in Macedonia—any more successful. Even in the wild uplands of Macedonia, where the Russians, with an inventiveness worthy of a better cause, put about the story of a miraculous picture of Lenin which had been seen to shed real tears at Tito's depravity, the population remained unmoved.

By the end of 1948 it had become apparent that Tito was unlikely to succumb to purely political pressure. He now even felt strong enough to admit frankly that his dispute was with Stalin personally, adding with the utmost confidence that he was right and that Stalin was wrong. The attacks made on him had served if anything to strengthen his position, rallying the party behind him and gaining him the added support of many non-Communists who had formerly disapproved of his allegiance to Moscow.

Always at his best in a crisis, Tito gave during these critical months the impression of a man supremely sure of himself. The doubts, the apprehensions, the uneasiness of the previous year had vanished. The stresses and strains of recent months had brought out all his fighting qualities. He was once again as calm, as resolute and as resilient as he had been during

* It is interesting to note that neither side let it be known at this stage that the Soviet letters had been signed by Stalin personally.

the war when confronted with what seemed insuperable odds. The scene, it is true, had changed. But despite his comfortable surroundings, despite his smartly cut summer suit and carefully chosen tie, there was something about Tito which left no doubt that here was a man who knew that he was up against it and who also had a pretty shrewd idea that somehow or other he was going to come out on top. The decision to defy the Kremlin had, he admitted, not been an easy one to take. "But now that I have taken it," he went on with a smile, "I have never been gladder of anything in my life."[4]

The dilemma which now confronted Moscow was an extremely serious one. The Soviet system was based first and foremost on authority, on the supreme and absolute authority of the Kremlin. Since June Tito had been openly challenging the authority and, what is more, challenging it with impunity. If the Russians were not to suffer a disastrous loss of face and diminution of authority, if they were not to risk losing what they had come to regard as an integral part of their empire, if—worst of all—they were not to risk the recurrence of this threat elsewhere, then Tito must be obliterated.

Political pressure, backed by intrigue, conspiracy and subversion, had failed to achieve this object. Another means had to be found. The Kremlin resorted to an all-out economic blockade. Barely three years had elapsed since the end of the war had left Jugoslavia, never a rich country, perhaps more dreadfully devastated than any other country in Europe. Barely one year had elapsed since Tito had launched his extremely ambitious Five Year Plan. For Jugoslavia the phase through which she was passing would at the best of times have been a critical one. The action which the Kremlin now took made it doubly so.

Since the end of the war the Jugoslav economy had been firmly orientated toward the East. The greater part of her trade had been with Russia and the satellite countries. She depended on them for numerous vital raw materials, for machinery, capital equipment and consumer goods. She likewise depended on them for markets for her own produce and for technical help and advice. Now, almost at one blow, she was deprived of all this. Abruptly Russia reduced her trade first to a mere trickle, then to nothing at all. One after another the satellites followed suit. Jugoslavia found herself isolated—economically, politically and militarily. Already shortages of food, of raw material and of consumer goods were causing discontent among the population. Any further deterioration in the economic condition of the country was bound to produce a reaction which Moscow would know all too well how to exploit. It was a situation which called for steady nerves and an agile mind. Fortunately for him, Tito had both.

From a relatively early stage in the quarrel it had been apparent to him that, should a complete breach with Moscow ensue, he would be obliged to reconsider Jugoslavia's international situation. A position of total isolation between East and West in a state of permanent and equal hostility to both, though in theory no doubt attractive to so independent a people, was not in fact practical politics—less still practical economics. Sooner or later, Jugoslavia, if she was to survive, would need to move closer to the Western democracies.

It seems possible that, from the first, Tito was encouraged in his resistance to Soviet pressure by the feeling that there was, after all, another alternative, by the recollection of the not unsatisfactory relations which he had maintained with the West during the war. Even so, the transition, for a number of reasons, would not be altogether easy. First of all, there was no reason to assume that the democracies, on whom for three years he had heaped every possible insult and affront, would now be ready to welcome him with open arms. And, even if they were, it seemed probable that they would only be prepared to do so on certain terms, political and economic, which he for his part would not be able to accept. It was, after all, in order to preserve Jugoslavia's national independence that he had broken with Moscow; he could not now sacrifice that independence in order to buy help from the capitalist West. He also had his own internal position to safeguard; he had the party to carry with him. The Russians had said that he was turning Jugoslavia into an "ordinary burgeois republic," "a colony of the imperialist powers." He must at this stage be careful to do nothing that would lend the slightest substance to these allegations. Meanwhile, the inescapable economic facts stared him relentlessly in the face.

Jugoslavia's immediate need was for financial and economic aid to fill the aching void which had resulted from the economic boycott imposed on her by Russia and the satellites. This Tito on inquiry now found the democracies ready to grant him. Trade agreements, credits and later loans were followed in due course by direct aid. What is more, the democracies were prepared to help him without, as he had feared, seeking to impose political conditions. For them the fact that he was endeavoring, with some prospect of success, to assert his independence from Soviet domination was in itself sufficient reason to help him. From the first his new relationship with the West was based on the firmest of all foundations—common interest.

This suited both parties. It left Tito free to proclaim his independence to his heart's content and even to make, for the record, an occasional public attack on his benefactors, who, as he never tired of pointing out, were, by helping him, in reality only furthering their own interests. At the same time it enabled the Western powers to explain to their own public opinion that, while admiring Tito for his stand against Russia, they had no liking for the way in which he conducted his internal affairs. On this essentially realistic basis the relationship prospered. Gradually, as they came to realize that it was possible to have normal relations with the Western powers without necessarily becoming a Western satellite, the Jugoslavs grew less suspicious and more co-operative, and there was at the same time a corresponding decrease in Western suspicions of Jugoslavia. Imperceptibly, despite ideological differences, a closer understanding began to grow up between Jugoslavia and the West.

By the middle of 1949 it had become apparent to the Russians that their economic boycott was unlikely to achieve its object. Jugoslavia was, it is true, under severe pressure. But it seemed clear enough that in the long run she would, with Western help, succeed in weathering the storm. In particular there was no sign that either economic stress or the subversive activities of Soviet agents had anywhere produced any serious unrest among the population—none, at any rate, that an active and vigilant security police were not well able to deal with.

The situation confronting Stalin was now more serious than ever. For a whole year Tito had defied him with impunity. There was clearly a grave danger that this might encourage other satellite leaders to follow his example. Already at the Cominform meeting of June, 1948 there had not been complete agreement as to the action to be taken against the Jugoslav Communist party. Some of the delegates had favored milder measures. Now there were signs of what the Russians, justifiably or not, chose to regard as a "Titoist" frame of mind among the Communist leaders in several other Eastern European countries. As early as October, 1948 General Koci Xoxe, the Albanian Minister of the Interior, had been arrested as a Titoist. In January, 1949, Gomulka, the Secretary

General of the Polish Communist party and Deputy Prime
Minister of Poland, was disgraced and stripped of his offices.
In February the Greek rebel wireless had announced the
downfall of Markos Vafiades, the leader of the Greek Communist guerillas. In March these were followed by Kostov,
the Secretary General of the Bulgarian party. And in June,
Rajk, the Hungarian Minister for Foreign Affairs, had gone
the same way. In due course trials and executions followed
the arrests. Koci Xoxe was shot as a Titoist in June, 1949.
Rajk was hanged on the same grounds in October and Kostov
in December. In Poland, for the time being, no more was
heard of Gomulka, while in Greece Markos Vafiades vanished
completely.

At their trials, Rajk and Kostov and their codefendants con-
fessed to having been involved in numerous plots and con-
spiracies in which Tito was alleged to have played a leading
part. On the face of it, the story unfolded seemed highly
improbable. But, like their Soviet prototypes, these trials dealt
not so much with actual, as with potential or hypotheical
events—with what might have happened rather than with what
had happened. Their purpose was at once to deter and to
instruct; their purpose, above all, was to blacken Tito. Stalinist
logic demanded that the heretic who had questioned the un-
questionable and sought to prove the fallibility of the infallible
must sooner or later be liquidated. Meanwhile it was necessary that he should be shown up in his true colors, as a
symbol of all the vices, a traitor and a renegade.*

* On one reader, at any rate, the effect seems to have been
exactly the opposite. While in prison, Black Zujovic was allowed
to read the published record of the trial of Laszlo Rajk. According
to his own account, the "slanderous attacks" which it contained
on the Jugoslav Communist party "brought him to his senses."
He saw the error of his ways, formally renounced Stalinism, and
shortly afterward was set free.

Hebrang, his fellow conspirator, ended differently. According
to official Jugoslav sources, further investigation revealed the
following story. At the end of the war the Russians had come
upon conclusive evidence that during the war Hebrang had worked
for the Ustaše and the Germans. After the Ustaše had captured
him in February, 1942, he had, it appeared, agreed to work for
them. On this understanding he had in September, 1942 been
included in a specially arranged exchange of prisoners and had
returned to Partisan Headquarters, where he had acted as an
enemy agent for the rest of the war, betraying vital information
to the Ustaše and Germans by means of a secret wireless link.

To such experienced stage managers the latter task presented no great difficulty. A much more formidable problem was how to liquidate him. Tito was not an easy man to get rid of. The political weapon had failed. The economic weapon had also failed. Assassination, if it had been tried, had not succeeded. The intended victim was still alive, impenitent and in power, in his own country and at the head of his own army. Only one possibility remained: armed invasion.

There can be little doubt that by the summer of 1949 the Russians were actively weighing up in their minds the relative advantages and disadvantages of adopting such a course. The tone of their official communications became more and more menacing. Their propaganda contained increasingly frequent references to the approaching day of retribution, there were more and more frontier incidents and more and more Soviet and satellite troops were moved to within striking distance of the Jugoslav border.

The trouble from the Russians' point of view was that already they had waited too long. And the longer they waited, the greater became the risks involved. Had they made up their mind to use armed force in the summer of 1948, immediately after the publication of the Cominform communiqué, they might have achieved their object without much difficulty. At that time a sudden attack would have taken Tito unawares and unprepared. He would have had no time to rally his supporters in the country, while internationally the attack would have found him completely isolated. But now things had changed. Tito had had a year in which to consolidate his position and adapt himself to the changed situation. Although in pitched battle his forces could not hope to hold their own against the overwhelming strength of the Red Army, they could in case of invasion once again take to the forests and mountains and there wage the kind of warfare by which for over three years they had succeeded in containing a dozen or more Axis divisions. Nor could the Russians now be sure that Jugoslavia, if attacked, would stand alone.

Already there were signs of a radical change in Tito's rela-

Instead of telling Tito of their discovery, the Russians had subsequently used the hold which it gave them over Hebrang to force him to serve as *their* agent in the Jugoslav Central Committee. This he had done until 1948. In 1952 it was officially announced that, after many months of interrogation, Hebrang had strangled himself in prison.

tions with the West. Economic co-operation had been followed by closer political relations. As early as May, 1949 Tito had privately given the British Government the express assurance that he would close the Greek-Jugoslav frontier and give no further help to the Greek Communist guerrillas. He had kept his word and there can be no doubt that his action served to accelerate the end of the Greek civil war and the victory of the Royalist forces. At international conferences the Jugoslav delegates did not now always vote on the side of the Soviet bloc. As its attitude toward Soviet Russia gradually sharpened, the Jugoslav press progressively toned down its abuse of the West to what could almost be described as friendly criticism. Meanwhile the public utterances of British and American statesmen made it clear that the Western powers would not remain indifferent to a Soviet attack on Jugoslavia. The summer of 1949 went by, and still the Soviet threat did not materialize.

In the summer of 1950 the world situation was completely transformed by the Communist invasion of South Korea and the immediate and vigorous reaction of the Western powers. The temperature of the Cold War rose sharply. Western rearmament went forward on a greatly increased scale. It became clear that Soviet Russia would no longer be allowed to eat up one country after another. The line had at long last been drawn. Henceforward an act of war would be met by another act of war.

In these changed circumstances a position of isolation between East and West became ever more impracticable for Jugoslavia. Western economic help had greatly increased in scale and relations in general were becoming steadily friendlier. Tito, while accepting economic help, had hitherto refused all military assistance from the West. He now changed his mind and let it be known that he would welcome British and American aid in re-equipping his army, which was still using a mixture of out-of-date British, German, Italian and Russian weapons and equipment. His request was granted and thenceforward a steady stream of arms and equipment flowed into Jugoslavia from the West. Soon she was in a position to put into the field thirty well-trained divisions, which, in addition to the natural fighting qualities of their troops could boast first-class modern arms and equipment. The Soviet Union, meanwhile, had been pressing on with the rearmament of the neighboring Cominform countries. Each summer there were menacing troop movements in the frontier areas and the threat of invasion was renewed. But Jugoslavia now no longer stood alone.

The *rapprochement* was soon to be carried a stage farther. In September, 1952, in response to a personal invitation, the British Foreign Secretary, Mr. Eden, paid a highly successful visit to Jugoslavia. In March, 1953 Tito paid a return visit to England, his first to any foreign country since 1948. Although it aroused vigorous opposition on the part of certain sections of opinion, notably the Roman Catholic community and the Communist party of Great Britain, this proved in the event an undoubted success. Arriving in London by river on March 16, Tito was met at Westminster steps by the Duke of Edinburgh, Mr. Churchill and Mr. Eden. During the week that followed, he lunched with the Queen at Buckingham Palace and dined at 10 Downing Street with Mr. Churchill and at Carlton House Terrace with Mr. Eden. He was taken to the ballet by Field Marshal Alexander and to an air display by the Secretary of State for Air. He visited the British Museum and the Tower of London and the London County Council and Hampton Court and Windsor Castle. He also had a number of official conversations with Mr. Churchill and Mr. Eden at Downing Street and with Field Marshal Alexander and his Service Ministers at the Ministry of Defence.

Tito was clearly impressed and delighted by what he saw, by the attention that was paid to him and by the respect with which he was treated. Those who met him were struck by his friendliness and good humor, qualities hard to reconcile with the idea which many of them had formed in advance of this Communist dictator from the Balkans. As he drove rapidly from one place to another, dressed sometimes in uniform, sometimes in day clothes and sometimes in evening dress with a lavish sprinkling of orders and decorations, he was escorted by a screen of mobile police outriders on motor bicycles, for the British security authorities were taking no chances with a visitor whose death would have given such pleasure to so many people. With him went his old friends and associates, Koča Popović, who had recently exchanged the post of Chief of the General Staff for that of State Secretary of Foreign Affairs, and Vladko Velebit, now Jugoslav Ambassador at the Court of St. James's.

Perhaps the thing that struck Tito most during his visit to England was the way in which he was received—with that odd mixture of traditional pomp and friendly informality which exists in no other country in the world. It was something which, despite differences of background and outlook, Tito, with his natural gift for human contacts, could readily understand and appreciate. It was, he realized, something very different from what he had found in Moscow. "We really knew," he said on his return to Jugoslavia, "that we had come to a friendly and allied country. . . . We found a common language in all matters. . . . We were treated as equals, and not with the arrogance we saw in the East." But Tito took away with him more than just an agreeable impression; he took away the feeling that, in the event of a Russian attack on Jugoslavia, he could count on active British support.

The improvement which had taken place in Jugoslavia's relations with Great Britain and America was followed by a corresponding improvement in her relations with the rest of the non-Communist world. Most important of all, she now moved steadily closer to Greece and Turkey.

On February 28, 1953, a Treaty of Friendship and Co-operation was concluded between the three countries at Ankara and this was followed by regular consultations between the three governments and their general staffs on subjects of mutual interest. Early in 1954 Tito paid successful state visits to Turkey and Greece, where he was received by President Celal Bayar and King Paul with all the pomp and ceremony due to the head of an allied state. Finally on August 9 of the same year a twenty-year treaty of alliance, to be known as the Balkan Pact, was signed at Bled by the three foreign ministers, providing for mutual consultation in the event of a crisis and for mutual armed assistance in the event of an attack on any of the three. It also provided that a permanent council, comprising the three foreign ministers, should meet at least twice a year.

By the mere fact of its existence the Balkan Pact radically altered the political and strategic situation in the Near East. Instead of standing alone, the three Balkan allies now presented a united front against aggression, a front which had the backing of over seventy well-trained and well-equipped divisions. Unlike her Greek and Turkish allies, Jugoslavia was not a member of the North Atlantic Treaty Organization, but through her connection with them she was now indirectly associated with the Western system of defense.

In contrast to Jugoslavia's *rapprochement* with Greece and Turkey, it was some time before there was any corresponding improvement in her relations with Italy. At the root of the trouble was the old problem of Trieste. Pending a final agreement, the Jugoslavs had since 1945 remained in possession of Zone B, while an Anglo-American force had continued to occupy Zone A including the city of Trieste itself. In March, 1948, at the very moment when Tito's dispute with the Kremlin was approaching its climax, the British and American Government had, in a somewhat obvious attempt to influence the outcome of the impending Italian elections, given formal expression to the view that both zones and Trieste itself should go to Italy. Their action, understandable so long as Jugoslavia remained a Soviet satellite, now became a cause of considerable embarrassment to them. Encouraged by the declaration of March, 1948, the Italians dug their toes in, demanding, as of right, the whole of both zones. The Jugoslavs were equally unyielding, vigorously maintaining their right to Zone B and, in moments of enthusiasm, to Zone A as well. Despite numerous attempts at mediation, little progress was made toward the solution of the dispute, the situation being further aggravated by the repeated charges of ill faith and worse publicly leveled at each other by the rival claimants. And so the dispute dragged on to the constant irritation of all concerned and to the satisfaction of no one save the Russians.

In October, 1953 a well-meaning attempt on the part of the British and American Governments to impose a rough and ready solution on both parties by announcing their intention of withdrawing their troops from Zone A and of handing it over to the Italians, while leaving the Jugoslavs in possession of Zone B, was neatly frustrated by Tito, who at once announced that if Italian troops entered Zone A, he would chase them out again. Troop movements and a crisis ensued and the British and Americans were roundly abused for their pains by both the Jugoslavs and the Italians. After which a deadlock again set in.

Jugoslavia's strained relations with Italy served still further to aggravate the tension already existing between the Jugoslav Government and the Vatican. In December, 1951, as a concession to opinion at home and abroad, Tito had released Archbishop Stepinac from prison and allowed him to resume his duties as a priest, while still declining to recognize him as Archbishop of Zagreb. But the Vatican's refusal to accept a solution on these lines or otherwise to modify their attitude, and the Archbishop's subsequent elevation to Cardinal only convinced him that there was nothing to be gained by further concessions. In December, 1952 he broke off the formal dip-

lomatic relations which he had hitherto maintained with the
Holy See. Simultaneously there was a marked hardening of the
Jugoslav Government's attitude toward the Catholic Church
and a correspondingly hostile reaction toward Jugoslavia on
the part of Catholics all over the world.

In October, 1954, however, a compromise agreement over
Trieste, under which the Jugoslavs kept Zone B and the
Italians occupied Zone A, at long last paved the way for an
improvement in relations between Italy and Jugoslavia. With
the removal of this contributory cause of tension the way now
seemed open for a new approach to the vexed problems of
Jugoslav relations with the Vatican. Though the treatment of
the churches in Jugoslavia still left much to be desired, and
though the party leaders, while talking a great deal about
freedom of conscience, still clung to their anticlericalism
as though to a talisman, it seemed possible that the gradual
change now taking place in the character of the regime,
coupled with the improvement in Jugoslav-Italian relations,
might in the long run lead to a greater measure of religious
toleration and to better relations with the Catholic Church.

Having reached agreement with Italy, Tito had now established satisfactory relations with all the Western powers. From
Great Britain, France and America he was receiving a substantial measure of financial, military and economic assistance.
He also knew that he could count on their active support in
case he was attacked. With Greece and Turkey he was directly
linked by a regular military and political alliance; which at
the same time provided an indirect connection with the North
Atlantic Treaty Organization and with the Western defense
system as a whole.

That Tito should have achieved this transition from the
perilous isolation of 1948 to virtual alliance with the West
on terms favorable to himself, without loss of independence or
dignity, and without forfeiting the support of his colleagues
in the government and in the party, bore witness to a high
degree of astuteness and political skill on his part. It also bore
witness to considerable clear-sightedness and restraint on the
part of the Western powers.

XV ꙅꙅꙅꙅ SCYLLA AND CHARYBDIS

DURING the years that followed their break with Moscow the Jugoslav Communists had had plenty of time to take stock of their ideological position. Of one thing they were from the first characteristically certain, that, on the immediate issues under dispute, they were right and Stalin was wrong. As their confidence increased and the strength of their position became apparent, they were emboldened to carry the theoretical controversy into wider fields. It would perhaps be an exaggeration to say that their new ideology was created after the event to meet the new situation which had arisen. But there can be no doubt that, as so often happens, the crisis through which they had passed was of considerable help to them in clarifying and crystallizing what was already in their minds.

At the bottom of their dispute with the Kremlin lay Tito's claim that "The Jugoslav brand of Communism was not something imported from Moscow but had its origin in the forests and mountains of Jugoslavia," the contention, in other words, that Marxism-Leninism was not unalterable dogma, but "leadership for action," something they could adapt to suit their own particular needs. It is easy to see how this line of thought soon led them, as the controversy grew more embittered, to criticize the way in which the Russians had adapted Marxism-Leninism to meet *their* own particular requirements. Instead of gradually withering away, as Marx had intended it should, the Soviet State, they pointed out, had under Stalin become more and more powerful, more centralized and more bureaucratized, until in the end it dominated everything. Soon, the original ideas from which it had sprung had been lost sight of or perverted; today its guiding motives were "bureaucratism," state capitalism and, in relation to other countries, the most brutal kind of imperialism. They, for their part, were determined henceforward to avoid these mistakes in Jugoslavia. The term "Titoism," with its hint of deviation, they indignantly rejected. They were no deviationists, but were guided by the purest Marxism-Leninism; what they were building was the only true Socialist state in the world. It was Stalin who was the deviationist. Indeed, as a rough rule of thumb, there was much to be said, when in doubt, for finding out what line the Russians were taking on any given subject and then doing the opposite.

Once again, the pace at which any changes could be accomplished was largely dictated by the need to avoid a course of action that might shock the less agile minds in the party or lend the slightest verisimilitude to the Soviet charges that Jugoslavia was being converted into a Fascist or capitalist state, an appendage of Wall Street or an annex of the Vatican. "For years," Moša Pijade confided to a friend, "we trained our party in the rigid orthodoxy of Moscow. Now we are having the devil of a time teaching them to think for themselves again."[1]

But, although gradual and at first largely one of atmosphere and emphasis, the change which now came over Jugoslavia was nonetheless very real. As lately as 1950 everything had still been overshadowed by the grim "monolithic" structure which orthodox Stalinism had imposed on Jugoslavia in the years before 1948. By 1952 it was clear that a new spirit was abroad. In the towns and villages, people seemed gayer, more carefree, less inhibited. There were fewer signs of interference by the state in their private lives. The Security Police, whom both Tito himself and Marko Ranković had publicly warned against exceeding their duties, were, in particular, far less active. In public places there was more laughter and noise. Everywhere animated arguments and conversations were in progress on a variety of subjects. Everywhere the prevailing mood was one of expectancy, expectancy of something better. The Stalinist framework was still there, but it had fallen into disrepair and disrepute and loomed unheeded in the background, like the vast cement headquarters which in their unregenerate days the Jugoslav Communist party had started to construct for themselves in a swamp outside Belgrade and had then left to molder half-built and half-demolished, a salutary reminder of past follies.

In the economic field, where detailed central planning had proved anything but successful, the emphasis was now on decentralization, enterprise, initiative, the profit motive. How some of these ideas, notably the principle of profitability, could be reconciled with orthodox Marxism would have presented a difficult problem to any but a Jugoslav ideologist. But fortunately Karl Marx, like other prophets, had written so copiously and as often as not so cryptically that a text could be found to justify almost any interpretation of his teaching. There was, too, always the heaven-sent apothegm that Marxism was "not dogma, but leadership for action." And then, as Tito had once characteristically observed, was not Marxism in any case "nine-tenths practice and one-tenth theory"?[2]

At least the new trend took more account of human nature and bore more relation to reality than anything that had gone before. Tito himself now publicly condemned the "megalomania" of recent years, decreeing that, in future, "the only projects to be initiated will be those for which it is known that there is financial backing at home or abroad and which are technically and economically justified." Even the Five Year Plan was scaled down to a number of more or less feasible key projects.

The theory behind the new policy was that the central bureaucracy should relinquish its hold on the administration of the nationalized industries and hand over control to the workers. This, it was explained, was a first step toward the withering away of the state. Henceforward instead of being controlled from Belgrade, economic enterprises were to be owned by the public and run as far as possible by the producers themselves. A law passed in June, 1950 provided for the election in all economic concerns of Workers' Councils responsible for approving the basic plan of work and for the distribution of final disposable profits, and, after an initial period of trial and error, a system was evolved which indeed placed a premium on efficiency and encouraged enterprise and initiative.

In agriculture, the government abandoned the policy of trying to force the peasants into co-operative farms against their will. Forced purchases of farm produce by the state ceased and the peasants were henceforth allowed to sell their produce for what it would fetch on the free market. In the spring of 1953, after much hesitation, the unscrambling process was carried a stage farther and peasants who had already been collectivized were given permission to leave the co-operatives. Large numbers promptly availed themselves of this opportunity and by the beginning of 1954 barely a thousand co-operative farms were left in the whole of Jugoslavia. No less than 82 per cent of the land was now under private ownership. By these measures and by a considerable increase in agricultural investment the government showed that they had at long last begun to realize the importance of agriculture to the national economy as a whole and the inadvisability of deliberately antagonizing nearly three-quarters of the population by means of an unpopular and therefore unworkable agricultural policy.

By the end of 1954 Jugoslavia was still seriously short of foreign currency and came nowhere near balancing her payments. But already the results of Western aid, intensive investment and the government's new economic policy were beginning to make themselves felt. The agricultural outlook was brighter than at any time since the war and the country's industrial potential had increased considerably. Most of the key industrial projects had by now either been completed or were approaching completion and the goods produced for home consumption had improved alike in quality, quantity and range. Throughout the country, while the standard of living was still low, there were signs of greater prosperity: better goods to buy in the shops at lower prices; better-fed and better-dressed crowds in the streets. Here and there privately owned shops and restaurants had reappeared. Even the peasants, many of whom remained basically hostile to the regime, were prepared to admit that things were better, that there was more to buy and more money to buy it with. What is more, their happier frame of mind was reflected in a greater readiness to co-operate with the government and in a higher level of production.

The Iron Curtain, too, had been lifted. Jugoslavia was in a receptive mood and the Jugoslavs were ready once more to throw open their country to the outside world. Everything was now done to attract foreigners and each summer many thousands of foreign tourists traveled freely all over Jugoslavia. In the cinemas British and Amercian films predominated and foreign books of all kinds were translated into Serbo-Croat. As yet relatively few Jugoslavs were given permission to travel outside their own country, but the numbers were steadily increasing. The carefully preserved vacuum in which Jugoslavia, like other Communist countries, had once existed, was being deliberately destroyed.

At the Sixth Party Congress, held in Zagreb in November, 1952, most of these new trends had received the formal blessing of the party. The party itself changed its name, its statutes and its program. It now became the Communist League, part of the larger Socialist Alliance, as the People's Front was henceforward to be known. From executive, its function became, in theory at any rate, mainly educational. The Congress was opened by Tito wearing a smartly cut blue suit and was made the occasion for a series of slashing attacks on the Soviet Union. The Russians, the assembled delegates were told once more, had betrayed Socialism they had degenerated into the worst sort of imperialists and state capitalists. Having successfully shaken off the "terrible delusion" under which they had once labored, the Jugoslav party had now become the only true exponents of Marxism-Leninism. What is more, they were ready, indeed anxious, to cooperate with Socialists and "progressive elements" all over the world. The Congress, which in this manner set the seal on the comparative liberalization of the regime and on friendlier relations with the West, took place in an atmosphere of easy informality, its proceedings being at one moment considerably enlivened by a high party official who broke off his speech in the middle in order publicly to accuse an even more distinguished colleague of having stolen his wife.

Two months later, in January, 1953, an entirely new state constitution, bearing a limited resemblance to that of the United States, was adopted in place of the old Soviet-style constitution —Tito being formally elected President. Under the new order the authority of the top-heavy central government was drastically curtailed and more real power granted to republican and local authorities. Politically as well as economically the accent was on decentralization and "Socialist Democracy."

Some Western observers, excited by the discovery that a change was in progress, were inclined to jump to the conclusion that Jugoslavia was already well on the way to becoming an ordinary parliamentary democracy. Such a conclusion was, to say the least of it, premature. It has been said with some truth that democracy can only exist in a community where everyone is agreed on essentials. By Western standards Jugoslavia had never been a democracy. Before the war King Alexander had, as we have seen, been obliged to suspend Parliament and the Constitution on account of the shooting which took place across the floor of the House. Nothing that had happened since had smoothed the way for democratic institutions. King Alexander, like so many of his predecessors, had been murdered; Prince Paul deposed; King Peter eliminated. Tito had seized power after three and a half years of bitter fighting, much of it against his fellow countrymen. He had remained in power despite the resolute attempts of the Soviet Union to dislodge him. He was a revolutionary, with, as he conceived it, a revolutionary program to carry through. Much of his life had been spent, both figuratively and literally, on the barricades. Recalling the dictum that there are only two sides to a barricade, he was not likely to give to those who stood on the other side of the barricade, and who to him were traitors, the opportunities enjoyed in Great Britain, for example, by Her Majesty's loyal opposition. Discussion there might be—within limits. Both in the Assembly and at party meetings controversy was encouraged on questions of method and detail and Milovan Djilas, now one of the chief dialecticians of the party, was for ever talking of "the clash of ideas." But that Tito would allow Cominformists publicly to advocate Jugoslavia's return to the status of a Soviet satellite, or monarchists the return of the monarchy, or Croatian separatists the establishment of an independent Croatia, was at this stage inconceivable.

If not parliamentary democracy, what then was to take the place of the Stalinist state which was now being so enthusiastically demolished? The builders left no doubt as to the basic character of the new structure. It would be the first truly Marxist state in history and would demonstrate once and for all the utter depravity of Stalinism and indeed of all other existing political systems. So much was clear. Exactly what lay beyond this basic idea was a good deal less clear even to those most closely concerned. No sooner had their new Socialist state begun to take shape than the Jugoslav ideologists led by Djilas, were already talking of its "withering away" in true Marxist fashion. And not only the state. In due course the party was to wither away too. "From now on," said Djilas in 1951, "the party line is that there is no party line." And Tito himself went even further. "If the state really withers away," he said. "the party must necessarily wither away with it . . . The one-party system, having succeeded a multi-party system, will in turn vanish."

But not yet. A fairly robust central structure, a fairly strong central control, would in reality be needed for some time to come. For one thing, the party itself did not relish the idea of its own early dissolution. It was this reluctance on its part to disappear, or indeed to surrender any substantial part of its hard-won privileges and power, that underlay the sudden crisis that rocked it to its foundations at the beginning of 1954.

For all the caution with which it had been introduced, the policy of liberalization, decentralization and ever closer co-operation with the West initiated by Tito after 1948 and officially promulgated at the Sixth Party Congress of November, 1952 had nonetheless aroused misgivings in certain quarters. There remained in the party elements who, while grudgingly accepting the need for a change, still, at the bottom of their hearts, regretted the greater ruthlessness and rigidity of the early days, who viewed without enthusiasm the recent concessions to common sense, who even felt a half-suppressed nostalgia for the old connection with Russia and regarded with distaste the increasing cordiality of their country's relations with the capitalist West.

In his conduct of affairs, Tito, dependent as ever on the united support of the party and as alive as ever to the dangers of "fractionalism," was obliged to take the attitude of these elements into account, to hold the balance between them— the "reactionaries," as he called them—and, at the far end of the scale, those other elements who, if given the chance, would sweep gaily on toward who knows what anarchist utopia. For this and for other reasons, Jugoslavia's progress away from Stalinism and toward her own brand of liberal Leninism could be neither smooth nor consistent. As often as not the government were forced to take one step backward or sideways for every two steps they took forward. In order, for example, to pacify those elements of the party who disliked their increasingly liberal agricultural policy and the virtual abandonment of collectivization, they had been obliged in the spring of 1953 abruptly to limit the extent of individual small holdings to twenty-five acres. In June a plenary session of the Central Committee held on the Island of Brioni had reasserted the need for regular disciplined activity by all party members and issued a definite warning against "Westernizing" deviations. And in October, six months after Tito's visit to England, the Trieste crisis had led to a sudden revulsion of feeling against the West and, by implication, against the government's pro-Western policy. Despite occasional setbacks, however, the trend toward greater liberalization and closer cooperation with the West remained predominant. It was against this background that toward the end of October, 1953 there began to appear in *Borba*, the official organ of the party, a portentous series of articles by Milovan Djilas, in which the author set out to survey at length in his own turgid and confused style the problem of the future of the party.

As Secretary of the Executive Committee of the Central Committee of the party (formerly the Politburo) and Vice-President of the Federal Executive Council, Djilas, now in his early forties, stood with Kardelj and Ranković immediately after Tito at the head of the party and government hierarchy. His wiry black hair was graying a little at the temples and his sensitive, firmly modeled face had grown a little haggard, with deeper lines round the eyes and at the corners of the mouth. But, for all the stresses and strains he had endured, for all the responsibilities he had assumed, he had lost none of his old innate Montenegrin enthusiasm or exuberance. As he sat in cafés, smoking a pipe, drinking and arguing, he was still at heart a Bohemian—a revolutionary. Of recent years he had come to be accepted as a leading propagandist, literary pundit and ideological thinker of the regime. Without routine administrative responsibilities, he was now free to devote most of his considerable energies to writing and speaking and traveling abroad on party or government business. His long, rambling articles filled the daily papers and monthly reviews. He had played a prominent part in the dispute with Moscow and in the propaganda battle which had ensued. It was he who had drafted the all-important Resolutions of the Sixth Party Congress, promulgating the latest party line. He had lectured at Chatham House. He had represented Jugoslavia at the Asian Socialist Congress at Rangoon early in 1953 and at the Coronation of Queen Elizabeth in Westminister Abbey later the same year, while that autumn he had entertained Mr. and Mrs. Aneurin Bevan at a luxury hotel on the lower slopes of Mount Durmitor. During the Trieste crisis at the beginning of October he had delivered some of the sharpest attacks on the West. His views were always a little in advance of anybody else's. Both in party circles and in the country at large and most of all in his native Montenegro he enjoyed prestige and authority.

At first Djilas's articles, which appeared at the rate of one or two a week, did not cause any particular stir. Large parts of them were devoted to the lengthy recapitulation of past events, to vague ideological generalizations and to surprisingly naive excursions into the realms of philosophy and metaphysics which the average reader with anything better to do would have felt amply justified in skipping.

But, as the weeks and months went by and article followed article, a phrase here and there began to point more clearly to the theme that inspired them. "The Revolution," wrote Djilas, "cannot save itself by its past. It must find new ideas, new forms, a new appeal. . . . If it is to survive, the Revolution must transform itself into democracy and Socialism." And in subsequent articles he elaborated at great length upon the new forms and new ideas which were to "transform" the Revolution. In a private letter to Tito, Djilas asked him what he thought of the articles. "They contain some things," the Old Man replied, "with which I do not agree. But in general they have many good points and I do not think that the other points are reason enough to stop you from writing. Go on writing."

Djilas went on writing. His output increased. He wrote more articles and longer articles. He also made his meaning clearer. Developing and expanding the resolutions of the Sixth Party Congress, he wrote in increasingly strong terms of the "bureaucratism" and other shortcomings of the regime, of the need to break the political monopoly of the party. He even hinted that the time had come when non-Communists might be allowed to play some part in affairs, when, in the eyes of the law, they might be regarded as having the same rights as party members. "Today," he wrote on December 20, "no party or group, not even the working class itself, can claim to express the objective needs of the whole society. . . . The only possible answer is more democracy, more free discussion, freer elections." "New ideas," he wrote two days later, "have always started as the ideas of a minority. All new ideas at first strike the majority as stupid, mad and illogical. . . . But today the most important thing is not new ideas so much as freedom of opinion, the freedom to hold ideas."

By now Djilas's articles had begun to produce a reaction, favorable in some quarters, much less favorable in others. Kardelj, for one, told him straight out that he did not agree with what he had written. This led to a heated argument in the course of which Djilas went further than ever. Tito, he declared, was on the side of bureaucracy and sooner or later he, Djilas, would have to fight it out with him. He knew that Kardelj and Ranković felt as he did himself, but were too opportunist to disagree with Tito. He, for his part, foresaw the emergence of a new left-wing Socialist party, in fact of a two-party system. Later in the conversation, it is true, Djilas went back on much of what he had said and Kardelj hoped that he had heard the last of the whole distressing matter. But two days later, on December 24, when he opened his copy of *Borba*, it became quite clear to him that he had not.

Under the heading "A Reply," Djilas proclaimed to all and sundry that his articles had been criticized and that he would now answer his critics. He was not, as had been suggested, a mere abstract philosopher. His intention, on the contrary, had been "to leave the unreal world of the chosen and predestined few and to penetrate as deeply as possible into the real world of the ordinary working people," to "abandon the closed party circle for the ordinary world outside." He had written in abstract terms because this was the "best way to shatter bureaucratic dogmatism, which was the last word in empty, primitive and malicious abstractness." He would not, he continued, defend himself against the charge that he was a heretic. His heresy was a splendid heresy and every Communist ought to be proud to join in it. For his part, he refused to accept second-hand Stalinist dogma as the ultimate truth. The manner in which he had been criticized clearly showed the "unprincipled, Stalinist, bureaucratic, pseudo-democratic character" of this criticism. It was nothing but "Jugoslav Stalinism," it had "the authentic Stalinist smell." "Whether the attacks on my views are justified or not," he concluded, "they cannot suppress the democratic struggle against bureaucratism, because it does not depend on this or that theory but on reality. . . . This struggle can be hindered and delayed, but it cannot be stopped."

Nor was this all. For the next fortnight fresh articles by Djilas continued to appear in *Borba*, at intervals of two or three days, further elaborating his basic theme and boldly launching into new realms of controversy. It sometimes seemed as though the author had not worked out all his conclusions beforehand but rather was being swept along who knows whither by the irresistible force of his own ideas. Ever sharper grew his attacks on the "closed circle" of the party, on its privileged position and isolation from the mass of the people, on its political monopoly, on its centralized control of everything "from morals to philately," on its artificial meetings with their "faked agendas and unwilling audiences," on its "dogmatic moralization and empty, idle and senseless discussions," on "the useless Party Youth Organization" and on "the petrified minds of our leading bureaucrats." All this, he wrote, might have been necessary while the Revolution was actually in progress. But now that the class struggle was at an end and the class enemy practically nonexistent, such a rigid machine was outdated and could only hinder progress toward true democracy. Already "strong new Socialist forces" existed outside the official party organization—in spite of it, one might almost say. "Man," he continued, striking a personal, a Promethean, note, "lives only by struggling and thinking, by explaining reality to himself and finding his way about in it. . . . New ideas are a product of the inevitable progress of society, of the struggle within society, of man's struggle against nature. . . . To the holders of the old ideas, new ideas will necessarily seem monstrous, immoral and unnatural. . . . They will be branded as 'anarchist, petit-bourgeois and Western.' " "To continue the revolution," he concluded, "means to renounce its obsolete forms for the purpose of developing its content, i.e. democracy, through new forms . . . . Today progress is possible in democratic forms only."

Thus wrote Djilas, the chief propagandist of the party, in the party's official organ, and at the end of December, as though to give official sanction to his ideas, he was unanimously elected President of the National Assembly.

By the beginning of the New Year, which Djilas celebrated by publishing three long, and even more outspoken, articles in a single issue of *Borba*, public opinion was in a ferment. Everywhere people from all walks of life gave free rein to their natural, but long repressed passion for political controversy. Excited meetings were held all over the country to discuss the articles. The newspapers carried whole columns of letters on the same subject from their readers. There was something more like a free exchange of views than Jugoslavia had known for many years. Opinion, it appeared from the press, was very largely on the side of Djilas. Some meekly accepted what they imagined to be the new party line. Others were genuinely enthusiastic "There can be no doubt," declared one veteran trade unionist, "that Djilas has hit the right spot at the right moment. I personally also think that the time has come to free political life from the dead hand of the party machine." "Djilas," wrote another reader, "is one of our greatest and freest thinkers. I am only a working man of average intelligence. But Djilas has given expression to ideas which have long been forming in my mind and the minds of others. He found the living word which we lacked." "Everybody I have spoken to," wrote a correspondent, "agrees that the time has come to change the present methods of political work. . . . Djilas has taken a revolutionary step forward." "The atmosphere at the meeting," wrote another, "was democratic and free. It promises a great deal for the future." "A Communist with twenty-nine years of party membership," went further still. After expressing himself forcefully on the subject of "obligatory attendance at voluntary meetings" and other abuses, "I consider," he wrote, "that the time has come for a party which has such obsolete methods of work to be relegated to a museum."

But if Djilas's ideas enjoyed support among the rank and file of the party, in one quarter they met with resolute opposition. At the highest, or almost the highest level, his articles had by now provoked a violently hostile reaction, a reaction which neither Tito nor his inner circle of colleagues could any longer afford to ignore.

A crisis was inevitable. Characteristically, Djilas precipitated it by publishing in the January issue of *Nova Misao*, the party's foremost literary and political review, a scathingly satirical sketch of life in higher party circles, "among those who own automobiles, travel in sleeping cars, buy their food and clothes at special stores and have become convinced that their exclusive right to these rare privileges is so natural and logical that only fools or the most hardened enemies could possibly question it." "Here," he wrote,

> the whole logic of the hierarchy becomes clear. It is to claw your way to the top and then kick down the "undeserving." This is what has made selfish monsters out of those who were once heroic men and women. . . . Almost all these women come from semipeasant surroundings and are semieducated. . . . Imperceptibly most of them have started to assume, not only externally, but internally an elaborate pseudo-aristocratic style and elaborately meticulous manners. . . . But the most grotesque thing of all is that some of them, with no taste whatever, have started collecting luxurious furniture and pictures, displaying not only their primitive greed and new-found pomposity but also the pretentious omniscience of the crassly ignorant.

The heroine of his little story was a beautiful young actress of humble origin who had recently married "a famous wartime commander," now "a high party functionary and important state official," and had immediately found herself snubbed and cold-shouldered by their new leaders of Belgrade society on the grounds that she had not fought in the war (she had been eight when it had started) and that she was in any case only an actress and therefore immoral. It described how on her wedding day her husband had taken her to the exclusive State Box in the Belgrade Football Stadium, where "a slender lady . . . the wife of an important economic official" had said to her "in a lazy drawl," "You are an actress, are you not? Other actresses married to our generals never come here .... You will never be acceptable company for our comrades"; and how afterward she had heard another woman say to the "slender lady" amid murmurs of approval from the other female occupants of the State Box: "You gave her a real telling off! And a good thing too!" It went on to describe in detail the other insults and humiliations which this poor innocent girl had undergone at the hands of "a caste, which, because it was newly arrived itself, was all the more stubborn and unyielding." "I smell the unpleasant odor of dissipation," one of them had said, "whenever I am in the same room with her." "We no longer know," said another, "who our women comrades are. It is hard to say who is a prostitute and who a woman comrade," while another added: "Her profession is such that she can only be a prostitute." The article then went on to imply that "these virtuous ladies" were themselves no better than they should be. And it ended with a highly dramatic portrayal of the beautiful young actress, desperately unhappy and now expecting a child, back on the stage, playing the part of "a gay, frolicsome soubrette."

> In the semidarkness of the boxes, she could see the hard faces of the sacred circle. . . . Her life, the theater, those cold women sitting out there, were all unreal. Only one thing was real—the pain that choked her and grew more and more unbearable as the child moved within her. As her gay song soared across the footlights, she shuddered, striving to hold back her tears. Then, when the curtain came down, she staggered to a sofa, hid her face in her hands and wept bitterly.

The effect of the article was electric. The characters and incidents which Djilas described were readily recognizable to all and sundry. The couple round whom the story centered were quite clearly Peko Dapčević, now Chief of the General Staff, and his strikingly beautiful young bride. The "slender lady" with the lazy voice was equally easy to identify. The party hierarchy, with its womenfolk to the fore, was thrown into an uproar. There could no longer be any question of delaying a decision. Immediate action was called for. A ban was at once placed on any further articles by Djilas. On January 9 his attitude was publicly denounced by the Central Committee, and a party inquiry ordered into the whole affair. Already the words "spy," "saboteur," "foreign agent" were being freely used.

The special plenary meeting of the Central Committee, called to inquire into "the Case of Milovan Djilas," was held on January 16 and 17 in Belgrade in a former bank building resplendent with marble and bronze. Most of the 108 members of the Committee arrived by car. Djilas, pale and haggard-looking, came on foot, accompanied by a solitary friend, Vlado Dedijer, who had long been closely associated with him in his literary and political work.

The proceedings on the first day were opened by Tito himself. It might be asked, he said, why nothing had been done about this matter sooner, why a solution had not been found without all this noise and trouble. He must himself admit to a share in the responsibility for what had happened. In the autumn Djilas—to whom he still referred by his old party nickname of "Djido"—had asked him what he thought of the articles and, while making it clear that he did not agree with everythng in them, he had told him to go on writing. It was only in December that he had realized that Djilas was going too far, that he was in effect attacking the party, undermining its discipline, destroying its unity and that of the country. The articles had been sharply criticized by leading party members. But Djilas had paid no heed and only taken a more extreme line. He himself had then felt obliged to intervene personally. But again Djilas, though aware of his leader's feelings in the matter, had nevertheless gone ahead with the publication of his article in *Nova Misao*, with the object presumably of forcing an issue. It would, Tito continued, be too much to assert that Djilas had realized from the first where his ideas were leading him. But he was out of touch with what was happening in the party and in the country. When he attacked "bureaucratism," he was storming an open door. Others had advanced many of these ideas long ago. "I myself," he went on, "was the first to speak of the withering away of the party, but I did not say that this must take place in six months or in one or two years. It is a long process. Until the last class enemy has been made harmless, until socialist consciousness penetrates the broad masses of the people, there can be no withering away of the Union of Communists." Djilas had preached abstract democracy, in other words anarchy. But there could be no democracy without Socialism and no Socialism without democracy. "The thing that worries me most in this case," said Tito, "is the incredibly low ideological and political standard of the members of our party who thought they saw in all this some sort of new theory concerning the further development of our Socialist system. No wonder there was such confusion. . . . I will say frankly that I would never have called a plenary meeting if I had not clearly seen the deplorable consequences which could arise from this state of affairs, consequences which were already increasing as fast as a snowball on a sloping roof." Djilas had of late drifted away from the friends with whom he had been working for the past seventeen years. In the past they had always talked things over among themselves and laughed and joked about them together and that had made everything easy. "We have never," Tito went on, "been against the free expression of thoughts, especially since our break with the Soviet Union: but these thoughts must be the fruit of common discussion." What had happened had demonstrated the full extent of their democratic tolerance. But they had now reached the limit. The time had come when they were bound to cry halt. Already the waverers and the reactionaries were raising their heads, already the West was hailing Djilas as the standard bearer of democracy. The post-revolutionary period, the period of gradual development and consolidation, was a difficult time for revolutionaries especially when progress was not as easy or as fast as some hoped. It was then that the weaker brethren threw in their hand or else demanded that things should be speeded up, without bothering to find out whether this was possible. That was what had happened to Djilas. He had had enough of painful reality. He had assumed that the class enemy no longer existed. But his own articles had shown how dangerous the class enemy still was. "Comrades," Tito concluded, "Djilas has made grave mistakes. But in my view it would not only be useless but highly obnoxious if we were to go to the other extreme and act as we did in our revolutionary days. Today we are so strong that we can deal with errors in a new and entirely different way, in our own way. We do not intend to destroy those who err but rather to help them to understand their errors and mend their ways."

The next speaker was Djilas himself. He was pale and haggard. "Looking back on my work," he said, "I cannot say that I have been among the best disciplined of Communists. But I am among those who fail to fulfill the tasks allotted to them. During the last few months I had begun to

feel that ideologically on a number of basic issues I was moving away from the theories generally held in our movement.
This was also the basic cause of my personal estrangement
from my closest friends on the Executive Committee of the
party. I arrived at my views after long and painful thought.
But I only put them forward for discussion. I do not claim,
even today, that all my ideas are absolutely correct, though
personally I am convinced that they are. . . . I came to the
conclusion that differences of opinion could best be settled by
verbal discussion, preferably in public. I believed that as a
movement and as a country we had reached a stage where
we might engage in such discussion without endangering our
unity. . . . My biggest mistake was to set forth my views without first discussing them with my colleagues, to think that
the time had come when I could make my personal views
public regardless of my official position. This gave rise not
only to organizational difficulties but unfortunately also to the
impression that the leadership was divided on political and
allied issues. I do not feel this to have been so. . . . I have
heard it said that I am against Comrade Tito. I cannot accept
that. . . . I shall always work in a disciplined way to carry
out the decisions of the League of Communists and of the
government. . . . I am ready to renounce any of my writings
which the leaders of the party consider politically dangerous.
. . . I have been since my earliest youth and I shall remain until the end of my life a free man and a Communist. I do not
see that the one excludes the other."

Djilas was followed by Kardelj, whose task it was to deal
with his errors from the theoretical point of view. Tito, he
said, had already disposed of the political aspects of Djilas's
opinions. The theoretical aspect was only of secondary importance. Indeed, had it not been for their political significance, the Central Committee would not have "broken in on
the theoretical meditations of Comrade Djilas." Having first
explained that he regarded Djilas's theories as "neither serious
nor scientific," he next proceeded to examine them in detail
and at great length, accusing their author of being at once
premature and behind the times, of tilting at windmills and
battering at open doors, of ignoring the working class and
"allowing idealistic dialectics to swallow up materialism," of
drifting away from Marx and falling into the errors of Bernstein, of dabbling in mysticism and existentialism, in liberalism
and bourgeois anarchy, of being, finally, arrogant and resentful of criticism. Continuing, he told of the conversation

which he had had with Djilas in December when the latter had announced that he would have to "fight it out with Tito" and had spoken openly of a two-party system. Though dumfounded, he had not, he said, reported Djilas's remarks to Tito, because he regarded them as "hasty and unpremeditated statements such as we have come to expect from Comrade Djilas" and because he hoped that in future articles he would pay more heed to the views of his friends in the Central Committee. He had been disappointed. Djilas's ideas, he concluded, were certainly harmful. But the struggle, they must realize, had to be waged on two fronts: against bureaucratic tendencies on the one hand and against the tendencies of anarchist elemental forces on the other. Some people were asking themselves whether, after this meeting of the Central Committee, Socialist democracy would be able to develop unimpeded. They need have no such fears.

After Kardelj came Dedijer, burly, confused and clearly unhappy. Of all who spoke, he came nearest to supporting Djilas, his old friend and associate. Having spoken of the "spiritual torment" through which he had passed and of the sympathy with which Tito, in particular, had treated him during these difficult days, he declared that in his opinion there was no substantial difference between Djilas's views and those of Tito and Kardelj. The trouble was that Djilas had "tried to systematize our theoretical thinking and in so doing had inevitably landed himself in difficulties." "Until a few days ago," he continued, with rather more frankness than tact, "the views expressed by Djilas in *Borba* were more or less accepted by all of us sitting here. We cannot deny this or try to excuse ourselves by saying that we read the articles too quickly. All of us, if we put our hands on our hearts, would admit it. Of course, those who read Djilas's articles thought that he had first discussed them with our Secretariat and that the Executive Committee was behind him. What does that mean? It means that people liked these articles, not because of their content, but because of the authority behind them. Now things have changed. People who earlier approved of Djilas have started throwing stones at him. . . . From this I draw two conclusions. First, the ideological level in our country is lower than I thought it was. Secondly (and this is a purely moral question), I think people will say that we say one thing one day and another the next." Djilas, said Dedijer, had been called a Trotsky. Why, he asked, was it necessary for people to attack a man so violently, just because he disagreed with them over questions of philosophy? By throwing mud at him, they were throwing mud at themselves and at their revolution. "I sincerely hope," he concluded, "that we shall find a sensible solution. There are few people among us of Djilas's caliber. Should we pass wise judgment, we shall succeed in saving this great and turbulent spirit. . . . Let us remember that our revolution has survived because it has not devoured its own children, and because the children of our revolution are honest."

Djilas himself now once more intervened in a defiant mood to confirm that, whatever Dedijer might say, his differences with the party were of an ideological and political and not just of a personal or emotional character. He accepted 90 per cent of Kardelj's arguments, but he was still not happy about the party. In his view it needed completely changing in character and organization. Most of its present members were not Communists at all. It was at present "the main obstacle in the way of democratic and Socialist development in Jugoslavia."

During the general discussion which followed some of the speakers admitted that they had at first agreed with parts of what Djilas had written, but the greater number simply echoed what had already been said by Tito and Kardelj, deploring Djilas's disregard of the working class, his lack of contact with reality, his tendency to anarcho-liberalism, the confusion which he had caused, and the harm which he had done to the ideological unity of the party. Several speakers referred angrily to the article in *Nova Misao*. One spoke of the influence exerted on Djilas by Mr. Aneurin Bevan. Others dwelt on the danger of "fractionalism," for so long the scourge of the Jugoslav Communist party. And here and there a note of personal animosity was clearly discernible.

By far the bitterest attack on Djilas delivered by Moša Pijade, his one-time comrade-at-arms in Montenegro and fellow *littérateur*. They had, said Moša, come together for the purpose, not of arguing with Djilas, but of condemning him. "I will not," he continued, "speak of the ideological aspect of his articles, which has already been faithfully dealt with by Kardelj. But I do want to say something about his immense conceit. In his first article he said that Jugoslavia was at the center of world affairs and that the whole world was breathlessly following the struggle of ideas there. And at the center of all this was Djilas, the man with the new idea, the 'Djilas idea,' to use his own phrase. And he is not only

Djilas, but the first Djilasist as well. Such extravagant vanity cannot be part of the equipment of a Communist. It can only develop in a petit-bourgeois writer, in love with himself and his own words." The article in *Nova Misao,* he went on, was nothing but political pornography. It meant the end of Djilas as a theorist and a political writer. But however hazy and confused his theorizing and his style might be, it was quite clear that his aim was to establish a multiparty or at any rate a two-party system. That idea was in his head from the beginning and remained his conscious aim. It was not a question of principles but of deliberate calculation. He had called himself "a free man and a Communist." In fact, however, he had ceased to be a Communist and he was free only in the sense that he had freed himself from all duties and obligations in the party and governments.

At the conclusion of the second day's debate, Djilas spoke again. This time he seemed in a more chastened mood. Since yesterday, he said, "something had snapped inside him." While sitting there he had felt "as though a devil had fallen from his soul." In his earlier statement there had been no sort of self-criticism; he had maintained his position. But during the night he had decided that he must stay with his comrades. That decision had brought him the first sound night's sleep he had had for some time. "I will tell you," he said, "what frightened me: I was afraid of the victory of bureaucracy in Jugoslavia. I took part in the anti-Soviet and anti-Cominform campaigns and afterward I began to criticize things in Jugoslavia. I saw many things in Jugoslavia that were similar to conditions in Russia. I feared that bureaucracy would get hold of our administration and it was my criticism of it that led me to establish my abstract democratic theory. This, as has been pointed out, would have meant the mobilization of the bourgeoisie and the petit bourgeoisie and Western social democracy. But I could never betray my Fatherland in the service of the enemy. Treachery has no place in my character. If I had continued in the path I had chosen . . . I should have reached the point where I should have become the leader of the opposition to Tito in Jugoslavia. This plenum has convinced me that in Jugloslavia there can be no victory for bureaucracy and for that reason I have regained my faith in the League of Communists, which yesterday I openly rejected. I will vote for the resolution with a clear conscience."

The resolution was now put to the vote and adopted unanimously. It declared that the views expressed by Djilas in his articles were basically contrary to the policy adopted at the Sixth Party Congress and had confused public opinion and done harm to the party. In these circumstances it had been decided to expel him from the Central Committee and punish him by giving him a final party warning.

It was left to Tito to sum up. They had, he said, been able to convince themselves that their party possessed an unbreakable and monolithic unity which nothing on earth could destroy. Djilas, too, had been able to convince himself of this. It should afford him strength and comfort in his time of trouble. Never, he continued, had there been more speculation abroad about events in Jugoslavia than at the present time. Some people said that they were becoming more, and others less, democratic; some that they were swinging closer to the West, others to the East. But he could tell them once and for all that nothing that was said abroad would influence them in the very slightest. They would continue to follow their own road to Socialism and Socialist democracy. In foreign policy they could co-operate with those countries with whom they had common interest, but they would not sacrifice their own views. Their aim, on the contrary, should be to influence others by their example. "We must never," he concluded robustly, "allow anybody to persuade us that we should accept any foreign ideas."

Djilas's expulsion from the Central Committee was followed shortly after by his resignation from his two government posts, the Vice-Premiership and the Presidency of the Assembly. From being one of the quadrumvirate who ruled Jugoslavia, he had in the space of a month become a private citizen without privileges or position. All that remained to him was a minister's pension and his membership of the party. Henceforward he took no part in public life. Inquirers were told that he was engaged on a novel, or rather a series of novels. From time to time he might be seen, haggard, disheveled and unshaven, standing in queues, doing his own shopping, or shoveling away the snow in front of his house. Visitors noticed that he now very markedly spoke of the leaders of the party and government as "They."

Toward the end of April came the news that Vlado Dedijer, who alone had supported Djilas at the meeting of the Central Committee in January, had now formally joined in recording his disagreement with him. A few days later a letter was handed in at the local Communist headquarters in a suburb of Belgrade. It was from Djilas. He enclosed his membership card, dating back nearly twenty-five years, and said that he no longer wished to belong to the party.

The party, meanwhile, with Tito at the helm, continued on its way towards its own Jugoslav brand of "Socialist democracy." Under its leader's experienced guidance, it had steered, or seemed to have steered, between the Scylla of bureaucratism and the Charybdis of anarchy, and had emerged, shaken but seemingly unharmed, into the calmer waters beyond. True, a comrade had gone overboard in the process. But what was the loss of one comrade, whatever his standing, as compared with the unity of the party as a whole? In the days before the war Tito's most notable achievement had been his triumph over "fractionalism." Again, after his break with Moscow, he had survived because in a difficult and dangerous situation he had succeeded in uniting the party and carrying it with him. Now once more he had shown in a crisis the same qualities of ruthless realism and skillful leadership which had stood him in good stead so often before. And once more the party had emerged united. That, he well knew, was what mattered most of all. His power, the power of his government, the stability of the whole regime was inescapably rooted in the unity and solidarity of the party.

It remained to be seen whether he would be equally successful in the future. The Djilas crisis had served to crystallize a fundamental problem confronting the rulers of the new Jugoslavia, namely how to reconcile the basically authoritarian and totalitarian character of their regime with their new policy of gradual liberalization and decentralization. Perhaps Dedijer had not been so far wrong when he had said that Djilas had "tried to systematize our theoretical thinking and in so doing had landed himself in difficulties." In order to give their government a broader political basis, in order to render it more viable economically, in order, finally, to show how different they were from the Russians, Tito and his colleagues had made a number of changes in the character of the regime which radically affected the role of the party in what was after all a one-party state. These changes had been given official sanction at the Sixth Party Congress, of which Djilas had drafted the resolution, and it had also fallen to Djilas, as the party's chief propagandist, to elaborate them and explain them to the public at large. The choice of interpreter had perhaps been a rash one. Like most Montenegrins, Djilas was by nature inclined to go too far. He was also apt to be carried away by his own ideas. The new line had been presented to the party (and to the public) in its most extreme form, carried through to what Djilas chose to regard as its logical conclusions. The manner of its presentation was disquieting enough. Still more disquieting had been the public reaction both inside and outside the party which conjured up disturbing visions of renewed fractionalism or even of a two-party system. The resulting crisis had forced Tito to choose and choose quickly between Djilas on the one hand and the party on the other.

The choice had not been a difficult one. Djilas had seemed about to arrogate to himself the position of leader of the opposition, and this was a conception which had as yet no place in Tito's scheme of things. Nor would it have been possible for Tito, even had he wished it, to fly in the face of the party. Of late, it is true, he had tended to address himself and more to the public as a whole, to speak as a national rather than as a party figure, with the result that he and his government had come to enjoy a wider measure of popularity in their own right than was accorded to the party as such. But for all this, in the absence of a nonpolitical civil service, the party remained the cement which held the whole structure together, the only link for administrative purposes between the government and the people, without which it must needs fall apart.

Such were the cogent "political considerations" which had caused the Central Committee to "break in on the theoretical meditations of Comrade Djilas." They also led to a marked change of emphasis: to a revision, a toning down of the new line, to a tightening up of party discipline and dogma, to an increased stress on the class struggle and on the dangers of "Western" and "Social-Democratic" influence. But, as the very handling of the Djilas case had shown, the fundamental reforms of the past six years still remained and with them the contradiction between the basically totalitarian character of the regime and the increasingly antitotalitarian trend of its rulers. The struggle, Kardelj had said, would have to be waged "on two fronts: against bureaucratic tendencies and against the tendencies of anarchist elemental forces." It was a new struggle, a struggle which had as yet scarcely begun and which, before it was over, would call for considerable qualities of leadership on the part of those conducting it.

And indeed before the year was out the rulers of the new Jugoslavia had once again been forcibly reminded of the persistent political and ideological problems which confronted them. It might have been thought that, after all that had happened, the last had been heard of "the Case of Milovan Djilas." But it had not. On December 22, 1954, the London *Times* published a message from their correspondent in Belgrade recording an interview with Vladimir Dedijer, in which he complained that he was being persecuted, that certain "pressures" were begin brought to bear on him, because of the line he had taken during the inquiry into the Djilas case and because of his refusal to join in the official boycott subsequently imposed on Djilas by his former comrades. He had, it seemed, been summoned before the Control Commission of the party and taken to task on account of his attitude. He had, however, refused to answer the charges made against him and had brought the proceedings to an abrupt close by walking out of the meeting a few minutes after it had begun. "I did not agree, and still do not agree," he told the *Times* correspondent, "with many of the theoretical theses of Mr. Djilas, but I have a great respect for him as an intellectual and humanitarian. I have spent twenty years of my life as his friend and we differ in many things, but I refused to join this boycott, because to do so would run contrary to my beliefs. . . . I cannot stop seeing a friend who is now so very much alone. In my view a Communist should be first of all a human being, and every political movement which puts aside ethics and morals carries within it the seeds of its own destruction."

Three days later, on Christmas Day, Dedijer's interview with the *Times* was followed by another interview, given this time by Djilas himself to the `Belgrade correspondent of the *New York Times*. The move against Dedijer, said Djilas, was "an attempt to frighten the democratic elements in the party." "Such elements," he continued, "exist, but they are unorganized, whereas the party itself is in the hands of undemocratic forces." He himself, he said, was frustrated and disillusioned. The liberalizing tendencies of the Sixth Party Congress had been nullified by the meeting of the Central Committee at Brioni ten months later. Power was in the hands of the most reactionary elements in the party who possessed a political monopoly. It was not his intention to lead a revolutionary movement against Tito. The country had had enough revolutions. But there must be freedom of discussion and a second party. If the free discussion and a second party were allowed, Djilas continued, the conditions necessary for political democracy might perhaps develop in ten years' time. He was, he admitted, taking a risk in being so outspoken. "But I think," he concluded optimistically, "that nothing bad will happen. It will mean a lot for our country to have a citizen say what he thinks."

The next move was with the government. It was impossible for them to ignore what had happened. In Tito's absence (he had left shortly before on a prolonged visit to India and Burma) Kardelj was in charge. In a speech made before the Party Congress of the Bosnian Communist party at Sarajevo on December 27, he vigorously denounced Djilas and Dedijer as "bankrupt politicians" who had lost all sense of responsibility toward their own people and who now hoped, with the help of the *Times* and the *New York Times*, to become "political figures" once again. "There are," he continued, striking an agreeably xenophobic note calculated to appeal to any Jugoslav audience, "people and circles abroad who are sympathetic neither to Jugoslav foreign policy nor to Tito's visit to India. For these reasons these two gentlemen have placed themselves at the service of anyone abroad who needs their services and by their false democratic phrases are seeking to hinder our progress toward real Socialist democracy in Jugoslavia."

It took more than a speech to silence Vlado Dedijer. On the very next day he rang up the principal representatives of the foreign press in Belgrade and informed them of his intention to hold a press conference the same evening at which he would reply in person to Kardelj's attack. But when that evening the journalists arrived at his house they found the entrance barred by half a dozen officials of the secret police who informed them that Mr. Dedijer would not be holding his press conference after all. Simultaneously, on the initiative of the public prosecutor, a measure was rushed through the Federal Council depriving Dedijer of his parliamentary immunity in order that he might face charges under Article 118 of the new criminal code dealing with propaganda hostile to the state and the people, and on December 30 it was officially announced that the investigating judge of the Belgrade District Court was opening proceedings against both Dedijer and Djilas under Article 118 because of their "hostile and slanderous propaganda" designed to "damage abroad the most vital interest of our country." Meanwhile at meetings held in different parts of the country the two defendants were freely denounced as "unscrupulous traitors."

The problem which now confronted Kardelj and his colleagues was by no means a simple one. A year earlier they had hoped that Djilas could be prevented from making a nuisance of himself, without its being necessary to place him under restraint and thus violate the new liberal principles of which they were so proud. They had hoped that under a ban of enforced silence and isolation he would soon lose such political significance as he still possessed. But their hopes had been disappointed. With the help of Dedijer, the irrepressible Montenegrin had re-emerged and the latest developments in "the Case of Milovan Djilas" were now exciting the liveliest interest not only in Jugoslavia but all over the world. Inevitably, a heavy sentence on the two rebels would be interpreted as a sign that Jugoslavia had relapsed into the rough and ready methods of Stalinism and that the Jugoslav Revolution was "devouring its own children." On the other hand, to allow the rebellion to continue unchecked, and possibly to spread, would be to take a considerable risk.

Following the example set by Kardelj in his speech at Sarajevo, the authorities in their pronouncements prudently concentrated on attacking the foreign press and "foreign circles" in general for interfering in what was a purely domestic Jugoslav problem and not a very important one at that. Djilas and Dedijer were meanwhile left at liberty to spend the holidays with their families and made numerous and much-noticed public appearances at theaters and concerts. Toward the middle of January it was announced that the preliminary investigation had now been completed and that their case would be tried on January 24. Dedijer, it appeared, was to be defended by the same Dr. Ivo Politeo who, with equal courage and disregard of the consequences, had defended Tito in 1928 and Archbishop Stepinac in 1946.

On the day of the trial it transpired that the proceedings were to be held *in camera*, the foreign press, now more than ever the villains of the piece, being specifically excluded from the court "because of the campaign they have conducted in connection with this case and because the court is not persuaded that they will truthfully report the proceedings." A crowd of perhaps a hundred people had gathered in the entrance hall and in the snowy street outside. When the defendants arrived, accompanied by their wives and lawyers, some youths crowded round them, booing and jeering. There were cries of "Traitor" and fists were shaken in Djilas's face as he made his way through the throng. But both he and his companion remained calm and composed, and as he was about to enter the doorway, a middle-aged man was seen to push his way toward him and shake him warmly by the hand.

The proceedings of the court lasted for sixteen hours and it was after midnight when an excited relative rushed out of the court building and embraced Djilas's old mother who, despite the bitter cold, had waited outside throughout the evening in a car belonging to a newspaper correspondent. A few minutes later Djilas himself appeared, smiling and composed, his wife clinging tightly to his arm, and, after pausing briefly to let himself be photographed, walked away in the direction of his home. He was followed by Dedijer, clearly exhausted and leaning heavily on his wife's arm, the limp left him by his war wounds more noticeable than usual. Both accused had been found guilty. Djilas had been sentenced to eighteen months' and Dedijer to six months' imprisonment. But the court had suspended the sentence for three and two years respectively and neither was in fact to be deprived of his liberty unless in the meantime he was deemed to have repeated his offense.

Commenting next day on the outcome of the trial, *Borba*, the official organ of the party, emphasized that the question at issue had not been the convictions or views of the defendants, but their attempts to seek "foreign support" for them and thus procure, for purposes of their own, foreign interference in the internal affairs of Jugoslavia. Apart from this, their political opinions, like those of any other Jugoslav citizen, were their own affair. They were free, said *Borba*, not only to express them, but to fight for them. What precisely was meant by this time alone would show.

XVI ⌘⌘⌘ THE RAZOR'S EDGE

> *C'est la déstalinisation qui déstalinisera les déstalinisateurs.*
>
> JEAN-PAUL SARTRE

WHILE the Jugoslavs, balancing precariously between tyranny on the one hand and anarchy on the other, were thus busily engaged in working out their own salvation in their own way, important events were taking place elsewhere, events which in the long run were to have the most far-reaching effects on the future not only of Jugoslavia but of the world at large.

Early in March, 1953, while Tito, as it happened, was on his way to England, the death had been announced from Moscow of his adversary and former leader, Josif Vissario-novich Dzhugashvili, better known as Stalin. For a quarter of a century, Stalin had held supreme power in the Soviet Union; power more absolute than that wielded by any of his imperial predecessors; power that reached out across the wide plains of Siberia and into the farthest valleys of the Caucasus and Tien Shan; power that regulated down to the last detail the life of the humblest Soviet citizen; power that controlled absolutely the conduct of orthodox Communists in every part of the globe. Of recent years this power had increased still further, extending beyond the frontiers of the Soviet Union to the satellite states of Eastern Europe and across Asia to Communist China. Never in the history of mankind had such total, such far-flung power, been concentrated in the hands of a single human being. But a human being nonetheless. And now, in the *Vozhd's* own words, "the laws of nature" had "taken their course" and Josif Vissarionovich had been called to his fathers, to those other Dzhugashvilis who, for their part, had never emerged from the remote obscurity of their native Georgia.

Tito, meanwhile, had followed the half-ironical advice which Stalin himself had given him in Moscow seven years before. He had "taken good care of himself." He had "seen to it that nothing happened to him." And now that Stalin was safely dead and embalmed, he "remained for Europe," firmly in power in his own country, on good terms with the West and ready, as he magnanimously announced, to "normalize" his relations with the Soviet Union, should the latter show signs of adopting a more reasonable attitude.

To normalize . . . The mere suggestion of such a thing had seemed in Stalin's day the last straw, the final insult, the ultimate impudence. It was as though Martin Luther had announced his readiness, in return for a full admission of guilt on the Pope's part, to overlook the grievous errors of the Supreme Pontiff.

But now things were different. Stalin was dead. No single successor had stepped into his shoes. His place had been taken by an uneasy oligarchy, riding, it sometimes seemed, on a looser rein. Some of the *Vozhd's* policies had been continued, others dropped. The line was now less clear, but also more flexible. In the Soviet Union itself and in some of the satellite countries there had been signs of a certain relaxation, of a letting-up of the pressure, though whether involuntary or deliberate was uncertain. Abroad the emphasis was now on "peaceful coexistence" with the capitalist world. And not only with the capitalist world. There were indications that the new rulers of the Soviet Union were ready, nay anxious, to coexist peacefully with Tito, with the arch-heretic; that they were ready, not only to let bygones be bygones, but to go futher: to admit that the fault, if any, had been theirs, to admit even that the Jugoslav ideologists had perhaps after all contributed something of value to Communist thought.[1] From the first it was the Russians who made the running, the Russians who announced their readiness to exchange ambassadors and restore trade between the two countries, the Russians who, abandoning their hostile propaganda, publicly drank to the health of "Comrade" Tito and wrote in their newspapers of their "old friendship for Jugoslavia."

Once bitten, twice shy. Tito's first reaction was one of extreme caution—as well it might be. Asked for his opinion of events in Russia, he spoke of a change of tactics rather than a change of heart. But, as time went on, his approach became rather more positive, he showed a greater readiness to admit that something might be happening in Russia after all. He did not reject the Russian overtures out of hand. He agreed to the reappointment of ambassadors. He agreed to

THE RAZOR'S EDGE 383

trade negotiations. He even sent a congratulatory telegram to Moscow on the thirty-seventh anniversary of the October Revolution. "We," he observed a trifle smugly, "are quite competent to recognize a trap."

It is hard to see what else he could have done. To reject the Russian advances would have been to lay himself open to the charge that he was looking for trouble, that he did not really want a peaceful settlement of the dispute. The Western powers traded with the Russians and exchanged ambassadors with them. Why should not he? Besides, from Tito's point of view, the latest situation presented certain not unattractive possibilities. After all that had happened, what could be more gratifying to him, as a Communist, than this half-admission from the Country of the Revolution that he had been right all along, than the implied suggestion that Titoism, or something very like it, might replace Stalinism as the central doctrine of Communism? "The Russians," a leading Jugoslav Communist said patronizingly toward the end of 1954, "stand today where we stood in 1950."

And then, coexistence. Was not "peaceful coexistence" in fact what everyone in the world really wanted? Tito had always been at pains to point out that he belonged to neither of the two opposing blocs. Might he not, poised between the two, be in a better position than anyone to mediate between them? Might he not thus earn the gratitude of the whole of humanity? And might not humanity someday be grateful to Jugoslavia for something else besides: for the fruit of her political, her social, and her economic experience? Might this not also help in some way to bridge the ideological gap which at present divided the world? These were tempting thoughts, thoughts which were to find a sympathetic echo in the questing minds of certain other unattached statesmen such as Pandit Nehru and U Nu, the Prime Minister of Burma, to whom Tito, ranging far and wide in the training ship *Galeb*, paid state visits at the beginning of 1955.

But, however attractive these ideas might at first sight appear, they were scarcely of a nature to turn the head of anyone so outstandingly hard-headed as Marshal Tito. As he himself had said, he and his colleagues were quite competent to recognize a trap. The resumption of normal diplomatic relations with Russia and her satellites was one thing. That Jugoslavia should herself willingly resume satellite status was quite another. There was all the difference in the world between normal diplomatic relations and the relationship which had existed before 1948. Having once safely extricated his head from between the monster's jaws, Tito was scarcely the man to put it back there of his own free will. Nor indeed was he likely to sacrifice without good cause the solid advantages derived from the Balkan Alliance and from his loose but mutually profitable connection with the West. The thought had perhaps crossed his alert and agile mind that the new interest being shown in Jugoslavia by the East might help to induce in the West a more proper appreciation of his country's value as a friend. But that, having at the cost of such superhuman efforts achieved security and independence, he should deliberately throw away all that he had gained seemed on the face of it highly improbable. "These countries," said Tito, speaking of the Western powers, "proved in most difficult times to be not our enemies, but our friends . . . we cannot allow the good relations which we have built up with them to deteriorate, simply in order to improve our relations with the countries of the Eastern Bloc."[2]

Such was the frame of mind in which Tito, in the early spring of 1955, a few weeks after Malenkov's resignation had again unsettled the balance of power in the Kremlin, received through the Soviet Ambassador in Belgrade a fresh approach from Moscow. The Russians, it seemed, were anxious to carry things a stage farther; they suggested a meeting, a meeting at the highest level; they expressed the hope (a hope not expressed since January, 1948) that he would visit them in Moscow, where, they assured him, he would receive a most cordial welcome.

Once again Tito, confronted with a situation abounding in potential pitfalls, showed that he possessed steady nerves and a level head. He replied that he was not prepared to go to Moscow, but would be glad if the Russians would visit him in Belgrade. And, once again, the outcome showed that his reaction, calm, logical and audacious, had been the right one. In due course the reply came back that the Soviet leaders would willingly accept his invitation, and in the early hours of May 14, 1955, it was simultaneously announced from Moscow and Belgrade that Khrushchev, the Secretary General of the Soviet Communist party, Bulganin, the Soviet Prime Minister, and Mikoyan, the Soviet economic chief, would shortly visit Belgrade for the purpose of discussing subjects of mutual interest to both countries.

The announcement, needless to say, gave rise to frantic speculation. To some it seemed to herald Jugoslavia's early return to the status of a Soviet satellite. But to those who stopped to think it was evident that in reality Tito had gained yet another tactical victory in his long-drawn-out contest with the Country of the Revolution. Had he not, only seven years before, been publicly expelled from the Communist fold as a renegade and a heretic? Had he not for seven years been vilified and abused? Had not Bulganin himself denounced him as "a Judas" and "a contemptible traitor"? Had not Khrushchev called him "a Fascist" and his government "a gang of hired Anglo-American spies and murderers"? And now, after all that had happened and after he had refused to come to Moscow to visit them, were not the masters of the Kremlin, the rulers of the mighty Soviet Union, the Secretary of the Soviet party and the Head of the Soviet Government, publicly eating their words and coming cap in hand to Belgrade to visit him and make their peace with him? What more striking vindication could there be of his total unwillingness to compromise, of his utter refusal to bow the knee? But it would have been unlike Tito to relax for a moment even in this hour of triumph. He remained, as always, on his guard, alert, wary and ready for trouble.

Punctually at 5 o'clock on May 26 the silver Ilyushin-14 touched down and taxied across the airfield to where Tito, in marshal's uniform, was sitting waiting in his big open Rolls-Royce. No sooner had the aircraft come to a standstill than the door opened and out skipped Khrushchev, small, perky and rotund in an ill-fitting linen suit. After him came Nikolai Bulganin, bearded, dignified and slightly ill at ease, and Anastas Mikoyan, dark and sardonic, both clearly in a subordinate role. With a radiant smile, Khrushchev shook hands vigorously with Tito, who had advanced majestically to meet him. Then he shook hands with everyone else in reach and patted them all on the back. "Everything," he announced smiling more radiantly than ever, "is going to be all right." After which, having rapidly inspected the guard of honor, he planted himself in front of a microphone, pulled his spectacles from one pocket and a typescript from another, and launched into a speech.

"Dear Comrade Tito and leaders of the Jugoslav Communist League," he began in a loud, rather raucous voice. Then, while Tito's face assumed a set expression, he embarked on an apology for Russia's past treatment of Jugoslavia, an apology so abject as to recall, curiously enough, the confessions of the accused at the Soviet State Trials of wreckers and deviationists. Jugoslavia's expulsion from the Cominform, he said, had been a terrible mistake. "We sincerely regret what happened," he continued, "and resolutely reject the things that occurred, one after another, during that period." The trouble, he said, had been caused by "the acts of provocation" committed by enemies of the people—Beria, Abakumov and others, since unmasked. "We have studied in detail," he went on, "the materials upon which the serious and insulting accusations made against the leaders of Jugoslavia were based. The facts show that these materials were fabricated by enemies of the people, condemned agents of imperialism who had by deceit penetrated the ranks of our party. We are deeply convinced that we have now left behind us the period during which our relations were darkened. For our part we are ready to do all that is needed to remove any obstacles standing in the way of the further normalization of our relations."

Having glanced at Tito, only to find his face still set in the same inscrutable expression, Khrushchev next went on to speak of the historic friendship which had existed between their two countries in the past and to express the hope that the success already achieved in normalizing relations would lead to further developments in the economic, political and cultural spheres. The Soviet Union, he added a little disingenuously "bases its relations on principles of equality, nonintervention and respect for sovereignty."

Before concluding, Khrushchev returned once more to what his opening words had shown to be the basic theme of his spech: the ideological link between the two countries. Once again he was addressing his "dear Comrade Tito" and not the head of a foreign state. The Russian Communists, he said, would be failing in their duty to the workers of the world, if they did not do all they could to establish mutual understanding between the Soviet Communist party and the Communist League of Jugoslavia, understanding based on the doctrines of Marxism-Leninism. The interest of the workers demanded that the leaders of Communist and Workers' parties all over the world should establish mutual confidence between themselves. It was the duty of the two parties to make common cause "in order to throw off the yoke of Captitalism." "Long live Tito!" he concluded, "Long live Jugoslavia!" and then, stepping back expectantly, offered Tito the microphone to reply. But Tito, his face as impassive as ever, simply motioned him to where the cars were waiting to take them up to the

White Palace for tea. As the long procession of Cadillacs, Packards, Buicks and Mercedes-Benzes drove by, it was noticeable that the crowds lining the streets cheered Tito, but entirely ignored the Russians.

Such was the start of the Soviet visit. Next morning at ten o'clock the two delegations opened their formal discussions in the great marble-pillared saloon of the Guards' Club. Across the conference table an unsmiling Tito, flanked by Kardelj and Ranković, faced Khrushchev, Bulganin and Mikoyan. Tape recorders kept track of every word that was said.

The discussions were held behind closed doors. But after two days an article appeared in *Borba* which made the Jugoslav attitude abundantly clear not only to the Russians but to the world at large. Jugoslavia, it announced, had no intention of joining Khrushchev's "Crusade for the overthrow of Capitalism." Her policy was one of "active co-operation with all countries, regardless of differences in their internal systems . . . a policy consistently opposed to joining any ideological bloc." Meanwhile, in conversation with visiting journalists, the Jugoslavs did not attempt to disguise their distaste for Khrushchev's shock tactics and clumsy attempts to involve them ideologically and poison their relations with the West, or for that matter, their disbelief of the story that, of the Soviet leaders, Beria and Abakumov alone had been responsible for the "misunderstandings" of 1948. The initial effect on the negotiations of Khrushchev's opening gambit had, it seemed, been far from happy, though once the Russians had realized their mistake and revised their attitude the atmosphere had improved and some progress had become possible.

The end of the first two days' negotiations was marked by a lavish evening party given by Tito at the White Palace. At this the Russians, ignoring the directions on the invitation and indulging in loud asides on the subject of "bourgeois formality," wore the crumpled, ill-fitting summer suits which they had had on since their arrival, while their less inhibited hosts sported faultless dinner jackets or glittering uniforms and Tito himself appeared in the full dress white summer uniform of a marshal of Jugoslavia.

Shortly after midnight a fleet of cars carried both delegations to the railway station, where a special train was waiting to take them on the first stage of their journey to Tito's summer residence on the Island of Brioni which was to be the scene of the next phase of their talks. After an all-night train journey, a seven-hour motor drive and a short sea crossing in the Presidential yacht, they reached their destination. The next day was spent in congenial surroundings partly in discussion and partly in relaxation. After this Tito dispatched his guests on an intensive two-day tour of "industrial establishments and places of cultural interest" in Slovenia and Croatia, while he himself made his own way back to Belgrade to await their return.

On Thursday, June 2, the two delegations reassembled for the last time at the Guards' Club. The Russians, it was noticed, looked somewhat battered after their two days of intensive industrial and cultural sight-seeing and another night in the train, and arrived an hour late at the conference table. After a further whole day of negotiation, agreement was finally reached on the terms of a joint Declaration of Friendship and Co-operation which was signed the same evening by Tito and Bulganin.

Perhaps the most significant thing about this lengthy but vaguely worded document, which was taken up for the most part with the enunciation of entirely innocuous "peace-loving principles," was the fact that it was signed, not by Khrushchev on behalf of the Soviet party, but by Bulganin on behalf of the Soviet Government, and that it contained no reference to Communism, Marxism-Leninism or inter-party relations. On the contrary, it expressly provided that "questions of internal organization, of different social systems and of different forms of Socialist development" should be "solely the concern of the individual countries." In other words, the Russians had failed in their principal objective, namely, to regain their ideological hold on Jugoslavia. Tito, for his part, in addition to the satisfaction which he could scarcely fail to derive from the turn which events had taken, received from the Russians a promise to "normalize" trade, practically non-existent since 1948, to negotiate a settlement of all outstanding trade questions, to repatriate the Jugoslav nationals still held by them and to cease from all hostile propaganda. In return, at no very great cost to himself, he associated with a passing reference to "the legitimate rights of the People's Republic of China in regard to Formosa." He also agreed, presumably with mental reservations, to allow the Russians, in return for the grant of reciprocal facilities in Russia, to re-establish an official information service in Jugoslavia and to encourage "a free exchange of opinions" between the two countries.

THE RAZOR'S EDGE 389

After the signing of the declaration both delegations repaired to a reception given by the Russians for a thousand guests including the diplomatic corps and a large number of foreign newspaper correspondents. The tables were laden with caviar and other specially imported delicacies. Vodka and sweet Soviet champagne flowed freely. Some selected members of the Soviet State Ballet had been flown in from Moscow. The atmosphere was pleasantly relaxed. "A ballerina," said Tito to Bulganin, as they sat watching the dancing, "is a more agreeable sight than a negotiator." "Yes," said Bulganin jovially, "Khrushchev never had legs like that."

Later Tito, his handsome new wife, Jovanka, and a few selected guests were taken off by their hosts to a special supper room. It was two in the morning before they reemerged. Tito and his wife were the first to come out, he in a beautifully cut dinner jacket, she in a low evening dress and diamonds. They made a striking and distinguished pair as they stood talking to the group of foreign correspondents who clustered round them. Then suddenly the door flew open and out came Khrushchev. Blinking happily at the assembled guests, he waved his hand and stumbled slightly as he crossed the threshold. "Journalists!" said Tito. "Very dangerous men!" Khrushchev rejoined merrily. Then, impulsively grabbing the correspondent of the *New York Herald Tribune* by the hand, "Who," he asked, "are you?" And, on being told that he was an American, "Oh," he shouted, "you Americans do not know Russia." At this the correspondent asked how his compatriots could get to know Russia if they were not given visas. "You can all have visas! You can all come tomorrow!" said Khrushchev. Mikoyan, dark and disapproving, now took his leader by the arm. "Come, let us go home," he said, "we have to be up early." But Khrushchev shook him off. "You can all come tomorrow! You can all come tomorrow!" he went on repeating. Then, once again brushing aside Mikoyan, he started to make a speech. "Our agreement," he bellowed, "contributes to peace and lessens international tensions." "What did he say?" a bystander asked Tito. "He said 'Peace'," Tito replied dryly. "Yes, yes," chimed in Khrushchev, "Peace! Peace!" This time it was Tito who intervened. "Come, Khrushchev," he said, "these journalists will take you prisoner," and, grasping him firmly by the elbow, started him on his way downstairs. "Peace! Peace!" shouted Stalin's successor with another merry wave of his hand, and, after successfully reaching the foot of the stairs, kissed every girl in sight, entered his car with the help of two sturdily built attendants and was driven rapidly away.

Next morning the red carpet was down once more at Belgrade airport and a brass band was playing cheerfully as Khrushchev, with his mackintosh over his arm and Bulganin and Mikoyan following along behind, hurriedly inspected the guard of honor resplendent in their electric blue tunics and then scuttled up the steps of the twin-engined aircraft which stood ready to take him back to Moscow by way of Sofia and Bucharest, where bewildered puppet governments anxiously awaited a new party line. Once more Tito, bronzed, correct and impassive in his marshal's uniform, stood to attention and saluted as the aircraft took off, and the visit of the Soviet leaders to Belgrade was over.

With the Soviet visit ended yet another phase in the life of Josip Broz, a phase on which, now that it was over, he could look back with unmixed satisfaction. From his trial of strength with the mighty Soviet Union he had emerged, not only unscathed, but triumphant. It had been the Russians who in the end had sued for peace. It had been the Russians who had come to Belgrade to make amends and publicly abase themselves. It had been the Russians who, swallowing their own words and abandoning their pretensions to infallibility, their claims to an exclusive monopoly of Marxist truth, had in the end accepted him on his own terms as an independent Communist and had been told in return that he might in due course be prepared to exchange views with them on the subject of "Socialist experience."

Nor was this all. Inevitably there was more to come. The sequence of events could not be checked. History would not stand still.

For twenty years under Stalin Soviet power had rested on firm principles: the personal dictatorship of one immensely formidable man, the absolute supremacy and infallibility of the Kremlin, its absolute control over Communists everywhere. On these principles depended the continuance of the appalling but nevertheless efficacious reign of terror under which the Russians had suffered for a quarter of a century and which more recently had been extended to large areas beyond their frontiers. Now at long last there were signs that these principles had been undermined and the massive edifice which rested upon them shaken to its very foundations.

Even before Stalin's death Tito's rebellion had struck a

telling blow at Soviet power. Its infallibility had been challenged and its monolithic character impaired. And now the giant had vanished and his place had been taken by lesser men, disagreeing among themselves and rightly suspicious of each other. He himself had no illusions about them. "You are blind like young kittens," he had said to the assembled members of the Politburo not long before his death. "What will happen without me? The country will perish because you do not know how to recognize enemies." And indeed under their auspices the undermining process was carried a stage farther.

For a time after his death, Stalin, lying in his twin glass coffin at Lenin's side, continued to be the object of modified glorification. But within a year or two, the new rulers of the Soviet Union, who had without exception been intimately associated with all the most unsavory aspects of their dead master's regime, began busily to demolish the shrine at which they had for so long worshiped. The cult of the individual, they announced, was at an end. Its place must be taken by Lenin's long-neglected principle of collective leadership.

Gathering force, the attack on the dead dictator reached its climax in a three hours' speech made to the Twentieth Party Congress in February, 1956 by Nikita Khrushchev. With a wealth of lurid detail, Khrushchev depicted Stalin and the regime he had established in something very like their true light. He spoke of the methods by which the *Vozhd* had achieved absolute power, of the treachery and deceit, the repression, the "violations of Soviet legality"; of the ensuing reign of terror, the purges of the 1930's, the terrible tortures used to extract confessions, the murder of countless innocent victims; of the tyrant's megalomania and brooding suspicion of all around him, of his willfulness and blunders in foreign policy and in the conduct of war; of the utter impossibility of reasoning with him. "But why didn't you kill him?" cried someone. "What could we do? There was a reign of terror," replied Khrushchev, bursting into tears. And he went on to describe how he himself had been publicly humiliated by Stalin. "Dance the *gopak*, Ukrainian!" the *Vozhd* had cried, and, puffing and blowing, Khrushchev had had to dance for his very life, kicking out his plump little legs for all he was worth.

. The impact of this astonishing speech, the contents of which soon leaked out, could only be tremendous. At one blow it demolished and trampled underfoot everything that up to then had been most sacred. Everything that had been done for the past twenty years had been wrong. Everything that had been said had been lies. Millions had died unjustly or in vain. Soviet policy had been one gigantic deviation. And Stalin, the Leader of the People, had been the biggest deviator of them all.

Time alone could show the full effects of the shock which Stalin's successors had thus administered to the Soviet body politic; had administered for that matter to Communist parties all over the world. At once, a sudden outburst of rioting in Georgia and widely advertised dissensions and disarray among Communists abroad gave a foretaste of what was to come. But already it was harder to turn back than to go forward. Willy-nilly the Soviet leaders were swept along by the policy of "de-Stalinization" and limited liberalization which they themselves had initiated.

In any other country the new regime would still have ranked as savagely repressive. In the fetid atmosphere of the Soviet Union, even a little freedom, even the slightest breath of fresh air, was something so new, so unheard of, as to be actively disturbing. Soon there were signs that here and there Russians were beginning to think for themselves, to think along lines which bore but little relation to ideological correctitude.

Nor was it only in the Soviet Union that the new tendencies made themselves felt. On the satellites, also, the heavy hand of the Kremlin now weighed a little less heavily, and here, too, the heady ferment of freedom began to take effect, and to take effect far faster than in Russia itself. "Their pace," said a member of the Polish Politburo, "will not do for us."

Such was the wider background against which in June, 1956 Tito, in response to a pressing invitation from the Soviet leaders, consented to return the visit which they had paid him the year before. Ten fateful years had gone by since he had last visited Moscow. Then, he had been treated with the distinction due to a leading satellite. Now, he was accorded honors of an entirely different kind. Whatever the innermost thoughts of the assembled leaders of the party and government who gathered at the station to greet him, they certainly allowed no hint of condescension to tinge their attitude toward him. On the contrary, they treated him as in every respect an equal—an equal whom they were anxious to conciliate and to whose wishes they were only too ready to defer. Already they had done much to make amends. In their speeches to the Twentieth Congress, Khrushchev and his colleagues had been careful to dwell at length on the "shamefulness" and "monstrousness" of Stalin's conduct toward Jugoslavia. In April they had disbanded the Cominform of unhappy memory. Gradually, they were weeding out the Stalinists among the satellite leaders and reinstating the Titoists, posthumously if necessary. And now, on the day before Tito's arrival in Moscow, they announced that they had dismissed their own Foreign Minister, Molotov, the signatory, with Stalin, of those ill-omened letters which had been dispatched to Belgrade in the spring and summer of 1948.

But more significant than any official tokens of regard, more significant even than these conciliatory gestures, was the reception accorded to Tito during his visit by the Russian people, by the common people of the Soviet Union, who for so long had been denied any opportunity of showing their true feelings, and who now cheered as they had never cheered before, cheered, not the picturesque foreign potentate, not the official guest of their government, but the rebel, the man who had defied the Kremlin and got away with it, the man who to them seemed somehow responsible for the strange wind of freedom now blowing through the Communist world. Wherever he went, from the moment when, grinning broadly and resplendent in a magnificent powder-blue uniform liberally garnished with gold, he alighted at the Kievski Station, until the moment, nearly three weeks later, when he stepped back into the cream and green Diesel train that was to take him home again, Tito was the center of an immense, wildly enthusiastic crowd. Everywhere, from the Gulf of Finland to the shores of the Black Sea, the same fantastic scenes were repeated. In Moscow, where hundreds of thousands of people lined the streets to welcome him and mobbed him wherever he went, where in the Dynamo Stadium a vast audience cheered him to the echo. In Leningrad, where amid scenes of wild enthusiasm he recalled his own part in the October Revolution. At the seaside resort of Sochi. In Stalingrad, where all security precautions were swept aside and a surging crowd of two hundred thousand people broke through the cordons of troops and police to acclaim him.

Fully to understand Tito's emotions at this reception, to grasp his feelings in regard to Russia itself, it is necessary for us to go back some way: to Feldwebel Josip Broz and to the revelation vouchsafed to him in Russia nearly forty years ago; to Party Member Broz, living "illegally" in Jugo-slavia and every night listening secretly on his wireless for the chiming of the great clock in the Kremlin; to Party Secretary Walter, looking steadfastly to Moscow for guidance and loyally carrying out the directives imparted to him *von oben;* to resistance leader Tito, fighting with might and main for revolution and for the Country of the Revolution; and so on, all through a life spent in the service of Moscow, until finally we come to alleged deviationist Tito, unjustly expelled from the Communist fold, reviled for a time as a Fascist Beast and a Capitalist Jackal, and now, at long last, admitted to have been right from the first and welcomed back to the fold and to the Country of the Revolution in triumph—a triumph aptly symbolized when Tito, visiting the grim basalt mausoleum on the Red Square, had paused briefly before Lenin's coffin and then turned contemptuously away from the other glass case next to it, the case in which reposed all that now remained of his one-time adversary, Josif Vissarionovich Stalin.

Such a triumph over his enemies, such a vindication of all that he had fought for, such a welcome from the Country of the Revolution and its people, was enough to turn anyone's head. Tito kept his.

He went, it is true, quite a long way—perhaps farther than he had originally intended—to meet his hosts' point of view. Indeed, to many observers it seemed at the time as though he had now irrevocably thrown in his lot with Moscow. "A broad similarity of views" was announced between the Soviet and Jugoslav Governments on a number of important topics. Fraternal relations between the two parties, broken off since 1948 and rejected by Tito in 1955, were now formally re-sumed. In any future conflict, announced Marshal Zhukov triumphantly, Jugoslavia and the Soviet Union would fight side by side. "I feel at home in the Soviet Union," declared Tito at Kiev, "because we are part of the same family, the family of Socialism."

But Tito was nothing if not a realist. There was all the difference between friendly, even fraternal, "bilateral" rela-tions between Jugoslavia and the Soviet Union and actual adherence to a bloc. The strength of Tito's position lay, as he well knew, in his "nonalignment," in his ability to maintain his hard-won independence, to maintain it and, if possible, to extend it to others. This he did not sacrifice. Neither, for that matter, did he leave Moscow empty-handed. In return for his more friendly attitude, for the use now and then of the word "Comrade," he had, after much hard bargaining, extracted from the Russians what seemed a notable concession.

At the Twentieth Party Congress in February, Khrushchev had enunciated the theory of "different roads to Socialism." Socialism, he had admitted, could be attained in more than one way, not necessarily or exclusively in the way taken by Russia. The declaration to which, with Tito, he now put his signature, was even more explicit. "Starting," it ran, "from the fact that any tendency to impose one's own views in determining the roads and forms of Socialist development is alien to both, the two parties agree that co-operation should be based on complete freedom and equality, on friendly criticism, and on the comradely exchange of views between them."

This, if it meant anything, which was admittedly doubtful, meant that the Kremlin was formally abandoning its claim to be infallible, to be the one source of truth and doctrinal authority. It meant that henceforth Belgrade's word would carry as much weight as Moscow's. It meant, in the ultimate analysis, that, not only Jugoslavia, but the other Communist governments of Eastern Europe were now free to work things out for themselves. Certainly this was what Tito took it to mean. "There are," he proclaimed in Bucharest on his way home a few days later, "no more satellites."

From the Russian point of view, as from Tito's, the resulting situation was full of possibilities, some promising, and some alarming. To tame Tito, to compromise him with the West, to lure him back into the fold, was something the Russians had long been trying to do. The question was: had they succeeded? And, if they had, what would be the effect on the fold? What would be the impact on the satellites of Tito's influence and ideas? How would they react when left to find their own way to Communism?

The outlook, on further inspection, proved anything but reassuring for the Russians. Already things were moving too fast and in a highly dangerous direction. That same summer, serious rioting broke out at Poznań in Poland. Clearly the brake must be applied. Indeed the engine must be put into reverse. If they had ever for a moment meant what they said, the Russians now had second thoughts. With belated prudence, they decided not to take any more chances. To the

Communist parties of the different satellite countries they dispatched a secret circular expressly warning them against following Jugoslavia's example and reminding them that, whatever they might hear to the contrary, the Soviet Union remained the only true example for all Communist movements and organizations, and the Soviet party the "directing party" for world Communism.

When, as it was bound to, the Soviet circular came to Tito's notice, he reacted violently. This was not what he had hoped for. This was not the freedom he demanded for each to find his own individual way to the common goal. This, on the contrary, was much more like old-fashioned Stalinist centralism, like old-fashioned Stalinist double-crossing. He put his point of view to the Russians in no uncertain terms and on September 19 it was announced that Khrushchev had suddenly arrived to spend a holiday in Jugoslavia.

The fiction of Khrushchev's holiday was only rather half heartedly kept up. From time to time he and his host would be photographed in suitably rustic surroundings. But soon it was freely admitted that talks were in progress, talks which involved the future relationship between the two countries, talks which, it began to seem, were not going any too well. Then, as though to confirm that something was badly amiss, came on September 27 the news that Tito, together with Khrushchev, had left at short notice for Russia by air. They were, it seemed, to spend another holiday together, this time in the Crimea. Meanwhile, in Belgrade a Jugoslav official spokesman let it be known that serious divergences of opinion had arisen between them, divergences which concerned the vital principle of different roads to Socialism and the whole future of the satellites. "Did the Jugoslavs propose to give way?" inquired a journalist. "The Jugoslavs," came the characteristic reply, "are not in the habit of giving way."

There followed more holiday pictures. Tito and Khrushchev had, it seemed, been joined by Bulganin and a number of other Soviet leaders and by a Hungarian delegation. Finally, on October 5, Tito returned home. To an expectant world it seemed probable that, whatever else might have happened at Yalta, Tito had not sacrificed his independence or, for that matter, abandoned his struggle for the vital principle of different roads to Socialism and for the right to propagate his ideas within the Communist fold. And, indeed, during the weeks that followed came reports of delegations from the Communist parties of Poland, Hungary, Italy, Bulgaria and

Rumania, wending their way, not to Moscow, but to Belgrade.

But already theoretical discussions on centralism, on different roads to Socialism, on Russia's control over her satellites, were fast being overtaken by events. A succession of dark and terrifying shapes were thronging forth from the Pandora's Box which Stalin's heirs had so imprudently opened. After smoldering for eight years, the spark which Tito had touched off in 1948 had been fanned into a blaze which no amount of negotiation or discussion could ever extinguish.

The Poznań riots had sounded a first note of warning. In October they were overshadowed by nation-wide risings in Poland and Hungary. By the end of the year order had been outwardly restored in both countries and normal relations with Russia re-established. But the Poles for their part had given nothing away, while in Hungary the Red Army could not by mere brute force ever efface the memory or rub out the consequences of those fateful autumn weeks.

What the ultimate outcome of it all would be was as yet impossible to say. The process was still continuing. But this much seemed clear. Recent events had profoundly shaken the authority of the Kremlin both inside and outside Russia. The vast military and economic might of the Soviet Union, its manpower and its natural riches, remained unimpaired. But the total power which Stalin had once wielded, the absolute control which he had exercised over the peoples of the Soviet Union and its satellites and over Communist party members throughout the world, was a thing of the past. His successors, swinging this way, or that, as the views of one faction or another prevailed, might yield ground, as they had done in Poland. Or they might temporarily impose their will by force, as they had done in Hungary. In the eyes of the world neither solution could be anything but an admission of failure. The fact remained that, after ten years of Soviet Communism, ten years of Soviet domination, the common people of Poland and Hungary had risen to a man and, fighting with rifles and hand grenades against tanks, artillery and aircraft, against the whole formidable apparatus of the state, had defied their oppressors and given them pause. Nothing could wipe out that inescapable, that triumphant fact. The spell had been broken, the vacuum destroyed, the fresh air let in. The fissure, which had appeared in the façade when Tito first defied Moscow and survived, had widened and deepened until Tito himself was frightened by it. Even in the Soviet Union there were signs that the same leaven of unrest was at work. "A specter,"

Karl Marx had written a century before, "is haunting Europe, the specter of Communism." Now, a hundred years later, it was the turn of the Communists in the Kremlin to be haunted —to be haunted by the unfamiliar, the avenging specter of Freedom.

For Tito, precariously balanced between East and West, between autocracy and democracy, between repression and the threat of anarchy, these events, following the changes which had taken place in Russia itself, were both exhilarating and at the same time alarming. What greater vindication could there be than this of his own revolt against Stalinism—a vindication so complete as to suggest that his rebellion had in the long run acted as a catalyst and precipitated the downfall and disintegration of the system which it had so successfully defied. But, on the other hand, how fraught with danger was the prospect which they revealed.

Up to now, with consummate skill, ruthlessness and restraint, he had managed to control and hold in check the liberalizing movement which he had initiated in his own country. But what had happened in Hungary showed only too clearly how easy it was for would-be liberalizers to be carried away and overwhelmed by the forces which they had themselves let loose. It also showed that, when they judged it advisable, the new rulers of the Soviet Union could use force to achieve their ends with a frank brutality which Stalin himself might have envied. Tito was above all a realist. Neither warning was wasted on him. He had no wish to be dislodged by an internal upheaval. Nor did he want his country to be overrun by a score of Soviet armored divisions. His conduct in this emergency, while resolute, was also prudent.

This prudence was cleaarly reflected in the official attitude of the Jugoslav Government toward Hungary. While approving the course of events in Poland and indeed in Hungary so long as they followed the National Communist model, Tito's attitude toward the Hungarian insurrection changed so soon as it became clear that a great number of the insurgents were opposed not only to Soviet domination but to Communism as such. Dislike of what he called the "reactionary forces" among the rebels, coupled with reluctance to disturb his relations with the Russians, led him to refrain from any further display of sympathy for the Hungarian insurgents and to confine himself to the mildest expression of disapproval of Soviet armed intervention. At the UN and elsewhere the

Jugoslav attitude remained equivocal, to say the least of it, and scarcely had the Russians announced the formation of Kadar's puppet government than the Jugoslav Government immediately gave it its public support.

But in the long run this attitude was to prove a difficult one to maintain. Any faith the Russians had ever had in Tito's repeated assurances that the satellites, if allowed to find their own way to Socialism, would become more strongly attached to the Soviet Union than ever had been shattered by events in Hungary. In their hunt for scapegoats it was not altogether surprising that they should now seek to blame what had happened on Tito. The opening shots in the anti-Jugoslav propaganda campaign that followed were fired by Enver Hodja, the Albanian Communist leader who had played a similar role in 1948. In an article published in Moscow by *Pravda,* Hodja sharply attacked those who "tried to invent new forms of Socialism for themselves," "sought to impose them on others" and, worst of all, "repudiated the example and experience of the Soviet Union."

This was too much for Tito and also for many others in the party whose opinion was bound to weigh with him. In a speech at Pula on November 11 he gave his views on the whole subject at some length. Hodja he simply dismissed as "that woeful Marxist who knows the words 'Marxism-Leninism' and nothing besides." With "the Soviet comrades" he was a good deal gentler, though inclined to be patronizing. He did not, he said, entirely despair of them. The trouble was that they were divided among themselves. They had made mistakes in Poland and Hungary because there were still Stalinists among them who imposed their will on the rest. But the good elements might well get the upper hand in the long run. It was not enough that they should condemn the cult of personality; their system itself was at fault. They must put it right. The issue was whether the Stalinist or the non-Stalinist way was to triumph in the long run. In Poland things had turned out happily. In future Jugoslavia and Poland would stand shoulder to shoulder in the fight against Stalinism and for more rapid democratization. He, for his part, had already given the Russians his views on Eastern Europe. It was their failure to listen to him that had led to the Hungarian disaster. The original Soviet intervention in Hungary had been a fatal error, though the second might to some extent have been justified by the need "to save Socialism." In the event, what had happened in Hungary had dealt a terrible blow to

Socialism, had sadly compromised it. But the sacrifices of the Hungarian people would not have been in vain if they caused the Russian leaders, perhaps even the Stalinists, to realize at long last that this sort of thing could no longer be done. Recent events, he added, had caught the fancy of certain unimportant elements in Jugoslavia, who liked fishing in troubled waters. But with a united party and a united people such elements had not got a chance. Jugoslavia, he concluded confidently, was different.

"The Soviet comrades" could hardly be expected to like this. Angrily they responded with comments which, as the Jugoslavs aptly pointed out, bore little relation to the "constructive criticism" provided for by the joint Moscow Declaration. Tito, wrote *Pravda* self-righteously, was trying to interfere in other people's affairs. His claim that the Jugoslav way to Socialism was the only true way ran directly counter to the Marxist-Leninist precept that each country could find the way for itself. To this broadside the Jugoslavs replied vigorously and soon an acrimonious exchange of dialectics was in progress, though it is only true to say that a milder tone, the retention of the word "Comrade" and an absence of old-fashioned zoological imagery distinguished the present controversy from the more violent exchanges of the Cominform period. But the spirit was the same. Nor were things improved by the brazen effrontery with which on November 22 the Russians openly kidnaped the unfortunate Imre Nagy, when, after sheltering for a fortnight in the Jugoslav Embassy in Budapest, he finally left it under a safe conduct granted by the Kadar Government. Soon there were signs that Stalin's successors were belatedly seeking to call a halt to "de-Stalinization," were seeking even to rehabilitate the *Vozhd*. "We are all Stalinists," said Khrushchev, "in the fight against imperialism," and thus sharply replied to Tito's suggestion that the Soviet leaders were divided among themselves. A month later he went even further. "As a Communist fighting for the interests of the working class, Stalin," he said, "was a model Communist."

For the time being at any rate, the latest Soviet-Jugoslav honeymoon was at an end. From Belgrade came indications of a desire to resuscitate the Balkan Pact and so, indirectly, to strengthen Jugoslavia's links with the West. Economic aid from America continued. Economic aid from the Soviet Union proved something of an illusion. Meanwhile Tito, reckoning no doubt that this was no time to take unnecessary risks, and resolutely refusing to allow his repeatedly declared enthusiasm for "rapid democratization" to run away with him, arranged for the rearrest and relegation to jail of Milovan Djilas who had recently published in an American magazine some pertinent criticisms of his policy toward Hungary.

Thus, neatly balancing on the knife edge which had for so long supported him, Tito emerged unscathed from yet another crisis, a crisis which, in one way or another, might well have been the downfall of a less agile statesman. Emerged to continue the propagation of the ideas for which he stood, ideas displeasing in many respects to East and West alike.

Today, in his middle sixties, the former Josip Broz gives an impression of exceptional mental and physical vigor. His zest for life is intense. He works hard, but not too hard. He takes pleasure in eating well, dressing well and living in agreeable surroundings. On his finger he still wears the handsome diamond ring which he bought in 1937 with the rubles he had earned by translating the official *History of the Party* into Serbo-Croat; it reminds him, he says, of those difficult early days. Everything interests him. His joy in some new acquisition, especially in anything of a mechanical nature, is like that of a child with a new toy. He possesses the invaluable gift of being able to set aside the cares of state and enter wholeheartedly into some frivolous pastime or pursuit. At heart a countryman, he is happiest in the country, shooting, riding or swimming. At his castle in Slovenia or at his villa on Brioni, he leads a patriarchal existence, surrounded by children and grandchildren, by dogs and horses and by a variety of hangers-on, most of whom were with him in the woods or worked with him underground before the war. Having divorced his second wife, Herta, he married in 1952 Jovanka Budisavljević, a dark, handsome Serbian girl in her twenties with a distinguished record as a Partisan.

His closest personal and political associates are still drawn from the little group which he formed round him before and during the war. With the passage of time it has grown smaller. Some of its members, like Ivo Ribar, were killed during the war, some like Kidrič, have died since. Others, like Žujović or Djilas, have for one reason or another been eliminated. Of the innermost circle of all, only Kardelj and Ranković remain, forming with Tito himself what seems at times a somewhat precariously poised triumvirate. But recent vicissitudes have further strengthened the bonds which unite these three men.

Now, as always, when there are decisions to be taken, they are taken jointly and after due consultation. Though Tito dominates it, the *kolektiv* is very much of a reality, and would in all probability survive were he to disappear. No one realizes better than Tito the importance of keeping in touch with the party and with public opinion, the importance of not becoming isolated. In his travels through Jugoslavia, he makes a point of talking to as many people as he can from all walks of life and from all parts of the country and of hearing for himself what they have to say. He also sees numerous foreign visitors, reads foreign books and newspapers, and has latterly traveled abroad in many different foreign countries.

With the years and with the experience they have brought, Tito's outlook has widened and become less rigid. Freed from the tutelage of Moscow, he has grown readier to experiment, readier to learn from the experience of others. His sense of humor, always a saving grace, has become still stronger. As a man, he has become calmer, mellower, less flamboyant and more even-tempered: less of a dictator and more of a human being. But he has lost none of his basic toughness and shrewdness, none of the qualities which have stood him in such good stead in the past. At sixty-five, he remains as alert, as decisive and as hard-headed as ever and as ready as ever to face resolutely, realistically and ruthlessly any situation that may confront him.

It is as yet too early to form a final estimate of Tito's place in history. "Remember," he said to me recently, "there may be more to come." And indeed, fresh vicissitudes may lie ahead of him no less astonishing than those which he has already experienced. His work, with its author and much else besides, may be swept away by another convulsion comparable to that which brought him to the surface. Or it may survive. We live in uncertain times.

Should he remain alive and in power for another five or ten years, it may well suffice him to consolidate what he has already achieved, to endow it with permanence and stability. He may be able to complete the task of welding into a coherent federal state the deeply divided nation in which he first took power and so give true substance to the phrase "Brotherhood and Unity." In a wider field, his example and experience have already had far-reaching repercussions. Viewed in its historical perspective, his break with Moscow, his defiance of Stalin and all that has followed since clearly mark a turning point in the history of Communism.

But, whatever the future holds in store, this much is certain. For his early plots and stratagems, for his leadership in the War of National Liberation, in those three and a half years of bitter strife, and, last but not least, for his stubborn defiance of the Kremlin and resolute rejection of Stalin's overlordship, Tito, like Czar, Lazar and Kara Djordje before him, will always be remembered in the history and legend of his own people. A typical South Slav, if ever there was one, his fame will be celebrated by future generations of South Slavs, the fame of his virtues and of his vices alike.

There is a saying in the Balkans that behind every hero stands a traitor.[3] The difficulty, as often as not, is to determine which is which. Again and again, there is something heroic about the traitor and an element of treachery in the hero. The early chronicles of the Serbs, Croats and Slovenes abound in such ambiguities. Nor is their more recent history lacking in examples. Take Tito himself. Seen from one point of view, he can be represented as a traitor to his king and country, as the agent of a foreign power, who ultimately betrayed even that foreign power. Seen from another, he appears as a national hero twice over. Take Draža Mihajlović. Is he to be regarded as a collaborator or as a resistance leader? And, if as a resistance leader, as a leader of resistance to whom— to the Germans or the Communists? Or was he perhaps not, on reflection, just a decent, well-meaning man who was overtaken and overwhelmed by events beyond his control? And Cardinal Stepinac, the prelate who, as a young Austrian prisoner of war, readily volunteered to fight for his emperor's enemies, the Serbs, and who later, as an Archbishop, clashed in varying degrees with three successive and contrasting temporal regimes, but remained relentlessly true to his Church. How is he to be regarded? As a martyr or as a war criminal? As a traitor or as a patriot? And Milovan Djilas, the Communist turned democrat? What of him?

All these characters—to take only three or four from among a multitude—have one thing in common: the courage of their convictions, political, ideological, religious; their readiness to die for an idea, though not for the same idea. It has been found possible, without doing serious violence to the facts, to present one or other of them as a hero and the rest as villains. I have preferred simply to set out the facts, insofar as I have been able to ascertain them, to place upon them what seems to me the most convincing interpretation, and to leave my readers to pass such judgment as they desire on men confronted with dilemmas and with conflicts of loyalty which they themselves, in all probability, have not yet had to face.

ᛒᛒᛒᛒ APPENDIX ᛒᛒᛒᛒ

(Page numbers refer to English edition if there is more than one edition.)

CHAPTER I

My principal source for my account of Tito's early life has been a number of conversations with Tito himself as well as research undertaken personally at Kumrovec, Sisak, Zagreb and elsewhere. I have also consulted for this and subsequent chapters:

VLADIMIR DEDIJER: *Josip Broz Tito—Prilozi za Biografiju.*
K. ZILLIACUS: *Tito of Jugoslavia.*
LOUIS ADAMIC: *The Eagle and the Roots.*

CHAPTER II

[1] Zilliacus, *Tito of Jugoslavia,* p. 64.
[2] Dedijer, *Josip Broz Tito—Prilozi za Biografiju,* p. 108.
[3] Zilliacus, *op. cit.,* p. 77.
[4] *Istorijski Archiv.,* Vol. II, p. 447.
[5] Several accounts of the trial are available, notably the official record and the accounts published at the time in *Novosti* and *Jutarnji List.* They do not differ materially. I have drawn on all three.
[6] Zilliacus, *op. cit.,* p. 81.
[7] *Ibid.,* p. 83.
[8] Conversation with the author, October 24, 1953.

CHAPTER III

[1] Adamic, *op. cit.,* p. 347.
[2] Zilliacus, *op. cit.,* p. 97.
[3] Kardelj, conversation.
[4] Dedijer, *Prilozi,* p. 187.
[5] Adamic, *op. cit.,* p. 363.

[6] *Ibid.*, p. 363.
[7] *Ibid.*, p. 367.
[8] Kardelj, conversation.
[9] Adamic, p. 368.

[10] Dedijer, *Prilozi*, p. 217.
[11] *Ibid.*, p. 219.
[12] Conversation with the author, October 24, 1953.
[13] Adamic, *op. cit.*, p. 378.
[14] Dedijer, *Prilozi*, p. 222.
[15] *Istorijski Archiv.*, p. 380.
[16] *Ibid.*, p. 344.
[17] Dedijer, *Prilozi*, p. 396. See also Zilliacus, *op. cit.*, p. 106 and Adamic, *op. cit.*, pp. 394-6.
[18] Conversation with the author.
[19] Dedijer, *Prilozi*, p. 241.

CHAPTER IV

[1] Dedijer, *Tito Speaks*, p. III.
[2] *Ibid.*, p. 114.
[3] Dedijer, *Prilozi*, p. 260.
[4] Conversation with the author.
[5] Dedijer, *Prilozi*, p. 224.
[6] *Nazi-Soviet Relations*, p. 2.
[7] Dedijer, *Tito Speaks*, p. 124.
[8] My account is based on information provided by Marshal Tito and Dr. V. Velebit.
[9] Report to Fifth Party Congress.
[10] *Komunista*, No.1. Belgrade, October, 1946.
[11] *The Soviet-Yugoslav Dispute* (Royal Institute of International Affairs), p. 46.
[12] W. S. Churchill, *The Second World War*, Vol. III, p. 140.
[13] *Ibid.*, p. 144.
[14] Ciano, *Diario*, Vol. II, p. 88.
[15] S. Clissold, *Whirlwind*, p. 98.
[16] A. Manhattan, *Terror over Yugoslavia*, p. 60. Also C. Fotitč, *The War We Lost*, p. 122.
[17] Ciano, *Diario*, Vol. II, p. 45.
[18] F. Cavalli, *Il Processo dell' Arcivescovo di Zagabria*, p. 74.
[19] Dedijer, *Prilozi*, p. 264.
[20] *Ibid.*
[21] Dedijer, *Tito Speaks*, p. 137.
[22] *Ibid.*, p. 138.
[23] H. F. Armstrong, *Tito and Goliath*, p. 24. See also F.

Borkenau, *European Communism*, p. 349. I understand from Mr. Stephen Clissold that the document quoted from on page 27 of his *Whirlwind* and mentioned by both these authorities is of doubtful authenticity.

[24] H. F. Armstrong, *Tito and Goliath*, p. 24.
[25] Report to Fifth Party Congress (1948).
[26] Dedijer, *Prilozi*, p. 270.
[27] Report to Fifth Party Congress (1948).

CHAPTER V

[1] Zilliacus, *Tito of Jugoslavia*, p. 106.
[2] Dedijer, *Prilozi*, p. 275.
[3] *Ibid.*, p. 271.
[4] *Ibid.*, p. 293.
[5] *Ibid.*, p. 296.
[6] *Ibid.*, p. 300. Tito, Report to Fifth Party Congress.
[7] My account is based on information given me by Tito personally. I have also consulted the account by Reiter published in *Politika* of September 15, 1951.
[8] Tito, *Borba za Oslobodjenje Jugoslavije*, p. 11.
[9] Conversation with the author.
[10] Tito, Report to Fifth Party Congress.
[11] *Ibid.*
[12] *Ibid.*
[13] *The Cetniks* (A.F.H.Q.), p. 11.
[14] *Ibid.*, p. 10.
[15] Christie Lawrence, *Irregular Adventure*, pp. 158-9 and pp. 230-3.
[16] *Ibid.*, p. 140.
[17] See page 347 below (Chapter XI).
[18] *The Cetniks*, p. 17. See also Christie Lawrence, *Irregular Adventure*, pp. 158-9 and pp. 230-3.
[19] Jasper Rootham, *Miss Fire*, p. 214.

CHAPTER VI

[1] Dedijer, *Dnevnik*, Vol. I, p. 64.
[2] *Ibid.*, p. 71.
[3] Ciano, *L'Europa verso la Catastrofe*, p. 703.
[4] Stepinac, *Diary*, p. 176. Book IV, March 28, 1941.
[5] *Nova Hrvatska*, February 25, 1942.
[6] F. Cavalli, *Il Processo dell' Arcivescovo di Zagabria*, pp. 219-21.
[7] *Ibid.*, p. 218.
[8] *Ibid.*, p. 217.

[9] *Ibid.*, p. 221.

[10] *Ibid.*, p. 222.

[11] *Ibid.*, p. 210.

[12] *Ibid.*, p. 175.

[13] *Ibid.*, p. 93.

[14] *Tajni Dokumenti o Odnosima Vatikana i Ustaške "NDH,"* p. 57.

[15] *Ibid.*, pp. 107-19.

[16] *Ibid.*, appendix.

[17] *Novi List*, July 24, 1941.

[18] F. Cavalli, p. 126.

[19] Dedijer, *Dnevnik*, Vol. I, p. 178.

[20] *Ibid.*

[21] *Ibid.*, Vol. I, p. 82.

[22] Tito, *Borba za Oslobodjenje Jugoslavije*, p. 71.

[23] Dedijer, *Dnevnik*, Vol. I, p. 206.

[24] *Ibid.*, Vol. I, p. 102.

[25] Ciano, *Diario*, Vol. II, p. 60.

[26] Tito, *Borba za Oslobodjenje Jugoslavije*, p. 70.

[27] *The Cetniks*, p. 53. See also D. Martin, *Ally Betrayed*, p. 145.

[28] *The Cetniks*, pp. 32 and 37.

[29] *Ibid.*, p. 53.

[30] *Ibid.*, p. 53.

[31] Dedijer, *Prilozi*, p. 308.

[32] *Ibid.*, p. 320.

[33] Moša Pijade, *About the Legend That the Yugoslav Uprising Owed Its Existence to Soviet Assistance*.

[34] *Ibid.*

[35] *Ibid.*

[36] *Ibid.*

[37] *Ibid.*

[38] *Ibid.*

[39] *Ibid.*

[40] *Ibid.*

[41] *Ibid.*

[42] *Ibid.*

[43] *The Cetniks*, p. 58.

[44] Moša Pijade, *op. cit.*

[45] *Ibid.*

CHAPTER VII

[1] Dedijer, *Dnevnik*, Vol. I, pp. 208-12.

[2] Moša Pijade, *About the Legend That the Yugoslav Uprising Owed Its Existence to Soviet Assistance*.

[8] *Ibid.*

[4] *Ibid.*

[5] Dedijer, *Dnevnik,* Vol. I, p. 297.

[6] Moša Pijade, *op. cit.*

[7] Tito, *Borba,* p. 70.

[8] *Ibid.*, p. 107.

[9] S. Clissold, *Whirlwind,* p. 113.

[10] Dedijer, *Dnevnik,* Vol. I, p. 366.

CHAPTER VIII

[1] *Goebbels' Diaries,* April 29, 1943.

[2] See *Tajni Dokumenti* and F. Cavalli, *op. cit.* These facts are, I think, not disputed, though they are clearly capable of various interpretations.

[3] F. Cavalli, *op. cit.*, p. 261.

[4] Ugo Cavallero, *Comando Supremo,* pp. 428-30; Dedijer, *Dnevnik,* Vol. II. p. 66; P. Tomac, *Cetvrta Neprijateljska Ofanziva;* S. Clissold, *Whirlwind,* pp. 116-19.

[5] Tito, *Borba,* p. 195.

[6] Moša Pijade, *About the Legend That the Yugoslav Uprising Owed Its Existence to Soviet Assistance.*

[7] Conversation with the author.

[8] *Hitler e Mussolini Lettere e Documenti,* p. 132.

[9] V. Terzić, *Cetvrta Neprijateljska Ofanziva.*

[10] *The Cetniks,* p. 60.

[11] *Ibid.*, p. 61.

[12] Dedijer, *Dnevnik,* Vol. II, p. 145.

[13] *Ibid.*, Vol. II, p. 160.

[14] Tito, *Borba,* p. 210.

[15] *The Cetniks,* p. 62.

[16] Rootham, *Miss Fire,* p. 160.

[17] *Ibid.*, p. 158.

[18] Leverkuehn, *German Military Intelligence,* p. 152.

[19] *Hitler e Mussolini,* p. 133.

[20] *Ibid.*, p. 143.

[21] Ugo Cavallero, *Comando Supremo,* p. 429.

[22] *Hitler e Mussolini,* pp. 156-8.

[23] Leverkuehn, *op. cit.*, p. 153. See also Hitler's letter to Mussolini of May 19, 1943, published in *Epoca* of June 27, 1954.

[24] Dedijer, *Dnevnik,* Vol. II, p. 194.

[25] Tito, *Borba,* p. 149.

[26] Dedijer, *Dnevnik,* Vol. II, p. 283.

[27] *Ibid.*, Vol. II, p. 290.

[28] *Ibid.*, Vol. II, p. 296.
[29] *Ibid.*, Vol. II, p. 296.
[30] Moša Pijade, *op. cit.*
[31] Dedijer, *Dnevnik*, Vol. II, p. 313.
[32] *Ibid.*, Vol. II, p. 310.

CHAPTER IX

[1] Conversation with the author.
[2] C. Fotitć, *The War We Lost.* Mr. Fotitć claims that the speech was inaccurately reported by Colonel Bailey.
[3] Moša Pijade, *About the Legend That the Yugoslav Uprising Owed Its Existence to Soviet Assistance.*
[4] Dedijer, *Prilozi*, pp. 353-4.
[5] *Ibid.*, p. 358.
[6] Dedijer, *Dnevnik*, Vol. III, p. 135.
[7] Dedijer, *Prilozi*, p. 365.
[8] *The Cetniks*, p. 36.
[9] *Ibid.*, p. 36.
[10] *Ibid.*, p. 39.
[11] *Ibid.*, p. 26.
[12] *Ibid.*, p. 22.

CHAPTER X

[1] Dedijer, *Dnevnik*, Vol. III, p. 185.
[2] Conversation with the author.
[3] I am indebted to the British Foreign Office for the text of these lecture notes.
[4] My account of Tito's visit to Moscow is based on Tito's own account quoted by V. Dedijer in Chapter XVI of his *Prilozi za Biografiju*, and on what Tito himself has on various occasions told me.
[5] Dedijer, *Prilozi*, p. 408.
[6] S. Clissold, *Whirlwind*, pp. 226-7.

CHAPTER XI

[1] W. S. Churchill, *The Second World War*, Vol. VI, p. 198.
[2] Tito, *Borba za Oslobodjenje Jugoslavije*, p. 259.
[3] W. S. Churchill, *The Second World War*, Vol. VI, p. 481.
[4] Tito, *Izgradnja Nove Jugoslavije*, Vol. I, p. 23. Also: *The Soviet-Yugoslav Dispute*, p. 35.
[5] *The Soviet-Yugoslav Dispute*, p. 36.
[6] *Ibid.*, p. 37.

7 Dedijer, *Prilozi*, p. 411.
8 *The Soviet-Yugoslav Dispute*, p. 39.
9 *Yugoslav White Book*, p. 368.
10 Tito, Report to Fifth Party Congress.
11 Tito, *Borba za Oslobodjenje Jugoslavije*, p. 245.
12 Tito, *Izgradnja*, Vol. I, p. 75.
13 D. Martin, *Ally Betrayed*, p. 343.
14 Dedijer, *Tito Speaks*, p. 255.
15 My account is based on that by Koča Popović quoted by Vladimir Dedijer in his *Prilozi za Biografiju* and on conversations with Tito himself.
16 Pattee, *The Case of Cardinal Aloysius Stepinac*, p. 423.
17 Dedijer, *Prilozi*, p. 396.
18 Dedijer, *Tito Speaks*, p. 331.

CHAPTER XII

1 *Borba*, June 30, 1948.
2 Dedijer, *Prilozi*, p. 422.
3 My account is based on that given by Dedijer in Chapter XVIII of his *Prilozi za Biografiju*.
4 Dedijer, *Tito Speaks*, p. 216.
5 Dedijer, *Prilozi*, p. 440.
6 See *Ibid.*, pp. 454-8.
7 See *Ibid.*, pp. 460-8.

CHAPTER XIII

1 Dedijer, *Dnevnik*, Vol. II, p. 602.
2 My account of the meeting is taken from that given by Dedijer in his *Prilozi za Biografiju*, pp. 470-2, which he states is based on the official record.
3 *The Soviet-Yugoslav Dispute*, p. 9.
4 I am indebted to Marshal Tito for a detailed description of this encounter.
5 *The Soviet-Yugoslav Dispute*, p. 12.
6 Dedijer, *Prilozi*, p. 477.
7 *Ibid.*, pp. 479-85 (based on the official record).
8 *The Soviet-Yugoslav Dispute*, p. 18.
9 Conversation with Djilas.
10 *The Soviet-Yugoslav Dispute*, p. 31.
11 *Ibid.*, p. 53.
12 *Borba*, June 30, 1948.
13 Dedijer, *Tito Speaks*, p. 365.
14 *The Soviet-Yugoslav Dispute*, p. 54.

CHAPTER XIV

[1] Dedijer, *Tito Speaks,* p. 372.
[2] Dedijer, *Prilozi,* p. 503.
[3] See *Politika,* June 2, 3, 4, 5 and 7, 1950; *Yugoslav White Book,* p. 367; Dedijer, *Tito Speaks,* pp. 396-8.
[4] Conversation with the author, May, 1949.

CHAPTER XV

[1] Zilliacus, *Tito of Jugoslavia,* p. 248.
[2] *Ibid.,* p. 236.

CHAPTER XVI

[1] Tito Speech of December 21, 1954.
[2] *Ibid.*
[8] Julian Amery, *Sons of the Eagle,* p. 44.

꒛꒛꒛ **BIBLIOGRAPHY** ꒛꒛꒛

Louis Adamic, *The Eagle and the Roots*. Garden City: Doubleday, 1952.

Filippo Anfuso, *Roma-Berlino-Salò*. Milan: Garzanti, 1950.

Hamilton Fish Armstrong, *Tito and Goliath*. New York: Macmillan, 1951; London: Gollancz, 1951.

Phyllis Auty, *Building a New Yugoslavia*. London: Fabian Research Series 165, Fabian Publications, 1954.

Elisabeth Barker, *Macedonia, Its Place in Balkan Power Politics*. London, New York: Royal Institute of International Affairs, 1950.

George Bilainkin, *Tito*. London: Williams & Norgate, 1949.

Franz Borkenau, *The Communist International*. London: Faber & Faber, 1938.

————, *European Communism*. London: Faber & Faber, 1953.

Ugo Cavallero, *Comando Supremo*. Bologna: Capelli, 1948.

Fiorello Cavalli, *Il Processo dell' Arcivescovo di Zagrabria*. Rome: 1947.

The Cetniks, A.F.H.Q. Handbook, 1944.

W. S. Churchill, *The Second World War*. Boston: Houghton, Mifflin Co., 1948-53; London: Cassell, 1948-54.

Galeazzo Ciano, *Diario*. Milan: Rizzoli, 2 vols., 1946.

————, *L'Europa verso la Catastrofe*. Milan: Mondadori, 1948.

Anton Ciliga, *La Yougoslavie sous la Menace Intérieure et Extérieure*. Paris: Les Iles d'or, 1952.

Stephen Clissold, *Whirlwind*. London: Cresset Press, 1949.

Edward Crankshaw, *Russia without Stalin. The Emerging Pattern*. London: Michael Joseph, 1956.

Basil Davidson, *Partisan Picture*. Bedford, England: Bedford Books, 1946.

Vladimir Dedijer, *Josip Broz Tito—Prilozi za Biografiju*. Belgrade: Kultura, 1953.

————, *Dnevnik*. Belgrade: 3 vols., 1945, 1946, 1950.

————, *Tito Speaks*. New York: Simon & Schuster, 1953; London: Weidenfeld & Nicholson, 1953.

413

Isaac Deutscher, *Stalin, a Political Biography*. New York: Oxford University Press, 1949.

Epoca, "Hitler-Mussolini Correspondence," June 27, 1954.

Konstantin Fotić, *The War We Lost*. New York: Viking, 1948.

Stephen Graham, *Alexander of Yugoslavia*. New Haven: Yale University Press, 1939; London: Cassell, 1938.

Walter Hagen, *Die Geheime Front*. Zurich: Europa-Verlag, 1950.

Hitler e Mussolini, Lettere e Documenti. Milan: 1946.

Harry Hodgkinson, *The Adriatic Sea*. London: Jonathan Cape, 1955.

————, *West and East of Tito*. London: Gollancz, 1952.

Istorijski Archiv Kommunisticheske Partije Jugoslavije, Tom II, Kongresi i Zemaljski Konferencije KPJ 1919-37. Belgrade: 1950.

Istorijski Atlas Oslobodilackog Rata. Belgrade: 1952.

E. Kvaternik, *Hrvatska Revija*. Buenos Aires: Articles, September, 1952, and June, 1953.

Robert Joseph Kerner, *Yugoslavia*. Berkeley: University of California press, 1949.

Josef Korbel, *Tito's Communism*. Denver University of Denver Press, 1951.

Christie Lawrence, *Irregular Adventure*. London: Faber & Faber, 1947.

Paul Leverkuehn, *German Military Intelligence*. London: Weidenfeld & Nicolson, 1954.

Richard Loewenthal, Contributions to *Twentieth Century* and *Der Monat*.

Fitzroy Maclean, *Eastern Approaches*. London: Jonathan Cape, 1949.

————, *Escape to Adventure*. Boston: Little, Brown, 1951.

Avro Manhattan, *Terror over Yugoslavia*. London: Watts, 1953.

R. H. Markham, *Tito's Imperial Communism*. Chapel Hill: University of North Carolina Press, 1947.

David Martin, *Ally Betrayed*. New York: Prentice-Hall, 1946.

Mile Milatović, *Slučaj Andrije Hebranga*. Belgrade: 1952.

Nazi-Soviet Relations 1939-1941. Washington: Department of State, 1948.

P. D. Ostović, *The Truth about Jugoslavia*. New York: Roy, 1952.

Michael Padev, *Marshal Tito*. London: Frederick Muller, 1944.

Richard Pattee, *The Case of Cardinal Aloysius Stepinac*. Milwaukee: Bruce, 1953.

Mosa Pijade, *About the Legend That the Yugoslav Uprising Owed Its Existence to Soviet Assistance.* London: 1950.

Jasper Rootham, *Miss Fire.* London: Chatto & Windus, 1946.

Erich Schmidt-Richberg, *Der Endkampf auf dem Balkan.* Heidelberg: 1955.

Hugh Seton-Watson, *The East European Revolution.* London: Methuen, 1950.

——, *Eastern Europe between the Wars.* Cambridge, England: Cambridge University Press, 1946.

Marko Sinovčic, *NDH u Svietlu Dokumenta.* Buenos Aires: 1950.

Boris Souvarine, *Stalin.* New York: Longmans, Green, 1939.

The Soviet-Yugoslav Dispute. London: Chatham House, 1948.

Edward Stettinius, *Roosevelt and the Russians.* Garden City: Doubleday, 1949; London: Jonathan Cape, 1950.

Tajni Dokumenti o Odnosima Vatikana i Ustaške NDH. Zagreb: 1952.

V. Terzić, *Cetvrta Neprijateljska Ofanziva.* Belgrade: 1946.

Josip Broz Tito, *Borba za Oslobodjenje Jugoslavije.* Belgrade: 1947.

——, *Izgradnja, Nove Jugoslavije.* Belgrade: 2 vols, 1947, 1948.

——, *Political Report Delivered at the Fifth Congress of the Communist Party of Jugoslavia.* Belgrade: 1948.

P. Tomac, *Cetvrta Neprijateljska Ofanziva.* Belgrade: 1951.

——, *Peta Neprijateljska Ofanziva.* Belgrade: 1953.

The Trial of Drajoljub-Draža Mihajlović. Belgrade: 1946.

Adam B. Ulam, *Titoism and the Cominform.* Cambridge: Harvard University Press, 1946.

Rebecca West, *Black Lamb and Grey Falcon.* New York: Viking, 1941; London: Macmillan, 1942.

Leigh White, *Balkan Caesar.* New York: Scribner, 1951.

Robert Lee Wolff, *The Balkans in Our Time.* Cambridge: Harvard University Press, 1956.

Konni Zilliacus, *Tito of Yugoslavia.* London: Michael Joseph, 1952.